HATE

Hate

GEORGE LINCOLN ROCKWELL AND THE AMERICAN NAZI PARTY

William H. Schmaltz

Brassey's

An Imprint of Batsford Brassey, Inc.
WASHINGTON • LONDON

Copyright © 1999 by William H. Schmaltz

All rights reserved. No part of this book may be reproduced by any form or by any means — electronic, electrostatic, magnetic tape, mechanical, photocopying, recording, or otherwise — without permission in writing from the publisher.

Editorial Offices:
4380 MacArthur Boulevard, N.W.
Washington, DC 20007

Order Department:
P.O. Box 960
Herndon, VA 20172

Brassey's books are available at special discounts for bulk purchases for sales promotions, premiums, fund-raising, or educational use.

Library of Congress Cataloging-in-Publication Data

Schmaltz, William H.
Hate : George Lincoln Rockwell & the American Nazi party / William H. Schmaltz. — 1st ed.
p.   cm.
Includes bibliographical references and index.
ISBN 1-57488-171-X
1. Rockwell, George Lincoln, 1918–1967. 2. American Nazi Party—Biography. 3. Right-wing extremists—United States—Biography. 4. American Nazi Party—History—20th century. 5. Subversive activities—United States—History—20th century. I. Title
E743.5.S35 1999
324.273'038'092—dc21
[B]
98-42520
CIP

Designed by Pen & Palette Unlimited

First Edition

10 9 8 7 6 5 4 3 2 1

Printed in the United States of America

In memory of
my aunt
Helen Klein
(1925–1995)

CONTENTS

LIST OF ILLUSTRATIONS

Look therefore
whether the light that is in thee
be not darkness.

— Luke 11:36

FOREWORD

In *Hate* there is much to shake the complacency of people who think a Nazi-like state and a holocaust "can't happen here." William Schmaltz's biography of the most charismatic American Nazi, George Rockwell, is a thoroughly researched, highly objective book that demonstrates what goes into a racist leader and what makes a hate movement work. In fine detail, it presents Rockwell, how he operated, and how he affected people. For those concerned about preventing another holocaust, it is most valuable reading. It is also especially important because Rockwell led the campaign in the United States to deny that the Holocaust happened. Since extermination of the Jews is the most intolerable part of Hitler's legacy, Aryan supremacists have worked to rehabilitate him by trying to prove it never happened—an effort that has fostered much doubt and confusion about the Holocaust.

Admirers and emulators of Hitler are drawn to him by similarities of personality. As the biography shows, when Rockwell was a small boy, his parents separated, and he was shifted back and forth between them, never having a home of his own, never developing a sense of worth, acceptance, or security. As in Hitler, these lacks were behind a lifelong struggle for a place, attention, and achievement. Rockwell literally created a home and an environment of his own by founding the American Nazi Party and living in its headquarters. And he found more than acceptance in the admiration of his followers. Like Hitler, he compensated for his sense of worthlessness by claiming membership in an elite—an imaginary super race of "Aryan" Americans—whose savior and grand leader he tried to become. Seeking acceptance beyond the Nazi Party, he campaigned unsuccessfully to become governor of Virginia and planned to become president of the United States. Security, he would never find.

The unconscious motivation for Rockwell's racism is revealed in a hoax that he perpetrated in his campaign of Holocaust denial. Under the name of a former member of the SS, he wrote a bogus article describing Germany's extermination of Jews and found a publisher for it. Then Rockwell exposed his own article as a fraud and cited it as proof that Jews use fraud to foster the "myth" of the Holocaust.

By adopting what he considered the deceitful methods of Jews—by putting himself in the position of a Jew posing as an Aryan—Rockwell identified himself with the people he hated. In addition he explicitly identified himself with black leaders Elijah Muhammad and Malcolm X, while advocating deportation of blacks from the United States and hinting he would have them killed when in power. He showed the same self-hating identification with people he meant to destroy that I found in leaders of the Third Reich.

Rockwell's experience of repeated abandonment by his family fostered deep resentment and an inability to trust people. These emerged during his twenties in increasingly critical views of the world and contempt for almost everyone. As with Hitler, his anti-Semitism developed suddenly in a paranoid awakening from "thirty years of political sleep" with the revelation of a Jewish conspiracy to destroy America and the "Aryan race." Thereafter he focused his hate in the idea of destroying Jews and then blacks.

Rockwell needed greatness so badly that he was unable to pursue ordinary employment or intimate relationships for long. He did marry twice and have seven children, but he abandoned his wives and children, devoting himself to a political crusade.

Being abandoned himself may also have contributed to abandoning his families and to sex- and gender-related positions he had the Nazi Party adopt—positions common to racist and other macho movements of the past. The sense of insecurity and vulnerability that Rockwell shared with Nazi colleagues was reflected in fears of contamination from Jews and blacks—contamination leading to moral and biological decay, ruining the United States. Their dread of "race mixing" had a long history. The historian Tacitus had explained what he saw as Rome's moral decay on the basis of intermarriage. To save Rome, he wrote the book *Germania*, in which he originated the notion of pure-blooded Aryan supremacy. In turn, *Germania* inspired the racism of the Third Reich and was copied by American Nazis. Following Tacitus and Hitler, Rockwell took on the role of saving "Aryan" women from "contamination" by Jews and blacks. He also advocated returning women to a position of subservience (a position that would hinder them from abandoning their children).

The deeper Rockwell got into his crusade, the more chances he took. Before his turn to Nazism, his life had been a series of starts and stops without direction. Afterward, it followed an unchanging course, with little regard for consequences. The Nazi Party grew, but the more Rockwell accomplished, the faster he rushed about to accomplish still more. Unfortunately, outward success without inner healing does not slow the treadmill.

Schmaltz takes us step by step through Rockwell's successes in building the party and in winning popularity as an orator. He also takes us through Rockwell's escalation from activities that annoyed his victims—from being a nuisance to society—to the recklessness that made him an embarrassment even to some of his Nazi colleagues, driving many of them out of the party and driving Rockwell to his own death. A lesson here is that racists should be watched, even when they are only nuisances, and that they should be controlled by full use of the law and by other institutions of social order when they go on to incite violence, as Rockwell did.

Schmaltz makes extensive and very effective use of Rockwell's words to reveal his personality, his thinking, and the power of his creed of hate. No matter how repugnant his words were, they had an insidious appeal—even to well-meaning people—as have the words of other racist figures through history, and as they still do.

Rockwell was highly intelligent and developed considerable charm, which he used to advance the Nazi cause. But, again like Hitler, lacking the patience to be thorough, Rockwell undercut his strengths by relying on superficial cleverness, tricks, and crude, malicious humor. These traits drew openly hostile people to him, but he provoked and alienated others sympathetic to his ideas. Even when he courted leaders of like-minded groups to forge alliances, he was apt to put them off by provocative behavior.

The self-destructiveness of such behavior was apparent in events leading to his discharge from the Naval Reserve. Informed that he was considered unfit for command because personnel serving under him would include ethnic groups he treated with contempt, he wrote back in words that could have come from Hitler:

> Throughout history, men who have stood uncompromisingly for unpopular and dangerous ideas have always had to suffer persecution and indignities, and I have and expect to suffer much worse than the withdrawal of my treasured commission because of my overwhelming concern for the safety of our nation which has fallen into the hands of traitorous conspirators. . . .

His defense suggested that his superiors in the Navy—the people deciding his status—were members of the conspiracy.

At a naval hearing held at his request, Rockwell responded to the charge of racism by parading his racism. The hearing was held shortly before he would become eligible to retire on pension. Not self-supporting, he would need his pension. But he disdained keeping a low profile even temporarily or promising the Navy that he would curtail his racist activities. Instead he increased them publicly at that very time. He provoked his discharge.

Rockwell was aware of his recklessness and of the price he paid for his crusade. He said, "Being prepared to die is one of the greatest secrets of living," and predicted his early death by violence. He also said, "[Devotion to the cause] has cost me the most beautiful wife in the world. Seven kids. All my relatives. I was a commander in the Navy and a half-year away from a pension. . . ."

And in fact he was killed at age forty-nine by a fellow Nazi because of his reckless anger. As Schmaltz recounts the events, John Patsalos, a man ashamed of his Greek identity, joined the American Nazi Party and embraced its "Aryanism," becoming a leader. He changed his name to the German-sounding Patler because it resembled Hitler. After years of serving the party, he withdrew temporarily from active participation to care for a sick relative. Feeling abandoned by Patler, Rockwell vilified him and threw him out of the party. In revenge, Patler stalked Rockwell and shot him to death. The stories of Rockwell and Patler typify the self-alienation, vulnerability, and destructiveness of people drawn to the Aryan supremacy, white supremacy, and Christian supremacy groups described in *Hate*.

Schmaltz ends his extremely valuable book with a sketch of Rockwell's legacy—of the Nazi and Nazi-like groups in the United States today. He stresses that these groups are small in membership and do relatively little harm. He also stresses that for one of them to become a threat to the nation requires only an economic catastrophe and the emergence of a highly charismatic leader—which could happen at any time.

I would stress also that Germany's Nazi Party was no larger than these groups when Hitler joined it and that during its early years it engaged in less killing than the American groups do. In the United States there are about five hundred such groups now, and they account for dozens of beatings and killings a year—hundreds in some years. That alone is more than enough cause to take them seriously and to seek effective action against them.

In addition, these groups do have a vast number of sympathizers—people who share their view that the nation is harmed by Jews, blacks, Hispanics, and Asians and would be better off without them. The ancient practice of scapegoating to solve personal and national problems remains strongly ingrained, needing only a national catastrophe to become rampant. Study of hate groups—as Schmaltz has done—is a key step toward countering them and the sympathetic response they evoke in non-members.

The next American Hitler may be less crude, less openly destructive, and less self-destructive than George Rockwell was. He may be a more effective person and a more charismatic leader. Most Germans recognized the danger in Hitler only when it was too late. The greatest contribution of Schmaltz's book is the help it provides to recognize the next Hitler and the threat he poses before he gains power—before it is too late.

George Victor
Author of *Hitler: The Pathology of Evil*

PREFACE

I get three types of reactions from people when I mention the name George Lincoln Rockwell. Some people recall that he was a Nazi and a publicity hound. Right-wingers—who refer to him as "Commander Rockwell"—recognize him as the first so-called neo-Nazi, the harbinger of an Americanized version of National Socialism, and one of the founding fathers of white supremacy. To others Rockwell is unknown, another identity lost in the shuffle of history through academic neglect, lack of interest, or a perceived insignificance.

As an undergraduate in history at the University of Wisconsin–River Falls, I "discovered" Rockwell by accident, on a reel-to-reel tape recording in the archives. Had there been a text on Rockwell and his American Nazi Party I would have read it and moved on. But there was no text, and that spurred my interest.

I submitted to the Federal Bureau of Investigation a Freedom of Information Act request for all the Rockwell files. The FBI took the next ten years to provide twelve thousand pages of previously unreleased documents; meanwhile I attempted to locate and interview Rockwell's former associates, scattered throughout the country. His wives, siblings, and children refused all requests for interviews.

My gratitude goes out to numerous people for their help on this project: Wayne A. Huppert, for his help as a "tour guide" on my research trips to the South; Greg Cox, review analyst at the FBI, for expediting my FOIA request; Barbara Blender for the use of her father's photographs; Stanley Tupper for sharing his memories of Rockwell's Boothbay Harbor years; Professor Stephen Feinstein for his helpful critique of this work; and David Feyereisen and Robert Kraske for their counsel.

Many thanks go to Rockwell's former associates for their help in piecing together the American Nazi Party (ANP) history: Roger Foss, Karl Allen, Bernie Davids, Matt Koehl, Ed Fields, Emory Burke, Schuyler Ferris, T. Eddy, Jerald Walraven, Mike Brown, William Pierce, Frank Smith, Chris Bailey, George Ware, Speros Lagoulis, DeWest Hooker, Colin Jordan, Alan Welch, and Barbara von Goetz.

My compliments to the many institutions that supplied documents for this project, especially the Stillwater and Washington County libraries, the Wilcox Collection at the University of Kansas, the Schomburg Center for Research in New York, the Bentley Historical Library at the University of Michigan, the American Jewish Archives in Cincinnati, the Virginia Room at the Arlington County Library, the Boothbay Region Historical Society and Museum, the Brown University Archives, and the University of Iowa.

Last, I want to thank Don McKeon, my editor at Brassey's, for his sharp pencil and attention to detail on this project. Special thanks go to my wife, Sally, for allowing me to put our lives "on hold" while I completed this book. She endured my continuous rambling about Rockwell, braved phone calls from extremists, and allowed me to deplete our meager savings on research trips—for a book that had no publisher. Thanks are due also to my children, Henry, Molly, and Karl, for their patience while I was "on the computer."

William Schmaltz, 1998
Stillwater, Minnesota
(wschmaltz@aol.com)

INTRODUCTION

On June 22, 1960, George Lincoln Rockwell, the leader of the American Nazi Party, flew into New York City to defend his application to speak in Union Square. Waiting for him at the airport was stormtrooper Roger Foss, who had hopped a bus from Washington, D.C., to New York City. They rode the subway to the New York State Supreme Court; there they walked cautiously through dozens of protesters standing outside the building. Nobody recognized Rockwell in a business suit—he looked more like a congressman than a Nazi.

The courtroom was in chaos. Six lawyers stood before the bench to oppose Rockwell's petition to speak; the gallery was filled with angry-looking members of the Jewish community. One by one citizens, attorneys, and pressure group representatives of New York City denounced Rockwell before the bench, claiming that his appearance would jeopardize the health and safety of the community.

Then it was Rockwell's turn to speak. The courtroom fell silent as he approached Justice Vincent Lupiano. Rockwell paused a few moments for dramatic effect before launching into a masterful soliloquy that utilized both legal citations and humor to disarm his opponents. Around the courtroom the lawyers and public officials stood open-mouthed; no one had expected such an effective performance.

Suddenly a bearded rabbi stood up in the back of the courtroom screaming of "Nazi atrocities." A heavyset Irish policeman yelled at him to "sit down and shut up," but the rabbi's hysterics intensified; he changed from broken English to Yiddish, waved his arms in wild gestures, and finally collapsed to the floor in convulsions. Bystanders and police carried the man off, but not before he had stolen the moment from Rockwell, the moment during which the entire courtroom had been hanging on his every word. The timing had been perfect.[1]

Judge Lupiano called a recess. Rockwell and Foss made their way out to the rotunda, where several television cameras were set up. The Nazis stood back to back, surrounded by an angry mob of 150 people. Rockwell told television reporters that the ANP was "growing every minute" but that his goals had been misrepresented by newspapers. "Contrary to newspaper reports we are not trying to exterminate anybody, but we are trying to eliminate communism. We want to shock the American people into the awareness of the extreme danger of what is going on."[2]

A reporter asked if he intended to gas Jews; Rockwell replied that he intended to gas traitors, Jews or otherwise. The reporter asked how many Jews that might be; Rockwell said, "Eighty percent." Immediately, shouts and curses rang through the rotunda. A spectator yelled, "If he'd go outside I'd break his neck for it! You dirty bum you! You call eighty percent of the Jews traitors!" The man lunged at Rockwell, but Foss grabbed his wrists and pushed him back. A television reporter asked, "Mr. Rockwell, how do you react to this kind of treatment?" "I'm used to it," shouted Rockwell. "They never make such a fuss over communists speaking; it's only when someone is an anti-communist."

A bystander half Rockwell's height wriggled through the mob to stand toe to toe with Rockwell. "Only dogs that spew disease all over the place, dogs like you that have the gall to come in here and do what you do." Rockwell kept his arms crossed, high on his chest so they would not be trapped at his sides if he had to start swinging his fists. Another spectator yelled, "How much do you get from the communists for fomenting this disorder, you animal?"[3]

The mob surged forward, surrounding Rockwell and Foss, pushing and pulling to get at them. Television cameras tipped over and crashed on the marble floor; reporters were knocked down and trampled under foot; the mob pressed in on Rockwell, shouting "Kill him! Kill him!" Security guards hustled Rockwell and Foss into an adjoining room to await the riot police. When order was restored the two returned to the courtroom, and the hearing commenced. At its conclusion, they were whisked off to La Guardia Airport under police escort and placed aboard an American Airlines plane bound for Washington.

The next day the episode received nationwide coverage in newspapers across the country; Rockwell had succeeded in forcing the media to give him publicity. He could not force them to be impartial, but the "facts" were irrelevant. The important thing was that his name was now synonymous with the American Nazi Party. Newspapers, television, and radio stations found it impossible to avoid mentioning his brash and daring exploits; editors and columnists could not resist the temptation to denounce him to their readers. More important to him personally, Rockwell could now claim leadership of the most infamous political party in America.

1

POLITICAL SLEEP

Without question Lincoln is the loudest talker on the
campus, the originator of more weird theories than
anyone else, and the Academy's outstanding artist. . . . We
have every assurance of his being successful because of
his incomparable personality and originality.

— *Green Parrot '38*
Yearbook, Hebron Academy, Maine

George Lincoln Rockwell was born on March 9, 1918, in Bloomington,
Illinois, the first of three children born to George Lovejoy Rockwell and
Claire Schade. His parents were vaudeville performers. His father had
joined vaudeville after high school and had toured extensively with the
B. F. Keith and Shubert circuits.

He was a rising vaudeville comic who overcompensated for his stocky,
diminutive physique—he was only five feet four inches tall—with a
repertoire of fast talk, quick jokes, improvised monologue, and a penny-
whistle dance routine.

Claire Schade was the youngest daughter of German immigrant Gus
Schade and Corrine Boudreau, of French ancestry. The older daughter,
Arline, was overbearing like her father. Claire was delicate and had her
mother's beauty, but she was also soft-willed and compliant to her
father's wishes and later to those of her domineering sister.

At six years of age, Claire was a natural for the stage. Gus built a family
act around Claire's ability to sing and toe-dance, and the family took to
the vaudeville circuit billed as "The Four Schades." The act prospered,
but the novelty faded when Claire reached adolescence.

In 1915, Claire met George. They quickly married and settled in
Bloomington, Illinois. Claire traveled with her husband on the circuit

but retired in 1918 with the birth of their first child, George Lincoln. In 1919 another son arrived, Robert, and a daughter, Priscilla, in 1921.

Rockwell, now a father of three, continued to work the vaudeville circuit with various troupes until one night in Hartford he concocted his famous "banana stalk" gag. On impulse he carried a whole stalk of bananas—left over from a monkey act—onstage as part of his tin whistle–ukulele act. He threw bananas into the audience in the direction of the greatest applause. The spectators loved the skit, so he added bananas to his routine.

One night in Cleveland his bananas disappeared; stagehands had eaten every one. Forced to improvise, he took the denuded banana stalk onstage and used it as a prop to demonstrate the human spine. Chiropractic was a popular and growing field, and he decided to ridicule the profession in his routine. He sat down on a small stool and "demonstrated," to the roaring approval of the audience, how the human spine "actually" worked. Holding out the stalk horizontally, he told the audience it was "the spine of a radio announcer who had died of inflammation of the vowels." With one malapropism after another he brought the audience to tears of laughter. From that day forth he dressed in a white lab coat and was known as "Doc" Rockwell. Doc worked the banana stalk routine for many years; at the height of his success he commanded $3,500 per week, an astronomical figure for the Depression era.

While Doc Rockwell's career was soaring, his marriage was in ruins. Claire was housebound with three young children while her husband had the time of his life headlining at the Palace Theater and Radio City Music Hall in New York City. In 1924 they divorced; George Lincoln Rockwell was six years old.

When the routine played out, Doc Rockwell came up with the "Glass Woman" for Billy Rose's "Seven Lively Arts," a skit that enabled him to continue his routine as a "doctor." The Glass Woman was a life-size, anatomically correct figure of a woman with internal lightbulbs controlled by his "nurse" assistant, Madelyn Merideth. While Doc delivered the monologue his nurse assistant would deliberately illuminate a wrong portion of the body, to set up the punch line. The racy routine was laced with double entendres and silliness; audiences loved it.

Eventually the vaudeville circuit began to die out, and Doc and Madelyn, his common-law wife, retired to their summer home in

Southport, Maine, where he concentrated on writing material for comedian Fred Allen and columns for several humor magazines. He took up lobstering, often telling people how nice a business it was: "You put your traps in the water and you're in business, you pull them out and you're out of business."[1]

Each summer George Lincoln Rockwell and his brother, Robert, traveled from their mother's home in Bloomington, Illinois, to live with their father and Madelyn in their large house on Southport Island, dubbed "Shipshod Manor." The rotation continued until the boys were in high school. The elder Rockwell boy preferred life in Maine, with its tall pine trees jutting from the rocky shoreline and the crashing ocean waves. His father led a nonconformist life, often taking his boys on deep-sea fishing expeditions in the chilly small hours of morning, all the while discussing the finer points of history, society, and art—unusual topics between adults and children. Above all, Doc Rockwell taught his boys to question everything: nothing was too sacred to be examined and judged, no authority too holy to challenge.[2]

There was also a dark side to life on Southport Island. The father-son relationship Lincoln fondly remembered was a one-sided relationship. Doc gave his boys attention as if they were a vaudeville audience, but love and guidance were missing from the relationship. Doc was an egomaniac. A nephew recalled that "the sun went up and down on what he was doing. Period." Another could not recall one instance of affection expressed by Doc toward Lincoln.

Doc Rockwell lavishly entertained show business friends who journeyed from New York to Southport for a little rest and relaxation. They included such well-known entertainers as Fred Allen, Benny Goodman, Walter Winchell, and Groucho Marx. One particular event, involving Fred Allen's wife, made a lasting impression on Lincoln. In the midst of conversation with other guests, Portia Allen uttered the word *shit*. The boy was so taken aback by this vulgarity—especially from a female—that he later questioned his father about the incident. Doc explained that Mrs. Allen was Jewish. Lincoln asked if Jewishness had anything to do with it; his father replied that Jews were very "sophisticated people" who meant no harm by such language.

There was a degree of anti-Semitism and racism expressed in all the households where Rockwell spent his youth. But it is not a likely catalyst for his later-life activities. Anti-Semitism and racism were not

Author's collection

Somewhere near Atlantic City, New Jersey, in the late 1920s. Rockwell, *left*, with his mother, brother, and sister, beneath whom on the photograph print he wrote "Mom, Tripe, Brat," respectively.

uncommon in the middle-class America of that era. Rockwell's cousins describe their family as "Archie Bunker types," very anti-Semitic, anti-black, anti-Catholic, anti-Italian, but ... these were feelings they "didn't talk about outside the family."[3]

In nearby Boothbay Harbor, Lincoln Rockwell was recognized as an insatiable extrovert, the center of attention in whatever he did. He organized a big band, the Phantoms of Swing, to showcase his talents as a self-taught reed player. His favorite instrument was the flageolet; he could play classic tunes like "Flight of the Bumblebee" as well as popular songs very well indeed.

To form the Phantoms, Rockwell recruited his friend Stanley Tupper, an accomplished Hawaiian guitar player, to play the stand-up bass. Rockwell taught Tupper twelve notes and a few bass runs for the left hand, and how to stroke the strings with his right hand. The Phantoms also had a piano player, who was quite good after a few drinks. That made three players out of twelve who could play their instruments; the others were hacks. But it didn't matter; everyone onstage and off knew who the leader was—Rockwell. He was a showstopper. The band played the local Grange halls and schools throughout Lincoln County, wearing Lone Ranger masks onstage to enhance the "phantom" image.[4]

One night at a Grange hall dance a local farmer asked Tupper why he was not playing his bass with a bow. Tupper had no idea the traditional method of playing the stand-up bass required a bow. Rockwell interceded and told the hayseed that bows were no longer in use; everyone used fingers to stroke the heavy bass strings.

Rockwell decided the Phantoms needed a promotional record. His father owned an acetate-cutting machine. Rockwell gathered the band in a large room, set up the microphone, and produced a recording of the "Beer Barrel Polka."[5] Unfortunately the record failed to bring fame or fortune.[6]

He was also a daredevil. He liked sailing his small skiff in stormy seas as a challenge against Mother Nature. The other boys watched from shore as Rockwell zigzagged across Boothbay Harbor, the waves crashing against his small boat. Somehow he would prevail and return to shore, boasting of his experience. On one occasion he completed an essay around Southport Island in very heavy seas, singing and howling at the wind with sheer animal energy while his younger brother, Robert, clung to the boat for his life. He recruited friend Eben Lewis to join him on a voyage to Pemaquid Point, a peninsula outside the harbor, far too distant for such a tiny boat.[7] On their return voyage high winds forced Rockwell to negotiate the small craft through a tortuous rock passage known as the "Threads of Life" in the dark of night, against the wind, in the rip tide.[8] These adventures became a benchmark for his life; defying the odds provided emotional catharsis, a triumph of the will.

He installed the largest engine available in his father's lobster boat, for the sole purpose of annoying tourists. If a tourist speedboat came too close while he was checking the family's lobster pots in Townsend Gut, he would shut down the winch, open the throttle, and chase the villain boat—not with malice but for fun.[9]

As a teenager he worked as a waiter in a small tourist hotel called the Green Shutters. The job provided ample opportunity to experiment not only with patrons but also with the waitresses. He reveled in both. The clientele of the hotel consisted of schoolteachers on holiday for the summer. Their empty chatter disgusted him: stories about tea shops, gift shops, and problems with other old ladies. Also, they badgered him with complaints of every sort. When their grumbling got on Rockwell's nerves he exacted revenge by pranks. His favorite trick was to wipe a sticky, syrup-soaked rag on doorknobs, pocketbook handles, light switches, anything the women might touch.

Notwithstanding, Rockwell was well liked by both men and women of the local community. Everyone expected great things. He was gregarious, clever, and always the center of attention. He seemed destined for show business of some sort—acting, comedy, band leading.

Beneath the surface was a young man with a fragile self-image. As Rockwell grew into manhood, his lanky six-foot four-inch frame towered over his sawed-off father, exacerbating Doc's own insecurity over his height. He made Rockwell suffer for it by cutting the boy's self-image to ribbons. Doc's hostilities created an emotional wasteland for Rockwell.

While Doc belittled his eldest at every occasion, Rockwell tried desperately to win his father's approval by emulating his father's mannerisms in every way. In the end, he became like his father. He was loud, talented, and self-centered; he was always "on," always trying to impress, and, if he could not impress, to intimidate.... One relative described him as "an opportunist, a con-man, just like his father."[10]

Each fall the boys returned to their mother's house. Claire moved from Bloomington to Atlantic City, New Jersey, to live with her sister, Arline. Living with his mother and domineering aunt was no picnic. Sister Priscilla recalls Aunt Arline being vindictive and determined to break Rockwell's willfulness. She beat him from age six to fifteen. Her psychological abuse—the name-calling, the taunts—continued until the day he left for college.[11]

Rockwell attended school in Atlantic City, where two particular events stand out: a hazing and a political standoff. The hazing consisted of a customary dunk in the ocean by the older students. Rockwell refused to be bullied into something he did not want to do, in spite of being outnumbered, surrounded on the beach by a gang of classmates. His reaction was immediate and ferocious: he fought off the entire gang. Fists flying, feet kicking, clawing, scratching, gouging, biting—he did whatever it took not to be thrown into the water. He prevailed. The boys abandoned their hazing attempt, but they held Rockwell in contempt for not "going along with the fun."

The following week, challenged and bloodied by a single classmate, he could not muster enough fighting spirit to handle one of the individuals he had tangled with the week before. He could not understand why he was able to fight off a gang of boys but was defeated by a single attacker. He concluded that fighting insurmountable odds brought out his true spirit, doing things, or going against things, in ways that others were afraid to try.[12]

During his senior year at Atlantic City High School, Rockwell engaged in his first political battle. Taking a course in "Problems of American Democracy," taught by a teacher named Schwab, he went "on strike." Schwab required students to transcribe large portions of their textbook word for word into their notebooks. While the students busied themselves with their transcriptions, Schwab would sit at his desk attending to his own pet projects. Rockwell despised this method of teaching. One day he brought a pulp Western to class, propped his feet upon the desk, and read while the rest of the class wrote verbatim from the textbook. When Schwab asked what he was doing, Rockwell responded that he was "on strike." At first Schwab was amused by Rockwell's impudence and did nothing, but after several days a few other boys joined in the strike. Schwab immediately went to school authorities, who told Rockwell he would not graduate unless he capitulated and began transcribing. When he still refused, the administration denied him the privilege of graduating. Rockwell was "sacrificed," but Schwab was called into conference with school officials and told to terminate his transcription methods and start teaching.[13]

Rockwell was growing more rebellious, focusing his anger and alienation on the power structure of the school. He could channel his resentment of his domineering Aunt Arline and his uncaring father against teachers and authority figures. It probably relieved some of his pain and stroked his own ego at the same time. It would become his characteristic behavior.

The next school year, Rockwell moved in with his paternal grandmother, Mary MacPherson Rockwell, and her daughter Marguerite in Providence, Rhode Island, to repeat his senior year of high school. He attended Central High School in Providence, became the editor of the school paper, and even wrote a few articles for the *Providence Journal-Bulletin*. After school he sold Electrolux vacuum cleaners door to door and studied for his Federal Communications Commission amateur radio license. He passed the examination and received the call letters W3GGN.[14]

His stay in Providence was one of the happiest times of his youth. Not only was he away from Arline, but Aunt Margie gave him genuine love. She listened to his thoughts, recognized his feelings, and provided affection that he desperately needed. His grades improved and he stopped antagonizing others.

After graduating, he took Harvard's entrance exams and completed the necessary paperwork, but as fall approached no admission papers arrived. Suspecting a mixup of some sort, father and son traveled to Harvard to rectify the situation. They discovered that his school records from Atlantic City (the school where he went on strike) had not been forwarded to the Harvard admissions board. Not wanting his son to miss a valuable year of schooling, Doc enrolled Rockwell at a prep school, Hebron Academy, in central Maine for the 1937 school year.

Life at Hebron was rigorous, but the teaching was good. Many of his classmates were upper-class toughs from Boston, sent to Hebron by their families as a last resort before reform school. Rockwell spent long hours reading such novels as Sinclair Lewis's *Arrowsmith* and John Steinbeck's *The Grapes of Wrath,* and a disturbing thought entered his mind. He sensed in them an attempt to convince the reader of social ideas not by force of reason but by emotional manipulation. He concluded that a reader is "mad to permit himself to be voluntarily hypnotized by a novelist, transported out of his critical faculties and thereby allow his mind to be powerfully conditioned by almost real 'experiences' which are nothing less than the invented devices of another human being." [15]

He also questioned his religious faith. Closer scrutiny of the Bible revealed conflicts he could not reconcile. A Catholic classmate suggested they see a local priest, who could answer Rockwell's questions and reveal his error. They journeyed through five miles of snowy backwoods to the church, but the priest was unable to resolve the biblical conflicts in Rockwell's mind; he gave up in exasperation, saying, "You just must believe. You have to believe." They skied back to Hebron in silence. Later that week the Catholic boy told Lincoln that because of their meeting with the priest he too had lost his faith. Rockwell felt he had erred in causing his classmate to fall. He made a commitment to himself never to discuss religion with anyone again. [16]

There were also some comic adventures at Hebron. Rockwell publicly challenged the largest man on campus to a nonsanctioned wrestling match. When the day arrived, dozens of boys gathered for the big match. The huge, six-foot-four football player, who outweighed Rockwell by at least fifty pounds, arrived in wrestling tights; Rockwell arrived in gaudy union-suit underwear. As the two entered the ring to square off, Rockwell's carefully orchestrated escape plan commenced. One of his friends came dashing up to the wrestlers, shouting, "The headmaster is coming! The headmaster is coming!" Everyone scattered. The entire match was a hoax. Rockwell had never intended to get twisted into a pretzel; it was simply showmanship to him. The football player never realized he had been tricked.[17]

On another occasion, this time a very formal school dinner with parents and teachers in attendance, Doc Rockwell began to cough and gag on his fish chowder. Rockwell and brother Robert jumped up and furiously slapped their father on the back, trying to bring up the bone. The entire dinner was disrupted as everyone watched in horror. Suddenly Doc reached into his mouth and pulled out an extremely long "gag" fishbone. The spectators gasped, then let out a roar of laughter. School officials were not amused.[18]

In the fall of 1938 the twenty-year-old freshman entered Brown University in Providence. The director of admissions at Brown, Bruce Bigelow, gave him his first clue that he "might be different from other people." The director purportedly told him he had the worst scholastic record of anyone ever admitted to Brown but that he had scored the highest grade ever given on the college aptitude test.[19]

Rockwell worked as art editor for the campus magazine, *Sir Brown!* He drew cartoons that ranged from campus-type humor to comic book horror for both *Sir Brown!* and the college newspaper, *The Brown Daily Herald.* His major course of study was philosophy, but like every freshman he had to complete the required "basic studies" before concentrating on it. He ran into problems with sociology. Unlike geography or psychology, where there were fundamental ideas and well-established facts upon which the science was based, he found the principles of sociology elusive. He could not get to the kernel of the discipline. The instructor's egalitarian beliefs confused him; he was sure that such beliefs could not be supported by facts. Surely the differences between the mental capabilities of individuals as well as the levels of development of societies could not be wholly explained by environmental effects. Were there no inherent differences in the quality of human beings?

When he confronted Professor Harold Bucklin with this premise, he was admonished before the class. Rockwell never "bought" the idea of human equality and the supremacy of environment. Instead, he attacked the ideology with his cartoons and columns for the school paper—many of which were "killed" by the editors. He was nearly expelled when he pushed it too far on a sociology paper. Assigned to write on the factors leading to criminality and delinquency, Rockwell wrote a fable about scientists in Africa studying "why ants acted like ants":

> They searched around until they found a lot of ant hills, observed them for many years and finally came up with the discovery that when ant eggs were hatched in tunnels in a certain kind of hill in Africa and grew up among six-legged creatures called "ants," they themselves were so affected by this strong environment that they became, themselves, ants and waved their antennae like ants, scurried around aimlessly like ants, looked like ants and were ants![20]

A Rockwell cartoon from his student days at Brown University foreshadows a life to come.

Rockwell never graduated from Brown, leaving to enlist as an aviation cadet in the U.S. Navy on March 15, 1941. Upon completion of flight training on December 23, 1941, he was commissioned as a naval aviator. He served aboard the USS *Omaha, Wasp,* and *Mobile* and saw action in both the Atlantic and Pacific theaters. His primary duties were photo reconnaissance, transport, and training. He took part in some combat flying on Guadalcanal, where he flew fighter-support missions and carrier air strikes against Japanese positions on the Philippine island of Luzon. In 1944 he also took part in antisubmarine action against Japanese vessels off the Alaskan coast.[21] In later years he publicly claimed that he helped kill German sailors in two separate U-boat sinkings in the Atlantic; the Navy has no evidence that he took part in any U-boat attacks.

In April 1943, Rockwell married his Brown sweetheart, Judith Aultman, in St. John's Church in Barrington, Rhode Island. They had a small wedding—which Doc Rockwell missed—and a disastrous honeymoon marred by fighting. Judith was not the submissive wife Rockwell expected. Although they had three daughters together, their entire relationship was strained and at times acrimonious.

In August of 1944 he was the officer in charge of a Support Air Control Team for the U.S. Naval Mission to Brazil. His impressions of the mixed-race Brazilians were not favorable. In later years he stated that pure-bred Africans were physically superior to the scrawny Brazilians, further proof for him that race mixing caused genetic confusion and weak, marginal beings. In September 1945, now a lieutenant commander in the Naval Reserve, he returned to civilian life.

In the summer months of 1946 and 1947 Rockwell made a living as a commercial artist in a small shop in Boothbay Harbor

As a young naval aviator.

while studying art at Pratt Institute of Commercial Art in Brooklyn, New York, during the school year. His partner in the "Maine Photo-Art Service" in Boothbay Harbor was Jack Myers; together they painted signs, developed film, and created a beautiful map called "Chart of the Boothbay Region." The chart was a three-foot-by-three-foot map of the entire Boothbay area, listing every house, waterway, island, and charter boat in the region.[22]

While attending Pratt he observed firsthand something he would later define as "the schizophrenic dichotomy of values characteristic of our exploding civilization." Half of the instructors were genuine artists with meaningful lessons; the other half, he believed, were charlatans pushing "modern art." He despised the modern art classes, which so neatly dispensed with the traditional tools of color, sensitivity, and drama in favor of shock, chaos, and disorder. He associated this type of modern art with "communism."[23]

Author's collection

Rockwell with mother *(left)* and first wife, Judy.

In one modern art class the instructor demanded the students create over the duration of the term a mural depicting workers, industrial strife, and maladies facing modern man. Rockwell rejected the idea, but he did not want to hold another "strike" and jeopardize the ninety dollars per month from the G.I. Bill. Instead, he and a few other classmates would check in, but then slip out the fire escape for coffee and "bull sessions." When the year was finished and the mural was due, he worked through the night to create the piece. He took a large illustration board, traced his foot with paint, drew a Marxist-looking chemist, mechanical gears, and a

While studying art at the Pratt Institute, Rockwell won an award for a macabre anti-smoking illustration.

Author's collection

freight train, then daubed and smeared primary colors to suggest "workers" and an "industrial cityscape." The next day the instructor praised the piece in front of the class and gave a lecture on its significance. He received a B for the work.[24]

In 1948, his second year at Pratt, Rockwell won the prestigious thousand-dollar first prize in a nationwide illustration contest sponsored by the New York Society of Illustrators. His winning work was an antismoking illustration for the American Cancer Society.[25]

The honorarium and national recognition should have opened agency doors where he could have developed a lucrative career. But Rockwell inexplicably quit school before completing his study. Instead he and two partners opened an advertising agency in Portland, Maine.

Maine Advertising, Inc., started fast, but a power struggle ensued, and Rockwell was bought out. In 1950 he established the Rockwell Publishing Company, Inc., in Portland. His product was a weekly tourist booklet called *The Olde Maine Guide*, a listing of happenings throughout the state, from bean suppers to tuna charters. The initial run of seven thousand copies was well received. The *Portland Press Herald* ran a photo of Rockwell and the governor of Maine, Fredrick Payne, holding an issue of the *Guide*.[26] His publishing business came to a halt on September 26, 1950, with a sudden recall to active duty for the Korean War. For the thirty-two-year-old artist California was about to become the first step on the long road of political extremism.

2

AWAKENING

> Word after word, sentence after sentence stabbed into the
> darkness like lightning bolts of revelation, tearing and
> ripping away the cobwebs of more than thirty years of
> darkness, brilliantly illuminating the heretofore obscure
> reasons for the world's madness.[1]
>
> — Rockwell's reaction to *Mein Kampf*,
> 1951

Rockwell's duty station was the naval air base at Coronado, California, where he taught Marine and Navy pilots the principles of tactical air support. For the next two years he and his wife enjoyed the economic security of an officer's pay and the stable life of the military. He was praised in his fitness report by his superior, J. D. McKinney: "Because of a tremendous enthusiasm for his subject matter coupled with an apparently inexhaustible supply of energy, Rockwell ranks as one of the better instructors at the Air Support School."[2]

While stationed at Coronado, Rockwell developed a keen interest in Wisconsin Senator Joseph McCarthy and in General Douglas MacArthur. He was swept up in the crusade to stop the rising tide of communism throughout the world. The Russians now dominated Eastern Europe and had just exploded their first atomic bomb, and China had fallen into communist hands in 1949. On January 21, 1950, a State Department official (and communist operative), Alger Hiss, was convicted of perjury. On February 9, 1950, McCarthy told an audience in Wheeling, West Virginia, that he had the names of dozens of State Department employees who were communists. The next day, Klaus Fuchs, a German-born physicist who worked in the U.S. atomic bomb program, admitted passing information to Russian agents at various times between 1942 and 1949. In March, Judith Coplon, a political analyst for the Justice Department, was convicted of passing secret documents to a Russian spy.

These events fed the public belief that the "godless" Russians planned to communize the world. They also explained why American foreign policy had failed in China and Eastern Europe—there were communists sitting behind desks in the State Department. The attorney general, J. Howard McGrath, charged, "There are today many communists in America. They are everywhere—in factories, offices, butcher shops, on street corners, in private business—and each carries in himself the germs of death for society."[3]

A movement was under way to get General MacArthur the Republican nomination in 1952. Rockwell liked the idea and made telephone calls to see what he could do to help. He read a letter to the editor in the *San Diego Union* by a woman asking for volunteers to help organize a MacArthur rally. Rockwell called her, and she invited him to her home to discuss the situation. There he told her his idea of renting a hall for the rally. The woman stopped him and with a sad face said, "No, you can't get a hall so easily, even if you pay. They won't rent one." "What do you mean?" Rockwell blurted. "Who won't rent one?" The woman glanced quizzically at her husband, took a deep breath, and said, "The Jews." "The Jews?" Rockwell burst out. "What have the Jews got to do with it? What do you care whether you get a hall or not?" "They hate MacArthur," was the reply. She unfolded a copy of the *California Jewish Voice* and pointed to an article condemning MacArthur. There were others like it. Rockwell sat in disbelief. It was too fantastic. He felt things were somehow being misinterpreted. The woman gave him some materials to take home and read.

One of the papers, "Common Sense," by Conde McGinley, detailed how Jews instigated the 1917 Russian Revolution.[4] Noting that the sources listed were the *Universal Jewish Encyclopedia* and the Overman Report to President Wilson, Rockwell decided to check the "facts" himself. He went to the San Diego Public Library and dug through journals to locate the citations in "Common Sense." The citations checked out. It suddenly occurred to him that if the woman was telling the truth about the Russian Revolution being Jewish led, perhaps she was telling the truth about an "international Jewish conspiracy" to destroy the civilization of the gentiles. So it was that in the basement of the San Diego

Public Library Rockwell awoke from "thirty years of stupid political sleep."[5]

He continued to visit the woman. Under her tutelage, he read more and more literature, until he came to the conclusion that Marxism was the organization of the world's inferior masses, attempting the overthrow of the elites of the world. He attended a speech by white supremacist Gerald L. K. Smith, director of the Christian Nationalist Crusade and publisher of *The Cross and the Flag.*[6] Smith implored his listeners to read the "holy" pages of Adolf Hitler's *Mein Kampf;* Rockwell scoured several San Diego bookstores until he found the book. He read it voraciously cover to cover, digesting its themes. He would later tell followers how the book delivered "mental sunshine which bathed all the gray world in the clear light of reason and understanding."[7] Rockwell the McCarthyite was now under the tutelage of Adolf Hitler.

He later said he now came to the realization that National Socialism was the only thing that could save white men from degradation and racial degeneration. Hitler became for him a Christ-like savior and *Mein Kampf* his new Bible. But he kept these discoveries to himself, telling no one, not even his wife, that he had become a believer in National Socialism. He focused his energies on reading all the extremist literature he could get his hands on. He carefully studied *The Protocols of the Learned Elders of Zion,* the same anti-Jewish book that Henry Ford Sr. gave away with each car for several years. Rockwell was unconcerned whether or not the *Protocols* was a forgery. The theme melded perfectly with his developing mind-set. To his wife he seemed preoccupied and distant. The few social events they attended turned sour when he attempted to "McCarthyize" the other guests. He was dismayed by the ignorance of even the best-informed people concerning what he now believed was the "battle for life and death of Western Civilization." He was appalled that learned people could read "reputable sources" like the *New York Times, Harper's,* and *Life* and believe they were truth. He reached the conclusion that Western civilization would be destroyed if the Jews were not stopped. He pondered the frightening magnitude of the task before him and wondered if his fighting spirit could take on such a difficult challenge.[8]

While he focused on the challenge of fighting communists, he was not up to the challenge his marriage presented. Rockwell and Judy now had three daughters, but their marriage was one fight after another. Nothing had changed from their honeymoon of 1943. Judy would never be the meek, passive mate he desired. They were a mismatch from the beginning, but he didn't want to put his children through the anguish of a divorce, as Doc had done to him.

In 1952 Rockwell, still a naval officer, received orders to report to Norfolk, Virginia, for further assignment. The family packed up the Nash and headed east, taking their time driving across the United States, camping in national parks, taking in the sights. He chose a northerly route so he could make a pilgrimage to Appleton, Wisconsin—Joe McCarthy's hometown.

When they arrived in Norfolk their excitement turned to gloom. Rockwell trudged out of the base with a sad look on his face; he had been assigned a one-year stint in Iceland. Since families were not allowed to transfer there, this did not bode well for his marriage. His wife and three daughters moved into a house next door to his mother-in-law in Barrington, Rhode Island, the last place he wanted his family to be.

Before he shipped out to Iceland, Rockwell visited with his cousin Pete Smyth. Smyth recalled that Rockwell became increasingly agitated as he described the magnitude of the "Jewish conspiracy" in America. Smyth was shocked by Rockwell's fervor as he went on and on about the wickedness and cleverness of the Jews. During the evening, as the two men got inebriated, Rockwell told his cousin about the need for an American Nazi Party—to rectify the error of fighting on the wrong side in the last war.[9]

He boarded a plane at Westover Air Force Base in Massachusetts for Iceland. When he stepped off the plane at the U.S. base in Keflavík, he had to brace himself against a tremendous wind. (Wind in Iceland often exceeded a hundred miles per hour, due to the convergence of the Gulf Stream and the Arctic currents at each end of the island.) Rockwell looked out at the colorless, barren land—no grass, no trees, no flowers, just dirty volcanic ash and bare ground. It looked like hell. He was detailed as executive officer of a fleet aircraft service squadron, FASRON 107. The squadron consisted mainly of patrol bombers, tucked away in a World War II hangar, surrounded by a few Quonset huts that housed the men.

Although Iceland was relatively isolated from the modern world and stateside amenities, there were consolations. Liquor was unbelievably cheap, and the beautiful Icelandic women provided carnal delights as a matter of social custom. Sex was like thirst or hunger: when they were hungry they ate, when they were thirsty they drank, and when they needed sexual pleasure, they indulged. It was not unusual for girls to take their boyfriends home for lovemaking while the parents roamed about the house. Parties at the base turned into orgies, with free liquor and free women. Even the most senior officers succumbed to temptation and partook in the frenzied activities. Rockwell later maintained that he rejected the debauchery and free-for-all atmosphere for asceticism, devoting his time to exercise, study, and writing.

After several months the Navy sent him back to the United States to tour a repair squadron in Rhode Island; he was eager to see his family, if only for a few days. When his wife picked him up at the airport she promptly informed him that she had learned to be "independent" and that there was no overcoming it. Their marriage had never been ideal. Throughout the years they clashed over control issues. Rockwell believed Judy suffered from the "common insanity" of modern education that made women feel inferior if they were housewives and mothers rather than career seekers. From time to time his college-educated wife would burst from the kitchen in anger and frustration to ask why *she* had to wash the dishes. They now argued about the house, the kids, the car, and his sexual passion, all of which made the visit uncomfortable and difficult for both of them. He slept on the couch, in the full realization that his marriage was over. When it was time for him to return to Iceland, his wife's relief was painfully obvious.[10]

He banished the agony of a broken marriage by redirecting his energies to study and writing. He reread *Mein Kampf* a dozen times, annotating and indexing the themes of the book. He wrote endless business plans for fictitious political organizations, along with propaganda and cartoons designed for mass consumption.

Rockwell took an interest in the language, culture, and history of Iceland, in particular the racial purity of the Icelandic people. He learned that Icelanders referred to Germany as the "people's defenders," in reference to their tribal memory of when Germans stood between the white men of Europe and the "savage hordes" of Genghis Khan. He attempted to learn the native language by talking with locals in and around the base, finally getting proficient enough to "shoot the breeze" at a little Icelandic grocery store.

One day he received an invitation to a diplomatic party at the

Norwegian Embassy in the capital, Reykjavík. There he met the most beautiful Icelandic woman he had ever seen. Tall, blond, aristocratic in looks and posture, she had "the face of an angel and the figure of a French model."[11] Captivated by her beauty, he asked her to dance. Margaret Thora Hallgrimsson was the twenty-three-year-old niece of the Icelandic ambassador to the United States. Thora, as she was known, had been educated in England and had traveled both the continent of Europe and the United States. She was divorced and raising a young son by herself. Over the next few months Rockwell made numerous jeep rides across the back-wrenching, icy roads between Keflavík and Reykjavík to be with her. In 1953 he asked his wife, Judy, for a divorce. She promptly agreed, demanding four hundred dollars a month in alimony.

On October 3, 1953, Rockwell and Thora, now two months pregnant, married in the national cathedral in Reykjavík. They honeymooned in the Bavarian Alps, visiting Hitler's former retreat at Berchtesgaden—"the Eagle's Nest." (Despite this choice of honeymoon destinations, it is not known whether Thora shared her new husband's enthusiasm for Hitler and his philosophy.) They returned to Iceland and settled into a family apartment on base. Only the highest-ranking officers were eligible for such luxurious quarters.

He asked the Navy for a one-year extension of duty, to November 1954, which the Navy immediately granted. On January 9, 1954, Rockwell was promoted to commander. On his fitness report his commanding officer, J. R. Wood, stated: "Rockwell has performed his duty... in an outstanding manner. He is very energetic, dynamic and persevering in whatever task he is assigned or undertakes. He is well liked and highly respected by both officers and enlisted men.... He knows how to lead men."[12]

During February 1954, he followed the newspaper accounts of the Zwicker hearings before Congress.[13] General Ralph Zwicker, a decorated World War II hero, was the commander of Camp Kilmer, New Jersey, where an Army dentist had been accused of being a communist. Zwicker had given the dentist an honorable discharge to expedite his removal from the Army; Senator McCarthy accused Zwicker and the Army of "coddling and honorably discharging a known communist."[14]

Disturbed by the accounts in the papers, he read transcripts of the proceedings in the *Congressional Record*. He immediately realized that the newspaper accounts and the *Record* were in contradiction. He concluded that American newspapers were suppressing the "truth" of McCarthy's statements; the Jewish-controlled media were deliberately slanting the news to make McCarthy look like a "bad guy" to the public. Even the Armed Forces Network was against McCarthy: the entire public information network was in a conspiracy to smear him. Why? he asked himself. Who had an interest in lying about McCarthy? He reasoned that anyone who was an effective anticommunist was labeled a hatemonger and a bigot. Since the "Jewish-controlled" media were against McCarthy, the Jews must be communist sympathizers. To Rockwell it made perfect sense: "communism was Jewish."

In May 1954 Thora gave birth to Lincoln Hallgrimmur Rockwell. After three daughters he was overjoyed to have a son. But their future clouded when on May 28 Rockwell received notice that the Navy was releasing reserve officers to inactive duty, effective October 1954. A financial disaster loomed if he could not find lucrative employment. Rockwell asked for two months' stateside duty so he could refamiliarize himself with the advertising industry (he had only watched television fifteen or twenty times) while conducting employment interviews. Captain Charles E. Perkins, the commander of the U.S. naval forces in Iceland, wrote an endorsement to Rockwell's request: "Rockwell is a writer of considerable ability. He is an outstanding caricature artist.... He is a keen-witted 'idea man' with the capability of turning out a compellingly worded pamphlet, complete with illustrations, in the shortest reasonable period."[15] The Navy granted his request for two months' duty in the United States and relocated him and his family to the naval air station in Brunswick, Maine, on August 28. He was released to inactive status on October 20, 1954.

Rockwell settled in Washington, D.C., where he put together a magazine directed at servicemen's wives, called U.S. Lady. His idea was to distribute the magazine free of charge to service wives. The large circulation base would make it attractive to advertisers. He hoped the magazine would provide not only a lucrative income for his family but a means of subtle political expression. He was also accepted into the Navy's Ready Reserve program, attached to FASRON 661 in nearby Anacostia. The first issue of U.S. Lady, in September of 1955, featured regular columns, "Menu of the Month," "Post of the Month," "U.S. Lady of the Month," and "Dress Parade," as well as household tips and service etiquette.

Rockwell published several issues of the magazine, but undercapitalization forced him to sell out in 1956. Although *U.S. Lady* was lucrative and a fairly successful business venture, the magazine was an inadequate vehicle for his anti-Jewish beliefs.

After sporadic employment he made a serious effort to establish a conservative newspaper that could be used as a national medium of expression. Such a paper, he believed, could organize and even discipline the "splintered and squabbling right-wing into a cohesive, effective organization."[16]

Under the aegis of the American Federation of Conservative Organizations, Rockwell created mock-ups for a newspaper to be called the *Conservative Times*. He held numerous public and private meetings in Washington and Virginia, where he met John Kasper, who referred to Hitler as "The Saint." Through Kasper he met Ezra Pound, the lunatic poet and broadcaster for Mussolini, now locked up in the mental ward of St. Elizabeths Hospital. Nonetheless, and although his premise for starting a conservative newspaper was sound, he was unable to persuade investors to provide the start-up capital for the operation.[17]

In 1955, Rockwell and others of like mind believed, the right wing had an opportunity to "sneak up" on the Jews by building a mass grassroots organization. Its strength would grow until one day it would turn on the Jews. This view was widely promoted, and although he would later call it a "coward's dream," he was at first as beguiled by it as anyone. They even talked of drastic "guerrilla" methods to "spill the beans" about the Jews, such as dropping pamphlets out of airplanes in crowded cities or raiding a major television network station at gunpoint and exposing to the masses the "fact" that communism was Jewish.

Rockwell felt, however, that his best efforts were useless, because the right wing consisted of "ninety-percent cowards, one-track minds, tightwads and worst of all, hobbyists." He now decided that their methodology was also wrong. The battle between ideologies had to be waged with force, terror, and power. Liberals had forced their way into power by daring minority tactics, not the excellence of their ideas or the merit of their work. They remained in power because conservatives were using the wrong methods. Rockwell believed the conservatives' motives were also wrong, that most were aracial. Their basic concerns were economic (taxes, government spending) and social (crime, morality); they were concerned about the erosion of their standard of living by the ever-encroaching welfare state. However, they had little concern about or knowledge of the "biological problem," of which the other issues, he believed, were manifestations.

Rockwell surmised that as long as conservatives focused on the economic-materialistic rather than the racial, defending a system rather than a race, they would continue foolishly to pursue spurious and superficial solutions rather than fundamental ones. In essence, he was falling into line with Hitler's doctrine:

> The instinct of preserving the species is the first cause of the formation of human communities. But the State is a folk organism and not an economic organization. A difference that is as great as it remains incomprehensible to the so-called "statesman," especially of today. They believe therefore, that they can build up the State by economy, whereas in reality it is always the result of the activity of those qualities which lie in line with the will to preserve the species and the race.[18]

His efforts to create the *Conservative Times* depleted his savings account to the point where he had to find some employment. He had no income other than his monthly Naval Reserve check. A mutual friend arranged a meeting between Rockwell and William Buckley, Jr., publisher of the *National Review*. Rockwell was overwhelmed by the intellectual prowess of Buckley and his staff—which included several Jews. He felt there was "more pulsating brain-power and genius surrounding Buckley than in any place else on earth."[19] Buckley would not discuss the "Jewish question," but he did hire Rockwell to promote *National Review* in colleges and universities. Their business relationship did not last long; Rockwell gave the job a halfhearted effort. Promoting conservatism was not his paramount objective. He wanted to fight Jews.

Rockwell decided to freelance his skills. He hired on with Robert Snowden, a wealthy plantation owner from Hughes, Arkansas, who ran a program called Americans for Constitutional Action. The official purpose of the group was to "awaken Americans everywhere to the dangers that are facing us at home as well as abroad," one of the dangers being runaway spending, which it believed was pushing the country down the road to socialism. The group focused on imposing limits on federal spending and taxation. Its strategy was to amend the Constitution with the approval of thirty-six states, thereby bypassing Congress. Its committee was one of the largest lobbies in Washington.

In the summer of 1956, Rockwell moved to Memphis, Tennessee, where he found Snowden's temperament not to his liking. Snowden assigned him only menial tasks and reneged on his promise to have Rockwell write film scripts, but Rockwell needed the $8,000 annual salary to support his current family and ex-wife. Rockwell was still flying one weekend per month, as commanding officer of FASRON 661, while working for Snowden. He was ordered to take a couple of reserve squadrons for two weeks' intensive flight training at Grosse Isle, Michigan. When he returned to Memphis, he and Snowden had a serious conflict; the men parted ways.[20] Rockwell purchased a towable forty-four-foot trailer so his family wouldn't have it so rough when he moved from city to city.

His next job was working for Russell Maguire, editor of *American Mercury* magazine. Maguire put Rockwell on his staff in New York City as his assistant to help promote the magazine, and Rockwell put total effort into his work. He was introduced to DeWest Hooker, a wealthy American with pro-Nazi leanings. Hooker had assembled some New York City toughs into a group called the Nationalist Youth League (NYL), which he used against communist meetings and leftist rallies. Rockwell and Hooker discussed using the NYL for anti-Jewish demonstrations, but nothing ever materialized, as Hooker soon went to Italy to operate a 7-Up soft drink bottling franchise.[21] Rockwell maintained contact with the members of the NYL.

At the end of 1956, Rockwell left the *American Mercury* after a row with Maguire. Nearly destitute, he took a job as a salesman for a management engineering firm in New York City, selling consulting services. Ironically, he was most successful selling to Jewish businessmen. He attributed this success to the fact that he understood them better than the average *goy*. He was direct, talked rough, and even pushed some of them out of their chairs.[22] This endeavor, however, also failed. The follow-up men from the consulting firm were unable to close the sales that Rockwell initiated, and he was let go.

Rockwell's foray into the right wing had not turned out as expected. He had made enemies of the very people he wanted to organize. But now DeWest Hooker got word to him about an upcoming meeting in Knoxville, Tennessee, to form the United White Party (precursor to the National States Rights Party), led by segregationists J. B. Stoner and Ed Fields. Rockwell traveled to Knoxville, arriving in time to attend an informal gathering the night before the event. Here Rockwell met the elites of the supremacist movement in the United States, including Stoner, Fields, Wallace Allen, and Emory Burke—the feisty founder of the Columbian Workers Movement.[23] After hearing Rockwell explain his "Lincoln plan" to repatriate blacks to Africa, Burke arranged for Rockwell to speak before the assembly. Burke was impressed by Rockwell's colorful personality and speaking abilities, but he cautioned him to leave the National Socialist jargon out of his speech; most Southerners made no distinction, he said, between National Socialism and communism.[24] The following day Rockwell gave his speech, minus the Hitlerism.

Wallace Allen, a well-to-do advertising man, took a liking to Rockwell and invited him to sell advertising with him in Atlanta. Rockwell moved his family to Atlanta. There he experienced a series of dreams, each a variation on the same theme. A man would approach him and say, "Someone wants to see you." The two would walk to a room, where Rockwell would open the door and find Adolf Hitler waiting for him; then he would wake up. Always a skeptic when confronted with the supernatural, Rockwell was shaken by the recurring dreams, omens that became for him a symbolic summons to a path not yet taken.[25]

Rockwell remained in Atlanta only a few months before the economy went sour and advertising sales dried up. In February 1958 he loaded his wife and their four children—Ricky, Lincoln, Jeannie, Evelyn—into their forty-four-foot trailer and drove to Newport News, Virginia, where he presented himself in naval uniform at the home of William Stephenson, publisher of the *Virginian*.[26] Stephenson purchased a few of his cartoons but never employed Rockwell directly. While freelancing for the *Virginian* Rockwell created "The Fable of the Ducks and Hens," an allegorical story that used farm animals to explore the "real world" relationships among whites, Jews, Germans, and Arabs. He was to employ this technique on numerous occasions in his writings in the 1960s.

Rockwell now met thirty-nine-year-old Harold Noel Arrowsmith, who owned the printing equipment used by Stephenson and bankrolled the *Virginian*. Arrowsmith was the son of the canon of the Episcopal cathedral in Baltimore, and he was reputed to be one of the owners of Dunn & Bradstreet. He lived with his mother in a large stone mansion in Baltimore.

With an estimated net worth of $150 million, Arrowsmith had no interest in pursuing a vocation. His life consisted of studying at prestigious universities and doing research in the Library of Congress. He held a degree from Johns Hopkins and had attended Cornell, Harvard, Stanford, the University of California–Berkeley, UCLA, and the universities of Mainz (Germany) and Oxford (England). A victim of chronic insomnia, Arrowsmith spent hour after hour, day after day, poring over microfilms in the Library of Congress, collecting what he believed to be official government documents "proving" a Jewish-communist conspiracy. He maintained numerous filing cabinets, each bulging with photocopies of declassified military intelligence reports, court records, and diplomatic correspondence. Unfortunately for Arrowsmith, his carefully documented findings were rejected time and again by scholarly journals. He decided to approach Rockwell with the proposition of printing, publishing, and distributing his materials. Rockwell was quite impressed with Arrowsmith, "the most violent Jew hater" he had ever met.[27]

Rockwell with his Icelandic second wife, Thora, and children in 1958.

3

1958: BATTLE CALL

I am anti-Zionist and anti-Communist-Jews, and any other
form of treason. I'm pro–American republic.
— Rockwell, FBI interrogation, 1958

On a Sunday morning in May 1958, Arrowsmith drove to Rockwell's
trailer in Newport News to discuss a partnership. Arrowsmith proposed
a dog-eat-dog plan to repossess the printing and photographic equipment that Stephenson used to produce the *Virginian* and give it to
Rockwell to establish an anti-Jewish publishing operation. Rockwell
liked the idea and suggested they locate in Arlington, Virginia, just
across the Potomac from the capital. They hoped the proximity to
Washington would ensure that their literature would get into the hands
of influential government officials. Arrowsmith wanted more than a
printing operation; he wanted street action—demonstrations and
protests—to coincide with their literature dissemination.

Rockwell had the foresight to realize there would be no turning back
once such a venture began; traditional employment would be difficult
to find if not impossible. This was a golden opportunity, a chance to
couple his anti-Jewish fervor with the financial backing of a millionaire.
He conditionally agreed to coordinate both printing and street action if
Arrowsmith supplied a home for his wife and children and an income
to support them. Arrowsmith agreed and countered with his final
demand: the name of the operation would be the National Committee
to Free America from Jewish Domination (NCFAJD). Rockwell disliked

the name, but he knew which side his bread was buttered on. They shook hands on their agreement.

Within two weeks they found a little suburban home in Williamsburg, a commercially zoned section of Arlington. The zoning provision allowed them legally to use the house as both a political headquarters and place of residence. Arrowsmith paid $15,200 cash down on the $23,000 purchase price and held the title; Rockwell would make mortgage installments and repay Arrowsmith the down payment from printing profits. Arrowsmith promptly repossessed his printing equipment from Stephenson and moved it to the new "headquarters," at 6512 Williamsburg Boulevard. Except for supplying the capital needed to run the operation, Arrowsmith wanted to be a silent partner. Rockwell could take the heat for operating the hard-core anti-Jewish organization.

The first project of the "National Committee" was a protest against the U.S. involvement in Lebanon. On July 15, 1958, President Dwight D. Eisenhower sent 3,500 Marines to Lebanon to help maintain the government of President Camille Chamoun, which was plagued by civil war between Christians, who wanted a pro-Western independent Lebanon, and Muslims, who demanded closer relations with Gamal Abdal Nasser's United Arab Republic. The prospect of a pro-Arab government coming to power in Lebanon was seen in Washington as a threat to Israel and peace in the Middle East. When the conflict reached critical mass and the Chamoun regime was near collapse, Eisenhower sent troops to stabilize it.

The news media spread the view that intervention was necessary to stop the spread of Nasser's influence, but Rockwell and Arrowsmith believed the U.S. military presence in Lebanon had been initiated by American Jews, who, using their "usual tactics of press distortion and secret pressure," wished to force the U.S. government into defending the Lebanese puppet regime against its own people.[1] Although the government of Lebanon had pledged war with Israel, Chamoun's regime was in fact resigned to maintaining the status quo with that nation. Thus it was in Israel's interest to support the regime; any additional Nasserite-type regimes on Israel's border would pose a serious threat to its security.[2]

Rockwell chose July 27, 1958, for the "coming out" of the NCFAJD. He printed large (three-by-five-foot) placards with the slogans:

Don't Fight Another War to Save the Jews.

Nasser has jailed his Reds, but Jews lie that he is Red.

Communism is Jewish. Twelve of thirteen convicted spies are Jewish. ROSENBERGS, GREENGLASS, SOBEL, GOLD, BROTHMAN, WEINSTEIN, MOSCOWITZ, etc.

The only communist party in the Middle East is Israel.

Jews won't dispute our facts. They must shut us up.

Zionism is causing trouble in Lebanon.[3]

Two of the signs depicted a large, hook-hosed man holding a pistol to the head of a caricature of President Eisenhower, with the caption "Save IKE from the KIKES."

Rockwell mobilized former members of Hooker's disbanded Nationalist Youth League from New York to picket the White House, and he arranged for simultaneous demonstrations by Wallace Allen and his associates in Atlanta, Georgia.[4] The New Yorkers arrived on a bus the day before the picket. Rockwell spread them out across Washington distributing thousands of handbills on the Lebanon situation. The next morning they became frightened—the leader of the group told the others they would be killed by "three or four hundred niggers." Rockwell told them he would go on alone if need be and that if they "chickened out" he would never want to see them again. A thin Greek youth, John Patsalos, stepped forward and said he would go with Rockwell. One by one, the others decided to stick it out; they packed up the placards and prepared to start. Rockwell held Thora and looked into her eyes for a long while. He too was concerned about violence; the "Kike" placards might cause a deadly riot.[5]

When they arrived at Pennsylvania Avenue, police informed Rockwell of the rules for picketing the White House. Rockwell grabbed a "Kike" placard and with little fanfare stepped off a small curb—the first step in becoming the world's most notorious anti-Semite since Adolf Hitler. There were no mobs of screaming Jews, no "three hundred niggers" waiting to beat them. Their audience consisted of journalists and Anti-Defamation League photographers. After a peaceful demonstration,

Rockwell accompanied the youths to a motel to celebrate their success with a few beers.

Rockwell's criticism of Jews was so far limited to Israel, but there is no doubt as to the true motivations of a man using caustic epithets like "Kike" on protest signs. He hated not only Israel but American Jewry as well. Public criticism of Zionists may or may not be acceptable to American Jewry, but open hatred and condemnation of its heritage, its existence, will mark a man for life—Rockwell was marked for life. Crossing over the unmarked line into anti-Semitism is an act from which there is no return. A political career—other than that of an extremist—is no longer possible. Moreover, the family is held accountable and impugned for such actions.

The Arrowsmith-Rockwell partnership was short-lived. They quarreled and by August had gone separate ways. Arrowsmith believed he had been deceived by a "con man," because Rockwell had not printed as many leaflets as instructed but instead had used the printing equipment to create his own propaganda, under the auspices of a different organization, the World Union of Free Enterprise National Socialists (WUFENS). Rockwell was already toying with the idea of a Nazi revival in which national Nazi groups would operate under an international umbrella organization. Rockwell, however, felt he was the one betrayed. Arrowsmith's style was to flaunt his great wealth, dangling enticements in front of people, but never to dole it out. When it came to money, Arrowsmith was stingy. In September 1958 Arrowsmith filed suit against Rockwell to recover the house, printing press, and other equipment from Williamsburg Boulevard. Rockwell claimed "squatter's rights" and maintained residence.

On October 12, 1958, fifty sticks of dynamite exploded inside the Hebrew Benevolent Congregation Synagogue in Atlanta. Authorities arrested Wallace Allen, among others, in connection with the bombing. A search of Allen's property revealed a letter from Rockwell mentioning a "big blast" that would take place in the future. Rockwell admitted writing the letter to Allen but told the FBI that his reference was to the Lebanon picketing, not a bombing.

Rockwell provided the FBI a letter he had received from Allen that July, when they were discussing plans to coordinate several simultaneous anti-

Jewish demonstrations in the eastern United States. Rockwell believed the letter provided proof that Allen had not bombed the synagogue:

Dear Linc:

Congratulations on having obtained arms to fight the enemy. I hope the "Fat Cat" realized the necessity for a continuing and relentless assault, as for instance, a weekly attack by Truth against the Daily Liars. . . .

The exact method we will use here is still undecided and is entirely dependent on existing conditions which will be examined thoroughly. You will just have to trust we will do the best job possible with the means at hand. The Israeli consulate is next door to the F.B.I., if there is any significance to that. The Temple would be wrong since it relates to the religious rather than the political. Next is choosing picketers who are the most immune from Jewish economic retaliation etc. But I'll figure out something.[6]

Rockwell believed the sentence "The Temple would be wrong since it relates to the religious rather than the political" was proof that Allen would not bomb a synagogue, not even picket one. Allen was eventually cleared of all charges. Rockwell insisted to FBI agents that his own writings were not meant to incite anyone to violence, except when being attacked by Jews. "Literature setting forth the truth was worth more than 10,000 cross burnings or a bombing. Their fight was against the political Jews and not the religious Jews."[7] He tried to convince the press and the FBI he was not anti-Semitic. "I am anti-Zionist and anti-Communist-Jews, and any other form of treason. I'm pro-American republic."[8]

When his connection with the Atlanta bombing made the papers, Rockwell acted as if paranoid. One night a speeding car tried to "run him down" in front of his home as he crossed the street. In fact, however, a cherry bomb was thrown into his front yard by someone in a passing car. There were also scores of calls threatening his life. He boasted, on the other hand, of receiving several "God bless you" calls from supporters. He told reporters, "I have not and will not ask for police protection. If anyone's brave enough to stick their head in here we'll take care of them."[9] Behind the veneer of bravado were second thoughts. He told another reporter, "It's scaring the life out of me and my wife because we know what will happen. Our kids will be persecuted in school. . . . The income tax people will be checking on me. . . . I've seen what happened to other people."

He spoke of the World Union of Free Enterprise National Socialists as a legitimate political group based on free enterprise and racial nationalism. He displayed to FBI agents the cover of a book he was writing about the WUFENS movement; on it was a large, black swastika. The title was *Battle Call: Fight on Your Feet with the World Union of Free Enterprise Socialists or Live on Your Knees with the Jews.*[10]

When Arrowsmith read the Associated Press story about the Atlanta bombing and the mysterious letter from Arlington he went to the FBI to explain his relationship with Rockwell. He told the Bureau he was engaged in the "publication of suppressed documents" and had hired Rockwell as a printer who would be accustomed to this type of work.[11] The FBI launched a general investigation into anti-Jewish activities in the Washington area; its primary focus was Rockwell and his association with Arrowsmith.

In late October the directors of the B'nai B'rith Cardozo Lodge in Arlington asked for the resignation of an Arlington school board member, Helen Lane, because of her "association" with Rockwell. The statement asked Lane to resign "for the good of the entire community."[12] If she did not submit her resignation, the lodge indicated, it would pressure the Arlington County Board to oust her. Lane, who had previously renounced Rockwell's ideology, emphasized that she had met Rockwell and his family through a mutual friend. She denied any "connection" with the family other than "a personal one" and remained on the school board.

Rockwell filed a $50,000 libel suit in Arlington Circuit Court against Cardozo Lodge for their statements that he was an "anti-Semite." Rockwell contended that Semites are "mostly Arabs, for whom he has great sympathy of Jewish aggression so that he is actually pro-Semite and is not an advocate of hatred in any form."[13] The case was thrown out; Judge Emory Hosner ruled that it did not warrant argument on its merits.

Looking for a new issue, Rockwell discovered an article in the *Northern Virginia Sun* about an upcoming fund-raising dinner at the Arlington Jewish Center where Israeli government bonds could be purchased to help finance a village in Israel to be known as Arlington-Fairfax Village. Hopeful that the fund-raiser might violate U.S. law, Rockwell paid a visit to Nathan Lenvin, head of the Registration Act Section, U.S. Department of Justice. Rockwell told Lenvin a fictitious story of having been approached by representatives from the Egyptian embassy regarding a job as a propaganda agent for the Egyptian government. He told Lenvin he was planning to leave for Cairo to discuss arrangements and was concerned whether registration was required prior to his departure.

Lenvin advised Rockwell that registration was not necessary, since the Foreign Agents Registration Act of 1938 regulated only activities within the United States. However, should he agree to act at the "order, request, or under the direction of the Egyptian Government," he would be under an obligation to file a registration statement pursuant to the act's provisions. Lenvin gave Rockwell a list of all registered agents in the United States.

Rockwell perused the list and noted that Irving Berman, the chairman of the Israel Fund Drive, was not a registered agent for the Israeli government. Rockwell was now convinced the Arlington-Fairfax fund-raising dinner would violate the Registration Act. The next day he telephoned Lenvin, advising him of Berman's absence from the list of registered agents, and the FBI, furnishing information about the dinner. He expected the FBI or the Department of Justice to stop the event.[14]

The FBI checked its records on the activities of the American Financial Development Corporation for Israel (AFDCI), which handled the sale of bonds in the United States. In 1951 the Bureau had determined that the AFDCI, which had thousands of volunteers throughout the country, was a nonprofit organization. The Department of Justice had exempted the organization from the Registration Act, because its activities in trade and commerce aimed to relieve human suffering.[15]

On the morning of November 16, 1958, Rockwell distributed pamphlets titled "Who's a Hate-Monger?" around the Washington, D.C., area. The pamphlet, which credited Rockwell with authorship, was one of the first issued under the World Union of Free Enterprise National Socialists banner. The pamphlet read:

> We learn that Russian Jews control ALL our television networks, our movies, most of our giant newspapers, our theater, our concert stage, and the monster department stores in cities all over the country which support ALL newspapers with their huge advertising budgets.
>
> We discover with increasing concern that Jewish papers and leaders boast that it was largely through Jewish efforts that the Supreme Court was induced to render its integration decision and that it is the American

Jewish Committee and the Anti-Defamation League of B'nai B'rith which push so everlastingly hard for race mixing in our stricken U.S. South.

When we go to the JEWISH books and papers, we discover that, among themselves, the Jews make no bones about their program of hatred and suppression of US. They advise Jews, for instance, to work to get rid of our ancient and precious Christmas traditions in our public life, and counsel their "Brotherhood" workers to get in their efforts in JULY, not at Christmas time, so that we won't notice their activity. Imagine what any normal person would think of a Christian who went to Israel, was welcomed, and then began a careful, planned activity in SECRET to eliminate Yom Kippur from Israeli life! In short, when we examine the ACTIVITIES of most Jews, we discover that their CREED appears to be hate and suppression of US, and manipulation to gain our power, our money, and our very inheritance of Nordic blood![16]

In Iceland, Thora's well-to-do father received word of his son-in-law's activities. Concerned about the well-being of his daughter and grandchildren, he telephoned Arlington and pressured her to return to Iceland. The dashing naval fighter pilot she had fallen in love with was now an open National Socialist. Sensing Thora's reluctance, her parents flew to the United States to persuade her to return. At first Rockwell was against the idea of his family leaving; Thora was his only companion and he loved his four children dearly. Nonetheless, he knew they were leading a difficult existence; he agreed to let her return to her homeland with their children. They agreed that after one year, when he had found steady employment and a new home, she would return. Mr. Hallgrimmson bought plane tickets and made arrangements for her belongings.

In late November a moving van rolled to a stop in front of the Rockwell home on Williamsburg Boulevard. The men loaded boxes, and the family quietly helped them. When the loading was complete the family squeezed into their car and drove to Idlewild (now JFK) International Airport in New York. Rockwell took a final picture of his four children as they waited to board the plane, and looked into the tear-filled eyes of his wife. After a final hug and kiss, Thora herded the children into the plane and flew to Iceland. She would never return.

Rockwell trudged through the concourse, now totally alone—no family, no job, no money, his home in jeopardy, the ire of the Jewish community raised against him. As the days passed into weeks, Rockwell slipped deeper and deeper into depression. The house that had been alive with playing children was now quiet, cold, and empty. The sight of a doll or baby dress left behind brought him to the verge of sobbing. He spent Thanksgiving and Christmas alone. His fellow conservatives ostracized him. The utility company shut off the electricity and telephone.[17] On December 1, 1958, Rockwell's naval status was changed to standby reserve: no more weekend flying, no more monthly paychecks.

Rockwell's siblings were shocked by his actions. His sister Priscilla said they were "horrified . . . we wanted to crawl in a hole and hide . . . it was a nightmare." Most affected by his older brother's notoriety was Robert, a rising young businessman raising a family in New England. Robert offered to help pay for psychiatric treatment for what he believed was Rockwell's clinical paranoia.

Robert tried to force Rockwell into a decision by issuing an ultimatum to "immediately drop all political and racial activities for a period of two years . . . and see a recognized psychiatrist" for extended therapy. If Rockwell rejected the offer, Robert threatened to sever all ties with him.

Rockwell responded with a four-page letter mocking his brother's concerns and ranting about the "conspiracy" of forces committed to his destruction. He also hinted at the need for psychiatric help. "I have even made attempts to see if I could finance a psychiatrist, not because I really do think I am nuts, but because I recognize that every nut thinks he is RIGHT. If I am NOT right, and am heading for this HORRIBLE battle, I DEARLY wish to be disabused of my delusion."[18]

John Patsalos, the twenty-year-old from New York who had stepped forward to picket the White House earlier in the year and had since joined the Marines, was in Washington on a layover. He decided to stop by and visit Rockwell. As he walked up the steps to the house, he noticed the windows were all broken. Inside he found a dejected Rockwell, cold and hungry.

Patsalos could sympathize with Rockwell; his own life had been checkered by loneliness. He was the first of two sons born to Christos and Athena Patsalos. When he was five years old his father had murdered his mother, an act Patsalos described as a "crime of passion—one of those freak episodes in life when a man permits his emotions to blind his rational thought."[19] Christos had been convicted of manslaughter and sentenced to Sing-Sing penitentiary. John and his brother George were suddenly alone, surrounded by strangers in the slums of upper Manhattan. The boys lived in a tenement building with their maternal grandmother in a neighborhood teeming with street gangs. His grandmother ran a small stand on Park Avenue, where she peddled flowers. According to Patsalos, the Jewish merchants who dominated the market "ridiculed his grandmother's Christian faith." Sometimes the arguments between his grandmother and Jews had become so hot that she would swat them over the head with her broom.

Although they were poor, however, there was always food on the table, and they took pride in a hard day's work. John had learned to be quick with his fists, since his physical stature was less than imposing, but there was also a very artistic side to his personality. In junior high school he had become the editor and cartoonist for the school magazine, acted in school plays, and had a one-man ventriloquist act.

When their grandmother died, the Patsalos boys had gone to live with their paroled father in the Bronx. It had been a difficult adjustment to make, and soon John was in trouble with the law, for stealing a car. At Christopher Columbus High School he developed a keen political interest in Jews—the teachers were mostly Jewish, as were most of the students. When a Jewish history teacher condemned Hitler for his actions against Jews in World War II, John vehemently disagreed, saying that believing what a Jew said about Hitler was like believing what the Devil might say about God. He went to the library and demanded the librarian unlock the bookcase containing *Mein Kampf*. After reading Hitler's book he became reborn a National Socialist, at age sixteen.[20]

He had read everything he could find on National Socialism and Adolf Hitler, and Conde McGinley's magazine *Common Sense*. He socialized with people of a similar persuasion. He was introduced to DeWest Hooker, the tall, handsome, arrogant Ivy Leaguer who had organized and funded a small group of hoodlums into a "political action" group he called the Nationalist Youth League. Patsalos immediately joined, and he became an integral member—marching around New York City, picketing, fighting, and breaking up communist meetings. He was eventually arrested for distributing inflammatory leaflets and sent to the Mental Hygiene Clinic at Morrisania City Hospital for observation. There Patsalos had been evaluated by Dr. Pierre Rube, who was struck by his hatred, "his impaired judgment, his rigidity, his very immature emotionality, his narcissism, his irrelevant suspiciousness, his belief in his own righteousness."[21] Rube had surmised that Patsalos was a repressed homosexual and a potential murderer; he diagnosed him as suffering from acute paranoia.[22]

In 1957, the members of the NYL had gathered at Hooker's house for a farewell party. Hooker, moving to Italy, wanted to give the boys a bash. It had been a short but memorable party; Patsalos had been introduced to Commander George Lincoln Rockwell, U.S. Navy.

Patsalos now dug into his wallet and gave Rockwell a twenty-dollar bill. Rockwell snatched the money and ran to the store for groceries. Before Patsalos left to catch his connecting flight to New York City the two men sang a Nazi battle song.[23]

Rockwell picked up a few printing jobs and was able to get the power turned on. He spent hours in the library, reading law in preparation for the showdown with Arrowsmith's high-powered attorney for custody of the house. When the day in court arrived Rockwell was well prepared, and he convinced the judge that his binding oral agreement with Arrowsmith entitled him a year's use of the property.

Nevertheless, he continued to sink deeper into depression and self-pity. In time, however, a strange experience pulled him out of his misery. One morning he received a package from a "fellow traveler," James K. Warner. Inside he found a carefully folded Nazi flag, eleven feet long. He believed it was a stroke of destiny. He closed the living room curtains and hung the flag across one entire wall, placed a plaque of Hitler at the center of the flag and three lighted candles on a bookcase in front of it, then stepped to the other side of the room to "worship" at his shrine, his altar to Adolf Hitler.

He felt an upsurge in his soul, a religious-like power. Goose bumps covered his body, his hair stood on end, tears filled his eyes. He experienced a sense of being more than himself, communion with something vast and eternal. His purpose in life was now clear; he was filled with a sense of mission, a sense of destiny. He would fight Jews to the death. He snapped his heels together, raised his arm in salute, and shouted "Heil Hitler! *Heil Hitler! HEIL HITLER!*"[24]

4

1959: THE ARMOR
OF FEARLESSNESS

> When I was in the advertising game, we used nude women.
> Now I use the hackenkreuz [swastika] and stormtroopers.
> You use what brings them in.
> — Rockwell, opening of WUFENS
> Headquarters, 1959

The week after Rockwell's Nazi epiphany, two visitors appeared at his door: twenty-seven-year-old Eugene Colton, a right-winger of recent acquaintance, and a man Rockwell never met before, who went by the name J. V. Morgan. Morgan was shocked by the swastika flag and wanted to leave, but Colton convinced him to hear Rockwell out. Under the swastika Rockwell asserted to Morgan that the "nigger trouble" was due to communist Jews pushing integration. He illustrated with pictures of the president of the National Association for the Advancement of Colored People (NAACP), Arthur Spingarn, and the director of the Congress of Racial Equality (CORE), Marvin Rich—both Jews. In the course of the evening Rockwell converted both Colton and Morgan into Nazis.

This small cadre hereafter met each week, dressed in khaki shirts, swastika armbands, leather belts, and boots. Rockwell bathed the swastika flag with an infrared floodlight to accent the psychological effect of heat emanating. He opened the curtains for all to see, knowing this would be too much for the Jews to stomach. He waited for them to take the bait.

The press and the FBI established a close watch and attempted to discover any connections with Egyptian President Gamal Nasser. The *New York Daily News* published a series of articles exploring the ties between Arabs and American hate groups. The *News* postulated a "loose-linked network of American neo-Fascist groups" acting on behalf of the United Arab Republic that kept American "hate groups" supplied with UAR propaganda, using Egyptian military intelligence officers, who had diplomatic immunity, as contact men.[1]

The UAR officials denied any involvement, stating they would have nothing to do with "these scum"; "they would be kicked out, if they dared to cross the embassy threshold." A UAR official asked, "What can we do if these people want to tell our story? Is that our fault? You know as well as I do that the Jews control your so-called free press here. Only the Zionist voices are heard."[2]

On January 29, 1959, Rockwell made a visit to the UAR embassy. His purpose was twofold. First, the possibility of being on the Arab payroll as a foreign agent appealed to him; getting a salary to harass Jews was worth checking into. Second, he wanted to see if he would be "thrown out," as reported in the *News*.

He was introduced to Amin Mouftah, who promptly asked him to leave the embassy. Rockwell insisted he had vital information for the UAR, but Mouftah was not interested. He reminded Rockwell that the UAR had already become a "victim of vicious propaganda" based on allegations surrounding the bombing of Jewish institutions. When Rockwell departed, Mouftah telephoned the U.S. State Department and repeated his conversation with Rockwell.[3]

Incensed about his treatment at the Egyptian embassy, Rockwell sent a letter to President Nasser:

His Excellency President Nasser

There can be no doubt that you have seen the despicable articles in the *New York Daily News* pillorying us all as a gang of dirty "hate" conspirators against the poor, innocent Jews—so I will not waste your time with a recital of the contents.

However your representatives here in America have stated that they would throw such "scum" as myself out of their premises "bodily" and I cannot believe you have authorized such cowardly and traitorous utterances.

I know they are cowardly, because I have appeared at your Embassy in Washington to be thrown out as promised—and, while I was indeed dealt with most discourteously, I was NOT thrown out.

I am a Commander in the U.S. Navy—a fighter pilot—and I know you too are a military man. I am a man of honor and integrity and courage like yourself, and I cannot believe you will run like a rabbit because the Jews here snarl at us.

Can it be that the great character which was able to unite and defend his people against the Jewish Imperialist conspiracy has grown so soft and weak that he is now frightened to speak for those who are brave enough to fight the same thing you defeated? We mean to expose the vicious conspiracy which is destroying our people, as it almost did yours, and to drive the ugly thing to its well deserved death. We propose nothing immoral or illegal. On the contrary, we are prepared to expose the ILLEGAL fund raising here in the billions for Israel—and to STOP these illegal funds with the LAW. We are prepared to do this, honorably, openly, powerfully.

When a man is accused of being a hunchbacked monster, his best defense is to step into the light and demonstrate the TRUTH. We have been accused of being illicit, sneaky, cowardly conspirators.

I suggest that you instruct your people to see me openly, honestly, and that we join in an open, honest, and successful fight to destroy Israel the way it must be destroyed, by cutting off the parasite's blood.

> Respectfully and with admiration,
> Lincoln Rockwell[4]

In February 1959 the FBI opened a Registration Act investigation to ascertain whether or not Rockwell was engaged in activities on behalf of the UAR. The following memo was circulated among senior FBI officials:

From information in the "New York Daily News" it is clear that anti-Jewish literature prepared by Arab countries is being either reprinted or distributed in this country by hate groups which are anti-Semitic. . . .

It must be kept in mind that the Arab countries and the hate groups in the U.S. have one common enemy—the Jews. The adage "Politics makes strange bedfellows" actually holds true here as the above racists are all anti-Semitic (which by definition of the word means anti-Arab as well as anti-Jewish) and anti-Negro, which the Arabs would definitely not admit being.

This appears to be a case where both groups (Arabs and racists) are using each other against their common enemy, the Jews, in order to further their own individual interests. . . . The mere fact that propaganda material is being swapped and reprinted by each group does not in and of itself indicate such control or direction [as] to require registration.[5]

On at least two occasions Rockwell was approached by outsiders seeking his involvement in acts of violence. The first incident occurred a few weeks after Rockwell, Colton, and Morgan began meeting as Nazis. A man identifying himself as "Jake" arrived at Rockwell's house. He represented "the Colonel," who commanded a secret army of a thousand men and two million dollars' worth of arms. The group had plans for an attack and enough arms to conduct a "major operation." The purpose of Jake's visit was to persuade Rockwell to meet with "the Colonel." Rockwell was convinced that Jake was a "crazy" or an agent provocateur. Fearful that someone was trying to tie him into a conspiracy with people who advocated violence, Rockwell immediately informed the FBI of Jake's visit. He emphasized to the Bureau that he would have nothing to do with any acts of violence and did not allow his associates to talk of violence. Nonetheless, the FBI stepped up its surveillance of Rockwell; all of his telephone calls were monitored, and a twenty-four-hour watch was placed on his home. Rockwell never heard from the mystery man "Jake" again, and FBI files reveal nothing about his identity.[6]

On another occasion, Rockwell telephoned the FBI to report correspondence with an anarchist in San Juan, Puerto Rico. He had received a letter postmarked from Puerto Rico with a rambling narrative about fires and bombs. Rockwell told the Bureau that he did not want to correspond with anyone who might be involved with bombings and thought the Bureau should be aware of the letter. Another possible attempt to involve Rockwell in a conspiracy had failed.[7]

By late March 1959 Rockwell had codified his ideas in a pamphlet entitled "Program of the World Union of Free Enterprise National Socialists." The pamphlet explained that the "problem" was Marxism, which had grown from merely a scheme in the "twisted" minds of Marx, Engels, and a few other Jews into a scientific, terroristic monster, Jewish Bolshevism. Since no present organization or government was capable of stopping Jewish Bolshevism, Rockwell believed, the rise of National Socialism was necessary. He summarized the seven principles that formed the basis of his beliefs and the tenets of the WUFENS organization:

> An honest man can never be happy in a naked scramble for material gain and comfort, without any goal which he believes is greater than himself, and for which he is willing to sacrifice his own egotism. This goal was formerly provided by fundamentalist religions, but science and subversion have so weakened all traditional religions, and given man such an unwarranted, short-sighted conceit of his own "power over Nature" that he has, in effect, become his own God. He is spiritually lost, even if he will not admit it. We believe that the only realistic goal which can still lift man out of his present unhappy selfishness and into the radiance of self-sacrificing idealism is the upward struggle of his race, the fight for the common good of his people.

That society can function successfully only as an organism; that all parts benefit when each part performs the function for which it is best suited to produce a unified, single-purposed whole, which is then capable of out-performing any single part, the whole thus vastly increasing the powers of all cooperating parts, and the parts, therefore, subordinating a part of their individual freedom to the whole; that the whole perishes and all of the parts suffer whenever one part fails to perform its one function, usurps or interferes with the function of another part, or like a cancer, devours all the nourishment and grows wildly and selfishly out of all proportion to its task—which latter is exactly the effort on society of the parasitic Jews and their Marxism.

That man makes genuine progress only when he approaches Nature humbly and accepts and applies her eternal laws, instead of arrogantly assuming to ignore and conquer Nature, as do the Marxists with their theories of the supremacy of environmental influence over the genetic truth of race, special laws of biological equality for humans only, and their insane denial of the primitive and fundamental human institution of private property.

That struggle is the vital element of evolutionary progress and the very essence of life itself; that it is the only method whereby we have won and can maintain dominion over the other animals of the earth; that we must therefore welcome struggle as a means of testing and improving us, and that we must despise weaklings who run away from struggle. We believe that life itself is awarded by Nature only to those who fight for it and win it, not those who wish or beg for it as a "right."

That no man is entitled to the services and products of the labor of his fellow man unless he contributes an equal amount of goods or services of his own production or invention. We believe that the contribution by a member of society of nothing else but tokens called "money" is a fraud upon his fellows, and does not excuse a man capable of honest work of his responsibility to produce his share.

That it is to the advantage of society to see that every honest man has freedom and opportunity to achieve his maximum potentials by preserving his health, protecting him from unforeseeable and ruinous catastrophes, educating him to capacity in the areas of his abilities, and guarding him against political and economic exploitation.

Adolf Hitler was the gift of an inscrutable providence to a world on the brink of Jewish-Bolshevik catastrophe and that only the blazing spirit of this heroic man can give us the strength and inspiration to rise, like the early Christians, from the depths of persecution and hatred, to bring the world a new birth of radiant idealism, realistic peace, international order, and social justice for all men.

The tenets of the WUFENS organization were:

JEWISH PROBLEM

We shall investigate, try, and execute all Jews proved to have taken part in Marxist or Zionist plots of treason against their nations or humanity.

We shall immediately remove all disloyal Jews from positions where they can control non-Jewish thoughts or actions, particularly from the press, government, education, entertainment, and courts.

We shall expose the criminal nature of the hate-book of the Jews, the Babylonian Talmud, by wide publication of its actual vicious words of hate and extermination of all non-Jews.

We shall cancel all debts owed to Jews by non-Jews, where there is evidence of unfair or immoral business methods or conspiracy.

We shall establish an International Jewish Control Authority to carry out the above measures on a world-wide basis to protect the rare honest Jews from the wrath of the people newly awakened to the truth about Jews, and to make a long-term, scientific study to determine if the Jewish virus is a matter of environment, and can be eliminated by education and training, or if some other method must be developed to render Jews harmless to society.

We shall establish an International Treason Tribunal to investigate, try, and publicly hang, in front of the Capitol, all non-Jews who are convicted of having acted consciously as fronts for Jewish treason of subversion or who have violated their oaths of office, or participated in any form of treason against their nation or humanity.[8]

Rockwell spent the majority of his efforts recruiting what he hoped would be the "officer corps" of WUFENS. By April, nine members had been initiated and twelve others were awaiting the ritual. Promotion to officer's rank was totally at Rockwell's discretion. The initiation ceremony consisted of pricking the cheek with a razor blade, dripping a large drop of blood on the border of the swastika flag, and swearing allegiance to the party with the "Troopers Oath":

In the presence of the Great Spirit of the Universe, and my Loyal Party Comrades, I hereby IRREVOCABLY pledge:

To ADOLPH [sic] HITLER, the philosophical leader of the White Man's fight for idealistic and scientific world order against the atheistical and materialistic forces of Marxism and racial suicide, I pledge my reverence and respect.

To THE COMMANDER of Adolf Hitler's National Socialist Movement, I pledge my faith, my courage, and my willing obedience.

To MY PARTY COMRADES throughout the world, I pledge my absolute loyalty, even unto death.

To MYSELF, as a leader of the White Man's fight, I pledge a clean and manly life of honor.

To THE UNITED STATES OF AMERICA, I pledge my loyalty, and my careful compliance with its Constitution and laws until those which are unjust can be legally changed by winning the hearts of the people.

To MY IGNORANT FELLOW WHITE MAN, who will hate and persecute me because they have been so cruelly brainwashed, I pledge my patience and my love.

To THE TRAITORS TO MY RACE AND NATION, I pledge swift and ruthless Justice.[9]

Troopers were required to have code names; they had to have some relation to their real names, and they had to sound tough. A new recruit named Burchard suggested the name "Birch," to fit his last name, but Rockwell thought that not tough enough; he christened Burchard "Trooper Oak." (Trooper Oak, in fact, was a sophomore at George Washington University infiltrating WUFENS for a term paper on deviant subversive groups.)[10]

Manpower was a scarce commodity. The motley crew that formed his WUFENS membership consisted of racists, thrill seekers, spies, and ex-convicts. None of them knew the first thing about National Socialism, except what Rockwell told them. But his charisma and dedication were enough to string a dozen men along as his foot soldiers.

Rockwell attempted to distinguish his Americanized version of National Socialism from Hitler's in several ways. WUFENS was not Germanic—members were not allowed to wear publicly jackboots, German uniforms, or toothbrush mustaches. Rockwell did not believe in dictatorship; he supported an authoritarian republic as established, he believed, by the Founding Fathers—not an equalitarian republic, in which government decision making was spread among the populace. He denounced fascism as primarily an economic doctrine of state-controlled industry; free enterprise and private ownership were superior. Hitler's "racial nationalism" would be supplanted by "international racism" to "protect and promote the Aryan Race and its Western Civilization."[11]

The world had become too complex and interconnected for racial isolationism or hatred of Aryans who lived in other countries.

Rockwell believed that millions of people were either conscious National Socialists or were "only a synapse away from discovering that they were National Socialists—and never knew it—because they have never been allowed to know what National Socialism is."[12] To his way of thinking, National Socialism was the very essence of what conservatives desired, but they were afraid to examine the doctrine because of the propaganda campaign directed at it. Instead of examining the ideas of National Socialism as propounded by Hitler in *Mein Kampf*, they let their minds be fogged by the emotional baggage of "Hollywood Nazism." The constant images of gas chambers, ovens, and piles of corpses prevented any serious analysis of the doctrine. The media, in his view, never focused attention on the millions of executions by Russian or Chinese communists; in the public mind, only the German Nazi atrocities were remembered. Rockwell realized that the Holocaust had to be refuted or inroads could not be made. Without the Holocaust, Hitler was just another dictator and National Socialism another fascist form of government. Holocaust denial was unheard of in 1959. Only fourteen years had passed since the end of World War II, and the public was still coming to terms with Hitler's mass murder of European Jewry. Some of the culpable, like Adolf Eichmann, would not be brought to justice until years later.

Rockwell needed to refute the facts. The testimony of survivors, the photographs, and the presence of the actual concentration camp buildings used in the killings were of no concern. If the Holocaust could be disproved or even slightly discredited, National Socialism, Hitlerism, might become palatable, maybe even respectable, as an ideology. The massive amount of evidence did not deter Rockwell; it was simply a large stone that needed to be chipped away. Future generations could reduce it to rubble.

To establish a Holocaust-was-a-hoax theme, Rockwell fabricated a story for a seedy men's pulp magazine called *Sir!* The story, "by a former corporal in the SS as told to Master Sergeant Lew Cor" (Rockwell spelled backwards phonetically) related how the Nazis conducted vivisection on Jewish concentration camp inmates. The article was accepted, and Rockwell received seventy-five dollars in payment. When it was published, the editors used concentration camp photos alongside his story to enhance its appeal. To Rockwell's way of thinking, since the publisher had used bogus photos for a bogus story, the Holocaust must be a Jewish fabrication. Rockwell was to use the magazine article as proof of a "holocaust hoax" for the rest of his life.

Like Hitler, Rockwell believed there was no artificial line between man and the universe. Man's egocentricity needed rethinking, in much the same way as people in the Middle Ages needed to learn that the Earth was not the center of the universe. Men varied not only in quality as individuals but also by breed, like all other living things. Until 1900 the rigors of nature had ensured upward evolution of the species by natural selection of the strongest, but modern science and humanitarianism had started *reverse* selection, that is, of the weakest human beings. Rockwell, like Hitler, believed that if mankind fell victim to unnatural ideas of human equality and racial integration, it would breed itself back down to the barbarian. Nature favors the strong, and no race has a prior claim to the title of "chosen" race. All races must prove their worth in the eternal struggle of mankind—a struggle wherein borders are in a constant state of flux.[13] We see another reflection of the thoughts of Hitler, as laid down in *Mein Kampf:*

> Nature did not reserve this soil in itself for a certain nation or race as reserved territory for the future, but it is land for that people which has the energy to take it and the industry to cultivate it. Nature does not know political frontiers. She puts the living beings on this globe and watches the free game of energies. He who is strongest in courage and industry receives, as her favorite child, the right to be the master of existence.[14]

Bystanders outside WUFENS headquarters watched through the plate-glass window as members strutted about in their Nazi-style brown shirts and swastika armbands. Virginia law permitted "open carry" of firearms within property lines; the Nazis wore holstered revolvers or semiautomatic pistols slung from web belts. Outside the house, a U.S. flag flew from a mast. A swastika constructed of glowing white plastic was attached to the slate-black roof, for the benefit of air travelers.

In the evenings, swarms of Arlington high school students would congregate in front of the house. Some were invited in, handed packets of WUFENS literature, and indoctrinated. Other students were indignant, shouting taunts and jeers at the house or marching with signs reading "Go Home Nazi" and "Rockwell Go Home." Occasionally a WUFENS trooper would stand at the side of the house, rifle in hand, to intimidate the young hecklers. Even Rockwell himself would bolt out the front door with a pistol. The Arlington Police Department felt no obligation to disperse the crowd; agitation works both ways. The swastika, the stormtrooper regalia, the weapons, and Rockwell's pseudo-intellectualism made WUFENS headquarters irresistible to the students. It was like a repeat of history before their eyes, and they were drawn to the forbidden. Rockwell knew this. He told reporters, "When I was in the advertising game we used nude women. Now I use the hackenkreuz [swastika] and stormtroopers. You use what brings them in."[15]

In early April, Rockwell traveled to Chicago to meet Mr. S. A. Davis, once a follower of Marcus Garvey's Universal Negro Improvement Association movement. Photos were taken of Davis and Rockwell sitting together; Rockwell would use them in a pamphlet titled "We Challenge the Jews." Rockwell believed blacks were being denied the privilege of returning to Africa by Jewish groups, who used them as cheap labor and captive voting blocs. Rockwell's visit with the Garveyite was merely a publicity stunt; the two groups were never in contact again. But the idea of forming an alliance with black separatists remained with Rockwell and eventually came to fruition several years later with Elijah Muhammad's Black Muslims.

Acting as his own attorney, Rockwell filed several libel suits in the spring of 1959, including a one-dollar nuisance suit against Arlington Commonwealth Attorney William Hassan, the local prosecutor. The suit involved an article in the *Northern Virginia Sun* in which Hassan had reported an attempt to "indoctrinate" Arlington students by "foreign appearing and foreign dressed individuals who are handing out foreign alien hate literature."[16] The suit was continued several times and was finally dismissed "without prejudice" at Rockwell's request. When asked why he filed the suit in the first place, Rockwell stated, "Just for the pleasure of it."[17]

His next legal action was a $500,000 libel suit against his former partner Harold Arrowsmith, who had told the press that Rockwell was a "con man" and a "blackmailer." Several affidavits in support of the suit were filed in Baltimore Superior Court, including one from Arlington school board member Helen Lane, declaring that Rockwell was "a person of high moral character and personal integrity."[18] It was on this occasion that a group of Arlington citizens unsuccessfully demanded her resignation from the board.

Rockwell stands beside a Nazi shrine in his home on Williamsburg Boulevard in Arlington.

On April 21, 1959, William Hassan decided it was time to shut Rockwell down. His department had been besieged with complaints about WUFENS headquarters for several months; Rockwell's libel suit made it personal. Hassan convinced a grand jury to bring a two-count indictment against Rockwell, for maintaining a "public nuisance" at his home and acting to "corrupt public morals and outrage the sense of decency of others."[19] A conviction would carry a maximum fine of $5,000.

That evening, as Rockwell was printing leaflets in his basement, he was interrupted by a knock at the door. Sheriff Carl Taylor handed him a summons to appear in court and a search warrant for the property. Leading the raid was William Hassan. Rockwell inspected the legal documents, said "Thank you, sir," and invited the officers inside for a piece of day-old birthday cake.[20] Police declined the birthday cake, which was for Hitler.[21]

They spent three hours cataloging items and carrying out cartons of literature, eight swastika armbands, two pistols, one rifle, a tear gas pen, a bronze plaque of Hitler, and a five-by-eleven-foot swastika flag.

During the raid, J. V. Morgan drove up and muscled his way through the throngs of reporters. One of them asked him for an interview; Morgan roared, "Out of my way, you filthy Jew." The other reporters laughed. Morgan reached the doorway and yelled *"Sieg Heil"* in defiance.[22] Rockwell pointed out to reporters that the police had taken neither his American flag nor Bible. "I have done no more than anyone who was running a Republican or Democratic headquarters, which every man has a right to do in this country."[23] Rockwell realized he could make some cash on the raid by selling photographs of the event. He picked up his camera and followed the police from room to room, snapping photos. That evening they were used on television and printed in the *Washington Evening Star.*

The arraignment took place before Judge Walter McCarthy, who appointed attorney Charles Russell as a "friend of the court" to help weigh the sufficiency of the public nuisance charges. Rockwell, representing himself, filed two motions, one for dismissal of charges and the other for suppression of the seized evidence. Both motions were denied, and a trial date was set for June 8. Judge McCarthy instructed Hassan to furnish a "bill of particulars," at the suggestion of Russell; Russell had complained that the charges were too vague and would likely raise constitutional questions.

Hassan's presentment contained eight separate acts that he considered constituted a "public nuisance."

1. Displaying the swastika
2. Producing and distribution "un-American hate literature"
3. Encouraging the congregation of children and adults
4. Carrying and displaying firearms on his premises
5. Impeding traffic on Williamsburg Boulevard
6. Stopping vehicles in the street
7. Searching vehicles in the street
8. Wearing "stormtrooper" uniforms with swastika armbands

A month later, Charles Russell's memorandum of *amicus curiae* effectively disposed of the presentment against Rockwell. The charges outlined in Hassan's presentment were too broad and certainly unconstitutional.

Answering charge one—displaying a swastika—Russell wrote:

Since the swastika was used by the American Indian before the time of Columbus, and since evidences of its use over 3000 years ago have been dug up in the ruins of Troy, it would certainly be no more of a public nuisance to display it than the Democratic donkey or the Republican elephant, were it not for its unforgettable associations with the late Adolph [*sic*] Hitler. . . . The mere display of a political symbol, however abhorrent to the majority of people, is an element of that freedom of speech which may not be taken away. . . . The privilege of free speech carries with it freedom of choice as to the mode of expression that may be employed. It includes the use of mechanical and manual instrumentalities of communication, including signs, banners, placards, pamphlets, radio and the press.

On charge two—producing un-American hate literature—he wrote:

Unquestionably, the ideas and policies advocated in this literature are annoying and repellent to the vast majority of Americans. This, however, should not have the slightest effect on defendant's right to publish and circulate them. Expression of opinion is entitled to protection no matter how unorthodox or abhorrent it may seem to others and even though the ideas expressed may be objected to by the overwhelming majority of the American people. No matter how specious, how intolerant, how narrow, how prejudiced or how dogmatic the arguments of devotees of one belief may appear to others, the right of either so to express himself is so a part of public policy that it will be defended and protected to the uttermost. Falsehoods and fallacies must be exposed, not suppressed. . . . The Supreme Court has held that this freedom includes the right to criticize the American system of government, the government itself, men in office and government policies. The constitutional guarantee of free speech extends to more than abstract discussion unrelated to action, but included the opportunity to persuade to action, not merely to describe facts.

On charge three—encouraging the congregation of children and adults—his views were these:

The acts of the defendant in displaying the swastika, the wearing of uniforms, etc., and the invitation of persons to visit his home for the purpose of hearing speeches were not nuisances in themselves and cannot become nuisances merely because these acts may attract those who are curious or hostile.

Charge four was "carrying firearms on the premises." Russell remarked,

The second amendment to the Constitution of the United States protects the right of citizens to bear arms. Under the Fourteenth amendment . . .

no State may abridge the privileges or immunities of the citizens of the United States. This has been held to include the privileges and immunities contained in the first ten amendments. Thus the defendant has the right to bear arms on his premises or anywhere else, for that matter, although this right is subject to reasonable regulations.

Charges five through eight involved redundant point-of-law rulings and single-occurrence acts, which disqualified or did not support a "public nuisance" charge.[24]

Rockwell claimed the charges had had "no basis in fact" and had been brought only because Hassan was under pressure to close his political headquarters. Hassan insisted that Rockwell had not been prosecuted for what he believed but for "the manner in which he does it. The right of the community must be protected."[25]

In early June 1959, two of Rockwell's troopers made arrangements to rent a meeting hall from the International Order of Odd Fellows. Willard Thompson, president of the IOOF, told reporters the rental was strictly a business transaction and that the IOOF was in no way endorsing Rockwell, but the board of trustees thought otherwise and voted to cancel the agreement. Rockwell filed suit for $1,920 against Virginia Lodge 11 of the IOOF, claiming the Order had hurt his "political career" by canceling his use of the hall for a rally.[26]

His affairs turned sour in June. All but three of his troopers left the party, and his one-year use of 6512 Williamsburg Boulevard expired. More than a hundred people gathered in front of the house to watch him move out. Rockwell told reporters, "I don't know where I'll move to. I'll stay temporarily with one of my troopers, I guess."[27] Rockwell made an off-the-cuff remark to a reporter in which he referred to "my man in the White House."[28] The FBI sent a memorandum to the Secret Service on July 15 about Rockwell's alleged contact. The Secret Service advised the Bureau that Rockwell had never been in contact with anyone in the White House; he was "pulling their chain."

On August 21, 1959, Rockwell met with the public relations officer of the Reserve Officers Association regarding an anti-communist exhibit created by the Assembly of Captive European Nations (ACEN). Rockwell had previously telephoned this individual, giving his name as Commander Ridgeway of the United States Navy, but at the meeting he confessed that he had given a false name and that he was really George Lincoln Rockwell. Rockwell explained how they could both make thousands of dollars by duplicating the ACEN exhibit and sending it around the United States during the visit of the Soviet premier, Nikita Khrushchev, that September. Rockwell believed the exhibit revealed what Khrushchev, the Soviet Union, and communism really stood for. He was sure that Russell Maguire of *American Mercury* magazine would cover the cost. Rockwell told the public relations officer that he was anti-Semitic because "the Jews" had caused him to lose *U.S. Lady*, which had been bought by John Adams. (The officer knew John Adams, who was also in the public relations field, and to his knowledge, Adams was not a Jew. He also knew that when Adams purchased the magazine from Rockwell, he had voluntarily assumed a large amount of debt. This would not be the last time Rockwell would blame Jews for his own problems.) The officer did not commit himself one way or the other, but he did inquire later about the cost of reproducing the exhibit—approximately $600.[29]

In September, Arlington Circuit Court Judge William Medley dismissed all "public nuisance" charges against Rockwell. Rockwell was pleased, but his energy was at its lowest. With no financial backing, no headquarters or printing equipment, his stormtroopers dispersed, he was ready to "pack it in." He told a reporter he was "giving up on America" to go to Iceland and rejoin his family. He sold his television, furniture, and other belongings and bought a plane ticket to Iceland.

When he arrived in Reykjavík, Iceland, no one was waiting for him. Somewhat perplexed, he hitched a ride to the apartment where Thora and their children lived. He raced up the stairs to their apartment with a feeling of jubilation, knowing he would soon be hugging his children and loving his wife. Outside the door of the apartment, he could hear his children scurrying around inside. How happy they would all be to see him. He set down his luggage, including a toy steam shovel and doll, and knocked on the door. Thora opened the door and stepped back, a look of horror on her face. "You! What are you doing here?" His heart sank; his throat tightened up. Thora would not allow him entrance; he forced his way into the apartment. Thora called the police, who promptly removed him. In shock from the day's events, he bought a bottle of whiskey and stumbled around the cold, wet streets in a drunken stupor.

After a few days of attempts at reconciliation, he realized the futility of the situation and borrowed return plane fare from Thora's father. As he waited to leave Iceland, Thora arrived at the airport to say good-bye. With tears rolling down their faces, they hugged and sobbed for several minutes. Then it was over, and she was gone. He would never see Thora or his children again.[30]

Back in the United States, there was nothing left. All his possessions had been sold to pay for his Iceland visit. He moved in with J. V. Morgan, bought some wine, and fell into drunken stupors for days on end. The FBI closed its Registration Act investigation of him; the WUFENS organization was defunct. Like a gambler who puts his last chip on the table and loses, Rockwell felt he had lost his gamble to create a "legitimate" National Socialist organization. Now there was nothing left—no job, no party, no family. He was at the bottom, with nowhere to go but up.

He thought long and hard about his failures and came to the conclusion that they were due to his innate tendency to trust people—their promises, their loyalty, their love. He realized that he could no longer believe anyone just because they "loved" him or "promised" him something. He realized that Thora, by throwing him out of her life, had given him a "priceless armor of fearlessness," which he could carry forward into future battles. He threw the wine bottles in the trash.[31]

James Warner, the man who initiated Rockwell's "religious experience" a year before by sending him a Nazi flag, appeared at the house asking what they could get organized. Two supporters from Baltimore contacted him with the same request: to organize a party. He was at the critical juncture of his life. He could give up on politics and move on to another endeavor or begin serious agitation. He realized that he was caught in a dilemma: his opponents could label him an anti-Semite, but his own self-imposed wish to present a "respectable" National Socialist organization had prevented a frontal assault against his enemies. He turned to Hitler for the answer:

> Any man who is not attacked in the Jewish newspapers, not slandered and vilified, is...no true National Socialist. The best measure of the value of his will is the hostility he receives from the mortal enemy of our people....
>
> Every Jewish defamation and every Jewish lie is an honorary scar on the body of our fighters....He is nearest to us whom they abuse most, and he is our best friend whom they hate most naturally.[32]

An open commitment to National Socialism, it now seemed to Rockwell, was not only the strongest irritant to the Jewish community but the only realistic way of recruiting the type of men he needed if he was to build a viable, long-lasting organization. He made a strategic decision to drop the term National Socialism, dashing all hopes of respectability—even among fellow National Socialists—and openly call himself a Nazi. Among National Socialists, the "Nazi" is considered derogatory, similar to a Marxist being labeled a "Commie" or a "Red."[33] He realized the term would cause misunderstandings and suspicion among fellow sympathizers, but the shock value of a goose-stepping, uniformed, Hollywood-style stormtrooper would attract tremendous press coverage and nationwide notoriety. Once again, he used *Mein Kampf* for guidance:

> Whether they laugh or swear at us, whether they present us as fools or as criminals; the main thing is that they mention us, that they occupy themselves with us again and again, and that gradually, in the eyes of the workers, we appear actually as that power with which alone one has to reckon at the time.[34]

His first objective was to gain public recognition, to make the name "Rockwell" synonymous with the word "Nazi." With this as the foremost objective, he decided to concentrate on flaunting the swastika and creating public incidents, highly visible court cases, and wild public demonstrations. If he could provoke violent opposition, all the better. His goal was to become known as the opponent of the Jews and blame everything that was wrong with the world—communism, race mixing, unscrupulous capitalism, moral degeneracy, sexual perversion—on them.

His destiny was now in focus. He would flaunt his outrageousness across America like no other before him, preaching ideologies so extreme that his life would be in constant danger. In October 1959, Rockwell formed the American Nazi Party.

5

1960: THE ULTIMATE WEAPON

Lots of men come to talk but few stay to fight. If you
want to fight, this is the place for you.
— Rockwell, recruiting ex-paratrooper
Roger Foss, 1960

The critical component needed to start a party political was a stable
base of operation—not just a post office box. It might have been possible to operate from a rented storefront, at least for the duration of one
lease, but Rockwell preferred an entire building that could house printing presses, offices, and barracks. The problem was money; he had
none. His network of associates now connected him with Floyd
Fleming, a World War I veteran, expert house and sign painter, and former president of the Seaboard White Citizens Council. Although
Fleming and Rockwell did not see eye to eye on every issue, they both
realized that a partnership was necessary if they were to save the white
race. Fleming wasn't rich, but he found a way to invest in real estate
while advancing a cause; once he committed his capital, he became
totally immersed in the party and its objectives.

In early January 1960, Fleming purchased a two-story house at 928
North Randolph Street, zoned commercial, for $21,500. Two tenants
were already renting the second floor; Rockwell's Nazi operations would
occupy the first floor. Fearing possible lawsuit and legal attachment,
Rockwell made it his policy never to have tangible property—vehicles,
printing presses, office equipment—in his own name. The property was
leased to the newly commissioned deputy commander, J. V. Morgan.

On January 11 Rockwell applied for an occupancy permit to use the house as the political headquarters for the American Nazi Party. The realtor who had sold the property expressed shock at the intended use of the home: "They [Fleming and spouse] said they were going to live in the downstairs apartment and use the garage and sheds for his contracting business."[1] Norbert Melnick, the Arlington County Director of Inspection, sent a team to examine the property. It determined that the premises were in compliance with building codes, and the county granted a permit for the American Nazi Party to operate at the address.

On Christmas Day of 1959, the Cologne synagogue in West Germany had been defaced with anti-Semitic slogans and swastikas. The desecration was the first in a chain of anti-Jewish acts committed in Germany and thirty-three other nations, including the United States, where nearly six hundred incidents took place over an eight-week period. Rockwell proudly took full moral responsibility for the worldwide outbreak. Acknowledging that his actions and literature played a part in arousing anti-Jewish elements, Rockwell added, "I deplore the avenue some of them choose. I would not permit my troopers to paint swastikas on synagogues or churches. . . . It's not necessary here. It is in Europe, where there's no other way."[2]

In response to the synagogue vandalizations, the National Executive Committee of the Anti-Defamation League (ADL) authorized an investigation to discover the "underlying causes and factors" involved. The ADL developed a seven-point program focusing on "the impact of Nazism on American youth." It also initiated negotiations with the Survey Research Center of the University of California for a "definitive and comprehensive investigation of American anti-Semitism." The ADL committed $500,000 over a five-year period beginning in 1961 for the study of anti-Semitism in America.[3] The results described desecration as "epidemic" in the United States but as neither organized nor instigated by any group as part of a "centrally organized campaign." It concluded that the actions were the result of a "high level of latent and overt anti-Jewish prejudice existent in American society."[4]

In Washington, Isaac Franck, Executive Director of the Jewish Community Council of Greater Washington, released a statement to the press that the council was "deeply troubled" by the distribution of Nazi-like leaflets in the Washington area. Franck explained that the Washington representatives of the Jewish War Veterans, the American

Rockwell checks the mail at ANP headquarters in Arlington, Virginia.

UPI/Corbis-Bettmann

Jewish Committee, and the American Jewish Congress were working together to formulate a plan of action against Rockwell. They discussed with Navy officials Rockwell's commission in the Naval Reserve and met with the local chief of police and law enforcement officials to explore every possible legal means of "preventing the repetition of this literature distribution." Franck advised:

> We have reason to be confident that Rockwell's vicious propaganda efforts will fall on deaf ears. . . . There is no reason for alarm. Rockwell has no substantial following or any financial resources to speak of. . . . Rockwell is avid for publicity. It would be ill-advised and a disservice to the Jewish community to take any steps that would afford him such publicity or the public platform he so desperately seeks.[5]

On January 6 the Chief of Naval Personnel sent Rockwell a letter informing him that his discharge from the U.S. Naval Reserve might be warranted: "Your known views espousing race and religious hatred would render ineffective your status as an officer commanding men made up, at least in part, of members of the various races and religions at which your propaganda is aimed." He gave Rockwell the opportunity to defend himself before a board of officers.

Rockwell acknowledged the letter and requested the formal hearing. The tenor of his reply was martyr-like:

> Throughout history, men who have stood uncompromisingly for unpopular and dangerous ideas have always had to suffer persecutions and indignities, and I have and expect to suffer much worse than the withdrawal of my treasured commission because of my overwhelming concern for the safety of our nation which has fallen into the hands of traitorous conspirators.[6]

Awaiting his hearing, Rockwell created a pamphlet, *In Hoc Signo Vinces* (In This Sign You Shall Conquer), as a testament to his belief in the ultimate triumph of the swastika. The Latin title was appropriated from Constantine, while the text called for the advancement of Hitlerian ideology throughout the Aryan world. The first National Socialist polemic since 1945, it expressed Rockwell's belief that the white race had passed its zenith and that if it were to survive,

> [T]he White man will have to reconquer the earth once conquered and civilized at the cost of so much blood by his ancestors. Under the banners of international Jewry, the colored masses are threatening to return civilization to savagery. Under the Swastika banner of Adolph [*sic*] Hitler, White men around the world will master the planet to save civilization.... The Jews realize what we must realize: that they are playing for the highest stakes in the history of mankind—mastery of the whole earth.... If we are to survive, we too must have the wit and the strength of mind to face up to the deadly facts of the situation and act ruthlessly, rapidly and effectively.[7]

On February 1, Rockwell appeared before naval officers J. S. Fahy, E. A. Parker, and R. T. Kieling in an attempt to save his commission. He read an eight-page statement and brought as witnesses J. V. Morgan and Benjamin Freedman. Freedman spoke for forty minutes, alleging Anna M. Rosenberg (a former assistant secretary of defense) was a communist. Morgan told the officers their party did not advocate hate or violence. The appeal was futile. The Navy gave Rockwell an honorable discharge and issued a statement:

> Mr. Rockwell was discharged from the naval service because of his public and open espousal of race and religious hatred, which reflected upon his judgment as an officer of the naval reserve to such an extent as to raise serious question concerning his mobilization potential. As the naval service is comprised of persons of many races and religions, Mr. Rockwell's known views would render him ineffective as an officer commanding

men, many of whom would be members of those races and religions concerning which he has expressed these views.[8]

Rockwell was extremely disturbed by his naval discharge. Not only did he lose some much-needed income, but his dismissal came just six months shy of twenty years' service and a monthly retirement check. His commission had been the last remaining vestige of his pre-Nazi life. He had now forsaken everything—his family, wives, children, the Navy—to carry the torch of Adolf Hitler.

On the cold afternoon of February 6, Rockwell and Deputy Commander J. V. Morgan packed up some party literature and drove into Washington, D.C., for their regular Saturday distribution at the intersection of 13th and F Streets, N.W. Police kept close watch on the two Nazis as well as bystanders. The pamphlet they were giving to pedestrians was entitled "White Man! Are You Going to Be Run Out of Your Nation's Capital Without a Fight?" The pamphlet conveyed the idea that blacks were becoming the dominant race in the District of Columbia and that the Jews were responsible for the population changing from white to black. At the scene was Irving Berman, the former president of the Arlington-Fairfax Jewish Congregation in Falls Church, Virginia, accompanied by four friends. Berman bolted from the crowd of onlookers and pounced on Rockwell, seizing his bundle of handbills. Morgan grabbed Berman and wrenched the handbills from his grasp. A tug-of-war ensued before police moved in to separate the combatants, arresting them for disorderly conduct.

The American Civil Liberties Union (ACLU) made a great show of Morgan's disorderly conduct trial, sending a Jewish lawyer to defend him. David Israel Shapiro agreed to take the case at the request of the ACLU director, Larry Speiser. Shapiro took the case because of his concern about the erosion of individual rights under the Constitution: "I believe in that right, no matter how strongly I might disagree with the contents of the literature. And as distasteful as I found the literature in this case, I find even more distasteful any attempt to prevent its distribution."

At the hearing, after Rockwell finished testifying, he and Morgan emerged to talk to the press. "I believe that fellow Shapiro is really giving a good fight for us," said Morgan. "He certainly is," replied Rockwell. "And I've got unbounded respect for Berman, too. Indeed I do. We respect his guts. He's got plenty of money and he could have hired someone to do it, but he came right up to us himself. He attacked the

Nazi Party." As Rockwell, Morgan, and lawyer Shapiro parted at the courthouse door, Rockwell turned to Shapiro, raised his arm and shouted, "Sieg Heil!"[9]

Charges against Morgan and Berman were dropped; Assistant Corporation Counsel Clark King explained that "the evidence does not seem to justify prosecution." King was not certain a tug-of-war over pamphlets constituted disorderly conduct. Rockwell commented from headquarters that the government had "dropped a hot potato" in dismissing the charges. "Now I'm cleared to proceed with other activities. I'm applying to the Department of the Interior to use the Washington Monument grounds for a speech April 1." Berman was also satisfied with the outcome. "Maybe we've made some progress. The community had been alerted to this racial hatred and bigotry."[10]

The legality of hate literature distribution was clarified by Washington's chief legal officer, Corporation Counsel Chester H. Gray, who stated that the act of handing out hate literature was not in itself illegal:

> The peaceful distribution of leaflets is an exercise of the Constitutional right of freedom of speech and press and may not be suppressed by the police or other government authorities even though the opinions expressed may be obnoxious to most people, unless such distribution causes, or gives rise to a clear and present danger of substantial public disorder or interference with traffic or other immediate threat to public safety, peace, or order, or in other ways violates a valid and specific law.[11]

In response to criticism from the Jewish community, the ACLU published a memorandum explaining why it had represented the Nazis:

> The major danger from Rockwell's proposed distribution was the reaction of people who were so incensed by his ideas and their expression that they were inclined to prevent him and his supporters from disseminating such views, even if necessary by seizing the leaflets physically. We recognize the strong, emotional feeling of Jewish people about such leaflets.... Despite this understandable anger, the ACLU cannot justify suppression of Rockwell's views by physical attack.... We cannot abandon the principles of the Bill of Rights, which require the defense of everyone's rights, without distinction.[12]

On February 26, Rockwell appeared in Arlington Domestic Relations Court to answer nonsupport charges brought against him by his first wife, Judy. Rockwell had refused to provide the $200 per month support as ordered by the Maine Superior Court; the last money she had received was twenty dollars in September 1958. Rockwell told Judge Hugh Reid he was unable to find a job because of publicity surrounding his political activities. Judge Reid asked, "Has it ever occurred to you that you hold ideas that arouse indignation? . . . You are not morally free to devote yourself to an unpopular cause which cuts you off from income."[13] The judge ordered Rockwell to begin paying his ex-wife eighty dollars per month, increasing to $200 per month within a year.

Rockwell's actions in the District caught the attention of Soviet "mole" Roger Foss. In 1959 the wiry Norwegian from Minnesota worked as a cook in New York City. The ex-paratrooper was so distraught by the moral decay of the country that he made a visit to the Soviet embassy to inquire about emigration; a week later he was approached by a man from the embassy, Valentin Ivanov.

Ivanov offered Foss a vile-smelling cigarette and took him to a bar for some drinks. He suggested Foss could be of better service to the Soviet Union by getting a government job in Washington, D.C., preferably in the Library of Congress. This made sense to Foss: a communist revolution in the United States would overturn "law and order" long enough for the white race to reorganize and save itself from race mixing. When Foss agreed, "Val" gave him fifty dollars for moving expenses. Thereafter, Foss and Ivanov met regularly at a Chinese restaurant in the District of Columbia. The Soviet continued to forward money while Foss applied for government work. After a few months, Foss was getting edgy; he had been unable to secure a government job. He made an unauthorized visit to the Soviet embassy, which drew the ire of Ivanov. The embassy was under constant FBI surveillance, and Ivanov's position would be in jeopardy if Foss continued to make such visits. Ivanov advanced Foss another fifty dollars and told him to "lie low" in Florida for a while.

Foss sat in his low-rent room debating what to do. He read a newspaper article about a Navy commander by the name of Rockwell, fighting "communists" from a headquarters building in Arlington. Foss reconsidered his situation. If he joined Rockwell, he would still be working for a revolution and preservation of the white race; he was not changing anything working with the Soviets.

Foss hitched a ride to 928 Randolph Street to meet Rockwell. Trooper Dick Braun invited Foss into the building but insisted he wipe his feet on the "Jewish prayer rug"—actually an ark curtain stolen from a synagogue—in the entryway. This was the ANP method of uncovering Jewish spies. Braun escorted Foss into the shrine room, where the blood-red swastika flag hung on the wall.

"You should see the Jews scream when we unfurl that flag in the District—they go crazy," boasted Braun. "When we take over the White House we'll gas them and send the niggers back to Africa. Personally I think we should kill all the niggers too; I don't go for spending money to resettle them in Africa, they're a bunch of animals."

Braun was getting more and more worked up as he spoke. His eyes narrowed as his ideas got more radical by the minute. He rambled on: "Any white man who doesn't help us should get his nuts cut off. . . . And Eleanor Roosevelt, we ought to strip her, put her in a cage naked with a buck nigger and parade her through Washington. . . . We'll hang those crooked nigger-loving politicians from the street lamps on meat-hooks like they did in Germany. We'll need every pole on Constitution Avenue for them, they'll hang there as a lesson to everyone that we mean business."

Foss said nothing. He read party literature for a few minutes before Rockwell made his appearance. They spent a half hour talking about Jews and communism, then Rockwell put the question to Foss: "Lots of men come to talk but few stay to fight. If you want to fight, this is the place for you." Foss thought it over. He hated the government and wanted to see it overthrown, but joining Rockwell was sure suicide. Then again, Rockwell might be the only chance the country had. Foss agreed to move into the barracks as a full-time Nazi.

Braun led Foss upstairs to pick out a bunk in the barracks room. The renters had vacated the building soon after the Nazi occupation, creating space for additional live-in Nazis. Foss noticed there were no sheets on any of the beds. There were two other rooms on the second floor; one contained the national secretary's office, the other was Rockwell's. Foss noted that Rockwell kept the door locked and the air conditioner on high. The main floor of the headquarters consisted of a kitchen, work room, the shrine room, and an office.

Since the kitchen stove was broken, troopers cooked french fries and onions in an electric deep-fat fryer with pitch-black grease. They lived as ascetics; the future of the white race and America depended on them. Each morning Rockwell and a trooper, usually National Secretary James Warner, drove to Falls Church to check the party's post office box. Rockwell ripped open the mail with the excitement of a child opening a wrapped present. He stripped each letter of any currency, wrote the amount on the envelope, and handed the letter to Warner for shoebox filing and addition to the party mailing list. On the way back to headquarters they would stop at a diner for bacon and eggs, the best meal of the day for whoever went with Rockwell.

One day as Foss and Braun cooked french fries in the kitchen, Rockwell pulled aside a curtain revealing a pantry that had been converted into a darkroom. "You do your own developing, Mr. Rockwell?" Foss asked innocently. Rockwell stiffened into a rigid military bearing. "Don't call me Mr. Rockwell, call me Commander like the other men. We are like pioneers here, Foss, we don't have the money for nice equipment so we make do with what we have. The Jews are surprised at the quality of material we put out. And we do it all right here, everything homemade, from the enlarger to the developing trays."

The enlarger was an old "bellows"-type camera suspended from the ceiling. The darkroom door was sealed with olive-drab army blankets to keep out the light—crude but effective. The ANP would buy several sheets of cellophane art type in different fonts, shoot the originals, then print dozens of copies on regular paper, which it would cut and paste for layouts.

Warner gave Foss a tour of his national secretary's office, proudly pointing out his card file of supporters, which had doubled since he had taken over the position. "I know one thing, Roger. If I ever leave here, that card file leaves with me."

"You can't do that, Warner. . . . In any business the work that you do while employed is automatically property of the organization," replied Foss in disbelief. "I built up the file. If I go, it goes with me," insisted Warner.

That week Foss met Deputy Commander Morgan, a "mean looking bastard" with black hair, wide, stocky shoulders, and a Colt .45 revolver strapped to his waist, cowboy fashion. Rockwell introduced Morgan as his "right hand" man: "He's the kind of man I need, tough and not too smart." Morgan did not blink an eye, but the remark seemed in bad taste to Foss. Foss observed Morgan's wide cheekbones and dark complexion. "What are you, Morgan? You have some Indian in you?" Morgan smiled, seemingly proud. "Yes, I'm part Indian. I always say Cherokee because I'm from Oklahoma. Actually I'm not Cherokee, but no one has ever heard of the tribe I'm from."

"How do you feel about mixing of the races, Morgan?" Foss asked. "I'm against it!" Morgan said firmly. "The way I feel is that enough damage has already been done. We have to stop it before it destroys us. What's done is done, let's not make any more mistakes."

Another top man in the organization was Eugene Colton, mean looking like Morgan but seemingly more cultured. Both men were married and visited headquarters on weekends for pickets and demonstrations. The appearance of Morgan and Colton would signal a "bull session" over coffee in the kitchen. The discussions covered Nietzsche, Hitler, the Torah, and Jewish publications. Foss thought both men were exceptionally well read, that beneath their rough exteriors were highly developed intelligences.

During one bull session, Trooper Braun suggested that everyone suspected of being Jewish should be killed, to make sure there would be no "contamination" of the government. As a joke, Foss pulled out his membership card to the Jewish Community Center, emblazoned with a big red Star of David. "Are you Jewish?" asked Colton. "No, I'm not Jewish, but I like to work out in a gym to keep in shape. The YMCAs are so full of queers that I looked for another place and found this one on 16th Street, N.W., in the District. It's real nice; it's got punching bags and everything. They even have a swimming pool for male and female both. That's a hell of a lot better than the 'males only' sign at the YMCA. . . . I swear to God, the 'males only' sign is for the queers to watch the boys swim nude."

"We gotta gas queers too!" snapped Trooper Braun. "How can you get membership in the Jewish Club if you aren't Jewish?" asked Colton. "Anybody can walk in there and join," Foss answered. Warner's eyes brightened, and he said, "Wouldn't it be something if we sent all our Nazi storm troops over there to train?" The men laughed.[14]

In early March, the FBI concluded a wire-tapping investigation of Rockwell. In the previous month, Rockwell had an "insider" at the phone company place calls to two people simultaneously, neither of whom had called the other. The resulting baffled conversation was then recorded by the "mole" and given to Rockwell. Rockwell played the tape-recorded conversation at headquarters, and the FBI informant within his organization relayed this information to the Bureau.

Although Rockwell had technically violated section 605 of the

Communications Act, the United States Attorney's Office decided against prosecution, for several reasons. First, a trial would force the FBI to expose its ANP informant and all details relevant to his operations. Second, the case would have to exclude Rockwell's background, which meant that none of the party's leaflets or publications could be used as evidence to enlighten the jury about his "disposition." The final point was that no communication of any consequence had occurred during the phone conversation; a jury might conclude that no evil purpose had been meant, that it had been merely a prank played on two people at 2:30 in the morning. The case simply was not good enough to risk a publicized trial, *United States v. Rockwell*. A Rockwell victory would further his activities and bestow additional notoriety on the party.[15]

On March 6, the Executive Committee of the National Community Relations Advisory Council met in New York. In attendance were the leaders of the American Jewish Congress, the Jewish War Veterans, the Jewish Labor Committee, the Union of American Hebrew Congregations, the Union of Orthodox Jewish Congregations, the United Synagogues of America, and a dozen Jewish community councils from various cities. Rockwell's activities were carefully reviewed and analyzed at length.

The Jewish community was faced with a political conundrum: how could it advocate suppression of Rockwell without abridging the Bill of Rights? Encouraging the government to suppress civil liberties and persecute a minority viewpoint is a dangerous gamble; one never knows when a pogrom will be instituted. The same constitutional freedoms that protect hate-mongers from suppression protect other minority groups from arbitrary suppression. To arrest Rockwell would give him a platform from which to speak, a "field day" in court. A court battle would bring to Rockwell's defense civil liberties groups and provide him a "hero's role" in the eyes of his followers and like-minded constituents.

A plan of action was devised, and a memorandum was sent to all Jewish organizations advising:

1. Do nothing to play into Rockwell's publicity seeking.
2. Do not telephone or harass him—it only feeds his delusion of self-importance.
3. Do not attend his public meetings.
4. Never use physical force against the Nazis.

The memo closed with a plea for restraint against vigilantism:

The strength and security of American democracy, and the security of the Jewish community as of all other groups, rests upon the unimpaired integrity of American law. When there is defiance of the law, and disrespect for the law and order, we are among the first to suffer. . . . Jews ought to be the last people in the world to acquiesce in conduct which goes counter to the basic structure of American law under which the safety and freedom of all of us have their most secure protection.[16]

Rockwell sent a written request to the National Capital Parks Police (NCP) to use the Sylvan Theater on the grounds of the Washington Monument on April 3 to deliver a speech titled "Nazism, the White Man's Ultimate Weapon to Save His Race, His Republic and His Religion!" He detailed the "nature and purpose" of the meeting:

The speech will demonstrate factually the growing menace of International Communism, Zionism, and Jewish subversion of all white Christian ideas, institutions and peoples; the Jewish-led campaign to destroy the domination of the white race in western civilization; the Jewish campaign to subvert and destroy the Christian religion and Christian traditions like Christmas; and that deadly danger of the American republic and the constitution before the onslaught of a dishonest and immoral advertiser-dominated public press and information complex.

A positive program of enlightenment, social solutions, and justice for all groups in America will be offered in accordance with the printed program of the Party.[17]

When the NCP denied his request to use the Sylvan Theater, Rockwell advised he would speak on April 3 at the Park Reservation on the corner of Constitution Avenue and 9th Street, N.W.—one of four park areas where political rallies could be conducted without permission. Rockwell sent letters to the *Washington Post*, National Capital Parks Service, the Office of the Corporation Counsel, and the ADL informing them of his intention to conduct regular weekend rallies on the Mall. He appealed for the "lawless elements" of the citizenry to remain calm and for law enforcement agencies to uphold his constitutional right to speak in these free-speech areas. He also took the opportunity to outline for the "ignorant" public the beliefs of the party:

In spite of the many hysterical outbursts against us, the public, in the interest of preserving the peace should know that we are almost all veterans of World War II and/or Korea, we love the USA with all our hearts and are trying to protect it, not destroy it, we do NOT favor dictatorship but rather an authoritarian REPUBLIC, as established by our slave-holding forbears, we plan to achieve power ONLY by elective processes (which is why we MUST speak and win the attention of our fellow citizens), we do not "hate" ALL Jews—or ANY innocent individuals or groups, for that matter—but only TRAITORS to this Nation and the White Race which unfortunately and provably includes a huge proportion of Jews, along with guilty Gentiles—and we are not ashamed or afraid to say that our program boldly plans the legal trials and execution of these traitors to our Nation according to the U.S. Constitution.

We do not hold with those of the White Race who will not face up to the Negro and tell him what simply IS in the hearts of all but a few White Men, that the White Man IS, on the record of historical achievement, superior in every way to the Negro, and the White Man will NOT mix with or grant real social equality to the Negro—EVER. This does not mean we "hate" the Negro, which we do not—but only that we refuse to be HYPOCRITES and give him the false hopes which are leading directly to horrible mass violence all over our poor, torn Country. We believe the Negro has been rottenly cheated and persecuted, and wish to SOLVE this situation, not by forcing Negroes in among superior White Men, but by giving the Negro a real, square BREAK among his own people.

Finally, we do not hold with the so-called "Southern segregationists" who seek to circumvent the plain language of the Constitution and the laws in regard to Negro rights. As long as the Constitution and the laws prescribe equality and voting rights, etc., for the Negro, we support the FBI and other law-enforcement bodies in combating the foolish "segregationist" attempts to SNEAK around the laws they pay such fervent lip-service to.

Instead of this kind of illegal fighting for the White Race—we demand the removal of the insane amendments to the Constitution which presume to make a regular "American" out of a black African—an impossibility as silly as to claim you can make a Negro into a "Chinaman" simply by letting him be born in China or giving him a "certificate." Above all else, we believe in the utter annihilation of COMMUNISM, Marxism—which we see as the source of almost ALL the unrest and misery abroad on the earth today.[18]

The first American Nazi Party rally took place on the cold and rainy Sunday of April 3, 1960. Nazi rallies thereafter became regular weekend events throughout the spring and summer. The party rented public-address equipment to reach as many listeners as possible, especially the hundreds of tourists visiting the nearby Smithsonian Institution. Tourists and Jewish groups besieged the Park Service with complaints,

Author's collection

Roger Foss leads a parade of Nazis in the District.

but there was no way to deny Rockwell's right to speak. The NCP eventually banned the use of public-address equipment, which forced Rockwell to shout his message to listeners. Removal of the public-address system taxed Rockwell's voice and weakened his presentation; also, the party could no longer play loud German march music to attract tourists.

A typical Rockwell speech began with "My fellow Americans," followed by a cacophony of jeering by hecklers: "Rockhead, you're sick, Rockhead." Swarms of tourists watched from a distance. Rockwell would point at them and say, "You people up there by the trees, come down here and listen to what I have to say. Don't let these filthy Jews scare you away. I want to tell you about the communist-Jewish conspiracy to make your children go to school with a bunch of black apes."[19] The hecklers would scream and yell to drown him out. When the heckling subsided, Rockwell would begin again. "I want to tell you about the treason that is going on in this government." Again the hecklers would roar. Finally frustrated from the heckling, Rockwell would insult the crowd: "You vile filthy Jews. You filthy vile Jews." Hundreds of tourists watched the spectacle from Independence Avenue, drawn by the commotion and Rockwell's booming oratory.

On a trip back to Arlington after a Mall speech, Foss asked Rockwell why he did not move the party headquarters into the District. Rockwell turned to Foss and in a fatherly tone said, "There's an old saying, 'Don't shit in your own back yard.' Once we cross the Potomac, District Police would have a difficult time arresting us for anything. I purposely set up our headquarters in Arlington, so we would have a quiet place to retreat." [20]

After another Sunday rally a heckler in an adjacent parking space ridiculed Colton and Foss as they stowed party equipment in the trunk of their car. When the heckler drove out from his parking space Colton eased his car out and followed slowly, watching for policemen. After a few blocks Colton pushed the accelerator to the floor; the big four-door slammed into the rear of the heckler's car with a loud crash. Colton slammed the car again and again, making a noise so loud that people on the streets and sidewalks stopped to watch.

Coming to a quick stop, the heckler sprang from his car with a tire iron in hand. Colton stopped a couple of car lengths behind, got out of his car, opened the trunk, and took out a pistol. When the heckler saw the pistol he jumped back into his car and sped off; Colton gunned his engine to catch up. When the heckler stopped for a traffic light Colton slammed his car from behind, pushing it far out into the intersection and oncoming traffic. Colton knew he had pushed his luck to the limit; he disengaged and took side streets back to Arlington. [21]

The party launched the debut issue of the *National Socialist Bulletin* in early May, the first of several periodicals it published. The *Bulletin* was a small (five-by-seven-inch), fifteen-page booklet with black-and-white photographs, news clippings, and highlights of National Socialist activity from around the world. The *Bulletin*, issued eight times, was eventually superseded by the *Stormtrooper*. These subscription periodicals became an important link between the party and a web of sympathizers throughout the country, attracting both followers and new members to the movement.

On April 16, Rockwell mailed a letter to Gerald L. K. Smith suggesting they join forces and work together; otherwise Rockwell would "expose" Smith and his self-serving tactics. Rockwell had a love-hate relationship with Smith. On one hand he admired Smith's dedication and fiery oration; on the other he detested Smith for extracting huge sums of money from the right wing while providing weak leadership, if any, and no street action. Rockwell was poor and jealous of the monetary tribute that the pseudo-Christian "pay-triots" like Smith and Billy James Hargis received.

Rockwell offered his services to Smith not as one of the nameless millions but as "one who has already beaten and driven his way, without money or influence, to the TOP position on the Jew hate list, which should be a position of honor for any White Christian American."

> It would shake the Jews to their ROOTS were you to join forces with US . . . to form an IRON FRONT against the master criminals of all time! I beg you once more, for the last time—to make it possible for the American people to honor your declining years. . . . We have the YOUTH— you have the aged and the moneyed. Let us join and FIGHT, SIR![22]

Smith ignored all correspondence from Rockwell.

On May 11, 1960, Israeli commandos kidnapped Adolf Eichmann in Buenos Aires to stand trial for his participation in Nazi prison camp atrocities. The ANP reacted by sending seven stormtroopers to picket the White House, with placards reading:

IKE—Help Free Eichmann

Israel Violates International Law

Punish the Jew International Bandits

Eichmann Did Not Kill ANY Innocent Jews

If the Jews Can Kidnap Eichmann, They Can Kidnap You

The protest proved unsuccessful. Eichmann was eventually tried in Jerusalem, and he was executed in May 1962.

One of the first sit-in demonstrations in Northern Virginia began on June 9, when seven blacks and five Caucasians seated themselves at the lunch counter of a Peoples Drug Store in Arlington. The store management quickly removed all the remaining seats from the other stools and stopped serving customers, fountain employees left without serving the newcomers, and a "closed" sign was placed in the window. As evening approached, a large crowd of teenagers gathered inside the store to chide the demonstrators. Rockwell, neatly dressed in a suit and tie, and six crew-cut stormtroopers wearing khaki shirts and swastika armbands pushed through the crowd to confront the demonstrators. "Why do you go where people don't want you?" Rockwell asked protester Dion Diamond. A short while later, police ordered everyone to leave; the situation had become explosive.[23]

The incident provided Rockwell a chance to disseminate handbills to the high school–aged "toughs" heckling Diamond and to debut his Nazi stormtroopers in "street action." Counter-protests against civil rights demonstrations became the very cornerstone of his entire operation. Although this particular skirmish was insignificant in terms of results or press coverage, that would not be the case in the future when Rockwell had dozens of stormtroopers stationed in metropolitan areas throughout the country.

The Justice Department deliberated whether the ANP should be placed on the Attorney General's subversives list. The inquiry was in reaction to an ANP rally on Memorial Day at which Rockwell boasted to the audience that the man standing next to him, John Patsalos, was both a Marine and a member of the American Nazi Party. Someone among the spectators called the Shore Patrol about the Marine's participation. The Shore Patrol removed Patsalos to Quantico, Virginia, where he was questioned, but no disciplinary action was taken since the ANP was not listed as a subversive organization and Patsalos was not in Marine uniform during the rally. A week later, Congressman Seymour Halpern of New York asked Attorney General Rogers to accelerate the Justice Department's investigation of the ANP. "This is an outrageous situation that calls for immediate action."[24]

In spite of the weekly rallies on the Mall and periodic White House protests, most of the nation was unaware that there were uniformed Nazis at the capital. Rockwell needed more publicity to attract the manpower and donations the party needed.

He found the solution in Union Square, on the Lower East Side of New York City. Union Square, a mustering area for Union troops during the Civil War, had come to be known as "Communist Square" by right-wingers, because the communist newspaper *The Worker* and the Yiddish *Freiheit* were printed near there. The square was also well-known for its leftists and beatniks. Since communists used the square for rallies, Rockwell decided the ANP should too; he also knew that a Nazi rally in a city with such a large Jewish population would cause enormous turmoil and publicity. In mid-June he applied for a permit to speak in

Union Square on the July 4 weekend. The reaction was instantaneous.

Unlike the Washington, D.C., area, where Isaac Franck successfully kept the Jewish community in a no-action mode when Rockwell demonstrated, the Jewish community of New York played right into Rockwell's hand.

On June 17, the Public Awareness Society (PAS) filed suit in the State Supreme Court of New York to prevent the city from issuing a permit for the Nazi rally. The suit was in response to an announcement by Parks Commissioner Newbold Morris that he would approve the Nazi rally on the principles of freedom of speech and assembly. Harry Sadow, the PAS president, claimed a Nazi rally would "lead to riot and bloodshed."[25] The pressure group obtained an order directing Morris to appear in court to explain why he believed Rockwell should be given a permit to speak.

Several other organizations also complained to City Hall. The Emma Lazarus Federation of Jewish Women's Clubs and the Farband Labor Zionist Order joined a dozen other organizations calling upon the city to refuse the Nazi permit. A federation spokesperson stated, "We must not allow the resurgence of Hitlerism here or elsewhere."[26] Another group, the League of Ghetto Fighters, Concentration Camp Victims, and Partisans, adopted a resolution calling the rally "an insult to the sacred human feelings of all who suffered under Nazism[,] and a betrayal of democracy."[27] The *Day-Morning Journal*, a New York Jewish newspaper, ran an editorial which detailed a telegram it had sent to Mayor Robert F. Wagner, Jr., and Morris: "For a Nazi to come on this holiday of American freedom to preach Nazism is an insult to America and a slap in the face of every Jew."[28]

On the opposite side of the fence was Henry Schultz, national chairman of the Anti-Defamation League of B'nai B'rith. Schultz declared that his organization was "very much for upholding the Constitutional rights of everyone—even nuts. If the permit is granted, we hope New Yorkers will show their contempt by staying away in droves so that there will be no untoward episode which the Nazis can exploit."[29] The New York Civil Liberties Union also urged that the permit be issued, since a denial would violate constitutional rights of free speech and assembly.

On June 22, Rockwell and Roger Foss arrived in New York City to defend the application to speak in Union Square. After the hearing and the ensuing riot (already described) in the courthouse rotunda, Mayor Wagner held a press conference in his office where he read the following statement:

> I have the primary... obligation to the people of the city for the maintenance of law and order. A man named George Rockwell, of Washington, D.C., has applied for a permit to speak in Union Square on July 4. Information supplied to me by qualified sources shows clearly that Mr. Rockwell's intent is to incite a riot by preaching, in a city where people of all races live peacefully together, a philosophy of race hatred and extermination by violence. Left to their own devices, the people of the city will stone Rockwell out of town. There is not a decent responsible citizen in the city who would follow him in his preaching. There are millions who have friends and relatives who died because of this race hatred either as unarmed victims or soldiers fighting for freedom.
>
> We have in this city the largest and best police force of any municipality. It can quell any riot, but no police force in the world can stop a riot from starting. In this case, every fact we have shows Rockwell's presence as a preacher of race hatred will cause a riot the police will have to quell. This is an invitation to riot and disorder from a half-penny Hitler. The invitation is declined. Mr. Rockwell will not speak here on the Fourth of July or any other time in terms of race hatred and race extermination.[30]

The next day the American Civil Liberties Union and the ANP joined forces in the fight to get a permit for Rockwell's July 4 rally in Union Square. George Rundquist, executive secretary of the New York chapter of the ACLU, explained that "the basis for our action would be to protect his right of freedom of speech and assembly under the Constitution."[31]

On June 24, New York Democrats Irwin Brownstein and (State Senator) Frank Pino asked State Supreme Court Justice Louis Friedman for a restraining order to prevent Rockwell from engaging in "Nazi-type" political activities in the state of New York and to ban the use of the swastika as a political symbol during any litigation. The order also sought to restrain the ACLU from assisting Rockwell. Judge Friedman listened to their arguments and adjourned the hearing. He told the press, "I don't sit here as a Jew, I sit here as Justice of the Supreme Court, bound to protect the rights of everyone, including Mr. Rockwell, if he has any."[32]

On June 28, Lester Fahn of the Jewish War Veterans filed a complaint against Rockwell for causing "disorderly conduct" in the Supreme Court Building. The charges stemmed from the riot in the rotunda where Rockwell and Roger Foss had talked to reporters. A warrant was issued for his arrest anywhere in the state. Rockwell never spoke in Union Square, and the warrant kept him from entering New York City for several years.

Rockwell was gratified by all the publicity, but party funds were nearly exhausted. To capitalize on the commotion he sent Roger Foss back to New York City to extract money from sympathizers. Foss took a bus from the District of Columbia to New York, where he was met by the party's main organizer in the area, Seth Ryan. (Ryan was of Irish-Catholic descent, dark-haired, skinny, and pale. He was a gifted political strategist, but his weakness for alcohol and his willingness to "take the easy way out" of situations undermined his talent. He would eventually move into the headquarters in Arlington as a member of the officer corps.) Foss and Ryan stopped for lunch at a Jewish bagel stand before catching the subway to the office building of a sympathizer who published a newsletter called *The Atheist*. Ryan introduced Foss, and the three men retired to a private office. The sympathizer praised Rockwell's efforts but wanted clarification about the party's continual use of the phrase "white Christian America" in its literature.

Foss told the atheist that the party used the "white Christian America" line to appeal to the Christian segment of society. Most whites were opposed to atheistic communism, and the party wanted to play upon that fear. For some people the appeal of "racial pride" was enough to gain their support, but for others it was not. The "Christian America" theme was an appeal to their Christian pride, but it also helped further the notion that Jews were a different race than whites. Foss assured the gentleman that there were no Christians at Nazi headquarters; from the commander on down to the last stormtrooper, none of them would "worship a dead Jew on a cross." Foss explained that a substantial amount of the party's financial support came from "little old ladies" around the country who believed the party was carrying the cross of Christ into battle. The atheist nodded in understanding. He opened a drawer in his desk, took out fifty dollars in cash, and handed it to Foss as a donation.

That evening Foss and Ryan met a sympathizer who agreed to put Foss up for the night. The sympathizer was a medical doctor who lived with a Jewish woman. Foss was stunned by not only the woman's beauty but also the collection of watercolor swastikas she had created. A Nazi doctor on the Lower East Side of New York City with Jewish patients and a sympathetic Jewish girlfriend—the incongruity was unbelievable. He wondered if he would be murdered that night. The next morning "Herr Doctor" gave Foss a small contribution and promised to send regular contributions if the party took his name off the mailing list: he was skeptical of ANP security and needed to protect his privacy. He preferred to pick up his literature directly from Seth Ryan.[33]

Activity at ANP headquarters was picking up. There were several live-in stormtroopers and numerous weekend-only Nazis. A party member brought a set of eight-ounce boxing gloves to headquarters; Foss, the most experienced boxer present, began training the men in the art of self-defense. They affixed a heavy punching bag outside the building and drew a caricature of a stereotype long-nosed Jew on the canvas. For psychological effect the troopers timed their boxing and punching bag work for 5:00 P.M., to coincide with quitting time around Arlington; local men on their way home from work could see the Nazis hammering away at the bag. The stormtroopers already had a reputation in the District; now Arlington residents could see the Nazis training.

Most of the troopers believed they were tough street fighters. Trooper Richard Braun, a tall, skinny fellow, was always talking about street fighting: "If you don't get a bloody nose or a black eye, it proves you weren't fighting hard enough. . . . When I fight a guy, I'm going to mangle him. When I'm through he's just a mess, that's all. No good for nothing." Foss boasted he only needed three punches: "Two hit the man and the third hits the air."[34]

Most of the troopers were in their early twenties. Some were military veterans or ex-convicts. With such a mix, it was not long before enmity between cliques resulted in fistfights. Rockwell seldom interceded; his men could settle disputes with their fists.

One of the frequent weekend visitors to the ANP compound was a pudgy, squirrel-cheeked ex-paratrooper named Dan Burros. Rockwell was very impressed with Burros's fervid passion for Nazism and his skill as a trained printer and expert office machinery operator. He was a rare individual in Rockwell's eyes; most of the visitors claiming allegiance to the cause offered no skills and little ability. Burros was different—a little too fanatical, but Rockwell was glad to have him.

Roger Foss, the newly promoted "security officer" at headquarters, decided to conduct background profiles on all party members. He asked Rockwell if a refusal would justify discharge from the party.

Rockwell replied, "If they won't provide the information, they will have to leave." The men cooperated with Foss's background information request, except Dan Burros, who told him, "I can't give that to you, Roger." Foss assured Burros the information would be confidential—known only to himself, Rockwell, and Party Secretary James Warner—but Burros refused, even at the threat of having his ANP membership revoked. "I can't give you my home address, Roger, and I won't give it to you," said Burros matter-of-factly. "No one at headquarters must know where I live."

Foss brought the security file to National Secretary James Warner for filing and related Burros's failure to comply. Warner agreed that Burros should be dismissed; the two men went to Rockwell with the situation. Rockwell shrugged it off: "I need Burros, he is my printer. We will have to make an exception in his case."

"An exception?" Foss yelled. "Because he's your printer? I'll be damned if I haven't had as much training on the Davidson [printing press] as he has and more in composition!" Foss argued at length against Rockwell's decision to leave a "security risk" in charge of party printing: "Dan Burros is a nut! First of all he's a sadist, second it's quite obvious he's Jewish. How the hell can you trust a man who refuses to divulge such basic information? How do you expect to find a man if he runs off with vital information from headquarters?"

Rockwell had had enough. He fixed his eyes on Foss and told him, "I run this party; if I say we make an exception in Dan's case, then we make an exception." Foss said nothing. He returned to the printing room to tell Burros the commander was making an exception for him.[35]

Burros worked long hours on the printing press, cranking out stacks of propaganda, swastika bumper stickers ("Hitler Was Right," "Communism Is Jewish," "White Man Fight"), the "Jew Pass" (which entitled the bearer to wait until the end of the line for the gas chamber), soap wrappers marked *"Judenschlaffe"* ("Jew soap"), and the "Official Stormtroopers Manual." Most of the "merchandise" was sold through mail-order via the *National Socialist Bulletin.*

Another regular visitor at ANP headquarters was ex–National Youth League member John Patsalos. By 1960 Patsalos was at his last duty station, with the Marine military police in Quantico, Virginia. Since he was within thirty miles of headquarters he made regular weekend trips to attend party rallies. By summer the Marine Corps had discharged him on grounds of "unsuitability," because of his association with the ANP.

Patsalos changed his name to John Patler, because it looked and sounded more like Hitler. At five feet seven inches, 160 pounds, Patler had a slight physical build. With his dark hair and deep-set eyes, his Greek lineage was apparent. He was not to be underestimated. He had the nickname "Animal Trainer" for his ability to bring even the worst ex-convicts and least tractable party adherents to do his bidding. Patler shrewdly formed cliques within the party, secret alliances with men he could control. There were no neutrals; one was either with him or against him.

By 1960 he had married a blond woman of German descent and sired a son he named Horst Wessel, after the German Nazi "martyr." Patler and wife Erika eventually moved from New York City to Arlington so they could do more work for the party. Patler was a print-er by trade and quick with his fists, both of which impressed Dan Burros. One day Burros baited Patler and Seth Ryan into fighting in the back yard. Ryan's blood splattered onto Patler's shirt; the ghoulish Burros begged Patler to give him the shirt as a memento.[36]

Patler was jealous that National Secretary James Warner was the edi-tor of the *National Socialist Bulletin;* Patler felt that he was more quali-fied and could do a better job. One day Burros and Patler asked Rockwell for a private meeting regarding the *Bulletin.* The two men, who worked directly under Warner, were going behind his back to wrest con-trol of the party magazine. Warner was furious when he discovered their treachery, but he maintained his composure; with Rockwell one could never be sure of anything—he rarely followed procedure or protocol. Warner maintained control over the *Bulletin* for the time being.

Warner had some tricks of his own. One day he telephoned ANP headquarters from the plant of their commercial printer to tell Burros that a photo of him would not be included in that edition of the *Bulletin* because the black SS uniform Burros wore was German issue and not in compliance with party regulations. Burros was furious; he raced around the ANP compound kicking furniture and screaming obscenities about Warner. Rockwell finally calmed him down by instructing Warner to hold the press until another picture of Burros could be sent over.[37]

Troopers complained that the party dog, a mongrel named Gas Chamber, was eating better than they were (troopers regularly dined on corn flakes, chicken backs, and fried potatoes). Burros looked at the mutt and sneered, "That dog looks better all the time. . . . What the heck, we can take him out and chop his head off and have him for supper." Some of the troopers laughed, but others believed he would really eat the animal if given the chance.

Torture was one of Burros's favorite topics. He talked endlessly about inventing new torture devices to use on Jews. His favorite fantasy invention had electrical wires connecting the nerve endings of a Jew to a piano keyboard. He envisioned himself playing a piano that would cause the Jew to jump and twitch to the tune banged out on the keys.[38] He also carried a bar of soap in his pocket with a label reading "Made from the finest Jewish fat."

These were terrible thoughts from the sick mind of a Jewish boy from the Bronx. The contradictions pile up. Although Burros's Jewish heritage remained a secret for five more years, several party members were suspicious. Rockwell had allowed a self-hating Jewish man to become an integral member of his organization. Did Rockwell suspect Burros was Jewish, or did he maintain a "don't ask, don't tell" policy? If Burros was a spy for the ADL, what difference did it make? He was willing to operate the printing press and attend pickets and counter-demonstrations, and he had as much zeal for the cause as the other men.

One day a Jewish reporter drove his car up to the barracks. Rockwell raced down the stairs, yelling, "Why the sneaky little Jew. . . . Quick, call the police on him, get out the rug, hurry." When the reporter entered the doorway, Rockwell spat on the ark curtain and said, "Look here, why don't you wipe your feet on this Jewish floor mat?" The troopers howled in laughter. As Rockwell talked with the Jewish reporter, police arrived to issue a parking ticket on his car. When the reporter went outside to get the ticket the Nazis laughed and jumped for joy. "What a triumph!" yelled Rockwell. "That Jew got a ticket!"[39]

All party activity revolved around Rockwell. He was the heart and soul of the entire operation, and the men followed his lead. On Sunday evenings Rockwell presided over a "training seminar" in the shrine room at headquarters. He would read a passage from *Mein Kampf* and begin a discussion of what Hitler had been saying. Party members believed they would assume power in the depression they thought was coming; each ANP member would be assigned leadership in a different part of the country. It was imperative that each man understand Hitler's plan contained in *Mein Kampf*. The meetings also included progress reports from the national secretary, discussions of agitation techniques and political theory, and intraparty matters—promotions and discipline.

In June, Rockwell was busy working in the makeshift darkroom when Warner ran into the kitchen with a newspaper, yelling, "The niggers are picketing the Glen Echo Amusement Park!"

"They wouldn't dare!" shouted Rockwell. "Let me see that newspaper." Rockwell read the article, about daily desegregation pickets scheduled for the amusement park. "This is just what I've been waiting for," said Rockwell, briskly rubbing his hands together. "Imagine the white people out there just waiting for the Nazis to save them. We will be their white knights. Let's get going, men, we'll make up some signs and really shake up those coons."[40]

When they reached the amusement park to face off against the dozens of segregation protesters, they were shocked to see that the protesters were white. The fight went out of the troopers as they looked upon the white liberals—mostly women and children—protesting segregation. The Nazis were assigned a spot away from the park entrance. There were no clashes, except for occasional Nazi imprecations directed at the other protesters. One of the segregation protesters was a minister. ANP troops shouted various insults at him, but the minister only smiled, with what Foss called the "I love Jesus look" on his face.[41]

Rockwell's Sunday speeches on the Mall were drawing more and more hecklers and ever-increasing hostility. The Nazis knew that eventually the "communists" would attack. On the warm Sunday morning of July 3, the troopers massed outside headquarters at reveille for calisthenics. Nothing too strenuous—they would need their energy for the speech on the Mall. Each man walked around aimlessly, deep in thought, contemplating the bodily injury he might sustain if the mob decided to attack. Many thought this would be the day.

Rockwell held a brief swearing-in ceremony for eighteen-year-old Bernie Davids, who had been coming down from Baltimore on the weekends. (Davids was fascinated by the German aspect of the party; he quickly learned about right-wing politics, blacks, and Jews.) After Davids took the trooper's oath, J. V. Morgan called a "riot drill" in the back yard. The troopers practiced forming a "circle of defense" around Rockwell to protect him in the eventuality the mob came through their perimeter. The "circle of defense" gave the men a sense of security, but they all knew if the mob came through the roped-off perimeter it would be a free-for-all, every man for himself. The drill gave the men something to do before the actual event; every fighter knows that waiting for a fight can be as exhausting as the actual combat.

Shortly before leaving for the Mall rally, J. V. Morgan called Foss into the kitchen. Foss stepped into the kitchen and stopped in surprise when he saw Morgan cracking the seal on a bottle of vodka. Morgan wanted to show Foss the proper mixture of water and vodka for Rockwell's "water bottle." When the time came to leave for the Mall, the ten anxious men jumped into cars.

On the Mall, beside the Smithsonian Institution, hundreds of tourists and local citizens waited patiently for the Nazis. Most spectators positioned themselves well away from the roped-off twenty-five-foot ring the Park Service had provided for the Nazis, but just outside its perimeter were dozens of angry men waiting to heckle and intimidate the Nazis.

The Nazis walked in pairs from their parked cars to the roped-off area and set up their speaking platform and a podium, and strung a large swastika flag from two poles. The large red-and-black swastika floating in the air gave the men a surge of power, as if something holy were hovering over them, enabling them to exceed their human weakness and limitations, assuring them that their cause was race and nation.[42] The troopers formed up the "circle of defense" around the perimeter as Rockwell stepped to the podium to speak.

"My fellow Americans. . . ." He was immediately drowned out by a thunderous roar from the hecklers. "You're sick, Rockwell. Hey, Rockhead, you're sick." The biggest, beefiest hecklers pressed against the ropes shouting insults at the Nazis. "My fellow Americans!" Rockwell shouted again. The mob erupted with shouts, again drowning him out. "This is your last speech," called one heckler. "Today's the day, Rockhead," yelled another.

Troopers Morgan and Colton strode around inside of the roped perimeter, challenging anyone to step inside the rope. "Come on, you fat Jew bastard!" yelled Colton, shaking his fist at one particular irritating heckler. The heckler pointed at Colton and shouted, "That man is a Marine!" A police officer came through the ropes and asked Colton if he was a serviceman. Colton denied it, but the officer decided to remove him and check with military police. Now the Nazi ranks were thinned by one.

Surrounding the Nazi enclave were hundreds of weekend tourists. Instead of viewing the monuments to the Republic, they watched uniformed Nazis engage in public spectacle.

Rockwell instructed Trooper George Clifford (a *Washington Daily News* reporter working undercover) to inform the Park Police lieutenant that he would not speak until the mob was quiet. "I don't care what he does," the lieutenant told the undercover newsman.

An hour passed, and Rockwell had been unable to speak. Morgan jumped on the speaking platform to converse with Rockwell. "We ought to agitate them some more," said Morgan. "Go ahead," replied Rockwell. "You lowly, cowardly, filthy, vile Jews!" Rockwell screamed in his strongest voice. The line of men outside the ropes surged forward, testing the integrity of the posts and rope restraints. Rockwell yelled out to Morgan, "Major Morgan, where do Jews come from?" Morgan turned to Rockwell and shouted, "When you cross a hound dog with a nigger."[43]

The next moment, hecklers seized Morgan from behind and pulled him over the ropes. The ropes went down, and a wall of men came charging through. The "circle of defense" broke apart as each Nazi fought for his life. The mob overturned the speaking platform, spilling Rockwell to the ground. The melee lasted for less than a minute before the hecklers broke off the attack and ran for their cars to avoid arrest. One by one the Nazis picked themselves off the ground and surveyed their injuries. Rockwell got up and laughed aloud at the hecklers running to their cars: "Look at those filthy cowards run."[44]

Fifty feet from the ring, police were pulling hecklers off J. V. Morgan, who had had no chance once he was dragged outside the rope. He had taken the worst beating, with several kicks to the head. The other Nazis were in fairly good shape. Warner had had a chunk of his ear bit off and there were some bloodied lips and noses, but no real damage other than to Morgan.

The Nazis were puzzled by the mob's retreat; they could have been killed had the mob remained to fight. Rockwell surmised that the mob's intention had been to disrupt the speech and to fight just enough for police to dub the event a "riot." A "riot arrest" would establish a legal precedent for banning future ANP demonstrations.

Police put the Nazis under arrest, herded them into a paddy wagon, booked them at police headquarters, and locked them into cells. The Nazis claimed victory because they had stood fast while the attackers ran; they had beaten the "communists." To celebrate, they sang Rockwell's "National Socialist Battle Song," which he had adapted to the melody of the original "Horst Wessel Lied." Burros sang the words in German.

Colton, who was released by police (he was not a Marine), and Schuyler Ferris, who was not at the rally, came to the police station with bail money for everyone. "Are we going to forfeit the bond?" asked Warner. "No," replied Rockwell, "we're going to fight this in court. Otherwise the Jews will use this incident to prove we incite riots every time we speak."[45]

At headquarters that evening the party readied for the nightly picket at Glen Echo Amusement Park; Rockwell's appetite for publicity had not been satiated by the riot. He instructed the men to apply bandages of white rags with ketchup stains over some part of their body. Injured or not, everyone got bandaged, on the head, arm, or leg. Morgan did not need any fake bandages; he went to the picket on a set of crutches, with severe bruises on his ribs and skull.

Burros, "the Ghoul," collected samples of blood from the injured Nazis to smear on the party's swastika flag (intended for the party museum), along with bloodied shirts for his private collection. The next morning most of the major newspapers carried the story of the "Nazi riot on the Mall."[46]

On July 4, Rockwell and troopers assembled on the National Park grounds near the Smithsonian for another rally. The melee the day before had no effect on their plans for a demonstration. As Rockwell readied for his speech, he was given an order signed by the acting secretary of the interior, Elmer Bennett, declaring the Smithsonian grounds off-limits for public assemblies. Rockwell inquired where "free speech" was still allowed; the Park Police officer directed him to Judiciary Square.

The Nazis gathered their equipment and marched to Judiciary Square. With no public address system and no speaking platform, Rockwell mounted an upturned pail and addressed the crowd. He talked a short while before he was drowned out by hecklers. In a surprise maneuver, he ordered the ten stormtroopers fanned out in front of him to turn their backs. He lit a cigar and folded his arms to drama-

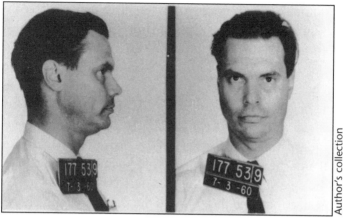

Author's collection

Two of Rockwell's many mug shots. This time he was arrested after one of his Sunday speeches on the Washington Mall turned into a brawl.

tize that he was not trying to speak or provoke the audience. As police walked through the crowd the heckling died down, and the mob lost its cohesion. After an hour Rockwell ordered his men to face forward, and he began his speech again. There were sporadic outbreaks of yelling, but Rockwell had beaten the mob by superior tactics.[47]

July 4 also marked the end of a five-day antisegregation demonstration at Glen Echo Amusement Park by members of NAACP and CORE. Rockwell and the stormtrooper entourage arrived before dusk to begin a counter-demonstration, their second street action of the day.

Rockwell believed that the hecklers attending ANP rallies were part of an organized plan of disruption. He theorized that the Anti-Defamation League was organizing hecklers and conspiring with U.S. Park Police to deprive him of his civil rights. He notified the FBI Washington field office, requesting its help in determining the degree of conspiracy between the ADL and the U.S. Park Police. The Bureau gathered relevant testimony on his request, but the matter was eventually dropped.

There appears to be some credibility in this conspiracy theory, as one U.S. Park Police officer gave testimony supporting Rockwell. The officer told the FBI that the same group of individuals appeared at consecutive Rockwell talks and were well organized. They continuously yelled and made noise while Rockwell was speaking, and the majority of the time their noise drowned out the speech. The officer stated that the usual interpretation of the disorderly conduct statute made it a violation for anyone to make loud noise or other disturbance. Preceding each Rockwell speech, U.S. Park Police were briefed by superiors to not make any arrests for heckling or loud talking except in the case of profanity, violence, or weapon use. The officer added that when black singer Paul Robeson had spoken at the Sylvan Theater, the USPP had taken action to prevent any loud noise or disturbances. The officer felt there should have been equal application of the law. Since the Interior Department had granted permission for Rockwell to speak and had provided a roped-off area, he felt, Park Police should grant him the right to speak without being disturbed by organized hecklers.[48]

A conspiracy between the ADL and the U.S. Park Police, nonetheless, is highly unlikely, even though the ADL was exchanging information with the Park Police as to the places and times of Rockwell's rallies. In fact, Park Police turned a blind eye to the heckling simply because Rockwell was perceived as an agitator; protecting him from verbal agitation was not of paramount importance.

On July 6, Rockwell appeared in court on the disorderly conduct charge stemming from the fight on July 3. During the hearing, Assistant Corporation Counsel Clark King questioned Rockwell's sanity: "We have grave doubts as to the man's competency. We feel he should be sent for a mental examination."[49] King demanded a $300 cash bond, along with an additional bond to be posted by a bondsman in case Rockwell decided to leave town. Judge George Neilson agreed.

Rockwell stood before the bench in silence, his eyes roaming the courtroom with a dazed and confused look—he was in over his head. The troopers in attendance consulted with each other; they could never raise Rockwell's bail money. In the rear of the courtroom, a man beckoned to Foss. Foss approached, and the man whispered that he could get the money for Rockwell's bail later in the day; he instructed Foss to meet him at the Library of Congress that evening. Foss asked Colton and Morgan if either of them knew the mystery man; neither did. They tried to think of any possible ulterior motives he might have.

With no other options, Morgan drove Foss to the Library of Congress to collect the money. Foss walked up the stone stairway into a deserted hallway, wondering if he might be gunned down. He walked slowly down the hallway, all senses at "battle stations"; finally the mystery man stepped out from behind a column and waved. He handed Foss a thick white envelope stuffed with twenty-dollar bills. "What do you want in return?" Foss asked skeptically. "Tell no one who gave you this money," replied the man. Foss returned to Morgan, and the two men drove to a bond company to make arrangements for Rockwell's release.[50]

The court appointed attorney O. B. Parker to defend Rockwell at his sanity hearing on July 27 in Municipal Court. Judge George Neilson wanted Rockwell to undergo psychiatric evaluation at District General Hospital on an outpatient basis, but hospital authorities refused, claiming inadequate facilities. Rockwell found two doctors from St. Elizabeth's Hospital who agreed to provide the examination. Rockwell told reporters he had never been under psychiatric care and predicted that after the examination the psychiatrist would become a Nazi.

With Rockwell free on bail, the ANP targeted African-American actor Sammy Davis, Jr., for their next protest. Davis was appearing at a night-club called the New Lotus, on 14th Street, N.W. Troopers marched outside the club with placards mocking Davis for his conversion to Judaism and for his engagement to white actress Mae Britt. The Nazis brought the dog "Gas Chamber," their mascot, to the picket with a cloth band wrapped around his midsection with a sign that read, "I'm black too Sammy, but I ain't a Jew." The next week they went after Davis again. Davis was scheduled to appear at the Black Saddle Restaurant in Washington for an interview with Steve Allison, to be broadcast over radio station WWDC. Several stormtroopers were in the restaurant that evening to heckle Davis, but Allison had received a tip they were coming and had canceled the show.

On July 24, for the second time in July, Rockwell and stormtroopers were arrested for disorderly conduct. As he addressed the dozens of spectators in Judiciary Square, two hecklers continually disrupted him. At Rockwell's signal, six stormtroopers moved into the crowd to circle the hecklers and shout them down. There was some pushing and shoving, and the park and metropolitan police immediately went into action and arrested all the Nazis for disorderly conduct.

Judiciary Square became the regular venue for the ANP. Troopers practiced public speaking in the empty square during the week, especially on the hot summer days when all the windows were open in the adjacent federal buildings.

Rockwell boasted in party literature that the "cops are with us." Almost without exception, someone from the ANP would telephone the local police, the press, and the FBI to inform them of upcoming speeches or demonstrations. This insured police protection at the scene—in case a mob attacked—and also increased the drama and fanfare of the event.

—————

The party had numerous run-ins with Arlington and Washington police, but its strongest opposition came from the Anti-Defamation League of B'nai B'rith and its chief investigator, Jason Silverman. ANP members respected Silverman and often speculated about their dossiers in his office. Rockwell would telephone, say "Hello, Jase," and inform him of the latest Nazi foray. Silverman had been selected by the Army at the close of World War II to interview Nazi prisoners of war interned at Fort Robinson, Nebraska, to probe the causes and motivations of Nazism in the German soldiers. The goal of the program was to develop a "reorientation (denazification) program" for the returning Nazis. In 1946, he had joined the ADL.

On July 26, Burros and Patler went to ADL headquarters in Washington to cause trouble. They rode the elevator to the fourth floor and asked Rose Gordon, executive assistant to Jason Silverman, for the latest copies of the *ADL Bulletin*. She recognized both men as Nazis and told them there were no copies of the *Bulletin* available. After a few minutes Ms. Gordon pressed the button for the elevator; she wanted to make sure the Nazis left the building. When the doors opened her eyes were immediately drawn to a red swastika sticker, saying "We are back" on the back wall of the elevator. She called the police, and a warrant was issued for the arrest of Burros and Patler, for defacing private property.[51]

The next day, Rockwell's sanity hearing commenced. Fearing committal, Rockwell readied the troopers for a demonstration; he instructed them to picket the White House but stay out of trouble until he returned. The hearing before Judge George Neilson commenced, and dozens of spectators watched the day-long inquest that would decide if the American Nazi Party leader would be locked up for a thirty-day psychiatric evaluation.

ANP literature and cartoons drawn by Rockwell twenty years earlier at Brown University were introduced as evidence against him by Clark King. King's chief witness, Dr. John Schultz, medical director of District General Hospital, testified that the literature and cartoons indicated a high probability that Rockwell was of unsound mind. Schultz testified that the nature of Rockwell's "illness" made him "very dangerous."[52]

In defense, five Nazi Party members vouched for Rockwell's sanity and competence to stand trial; there was also a letter from a private psychologist, Thomas Murphy, affirming his competence. Rockwell took the stand in his own defense, saying, "I feel the only thing between me and the bughouse this minute is the Constitution. If the government is permitted to put me under lock and key for thirty days, this will be a gross violation of a person's right to speak his ideas."[53] Nonetheless, when the testimony was finished Judge Neilson ordered Rockwell committed to District General Hospital for thirty days. The civilized courtroom was replaced for Rockwell by the putrid reality of a cell. Two overweight deputies whisked Rockwell from the courtroom and locked him inside a holding tank that reeked of urine and vomit.

After a few hours Rockwell and several black prisoners were herded into a vehicle for their trip to the "loony bin." The steel-walled wagon was stifling; the black paint absorbed the ninety-degree Washington sunshine, turning the inside of the wagon into a broiler. The unwashed prisoners all sweated profusely, making a stench so powerful that Rockwell's olfactory senses were overwhelmed. The only ventilation came from four slits in the metal. The guards compounded the misery by stopping for refreshments, paper transfers, and prisoner exchanges along the way.

In the psychiatric ward of the hospital the new inductees were greeted by an all-inmate welcoming committee composed of several alcoholics and a pock-faced junkie. Rockwell was handed pajamas and led to his room. There were locks on every door and a ceiling-mounted closed-circuit television camera in each room.

As he lay on his assigned bed, the reality of his predicament sank in. It was clear to him that Dr. Schultz and the ADL had "railroaded" him this far. What would keep Schultz—working in his own hospital—from "diagnosing" him as a lunatic? He could use injections and electro-shock "therapy" to make Rockwell appear insane. He could lock him up for life or, worse, yet, perform a frontal lobotomy. Rockwell needed a plan.[54]

In reaction to Rockwell's commitment, Burros, Patler, and Foss, accompanied by mascot Gas Chamber, picketed the White House with placards reading:

If you don't love Jews and Niggers, you're nuts
Free Speech for Reds, insane asylum for Rockwell
Free Speech? Free Rockwell
IKE free Lincoln Rockwell
Rockwell put away. His crime? Fighting Communism
Help free Rockwell, call JA4-5831

They marched all day, back and forth in the hot July sun. Nearby, a police officer watched from his squad car. After seven hours, the Nazis called it quits. As Burros and Patler were about to leave the police officer put them under arrest for defacing private property—the ADL headquarters. The two Nazis were furious that the officer had let them picket all day until their feet were swollen and sore before making the arrest.

Foss went to jail to talk with them. Patler was sitting on the bed, while Burros paced the floor. Burros asked, "Did you bring the money to get us out, Roger?" "We haven't been able to raise the money yet. Morgan says to sit tight. We may be able to raise it by Monday," replied Foss.

"I won't sit in here that long!" shouted Burros. "Look, Dan," sneered Foss, none too happy with Burros's indignation, "it's your fault you're here in the first place, don't yell at me. You went against party orders for even going down to ADL headquarters. You guys goofed. Now the least you can do is to sit here like men and wait until we can raise the money." Patler called Burros over to the bunk to confer for a moment, then walked over to the bars and told Foss, "You can go back and tell J.V. that if he doesn't have our bail down here tonight we will give enough evidence to the ADL to have every man in the party put in prison for life."

"Do you realize what you are saying, Patler?" asked Foss. "Do you realize that this is the highest form of treason? Do you mean to say that you two tough Nazis can't sit here in jail until Monday?" Both men were insistent that their message he relayed to Deputy Commander Morgan.

Morgan and Warner were waiting for Foss back at headquarters. There was nothing Morgan could do about raising bail money before Monday. The party was in crisis, and Rockwell had not even been gone a day. Burros and Patler finally made bail, but not through party channels; Erika Patler was somehow able to get a Jewish bondsman to post bail.[55]

In District General Hospital, Rockwell devised a plan to beat the "Jewish conspiracy" that had "railroaded" him there. He knew the conspiracy was not total; only a few of the top Jews were in on the plan. Most of the people he would deal with in the hospital would be sincere, but misguided. His strategy was to cooperate: no antisocial behavior, no fighting, no arguing. The next day he volunteered to help as a social worker in his cell block for the insane. He drew pictures for the inmates, helped them write letters to their families, and talked with them. When the psychiatrists gave him ink-blot tests he saw birds with beautiful feathers and Japanese dancers with flowing kimonos, not the wreckage, blood, bodies, and carnage he presumed they wanted him to see.[56] After ten days the doctors pronounced him "of sound mind and mentally competent to stand trial."[57] Rockwell later wrote a synopsis of his psychiatric experiences in a pamphlet called "How to Get Out or Stay Out of the Insane Asylum."

When Rockwell returned to headquarters he suspended Patler and Burros pending the outcome of their trial, then changed his mind and reinstated them, because he was "convinced of their innocence." The Burros/Patler defacing trial was heard by Judge Milton Kronheim on September 20. Judge Kronheim, a member of B'nai B'rith, asked the court-appointed attorney representing Patler and Burros if he had any objections with his, Kronheim's, trying the case. The attorney, James Jones, had no objections to the obvious conflict of interest. The trial lasted a few hours, but the jury only took twenty minutes to return a guilty verdict. The judge sentenced the Nazis to pay a hundred dollars or spend ten days in jail, with six months suspended. They paid the fine; Patler filed an appeal, which was later rejected.

With the government considering a subversives investigation, Foss decided it was time to clear the air with Rockwell about his previous involvement with the Soviets (his attempt to become a paid informer within the government). In early July, when Rockwell heard Foss's story, he escorted him to FBI headquarters to offer his help in breaking up the Soviet spy ring, his real reason being to protect the party. Foss concurred, later explaining, "We didn't want my past to give the Party a black eye." The FBI declined Rockwell's offer to break up the spy ring; the link between Foss and his onetime handler, Ivanov, was already under investigation. The Bureau told Foss to register as a foreign agent since he had accepted money from a foreign government.[58]

In early August the FBI sent Foss a letter formally requiring him to register as a foreign agent, and within ten days. Rockwell and Foss had kept the Soviet information confidential in order to allow the Justice Department to build a case against Ivanov. Rockwell decided it was time to go public. He worked out an agreement to give Les Whitten, a reporter for the *Washington Post,* an exclusive exposé on the Soviet "spy ring" if it was given full treatment in the *Post* newspaper and its radio and television affiliates. That night the local television station flashed pictures of Foss and Ivanov. The *Post* headlined the story, with pictures.

Tom Kelly, editor of the *Washington Daily News,* called Rockwell for the story. "Sorry, Jew," chuckled Rockwell, "you'll have to read about it in the *Post.* They have an exclusive."

At headquarters the men were ecstatic. "Well, Foss," said Rockwell victoriously, "that exclusive will force the Justice Department to take some action. I wouldn't be surprised if the FBI is snickering right now." Rockwell believed the FBI was an intelligence-gathering organization, its actions dictated by the elites at the Justice Department who were crypto-communists. Their failure to act against Ivanov proved it. Higher-ups in the department—most likely Jews—were working a deal for Ivanov and squelching the spy accusations. Publicizing the information would put an end to any "deals."

On August 12, 1960, one day after the *Washington Post* reported his link to Roger Foss of the ANP, the State Department ordered Valentin Ivanov out of the country. The State Department called in the Soviet ambassador, Mikhail Menshikov, to tell him that Ivanov had "grossly violated the established norms of diplomatic behavior."[59] Ivanov became the highest-placed Russian diplomat expelled from Washington in America's twenty-seven-year relations with the Soviets and the second Soviet expelled that summer (the Third Secretary, Petr Ezhov, was ordered out July 22 after he paid $1,000 to an undercover FBI agent for aerial photographs of U.S. naval bases).

The Russians retaliated by expelling a U.S. air attaché from Moscow for making "intelligence trips." Two American tourists were also told to leave Russia for anti-Soviet activities. The State Department described the actions as a "somewhat hysterical" campaign to set the stage for the upcoming espionage trial of U-2 pilot Francis Gary Powers, who was shot down over Russia by a Soviet SA-2 missile in May 1960.

Rockwell asked Foss to come up to his room for a private discussion. Foss was stunned by the chill from the air-conditioning in the room; Rockwell claimed it helped his "asthma" (he did not suffer from asthma).

Rockwell sat by his typewriter wearing khaki pants and a dirty T-shirt, puffing slowly on a corncob pipe for emphasis. "Foss," Rockwell began, "in New York City I mentioned to you that I needed a woman. I love my wife dearly and I miss her very much. What do you think the men would say if I took a mistress?"

"Why would they say anything?" Foss asked.

"In my position here at headquarters I have to keep a sort of image in front of the men. You know how it is in the service, Foss, an officer is supposed to do his personal things separate from the men. We eat separately, we shit separately, it's important that the men have respect for an officer. Here at headquarters that's nearly impossible; they see me as only a noncombatant orderly should see me.

"There are several women who have made it clear to me that they would desire an intimate relationship. There is one in particular that has the necessary qualifications to be my mistress: she is intelligent, poised, attractive, and very dedicated to the cause." Foss convinced Rockwell there would be no problem from the men about a mistress.

From then on one of Foss's duties as security officer was to escort Rockwell to the home of the mistress. She had recently moved from the District of Columbia to a chalet-style house in a residential area in nearby Falls Church. One morning Rockwell was not quite ready to leave when Foss arrived with the car. Foss was waiting inside the home, admiring the large swastika flag hanging on the wall of the living room, when the doorbell rang. Foss found two well-dressed women holding wicker baskets on the doorstep. One looked Jewish. "What do you want?" Foss demanded.

"We are from the Welcome Wagon Committee and we have come to welcome you into the community. Is your wife home?" Before Foss could answer, the Jewish-looking woman peeked her head inside the door to ogle at the furnishings. Her eyes locked onto the swastika flag for several moments, staring in disbelief. Without warning she dropped her basket, screamed, and ran down the steps out to the street. Her companion, completely dumbfounded, made a slow retreat. Rockwell and his mistress walked out on the balcony to see what had happened. When Foss related the story, they both doubled over with laughter.[60]

Another incident occurred that week when Rockwell decided to treat his men to some pizza at Mario's Pizza House in Arlington. They were refused service because the proprietor, Howard Levine, claimed

Rockwell had used "lewd, obscene, and heinous language" in his establishment in the past. Rockwell stormed out of the pizza house and returned a short while later with several picketers. One of Mario's employees turned on the garden hose outside the building and sprayed the Nazis with water. Police Lieutenant Elmer Redmond was on the scene but denied seeing the incident. Rockwell lodged a complaint with Captain Raymond Cole of the Arlington police but decided against bringing charges against Redmond before a grand jury. He simply wanted the Arlington police to furnish the same protection given to other citizens.

On August 24, New York State Supreme Court Justice Louis Friedman granted an extension of an injunction to keep Rockwell from holding a rally in New York. The original injunction had prevented Rockwell from holding a July 4 rally. The new extension, good until September 8, prevented Rockwell from holding a Labor Day rally as well. At the end of August, Justice Henry Epstein of the same court dismissed Rockwell's petition to compel the city to grant him a permit to speak in Union Square. Epstein ruled, "It is not within the reasonable scope of the Bill of Rights amendment here relied upon to loose self-confessed advocates of violence upon a community at a time and place where it is inevitable that public disorder and riot will result." Epstein further stated that the New York Civil Liberties Union had misread the Constitution and legal precedents in seeking the permit.[61]

In the District of Columbia, the trial for both disorderly conduct arrests the past July got under way. The Nazis were found guilty by Municipal Court Judge Mildred Reeves of disorderly conduct. Rockwell was sentenced to pay a hundred-dollar fine or spend thirty days in jail. Stormtroopers Dan Burros and Roger Foss were fined twenty dollars or ten days in jail for their actions on July 24. The other troopers were each sentenced to pay a ten-dollar fine or five days in jail. During the closing arguments Rockwell told the court that the issue was whether "an unpopular group has the right to go out and preach unpopular ideas under our Constitution."[62] Judge Reeves told Rockwell that speaking on political ideas is one thing but that when personal abuse is interjected, it does not come within the realm of freedom of speech. Rockwell asked why he had been permitted to speak for so long and had not been charged with inciting a riot. Reeves replied that on the basis of testimony he was in fact guilty of inciting to riot with his talk; the prosecutor was simply being lenient.

Rockwell appealed the decision but was denied a new trial by Judge Reeves. All charges against the six men accused of heckling Rockwell during the July rallies were dropped by Assistant Corporation Counsel King. Rockwell appealed to another court, but his conviction was upheld in the summer of 1961. By a 3–0 ruling the court noted that freedom of speech does not give a person "an unlimited license to talk." The judges leaned on a Supreme Court ruling in which the use of "epithets of personal abuse is not in any proper sense communication of information or opinion safeguarded by the Constitution."[63]

Rockwell had learned a valuable lesson on the limits of the First Amendment. Freedom of speech remained his primary weapon, but never again would he shout "dirty, vile, filthy Jews" in public. The ADL believed that his public denunciations of Jews and "niggers" were "fighting words" and did not entitle him the protection of the First Amendment. Conversely, civil libertarians believed that silencing him would cause greater damage to civil liberties than if he were allowed to speak. Rockwell gathered a list of names of every civil liberties lawyer and organization that might defend him in court.

The local community of Arlington began to harass Rockwell in early September. Commonwealth Attorney Hassan advised him that the county would no longer tolerate the usage of ANP headquarters as a "flop house." No more than three guests would be allowed to reside there at any one time. Rockwell reviewed the code for Arlington County and ascertained that it was permissible for him to have "domestic employees." He informed the county that besides himself, James Warner, Roger Foss, and Dan Burros would reside in the building, but also a cook, maid, and janitor from Chicago. This way he could skirt the law and retain other members at the headquarters under the guise of domestic employees.

Foreclosure proceedings against the headquarters building commenced on September 9, due to Floyd Fleming's failure to insure the property as set forth in the purchase agreement; twenty-two firms had rejected Fleming's requests for insurance because of the ANP occupancy. A property auction was scheduled for September 15, but Fleming avoided the sale by paying off the Deed of Trust note, in the amount of $4,167.

On October 2, Rockwell was assaulted at the annual picnic at the German Orphans Home in Prince George's County, Maryland. He was mugged without provocation in the kitchen of the home, out of sight of the hundreds attending the picnic and his stormtrooper bodyguards. He refused hospital treatment for black eyes and facial cuts. Foss was furious that the troopers had failed to protect their commander. The next day Rockwell requested permission to carry a concealed handgun; it was denied by Hassan.

Two weeks later the ANP made a show of force at the "Kennedy for President" headquarters on Connecticut Avenue and K Street, N.W. Seven troopers marched in front of the headquarters at noon and again at 4:30 P.M. Rockwell attended the noon demonstration but did not picket. He filmed the event with a movie camera in case the troopers were arrested.

"I want to show we're producing no violence and speaking no words. I'm not walking the picket line myself, because I've got all I can handle now. I can't handle any more jails or bug houses or anything else." [64] He instructed the seven picketing brownshirts and his two bodyguards not to talk with anyone except reporters. The demonstrators carried placards which read:

Thank God Nixon Won't Apologize to Reds
Judas Johnson
We Don't Need Another Mr. K.
Kikes for Kennedy
Nazis for Nixon
I am thinking mean thoughts about Kennedy

A huge lunch-hour crowd of nearly a thousand clustered around to watch and jeer. When traffic backed up, police asked the Nazis to disperse, and they complied. When the Nazis began their second demonstration, at 4:30 P.M., police again asked them to leave, because of the threat of violence. They all obeyed except for Roger Foss, who stayed on to test the legality of their protest. Foss was arrested and charged with disorderly conduct.

In a surprise move, Clark King filed charges against Rockwell and five other troopers for picketing, even though they had disbanded at police request. King reasoned that the picketing was done as "an organizational matter," so all pickets were equally responsible. The others arrested were Troopers Roy James, Ralph Grandinetti, Ralph Hassinger,

Tony Wells, and John Pall. Rockwell and four troopers were acquitted by Chief Municipal Judge John Lewis, Jr. Foss was sentenced to ten days in jail or a twenty-five-dollar fine; John Pall was deported.

Immigration officials had started deportation proceedings against Pall immediately after his picketing arrest. Pall, a Hungarian, had emigrated to Canada in 1951 and had become a naturalized citizen. He had come to the United States in September 1960 and joined the ANP. The forty-five-year-old told a reporter he had read of the Nazi Party and wondered why a former U.S. Navy officer who had fought against Hitler would be leading it. He had made a visit to the Arlington headquarters and decided to stay, but he had neglected to get permission from U.S. immigration authorities. He was deported to Canada in December.

In Hollywood, California, four stormtroopers from an independent group, wearing khaki uniforms and swastika armbands, marched in protest at the Huntington Hartford Theater, where Sammy Davis, Jr., was performing. The troopers had called the Hollywood police station earlier in the evening and announced their plans to picket the theater. Police had told them it was legal to do so but had advised against it.

When the Nazis started picketing an angry mob of a hundred men attacked. One trooper ran from the scene as the screaming, jeering mob caught the other three and battered them about the face and head. One of the attackers grabbed a length of two-by-four lumber from a construction site and took a swing at the head of one of the troopers before being disarmed by police. Police interceded and shoved the three troopers into a squad car and raced away from the theater. Three men were arrested.

One, Leonard Holstein, was the leader of Nazi activities in California. At the time of the theater protest none of the men were official party members, because they had not paid dues. Their swastika armbands had been purchased from ANP headquarters for $1.50. Holstein's Nazi activities had started at an early age. When he was thirteen years old he had begun reading books on Hitler. By age seventeen his Nazi interests had resulted in numerous fights; he was placed in a juvenile home. He had transferred to a mental hospital but had not responded to treatment. Upon release he had continued talking about a "master race" and the elimination of Jews. His mother believed he was in need of psychiatric care: "It's crazy. The whole thing is crazy. When he parades around with that swastika, he doesn't realize what he's doing to his family. And to himself. He's committing suicide—we're a Jewish family."[65]

On November 30, five members of the ANP filed a $550,000 suit in District Court charging various federal and District government officials and others with violating their civil rights. The suit named fourteen defendants, including Interior Secretary Seaton, three District commissioners, Assistant Corporation Counsel Clark King, Chief Harold Stewart of the National Capital Park Police, three officials of ADL, and Dr. John Schultz (medical director of District General Hospital) with conspiring to arrest them illegally on disorderly conduct charges at rallies held by the ANP on the Mall and at Judiciary Square. Nothing ever came of the suit, which was thrown out in March 1961 by District Judge Leonard Walsh.

The year ended with the creation of an ANP front group. Rockwell and a Chicago sympathizer formed the Fighting American Nationalists (FAN) in late 1960. The genesis of FAN took place at a saloon on the North Side of Chicago called the College of Complexes—Headquarters of the American Beatnik Party. Rockwell despised the beatnik movement, whose adherents embraced rootlessness, unconventional clothing, drugs, alcohol, and a craze for Eastern religion and philosophy. A Nazi sympathizer made arrangements for a Rockwell appearance. On the night of the event the saloon filled to capacity—including forty police officers and another 150 people outside the saloon. Rockwell drove around the block several times, analyzing the situation. With no entourage to shield him from the beatnik enclave, he decided to pass up the appearance. He arranged for a private gathering at the home of a sympathizer, where he gave a presentation of the situation in America and outlined ANP goals.

There he found support for his ideas but not enough manpower to create a functioning headquarters unit. The idea was presented of creating FAN to recruit a larger circle of adherents without the Nazi trappings. Rockwell supported the plan, and the first FAN unit was officially founded. Separate groups sprang up in New York, Pennsylvania, Louisiana, Ohio, and Maryland. The ANP guided and directed FAN units throughout the country, with the exception of the Maryland cell, which operated independently. The FAN agenda mimicked that of the

ANP: condemnation of race mixing, communism, and the "Marxist" United Nations. The Chicago branch attained the highest membership, with forty supporters. FAN activities consisted of handing out literature while picketing communist organizations and racial integration events. Each member wore a red, white, and blue armband with the initials "FAN." Although FAN proved useful as a recruiting tool for the ANP, Rockwell always referred to the group in derogatory terms, calling the members "sissies" or "Future American Nazis."

Attending the FAN formation meeting was a twenty-five-year-old Milwaukee native, Matt Koehl, already a veteran of numerous right-wing campaigns. The FAN meeting was the turning point of his political career. In 1956 Koehl had attended the "We the People" convention at the LaSalle Hotel in Chicago. Koehl had no patience for "kosher conservatives" and had been probing about for a community of similar interests. At the convention he had made contact with a member of the Sons of the American Revolution who told him of a Navy fighter pilot who wanted to create a Nazi party. Koehl was a bit surprised—a Nazi party seemed a little too much—but he had hoped it was true.

The following year Koehl had attended the formation meeting of the United White Party in Knoxville, Tennessee, where Rockwell presented his "Lincoln Plan" to provide $10,000 to every black family willing to relocate to Africa. Koehl was impressed by Rockwell's presentation but opted to join Ed Fields's and J. B. Stoner's organization that shortly became the National States Rights Party. In late 1958, Koehl had moved to Chicago and had taken a job as a Compton Encyclopedia salesman while continuing to work with the local branch of the NSRP; meanwhile he kept hearing reports that Rockwell was serious, not a flash in the pan.

In late November 1960 Koehl decided it was time to join Rockwell's movement as a leader in the Fighting American Nationalists. He would eventually become second in command of the American Nazi Party.[66]

The year 1960 was a crucial, foundation-laying time for Rockwell and his party. Surmounting the arrests, his psychiatric commitment, riots, beatings, and court hearings was exhausting, but in the end it made

Rockwell stronger. The party made numerous gains. It now had a secure headquarters in Arlington. Its frequent demonstrations gave it local notoriety and considerable press coverage. Rockwell's court appearance in New York and the subsequent outrage among the Jewish community had produced the national media attention Rockwell was seeking. He had also defined for his purposes the limits of the First Amendment.

There were incongruities, too. This group of agnostic Nazis was fighting for a white Christian America. A Jewish stormtrooper was living at Nazi headquarters and fighting for Nazism; another was in California protesting inter-racial marriage. The party was led by only a dozen men with virtually no income. Rockwell, however, was proving a master at using guerrilla agitation techniques to exploit the media and gain free press coverage.

6

1961: THIS TIME THE WORLD

We only hate the things that every red-blooded American
should hate—Communists and race-mixing.
— Rockwell, Parish County Jail,
New Orleans, 1961

Communism moved forward on several fronts in 1961. Yuri Gagarin of
the Soviet Union became the first human in space. First *Sputnik*, then
Gagarin—the Soviets were clearly ahead of the U.S. in the race to claim
dominance of outer space. In mid-April, anti-Castro Cuban exiles,
trained by the CIA, attempted an invasion at the Bay of Pigs, in Cuba.
The attack was crushed when President John F. Kennedy reneged on his
promise of air support; the failure to retake Cuba was a blow to U.S.
prestige and strengthened Castro's regime. In December, Specialist
Fourth Class James Davis was killed by the Vietcong. He was the first
American killed in combat in Vietnam.

The American Nazi Party began the year with a well-publicized picketing in Boston of the movie *Exodus*, which was about the early years of the
state of Israel. On January 15, Speros Lagoulis, a sympathizer, put up several hundred dollars to finance the protest. Lagoulis had met Rockwell in
1960, and the men had taken a liking to one another. Lagoulis was
Rockwell's age and had some show business background. He ran a the-
atrical costume rental shop in Boston as well as the Joe McCarthy
Bookstore. Lagoulis suggested that Rockwell protest *Exodus* because it was
a "filthy Zionist movie," whose screenwriter, Dalton Trumbo, had refused
to testify at a congressional hearing on subversive activities.[1]

Early in the week, Rockwell notified the *Boston Globe* of the impending demonstration. The *Globe* ran articles about it, providing the advance publicity Rockwell desired.

The party rented a cargo truck to haul ten troopers from Arlington to Boston, and it purchased airline tickets for Rockwell and four body-guards. The five Nazis flew into Boston and checked into a sixth-floor room of the Hotel Touraine, where Lagoulis had reserved rooms under the name "Nathan Ginsberg." From there they could observe the Saxon Theater, the site of their scheduled protest and rendezvous point for the stormtroopers driving up from Arlington.

Roger Foss and J. V. Morgan took turns driving the unheated cargo truck carrying the stormtroopers north from Virginia. They stopped at a restaurant in Manhattan so the troopers could warm up and eat a quick meal, then proceeded up the Massachusetts Turnpike, where they ran out of gas. Foss hitchhiked to the next exit and brought a service truck back with fuel.[2]

At 12:45 P.M., fifty anti-Nazi protesters arrived in front of the theater carrying placards that read:

Fight Nazism Now

No Nazi Dictator

Remember Auschwitz

Nazism Means War

Nazism Destroys Civil Liberties

Act Against Fascism

At 1:00 P.M., hundreds of anti-Nazi protesters swarmed the streets surrounding the theater. By 2:00 the crowd had grown to more than three thousand. The Nazis watched from the hotel windows, frightened by the sight of the huge crowd and puzzled by the absence of the other troopers. At 2:15 P.M. Rockwell told the other troopers he was going to protest alone; this was a suicide mission, and he would not command the others to follow. John Patler shouted, "No, Commander, you cannot go out there alone! We will go with you!" Rockwell exhaled in relief. "All right, if you insist, but leave your overcoats on over your uniforms."[3]

At 2:20 Rockwell and four stormtroopers, all wearing overcoats to hide their khaki uniforms and swastika armbands, walked out the side door of the hotel; they expected the worst beating of their lives. When they reached the front of the theater Rockwell removed his overcoat; the crowd let out a roar and burst through police lines. The stormtroopers tried to protect Rockwell by encircling him, but the onslaught was too much. They were all kicked, punched, and whirled about in a sea of mob violence.

Mounted police formed a flying wedge and galloped into the fray, splitting the mob in half. Police on foot fought off the remaining attackers and rushed the Nazis into a narrow alley adjacent to the Saxon Theater. This position was defensible: they could only be attacked from one direction.

The mob regained composure and resumed the attack, pelting the Nazis and police with rocks, eggs, tomatoes, and firecrackers. A patrolman went down when a rock caromed off his skull. Police reserves reinforced the alley where the Nazis were huddled. A sergeant unlocked a cellar door at the rear of the Saxon and led the Nazis behind the movie screen on which *Exodus* was playing, through a tunnel that passed under the Gary Theater (where John Wayne was killing Mexicans in *The Alamo*), into a waiting police cruiser that took them to South End station.[4]

The truckload of stormtroopers finally arrived from Virginia in downtown Boston, only to find the streets jammed with people. As they neared the picket site they could hear a mob of thousands chanting, "Kill him! Kill him!" They were too late to join Rockwell; Foss and Morgan discussed whether they should let the troopers out of the truck. If Rockwell was in protective custody, their mission was already a success—they would make headlines. If they released the troopers from the cargo bay to clash with the mob, there would certainly be injuries and arrests. Arrests meant bail money, something the party did not have. A policeman made the decision for them. Boston police knew what type of truck the ANP had rented and were waiting for it as it neared the protest area. A police officer climbed up to the cab and told them Rockwell was in protective custody. He escorted the truck to the police headquarters, where Rockwell and the press were waiting.

Rockwell thanked the police for saving his life and vowed to return to Boston. He told reporters he considered the swastika no longer a German symbol but rather a symbol of anti-communism. Asked about the riot, he said, "I think this will help my cause. I would have preferred to picket but I get more publicity from a riot."[5] Rockwell and four stormtroopers returned to Washington by plane, while the ten troopers who had missed all the action departed Boston by truck, only to run out of gas again on the Massachusetts Turnpike.

In Chicago a similar event took place when the Fighting American Nationalists held a protest at a theater showing *Exodus*. Fighting broke out between FAN members and bystanders, and police escorted the FAN members away from the theater and dispersed the crowd of two hundred.

On Southport Island, Maine, Doc Rockwell was devastated by the actions of his son. When the *Portland Press Herald* telephoned, Doc apologized for his son's actions, but he wanted to believe the whole Nazi business was Lincoln's idea of a morbid joke—"He gets off on these things every so often." [6] Locals in Boothbay Harbor noticed a spiritual and physical deterioration; neither Doc nor Madelyn was ever quite the same. Doc's good name had been ruined by his son's actions. The name "Rockwell," once known for the laughter and joy Doc created, was now a synonym for "Nazi." [7]

Back in Arlington, Rockwell received a long-distance telephone call from Arthur Smith and Graeme Royce of the Australian National Workers Party (ANWP), inviting him to Australia to address a rally in May 1961. The ANWP was seeking to promote a "Nordic Australia" by encouraging lawmakers to pass legislation to prevent Asians from immigrating.

When word of the invitation became public, the Australian prime minister, Robert Menzies, was so disturbed that he summoned the minister of immigration, Alex Downer, out of a bath to discuss the situation. Downer in turn directed all Australian consulates in the United States to forward any application for a visa by Rockwell to Canberra for a top-level decision. Their concern proved unnecessary; the ANWP could not find the funds to pay for Rockwell's visit. [8]

On February 1, 1961, Troopers Ralph Forbes, Raymond Goodman, and Schuyler Ferris were dispatched from ANP headquarters to picket the Boyd Theater in Philadelphia at the premiere of *Exodus*. Hundreds of anti-Nazi protesters and policemen awaited their arrival. Police went all out in their effort to prevent violence. They roped off a two-block section surrounding the theater, cleared coffee shops and luncheonettes of student agitators, and set up a roadblock at the Benjamin Franklin Bridge (which connects Philadelphia with Camden, New Jersey) to turn back both Nazi sympathizers and rabble-rousers. Police at the roadblock confiscated enough eggs, tomatoes, and tangerines to fill a small grocery store, as well as a sizable pile of bricks and rocks. One man was arrested for having two guns, a baseball bat, an iron pipe, four oranges, three tomatoes, and a sign reading "Nazis should get the gas chamber."

Violence erupted when police stopped a blue convertible with six youths carrying a pile of rocks and eight dozen eggs. Police pulled the passengers from the car and lined them up against a wall near the theater. On the other side of the street an anti-Nazi group mistook the youths for Rockwell's troopers and broke through police lines to attack them. The mob mentality went into effect, and another three hundred anti-Nazi protesters surged in on the youths and police officers. The youths from the convertible were severely beaten by the mob before they could be rescued. When the real Nazis arrived the remaining mob bombarded them with rocks and eggs. Police arrested sixty-four anti-Nazi protesters, most of whom were college students, for disorderly conduct and the three Nazis for breach of peace, inciting a riot, and disorderly conduct.[9] The three Nazis were locked up for thirty days before they were tried and found not guilty.

On February 14, 1961, Rockwell won a major victory in his year-long battle with the state of New York: the Appellate Court of New York reversed a lower-court decision to limit the right of free speech. The Appellate Division directed Park Commissioner Newbold Morris to allow Rockwell to file a new application to hold a rally in Union Square, and then to approve it. The court ruled the city had had no right to ban Rockwell from speaking in Union Square:

> The unpopularity of views, their shocking quality, their obnoxious and even their alarming impact is not enough. Otherwise, the preacher of any strange doctrine could be stopped; the antiracist himself could be suppressed.[10]

Justice Charles Breitel added,

> If he does not speak criminally, then, of course, his right to speak may not be cut off, no matter how offensive his speech may be to others. Instead, his right, and that of those who wish to listen to him, must be protected, no matter how unpleasant the assignment.[11]

When Rockwell was informed of the decision, he responded, "I want police protection, and, if necessary, the Army and National Guard troops. I'm going to need it. . . . If they can call out the National Guard and the Army for three Negro girls in Little Rock, they can call out the Army for me."[12]

The mayor of New York, Robert Wagner, directed the corporation counsel to appeal the decision to the State Court of Appeals, but that court unanimously agreed that Rockwell was entitled to speak in Union Square. The court thus upheld the Appellate Court ruling that the right of freedom of expression could not be subject to prior restraint "for contemplated violations of the law."[13]

New York congressman Frank Becker publicly urged an investigation of the ANP to ascertain if the group was subversive. Rockwell was disturbed by the demand; though previous attempts at such classification had failed, he did not want these investigations to be an annual event. He sent letters to Congressman Becker; the FBI; the Virginia State Police, Arlington County Police, and Metropolitan Police; and the Subversive Activities Control Board, inviting them to visit ANP headquarters to look over party records and conduct interviews with members to form their own opinions of the ANP. The offer was left on the table.

On February 20, 1961, the Jewish community responded. The Jewish Community Council of Greater Washington organized the other major Jewish organizations—American Jewish Committee, American Jewish Congress, ADL, Jewish War Veterans (JWV)—to promote self-restraint among the Jewish community, specifically to stay away from the scheduled ANP picket of *Exodus* in Washington, D.C. More than nine thousand copies of a joint memorandum were distributed among the various organizations urging people to stay away from the ANP picket. This was the first time the Jewish leadership had approached "the Rockwell problem" as a community, working unanimously toward the same goal.

The *Exodus* premiere opened in the District of Columbia with Rockwell and twelve troopers carrying placards reading:

Ban Exodus, Red Trouble Maker

American Legion Recommends Exodus Boycott

Exodus Was Written by a Red Jew

Israel Trades with Reds

Only seventy-five people congregated around the Nazis, far fewer than the party had expected. After just twenty minutes of picketing Rockwell called off the demonstration. That evening only one television station carried the event, and the story was passed over by the newspapers.

Isaac Franck, executive director of the Jewish Community Council, wrote a follow-up memo to the other national Jewish organizations, thanking them for their cooperation in the successful endeavor. Franck summed up the hysteria surrounding the ANP:

> Rockwell's is a two-bit operation, which combines petty racketeering, borderline psychopathology, and a sixth sense for irritating and provoking Jews into thoughtless action. The fact is that only Jews and a tiny handful of bigots have given him any attention. . . . Jews have been more steadfast and persistent than the bigots in the attention they give him.
>
> Rockwell has fed too long on the hysteria and alarm that has been artificially whipped up in the Jewish communities. If we succeed in "talking sense" to our Jewish community, and in effectively quarantining this tiny trouble-maker, we may be enabled soon to close the chapter in American Jewish History, entitled "The Rockwell Madness."[14]

The National Commission of the ADL adopted a more aggressive policy regarding Rockwell's activities:

> ADL regards freedom of speech as the cornerstone of American democracy. However, freedom of speech does not extend to one who incites violence or murder, nor does it provide immunity to a speaker who deliberately evokes a breach of the peace by threats and violent action.
>
> For these reasons, ADL has the duty to alert the public officials in any community where Rockwell [has] proposed to hold a public meeting, to advise them of the facts concerning past meetings held by Rockwell . . . and to urge them to take appropriate action for the purpose of preserving the public order and preventing the incitement of breaches of the peace.[15]

The year 1961 marked the beginning of a "press blackout" against Rockwell that the Jewish community instigated and maintained for the remainder of his life. The Jewish War Veterans remained reluctant partners but generally abided by the resolution. Slowly an incomplete, but largely effective, media quarantine descended around the ANP.

Rockwell's major advantage in dealing with the blackout was his ability to choose the battlefield. If the quarantine was too effective in one city, he simply moved to another. When one agitation technique failed, he dreamed up another. When he found a weakness or soft spot in the quarantine's coalition, he maximized his efforts at its weakest link.

Privately he agonized about it; publicly he criticized it as censorship. So did others. One critic of the quarantine, Ben Bagdikian, writing in the *Columbia Journalism Review,* called it "pernicious." He and other advocates of free speech believed the Constitution's First Amendment protected demagogues and that any exception jeopardized all citizens' rights. Bagdikian also criticized reporters and editors for filtering their stories to fit their personal moral agendas.[16]

James K. Warner, who had left the party in late 1960, wrote a booklet in January 1961 called *Swastika Smearbund*, an exposé of the inner workings of the party. Rockwell was in the process of writing an autobiography that expressed views on the right wing in America, views that Warner considered a smear. Warner believed Rockwell wanted to destroy any "real" patriots fighting communism in the U.S. who did not support his radical views. He felt Rockwell's book would "ruin many and drive others out of business."[17] Warner's motive for writing *Smearbund* was probably more self-aggrandizement than protection of "patriots": over the next three decades he peddled right-wing books through unscrupulously acquired mailing lists.[18]

In Warner's absence, Rockwell appointed Roger Foss to the post of national secretary, third-highest-ranking member of the party, just behind Deputy Commander J. V. Morgan. While serving as the national secretary Foss witnessed a rapid decline in party unity because of continual scheming by John Patler, Dan Burros, and Ralph Grandinetti. The trio constantly accused other members of "spying for the Jews," denouncing even Rockwell's mistress as being a spy. Suspicion was a cancer eating away at the party, but Rockwell was indifferent; he refused to intercede. Foss resented how Grandinetti, Burros, and Patler were always around when Rockwell wanted to play a game of chess or go out for a lavish meal at a German restaurant on party funds, while he and Seth Ryan, Roy James, and Dick Braun ate fried potatoes at headquarters. Rockwell had a knack for generating publicity, but when it came to judging men he was blind.

On February 12, Foss became the target of the three schemers. At the weekly Sunday meeting in the shrine room, a disciplinary action was initiated against him by Dan Burros and John Patler for "viciously beating a fellow stormtrooper." Foss was stunned by the accusation and explained his side of the incident.

Trooper Ralph Hassinger, a tall, emaciated ex–postal worker from Cleveland (he had quit the post office because the government was "hiring too many niggers"), had refused to take orders or do any work around the headquarters. Hassinger wrote letters late into the night and then claimed to be "too tired" to help around the building. After several weeks Foss, weary of Hassinger's excuses, confronted him. When Hassinger again refused to pull his weight, Foss slapped him with an open left hand three times across the face. Hassinger meekly backed off and retired to his bunk, knowing full well that Foss would otherwise beat him severely. Since American Nazis settled disputes with their fists, Foss thought this was the end of the matter—until Burros brought charges against him.

The party "court" found Foss guilty, so Rockwell reduced his rank from captain to lieutenant. During the hearing, a smirking Ralph Grandinetti reached for a pack of cigarettes from the table near Foss. Foss misinterpreted the movement as an attack and threw a left hook that caught Grandinetti squarely in the head. The other party officers interceded and ended the altercation.

Foss felt betrayed. The next week he found work at a print shop downtown, called a cab, threw in a suitcase, and moved out of head-quarters. Seth Ryan succeeded Foss as national secretary, John Patler became the editor of the *National Socialist Bulletin*, and Dan Burros became director of printing.[19]

On March 5, Rockwell furnished the FBI with sample application forms for joining the ANP:

> It is not easy to join the American Nazi Party. We purposely make it dif-ficult partly to protect the party from spies and agents provocateur, but also to weed out those who imagine this is a "club" or "gang" which can be joined lightly and frivolously.
>
> The American Nazi Party will one day assume the enormous burdens of leadership of the American Nation, and thus of the White Western World. This is not a task for any kind of "gang" or "mob" as we are often painted by the press. We are fighting and in training for statesmanship on a global basis and cannot tolerate weaklings, wise-guys, hoods, bullies or criminal saboteurs.
>
> Our vicious opponents, the Communist International, unhesitatingly demands its members submit the most intimate personal information to it before joining, much more intimate information than we demand here. The enemies' discipline also requires that a husband leave his wife without a word and move to another city, to kill and spy on orders from the criminal leaders in Moscow or New York.
>
> We are the ONLY real, fighting opposition to this gigantic Marxist machine which has almost taken possession of the whole planet. We cannot draw back from anything just because it is "embarrassing" or "trouble."[20]

Rockwell also provided the FBI with completed membership application forms. Under the heading "Reason for Joining the American Nazi Party," various ANP members had written:

I have joined the American Nazi Party to stop the Jewish plot for world domination by means of communism and Zionism. It is a political organization that has strength for decisions in addition to being able to cope with treasonous Jews and their nefarious activities.

I also am a believer in separation of the races as a means of survival for the White Race.

To preserve White Race of people and Western civilization and counter against Jewish communism and other treason.

I wish to preserve the White Race and combat the forces of Jewish Bolshevism which seek to destroy our race and nation.

Keen interest in politics, the American way of life, the White Race, etc.

I've always been a National Socialist.

I joined the American Nazi Party because it is the only political party that is offering any real opposition to communism and race mixing. It also is the only party that offers any real help to the people of this nation. This is the only party that recognizes the Negro Race problem and plans to mend the situation.

Because I'm a Nazi at heart.

To fight for white race and USA nation.

I want to join to fight Jewry, communism, capitalism, socialism, syndicalism, Satanism, immorality, and race mixing.

I am fed up with communist activity in the world and join this party with the hopes of restoring order and saving the white race from mixing themselves to death.

I am a member of the American Nazi Party because I believe the national socialism is the only form of government that can save the world from the total chaos of today and because it is the only form of government sworn to destroy the arch enemy of the white man, communism.

To help fight communism and further the white race.

Like a decent man that cannot sit down to eat with dirty hands until they are washed clean, I cannot and will not rest until America has been cleansed of communism and integration. I dedicate my life for all it's worth in the struggle against treason to the United States of America.

Due to my firm belief in the cause of the white man, the cause of honor as opposed to dishonor, of courage as opposed to cowardice, of decency as opposed to filth. I love my God, my family and my white brothers everywhere. To the enemies of these I pledge total destruction. To the banners of the United States and the Nazi Party I pledge my life. To my God I pledge my soul. Sieg Heil.[21]

Most of the men who joined Rockwell's movement were of similar mind-set: they were either anti-Jewish, anti-black, or both. Some were thrill-seekers, and some were simply attracted by the Nazi image. Many had experienced significant professional and personal failure; several were ex-convicts. Movements offer such people not only a sudden change in lifestyle but an enemy on which to focus their anger and frustration. Some type of intrinsic battle between good and evil is self-evident in most every movement, so there must be a "devil." When Hitler was asked whether he thought the Jew must be destroyed, he answered, "No. . . . We should have then to invent him. It is essential to have a tangible enemy, not merely an abstract one."[22] The ideal villain is ubiquitous and nefarious. This way, every failure within a movement is seen to be the work of the enemy, while every success is a triumph over his evil scheming. Through the process of renouncing the self for the collective, adherents can rid themselves of personal responsibility. There is no limit to the extremes of cruelty people will inflict when they are no longer in control of their own individuality.

On March 14, the American Nazi Party was granted a charter by the Virginia State Corporation Commission. The Nazi goal as set forth in the articles of incorporation was "the gaining of political power in the United States by all legal means and elective processes" and "the education of the American public to suppressed facts concerning the communist conspiracy to destroy us and the white race."

The corporate charter structured the ANP in the following manner. The incorporators—George Lincoln Rockwell, J. V. Morgan, and Seth Ryan—would serve as the board of directors. Rockwell was appointed chairman, with power to veto any nomination or election to the board of directors, and with sole power to appoint his successor. This would ensure his continual control over the party should a faction attempt to wrest it from him.

Incorporating the ANP provided not only validation of the party in Rockwell's and his followers' eyes, but also the legal rights, remedies, and shields that corporations enjoy. Rockwell was patiently laying the framework for what he hoped would be a lasting organization.

On March 28, Rockwell and Trooper Roy James traveled to Newburyport, Massachusetts, to attend a lecture by right-wing extremist "expert" Gordon Hall. They never got there: Massachusetts state troopers arrested them in Salisbury for violating the True Name Law. The True Name Law was an attempt by the state to reduce prostitution by requiring hotels and motels to register guests under their real names. Rockwell was accused of having signed into the Hotel Touraine in Boston as "Nathan Ginsberg" shortly before the riot outside the Saxon Theater. Rockwell and James were booked in the Topsfield State Police barracks, then were transferred to Boston's City Prison until they made bail.

When they appeared in Municipal Court, Rockwell denied registering under the name "Ginsberg." He told Judge Joseph Riley that a man "by the name of Christopher Snow" had registered him at the hotel. "I didn't know until I left the city and read it in the newspaper that I was registered under that name.... I would not have done such a thing, I had no intention of cheating or falsifying records."[23] They were each fined ten dollars.

On April 1, a "Witness for Peace" rally took place in Judiciary Square in Washington, D.C. Fourteen separate pro-disarmament organizations marched from the Pentagon to the square to publicize their belief that the United States should take greater initiative in disarmament by eliminating stockpiles of chemical and biological warfare devices. The highlight of the event was a talk by the writer James Baldwin, who attempted to link the peace movement with racial freedom. As the four hundred marchers mingled about Judiciary Square, a detachment of twelve ANP troopers in Nazi uniform heckled them, calling them "termites" and "communists." Rockwell did not attend the rally.

Two weeks later, on April 15, 1961, the Bay of Pigs invasion of Cuba began. Rockwell believed the failed invasion had been instigated by Jews who wanted Castro removed because he had nationalized their businesses. Castro was the "rarest of rare birds, a communist who is not crazy about Jews.... Castro is anathema to all the Zionist–Wall Street Jews for grabbing their business interests.... It is my belief... [that] Castro will be out, and a new, more Jew-loving, Trotskyite red will be installed."[24]

On April 8, the Chicago branch of FAN conducted a sympathy demonstration for Adolf Eichmann outside the consulate general of Israel. Demonstrators carried signs bearing the following inscriptions:

Israel Violates International Law

The EICHMANN Trial—The World's Most Publicized Lynching

If They Can Kidnap EICHMANN They Can Kidnap You

Stop EICHMANN Lynching

Zionist Hoodlums Defy Monroe Doctrine

Israelis Deny Jury for EICHMANN

Communes or Kibbutzim—What's the Difference

Try BEN GURION for Murder of 7,000,000 Arabs

What about Israeli Atrocities

Bigoted Judges to Try EICHMANN Says Chicago Tribune

Four days later the self-directed California Nazis staged a similar protest. Leonard Holstein and Jeff Skinner marched toward the Israeli consulate in Los Angeles with placards that read:

Free Eichmann Now—Israel Lynch Law Stay Out of U.S.A.

What's Wrong with Gas Chambers for Traitors

They were intercepted by police before they reached the consulate but not before their brief protest was recorded by television, radio, and press photographers.

The ADL was concerned that the Eichmann trial might cause repercussions against Jews throughout the world. Accordingly, it mapped out a strategy to act as a buffering force against anti-Israeli, anti-Jewish sentiments arising from accusations that Eichmann had been illegally kidnapped and that the law covering the crime was ex post facto.[25]

In the spring of 1961, James Farmer, the national director of CORE (Congress of Racial Equality) announced a new integration tool called the "Freedom Ride." His plan was to send a bus of integrated passengers through the South to New Orleans, in an attempt to bring about desegregation of interstate buses, terminals, and their restaurants.

In early May, thirteen passengers left Washington on this dangerous trip, intending to arrive in New Orleans on May 17, the seventh anniversary of the *Brown v. Board of Education of Topeka* decision in which the Supreme Court ruled that "separate but equal" was unconstituitional. When the first bus crossed the Alabama state line, a group of young white hoodlums boarded it and beat the "Freedom Riders" with chains, brass knuckles, and fists. One CORE member was knocked unconscious in the aisle, another was kicked repeatedly in the head. The bus continued to Birmingham, where another beating took place at the bus terminal. One CORE worker needed fifty-six stitches to close his head wounds.

When the bus reached the Anniston, Alabama, terminal, a mob of angry whites waited with weapons in hand. The Riders decided against integrating the terminal and remained on the bus; the mob reacted by slashing the bus's tires with knives and ice picks, then followed the bus as it limped out of town. The remaining tires blew out just outside the city limits. The mob surrounded the bus, pinned the doors shut, broke a window, and hurled a firebomb inside. The passengers narrowly escaped incineration by exiting through the emergency hatch. The first Freedom Ride was over.

Almost immediately another group of Freedom Riders departed from Nashville for Birmingham, Alabama. When the bus reached Birmingham the city's commissioner of public safety, Eugene "Bull" Connor, had them arrested. The next day the Riders were released and took another bus to Montgomery, this time with state trooper escorts. The escorts, however, departed halfway through the trip; when the bus reached the Montgomery depot there were no police, only an angry white mob. As the Freedom Riders go off the bus the white mob attacked with clubs and chains. Police appeared only fifteen minutes later, after the Riders had been severely beaten.

Rockwell decided to stage his own cross-country demonstration, in a Volkswagen van "Hate Bus" that trooper Schuyler Ferris had purchased and lent to the party. On May 22, Rockwell announced to the press that twelve members of the ANP would depart Washington, D.C., for New Orleans. He sent telegrams to the governors of the states along the route demanding protection from "Jew and Negro hoodlums." He told reporters the trip was being made to symbolize "the fact that decent Americans do hate and should hate communism and race-mixing."[26]

The Nazis left Washington in the two-tone green Volkswagen van followed by a green Chevrolet with more troopers. Affixed to the sides of the Volkswagen van were freshly painted signs: "Lincoln Rockwell's Hate Bus" and "We Do Hate Race Mixing." The Nazis were hoping to make newspaper headlines on each leg of their journey south and to solicit donations from white sympathizers along the way. They found neither. When they reached the racially troubled city of Montgomery,

Rockwell briefs stormtroopers before the "Hate Bus" departs Virginia for New Orleans.

Alabama, where they hoped to speak and collect donations, seven squad cars of federal marshals intercepted the van and escorted it through the downtown and into the southern section of the city. The Nazis were not allowed to agitate.

Meanwhile, Governor Jimmy Davis of Louisiana issued a statement calling for "outside agitators of either the extreme right or the extreme left" to stay out of Louisiana. Davis said that Louisiana was large and had room for many differences of opinion, "but, our state will never have room for those who seek to put race against race and add to the already strained conditions that face us."[27] The statement was directed at both the Freedom Riders and the Hate Bus.

On May 24, the Hate Bus approached New Orleans with Bernie

Davids behind the wheel and a phalanx of police cars following behind. Possibly unnerved by his escorts, Davids scraped a fender of the Volkswagen on a wall of the Lake Pontchartrain Causeway. The police arrested him for reckless driving.

The troopers continued on, disembarking in New Orleans to picket a theater showing *Exodus*. Rockwell, who had flown into New Orleans that morning, joined the troopers at the theater protest. The New Orleans Police Department quickly arrested all the participants for "disturbing the peace by the commission of an act in such a manner as to unreasonably disturb and alarm the public with conspiracy to provoke a disturbance of the peace and refusing to disperse and move on when ordered by police." The charge against the Nazis was the same as that used against integrationists for staging sit-in demonstrations at lunch counters. The Nazis pled "not guilty" to all charges.

Rockwell and the troopers staged a hunger strike in the New Orleans parish jail to protest their arrest, refusing food from May 25 through May 28. Rockwell told the press they would not post bail: "It's time the white man did the same as the niggers and stayed in jail to protest for our rights. If the niggers can do it for integration, then we can do it for segregation." He explained that the Volkswagen van was named the "Hate Bus" to discredit the word *hate*. "We only hate the things that every red-blooded American should hate—communists and race-mixing. The Freedom Riders are really the haters because they're stirring up violence."[28] He cadged a cigar off a reporter and continued talking. "This is the first night I've ever spent in jail, but we're doing it for a principle. We couldn't post bail if we wanted to.... We're broke." He told the reporter he would attempt to recruit followers for the party during his incarceration. "Some of our best recruits come from jails. It seems that the real red-blooded Americans seem to get in trouble with the beatniks and others of that ilk and get violent and are jailed."

On May 30, supporter Ray Leahart bailed Rockwell and Davids out of jail, and both men returned to Arlington. The next day Rockwell telegraphed the nine troopers still behind bars and told them to start eating—their trial date had been set. Over the next week all nine troopers were released on bail. Rockwell sent an affidavit to the U.S. attorney, M. Hepburn Many, of the Eastern District of Louisiana, in which he accused New Orleans city officials of depriving the ANP members of their civil rights. He also sent a telegram to the U.S. attorney requesting an investigation and action to halt violations of federal law and the U.S. Constitution by the officials of New Orleans.

On June 13, Judge Edward Haggerty found them guilty. Rockwell was sentenced to pay a fine of a hundred dollars and serve sixty days in the New Orleans parish jail; Seth Ryan, John Patler, and Roy James were fined seventy-five dollars and ordered to serve forty-five days in jail. The other troopers—Charles Beveridge, Tony Wells, Paul Dukel, Andrew Chappell, Ralph Hassinger, and Robert Johnson—were each fined fifty dollars and ordered to serve thirty days in jail. Rockwell filed a motion for permission to leave the jurisdiction on June 16; it was granted by Judge Haggerty. The charges were eventually dropped.

The Hate Bus adventure generated moderate press coverage and caught the attention of Karl Allen, who would become the next deputy commander of the party. But the party had also consumed its precious capital to pay for the trip and bail money.

One of the most important missions the ANP undertook in the summer of 1961 was an attempt to form an alliance with the Black Muslims and their leader, Elijah Muhammad. From its inception the ANP had referred to African Americans as "niggers" and had affirmed the premise that they were mentally inferior to whites, but Rockwell became enchanted with the idea of a coalition; Nazis and Black Muslims could be allies, since they both sought the same goal—separation of the races. Rockwell told his followers that Muhammad "has gathered millions of the dirty, immoral, drunken, filthy-mouthed, lazy and repulsive people sneeringly called 'niggers' and inspired them to the point where they are clean, sober, honest, hard working, dignified, dedicated and admirable human beings in spite of their color. . . . Muhammad knows that mixing is a Jewish fraud and leads only to aggravation of the problems that it is supposed to solve. . . . I have talked to the Muslim leaders and am certain that a workable plan for separation of the races could be effected to the satisfaction of all concerned—except the communist-Jew agitators."[29]

Black Muslim cooperation with Rockwell and the Ku Klux Klan went beyond ideology and rhetoric. There were practical implications. Like his white racist counterparts, Elijah Muhammad believed that interracial sexual relations were morally depraved and genetically destructive, for interracial sex "ruins and destroys a people." Rhetoric aside, he wanted to establish a truce between racists and his Southern mosques. To this end he sent Malcolm X to Atlanta to accompany Jeremiah X, the local Muslim minister of Atlanta, to a secret meeting with members of the Klan. Both sides discussed race relations. Malcolm described the integration movement as a Jewish conspiracy carried out by black stooges. The parties eventually hammered out the main issue: a nonaggression pact. If the Muslims did not aid the civil rights movement in the South, the mosques would be undisturbed.[30]

On Sunday, June 25, 1961, Rockwell and ten troopers attended a Black Muslim rally at Uline Arena in Washington. They watched in awe as convoys of chartered buses unloaded hundreds of passengers outside the arena and the Muslim vendors made a killing on official souvenirs and literature. The Nazis were frisked at the door of the arena by several well-dressed but stern-looking Fruit of Islam guards—the Gestapo of the Nation of Islam. A special guard greeted Rockwell, said into his walkie-talkie that the "big man was coming now," and escorted them to seats near the stage in the center, surrounded by eight thousand Black Muslims. They were encircled by black journalists, who wanted to know Rockwell's thoughts. He told reporters he considered the Muslims "black Nazis." "I am fully in concert with their program and I have the highest respect for Mr. Elijah Muhammad." Rockwell pointed out his only disagreement with the Muslims was over territory. "They want a chunk of America and I prefer that they go to Africa."

The Nazis were very impressed with the professionalism and stagecraft of the event, especially the Fruit of Islam guards, who maintained their positions throughout the lengthy program despite stifling heat in the auditorium. Eight thousand faithful followers of Elijah Muhammad waited six hours to hear him speak. After several introductory speakers, Malcolm X stepped to the microphone to deliver a talk entitled "Separation or Death."

"Muslims are not for integration and not for segregation." Looking up at the audience as if to beg the question, he asked what they "were for." The audience shouted, "SEPARATION." Rockwell and the troopers vigorously applauded. Malcolm told the audience, now quite restless in the ninety-degree heat, that before the climax of the program a collection would be taken. He told the two hundred white people sitting segregated in the center of the auditorium to chip in "and give us back some of that money they didn't give our ancestors. . . . I don't want to hear clinking, I want to hear that soft rustle."

Malcolm asked the audience for donations of one hundred dollars and got three. As Malcolm dropped his request to fifty dollars and then to twenty dollars, Rockwell pulled out his wallet and handed a twenty-dollar bill to the usher to be sent up to Malcolm. Malcolm asked who had given the money; a trooper shouted at the top of his lungs, "George Lincoln Rockwell!" This brought scattered applause and a covey of reporters and cameramen to Rockwell's side. At Malcolm's request, Rockwell stood up for applause, to which Malcolm said, "You got the biggest hand you ever got."[31] Rockwell was not amused, but he cracked a grin for the cameras.

Another speaker took the podium and announced that Elijah Muhammad would not speak because of illness. The audience began leaving the building, but the Nazis remained for the final speaker when they heard him begin to lash out at Jews. Outside the arena Rockwell lied to a TV reporter, telling him that many of the Muslims had urged him to speak. He would get his chance to address the Muslims the following year. Rockwell kept in contact with Malcolm X, with occasional telegrams and stormtrooper couriers when Malcolm was in the Washington area.[32]

On a muggy Saturday evening in July, a group of Arlington teenagers walked home after a dance at Washington-Lee High School. They paused in front of the ANP headquarters to gaze at the huge swastika flag inside the house. Suddenly the door flew open, and stormtroopers came charging at them. In panic, the youngsters broke and ran in all directions. One of the boys, thirteen-year-old Ricky Farber, was caught by a trooper. The Nazi twisted the boy's arm behind his back and marched him into Nazi headquarters, where he was handcuffed and interrogated.

The Nazis asked, "Are you Jewish?" Farber nodded. "Do you know what the blacks are doing over in Washington? They're driving out the white people," yelled a trooper. The boy returned fire, "No they're not." Another trooper shouted, "He's an integrationist."

At 11 P.M. the police arrived and the boy went home. The next week the boy's father, Hyman Farber, swore warrants charging troopers Robert Braun and Robert Garber with felonious assault. Both men were arrested and placed in jail. A few days later the Farbers received a cloth with a skull-and-crossbones insignia and the word *Juden*.[33]

When the trial commenced more than 250 people lined the court-house walls waiting for a seat in the courtroom. Only a select few were allowed to attend the hearing. When Rockwell arrived in court he glared at those already seated in the courtroom and said, "Look at that, they've let in all the official Jews."[34]

The Nazi defendants told the court that Farber had been throwing rocks at their headquarters and that they had apprehended him with the intention of handing him over to the Arlington police. The court had no sympathy for their story. Both men were convicted of simple assault and sentenced to the maximum under the law: a year on a chain gang. Neither man appealed the conviction, fearing the more severe charge of felonious assault. Trooper Braun told Rockwell, "I'll see you next year."

A week later an alleged teenage rock-throwing incident led to the arrest of three more ANP members. Stormtrooper Tony Wells caught one of the juveniles, a sixteen-year-old, and beat him about the face. Troopers Roy James and Charles Beveridge were also arrested, but only Wells was convicted of assault; he was sentenced to sixty days in jail.

By the end of July the citizens of Arlington had organized an ad hoc committee, called Citizens Concerned, to oppose the ANP; the recent arrests for assaulting children had provoked them to act. Their first objective was to strip the Nazis of their firearms. They demanded that state firearm laws be changed to prohibit the ANP (and all other Virginia citizens) from carrying firearms on private property. They also made a vain appeal to the U.S. Attorney General's Office that the ANP be placed on the subversives list. The committee unanimously agreed to delete "Lincoln" from any reference to Rockwell's name and refer to him as George Rockwell, "to protect the name of a great President."[35]

In reaction to Arlington's growing opposition, Rockwell tried to bargain with the city fathers at a county board meeting. He told the board he was very fond of Arlington and had thus far left it alone, "but if the community continues to agitate, I will have to educate them." "Educating" in this case meant Nazi parades, marching through the streets with loudspeakers, speeches, and mass literature circulation.

Board member Thomas Richards, his face twisted in anger, lashed out at Rockwell: "Your crummy, misbegotten organization is a shame upon our community. The thugs and hoodlums your organization attracts are a threat to our citizens. . . . I suggest that you disband this vile organization and crawl back into the holes where you belong." Rockwell lashed back, telling Richards there would be no problems "if Arlington simply will drop all this agitation to get rid of us. I don't expect to be persecuted, to be hounded, to have people issuing statements and making resolutions when they don't know what I'm for."

The meeting nearly erupted into a fistfight when Commonwealth Attorney William Hassan and Rockwell got into a shouting match. Hassan accused Rockwell of making false statements about court cases. While he was speaking, Rockwell walked away. "Don't you walk away from me, you faker, don't you want to hear the truth?" Hassan yelled. Rockwell spun around and said, "I'll go a round with you." Hassan moved to close the gap, but police Captain Raymond Cole restrained him.

Upon leaving the courthouse, Rockwell and his stormtrooper entourage were stopped by Arlington police as they attempted to drive away in their Volkswagen bus. The driver, Ralph Forbes, was arrested for driving without a registration permit, county tags, and a Virginia permit. Unable to post a hundred dollars bail, Forbes was jailed.[36]

When the Arlington County police impounded the bus, a reporter discovered the vehicle was registered to Schuyler Ferris. The press revealed that Ferris worked in the Army Map Service and held a security clearance. Immediately Congressman Seymour Halpern of New York blasted the Army Map Service in public statements and sent a letter to the secretary of defense, Robert S. McNamara, stating, "I do not understand how the United States Government can justify continued employment of an individual so unstable politically that he facilitates totalitarian extremism and propaganda."[37]

When asked if he had paid for the vehicle, Ferris replied, "It could be. I'm not saying one way or the other. This is rather explosive material." Rockwell told the press, "I have advised him to go to the Civil Service Commission with a complaint against the Army Map Service which is persecuting him." Ferris was eventually dismissed from his clerk position at the Army Map Service for "sleeping on duty, AWOL, and insubordination." Ferris believes he was terminated for his political beliefs.

Enough money was now coming into the party treasury from sympathizers to establish a second barracks. The headquarters building at 928 Randolph Street was so overcrowded that it was beginning to resemble a flophouse. The party found a perfect site at 6150 Wilson Boulevard, a heavily wooded, twenty-six-acre lot with a long driveway leading up to a large, secluded, three-story mansion. The mansion was built on the highest ground in Arlington; from the balcony on the upper floor all of Washington was visible. The property was owned by

FBI

ANP barracks on what the Arlington locals called "Hatemonger Hill."

the widow of Admiral Willis Kern; she rented the property to J. V. Morgan and let the party stay on even when it was delinquent with the two-hundred-dollar monthly rent payments. Located on one of the main roads of Arlington, the "barracks" was close to shopping centers, restaurants, and a Laundromat. It was a beautiful location, but the large woods and long driveway proved to be security problems.

Rockwell came up with an idea for gaining additional party income by creating a business called Homestead Builders. His idea was to bid low on yard work, painting, and chain-link-fence installation so inactive troopers could have day jobs and to reduce the monetary drain on the party. Bernie Davids and Roy James learned painting from Floyd Fleming, while Ray Goodman, J. V. Morgan, and some of the other troopers installed chain-link fences, but most of the troopers were not enthusiastic about having to work—they nicknamed the project the "Slavestead Company."

On August 9, the Justice Department decided the ANP would not be added to the subversives list. Attorney General Robert Kennedy told the press the Justice Department would continue its investigation of the ANP but that there was no need to place the party on the list. "Such action would not prohibit or even curtail the activities of the group, nor would it result in the imposition of any sanctions on its members," wrote Kennedy.[38] Kennedy's decision may have been influenced by the American Jewish Committee, which lobbied the Justice Department to leave the American Nazi Party off the list. The AJC feared that if the ANP was listed, Rockwell would take center stage in full Nazi uniform at congressional hearings, where he could defend his party while attacking Jews.

In Florida, Karl Allen decided to join the ANP. Earlier in the year, he had read about Rockwell's "Hate Bus" and had driven up to Arlington to see what the American Nazi Party was all about. He had picked up an application and some literature and returned to Florida. Joining the ANP was not a simple proposition. Family and loved ones would eventually find out and be subject to embarrassment.

As a boy, Allen had followed World War II on his map of Europe; he was ambivalent toward the Germans, almost neutral. In high school he developed architectural drafting skills, which he used working for the Florida Park Service during summer breaks from Florida State. After graduating from FSU he was hired by the Florida Development Commission to help promote the state's economy. One of the first projects he took part in was bringing Walt Disney to Florida. Later he worked on a committee to bring to the state nuclear energy, an industry he disliked. When the commission continued to pursue the nuclear industry business against his recommendations, Allen resigned and took up construction design work for his brother, until he read about the American Nazi Party.[39] Allen hitched a ride to ANP headquarters in early August and joined the party.

The first thing he noticed was Seth Ryan stumbling around headquarters with some nasty bruises on his face. Ryan and Patler had been in a fight, and Ryan had gotten the worst of it, but Patler's backstabbing had finally caught up with him. (Shortly after the fight with Ryan he packed up his family and moved back to New York City.) Allen wondered about the group: it appeared that Rockwell gave his blessing to men's beating each other to settle disputes. Allen coined a phrase that best described the experience of joining: "No one knew what to expect, but everyone agreed it was not what they expected."[40]

Because of Allen's prestigious credentials, the party officers suspected him of being a spy. They asked him to fill out a second application blank (to compare against the first application), and arranged a bogus mission (a second Hate Bus run) to see if Allen would leak information. Allen moved into a small room at headquarters and found outside work so he could be self-sufficient and not a drain on the party. Being several years older than the other troopers and highly educated, Allen moved up fast in rank. His first assignment was organizing the three shoeboxes of donation receipts collected by the former national secretary, James Warner. Neither Seth Ryan nor Dan Burros had been able to piece together Warner's jumbled records.

As usual, cliques developed within the party. Seth Ryan, Ralph Forbes, and Roy James formed the first "anti-Allen" clique. Although they would later become good friends, they were suspicious of Allen's stellar background. He was simply too good to be true: intelligent, methodical, a capable leader, physically and mentally self-assured. Rockwell recognized these attributes and put Allen in charge of headquarters. The two men rarely spoke to each other on personal matters. Allen took charge of the headquarters and ran the operation as a business entity.

In mid-September, party member Charles Beveridge was arrested for statutory rape of a fourteen-year-old Arlington girl. Her parents pressed charges against the Nazi after learning of the incident. Beveridge and the high school student had gone on a picnic and had sex in a field of tall grass. Since the girl was a minor the charges were very serious, but Beveridge, acting as his own attorney, persuaded the court to drop the charges after cross-examining the girl on the stand. She told the court the two planned to wed and had applied for a marriage license. Police confirmed the application was on file and that her age was listed as eighteen.[41]

A few weeks later another Nazi was arrested for a sex crime; this time, Trooper Bob Bigley was charged with having carnal knowledge of a fourteen-year-old girl. The charges stemmed from an encounter between Bigley and the girl in a car parked in Prince George's County, Maryland. Bigley was the sixth Nazi arrested for incidents involving teenagers.

In other court action, Rockwell was found in contempt of court for failure to make support payments to his first wife. Commonwealth

Attorney Hassan blasted Rockwell for failing to pay the $150 a month; his first wife and three daughters were living a cruel existence in Connecticut in a home without proper heat or sanitary conditions. Rockwell presented Karl Allen as a witness in his behalf, describing him as a graduate of Harvard Business School and the party bookkeeper. After hearing Allen's testimony about the books and the party income of $11,870, Judge Hugh Reid commented, "If this is the Harvard system of bookkeeping, I'm glad I sent my son to Randolph-Macon."

The hearing developed into a verbal joust between Rockwell and Judge Reid. Rockwell contended that despite the donations received he could not make payments because the bulk of his receipts were used to further Nazi political aims. Judge Reid rejected his argument, telling Rockwell that the Nazi Party and Rockwell were one and the same; Rockwell could do with the money as he pleased. Judge Reid sentenced Rockwell to thirty days in jail for failure to make support payments but suspended the sentence for three months on the condition that future support payments be made promptly. Near the end of the hearing the fourteen Nazi stormtroopers in attendance laughed at the proceedings. Judge Reid angrily ordered the Nazis out of the courtroom. A fight nearly broke out when the unruly stormtroopers shouted racial insults at several spectators. Security forces quelled the disturbance and ejected the Nazis from the building.[42]

William Hassan hated Rockwell. He was always badgering Rockwell, even for the slightest infraction, like failure to use a turn signal. Hassan's courtroom demeanor was characterized by yelling and shouting at defendants and witnesses in a very abusive manner, sometimes getting red in the face. Defense attorneys despised his courtroom mannerisms but could do little to tone down the hot-tempered Irishman.

One day hecklers stopped in front of ANP headquarters and threw a bottle at the building. Duty Officer Gary Smith ran from the headquarters to get the license plate of the vehicle. Unfortunately for the hecklers, their car stalled as they attempted to speed away. Smith approached the car and punched the driver's window out with his bare hands to get at the driver. When Smith was brought to trial for the incident, Hassan went into his usual tirade about the severity of Smith's crime. Smith waited until just the right moment, then stood up and shouted, "Mr. Hassan, don't yell at me!" The entire courtroom went silent, except for some snickering by defense attorneys. The judge let Smith go free.[43]

The West Coast Nazis went into action in late October. Leonard Holstein led two other stormtroopers in a picket of the Los Angeles County Board of Education, protesting the school board's decision to use six films and a film strip to teach communism in the classroom. (The board eventually promised the films would not be shown in secondary schools until teaching guides were prepared by a committee of "expert teachers.") Holstein told reporters that their demonstration had been a reminder to the citizenry on the danger of "propaganda films." The Nazis carried placards that read:

> You Know Who Fought the Communists First,
> Stand with Us This Time
>
> Get the Reds and Their Films Out of the Schools
>
> 6,000,000 Nazis Died Fighting Communism. Join the ANP

Considerable coverage was given by local TV, radio, and newspapers, but very few bystanders took notice of the event.[44]

The *National Socialist Bulletin* came to an end in October, when the party introduced *The Rockwell Report*. The early *Rockwell Report*s featured outrageous charcoal drawings by Rockwell on the cover, typically caricatures of Jews stealing the wealth or running roughshod over the political system in the United States, with bold headlines like:

> THE JEW FRAUD OF DEMOCRACY!
> SMASH THE NIGGER REVOLUTION NOW!
> IS MARTIN LUTHER KING A COMMUNIST?

The *Report* was a full-size, eight-by-eleven-inch magazine with a bright, two-color, professional-looking format. Its purpose was to inform the "middle-class" reader of National Socialist ideology, current events, and prognostications. The length varied from four to thirty pages and the frequency of publication from semimonthly to monthly; when money was tight, bimonthly. The magazine was printed for seven years.

By late 1961, intraparty affairs were not going well. The Nazis lived in a depressive-paranoiac atmosphere at the barracks, engaged in constant bickering, feuding, and treachery. Rockwell talked constantly about traitors. His fears were justified; some of his members were actually anti-Nazi undercover agents from law enforcement agencies, or newspapers, or from other fringe groups. The few donations that came in went for bills and alimony payments. Rockwell trudged around the barracks complaining of headaches, toothaches, and fatigue. Several members left the organization. Leaving the party was not easy; a face-to-face encounter with Rockwell took considerable courage. Desertion was common, usually at night through a window. Anyone who left the party was instantly tagged a treacherous, cowardly rat.

In November, Dan Burros left the party to join John Patler in New York. Patler and Burros had caused considerable friction within the party, and their arrogance had caused Rockwell to reach his breaking point. In the party's *Official Stormtroopers Manual* Burros had included his photo and had taken not only authorship credit but had copyrighted the booklet in his own name; Patler's photo had also been included with a byline for "layout and design." This type of self-promotion had not sat well with Rockwell; he was the focal point of the party and demanded deferential treatment. In New York the two ex-Nazis started their own group called the American National Party and published a small hand-typed magazine, *Kill!*

There was no heat in either the headquarters or the barracks that winter, because the party had no money for fuel oil. Although Virginia winters are fairly mild, only Roy James stuck it out in the barracks; everyone else fell back to headquarters, where there was electricity. On one occasion a freezing trooper ignited a charcoal grill on the first floor of headquarters to keep warm while standing guard duty. The tenderfoot lit the charcoal briquettes on fire and slept next to the coals all night. When morning arrived the men upstairs awoke with splitting headaches. They were lucky to wake at all; carbon monoxide fumes given off by the charcoal had traveled upstairs and could have killed them in their sleep.

In December, Rockwell provided the FBI with an updated list of active ANP members. Manpower turnover being frequent, Rockwell wanted the FBI to know who was no longer an ANP member. He did not want the actions of nonmembers, especially those of Patler and Burros, to be associated with the ANP.

No recruiting occurred that winter, as party members busied themselves at headquarters printing the first edition of Rockwell's autobiography, *This Time the World*. Trooper Bill Cody taught the men how to bind the book by hand. Three hundred and eighty copies were printed and sold.

Party expansion had been achieved on several fronts in 1961: a corporate charter from the state of Virginia, the opening of a large barracks in Arlington, and the continued activities of units in California and Illinois. The Nazis had stepped up their publication quality and frequency with the issuance of *The Rockwell Report* and Rockwell's autobiography.

They had received national press coverage for their "Hate Bus" trip to New Orleans, the *Exodus* riots in Boston and Philadelphia, and the Eichmann kidnapping protests. Rockwell had also won the right to speak in Union Square in New York City, an important affirmation of the First Amendment. He had also begun his flirtation with Elijah Muhammad's Black Muslim movement.

There were negatives for the party, too. It had experienced tremendous friction with the community of Arlington over the physical and sexual assaults by troopers against several minors. It had also come face-to-face with the first effective "press blackout" organized by Isaac Franck and the Jewish community in Washington, D.C. Press blackouts would gain momentum as the most effective way of curtailing Rockwell's exposure to the public and curbing his effectiveness.

The manpower shuffle had continued. Burros, Patler, and Roger Foss had left the party; others had gone to prison. But new men had arrived to take their place. Karl Allen, Ralph Forbes, and Bernie Davids had assumed leadership roles from the day of their arrival. The revolving door was simply a given, as there was very little the party could offer in material comforts. There was no pay, poor food, and ramshackle living conditions, and the threat of violence was always close at hand. Only men with a certain type of mettle and worldview could live in such conditions, those who believed in Rockwell's battle call to "save the race and nation."

7

1962: A WORLD UNION OF NATIONAL SOCIALISTS

> If you're a fanatic you'll produce something great, you'll
> create. . . . We are ideological and idealistic fanatics, just
> like the Communists. . . . In between the Nazis and the
> Communists is the great mass of non-fanatics, the TV
> watchers and the comic book readers.
>
> — Rockwell, Carleton College
> Northfield, Minnesota, 1962

On January 31, 1962, Rockwell was scheduled to appear at Bucknell University in Lewisburg, Pennsylvania, but the invitation caused such a clamor among Lewisburg residents and patriotic groups, like the Veterans of Foreign Wars, the American Legion, and the Daughters of the American Revolution, that the school capitulated and revoked it.[1] Rockwell dispatched Roy James and Karl Allen to Lewisburg to try to persuade the student organizers to overturn the decision. Their efforts were in vain, but Rockwell was adamant about speaking in Lewisburg. Once again he dispatched Allen and James, this time with Seth Ryan, to Lewisburg to distribute handbills announcing his intention to give an outdoor speech on February 4. Ryan was arrested in Sunbury, Pennsylvania, for illegal distribution of handbills, fined twenty-five dollars, and released.

On February 2, Lewisburg officials dispatched a telegram to Rockwell asking him to abandon his appearance, since they could not guarantee his safety. A reporter from the *Sunbury Daily Item* telephoned Rockwell for his reaction; Rockwell read a telegram he was sending to Lewisburg officials:

I appreciate your concern for my safety. I have already risked my life as a Navy flyer in combat and in two wars to protect my country, my Constitution and my people. In the past three years I have many times faced riotous mobs who were falsely agitated by infamous lies about me and my program and I have never yet been intimidated from what I believed was my duty nor have I run....

I sincerely regret the difficulties this situation is causing your community but it was started by the intellectual lynch mob which "welcomed" Benjamin Davis, the communist traitor, to Lewisburg and used pressure and terrorism to suppress the honest speech of an American citizen and veteran of almost 20 years service in the U.S. Navy.[2] In defending my right to speak, Lewisburg defends our Constitution, its citizens and its honor. I cannot believe it will fail.[3]

On Sunday morning, February 4, Rockwell, accompanied by Troopers Schuyler Ferris, Brent Bell, and Andrew Chappell, departed Arlington for Lewisburg. Meanwhile, a squad of ANP troopers was already in Lewisburg, going door to door to slide leaflets under the Sunday papers. This type of neighborhood canvassing was the least-favorite activity for troopers because it involved so much walking, but the publicity return usually justified the endeavor.

When Rockwell's entourage arrived in Lewisburg, Chief of Police Gordon Hufnagle and Mayor Tom Summers told him the city lacked adequate facilities for a speech. Someone in the crowd mentioned "the monument," a Civil War statue a few blocks away. Rockwell and troopers made their way there, followed by dozens of people waiting to hear his talk.

He began his speech at 1:58 P.M. and terminated his talk at 2:10 P.M. In that short time he mentioned Benjamin Davis's appearance at Bucknell and warned the citizenry about the dangers of communism. He briefly explained that his Nazi movement was not designed to overthrow the government of the United States but to fight communism. He claimed that he bore no malice against Jews as a race, and bragged that his top man in California, Leonard Holstein, was Jewish.

The crowd was very hostile, shouting and jeering at everything he said. Rockwell had to shout at the top of his lungs in order to maintain control over the crowd. He ended the spectacle after just twelve minutes because he had "no prayer of convincing a mob such as this," but he vowed to return to Lewisburg at a later date. Lewisburg police placed Rockwell and associates in a van and drove them out of town to their waiting cars. The entire affair was covered by Lewisburg police, Pennsylvania state police, and sheriff's deputies from the surrounding communities, as well as the wire services and local television reporters.[4]

Rockwell received an invitation to appear in Los Angeles on March 2 on KTTV's controversial television program "The Tom Duggan Show." He was ecstatic about the opportunity to convey party ideas to millions of television viewers—a publicity jackpot. Most promotional opportunities came by way of arrest or academic invitations; media invitations were extremely rare. He quickly put together an itinerary composed of speeches and party rallies to offset the travel costs of a West Coast tour. The first stop was O'Hare International Airport in Chicago. A squad of ANP stormtroopers drove him to the Chicago headquarters, at 2124 North Damen Street.

The Chicago FAN unit had transmogrified into an ANP unit, operated by Captain Eugene "Mal" Lambert and Lieutenant Matt Koehl. The Chicago headquarters was a two-story brick row house. The ground floor contained a small right-wing bookstore (called the Vineland Bookstore) and a meeting hall; the barracks and kitchen were on the second floor. The unit held a welcoming party for their commander and a photo shoot around the swastika flag. One of these photos would grace a page of the next month's premier issue of the *Stormtrooper.* Rockwell congratulated the men for their street action and for securing such a fine headquarters. He emphasized the importance of maintaining a barracks in each part of the country to provide housing for troopers as they crossed the country for agitation.

On February 25, Rockwell and a contingent of ten stormtroopers walked into the Chicago International Amphitheater, where more than twelve thousand Black Muslims were gathered for the Savior's Day convention. The Nazis were searched by the Fruit of Islam guards and escorted to the front row. Malcolm X spoke to the audience before introducing Elijah Muhammad. When Muhammad finished his talk, Rockwell was invited to speak. Dressed in full Nazi uniform, flanked by two stormtrooper bodyguards, he told the audience he was proud to stand before them and that he considered Elijah Muhammad the Adolf Hitler of the black man. He told the audience they had been getting a raw deal in America and that it was the fault of the Jews for "exploiting your people and my people." He asked the audience if Negro organizations needed Jewish leadership; the throngs of Muslims shouted "No!"

"You know that we call you niggers. But wouldn't you rather be confronted by honest white men who tell you to your face what the others

Author's collection

Rockwell prepares to speak at a Black Muslim rally in Chicago.

all say behind your back? Can you really gain anything dealing with a bunch of cowardly white sneaks? The yellow-liberals who tell you they love you, privately exclude you every way they know how. I am not afraid to stand here and tell you I hate race-mixing and will fight it to the death. But at the same time, I will do everything in my power to help the Honorable Elijah Muhammad carry out his inspired plan for land of your own in Africa. Elijah Muhammad is right—separation or death!"[5]

During his talk some members of the audience grumbled and booed, but Elijah Muhammad and his top aides applauded enthusiastically.[6] His thoughts were encapsulated in the April 1962 issue of *Muhammad Speaks:*

> Mr. Rockwell (American Nazi Party) has spoken well. He has lived up to his name. He is not asking you and me to follow him. He endorsed the stand for self that you and I are taking. Why should not you applaud? No other white people want you to do such a thing. His own people will hurt him or try to hurt him, you heard what he said, just because they have taken a stand to see that you be separated to get justice and freedom....
>
> What right have you to sit there and hold your hand when you know he is telling the truth. No, the trouble of it is you are scared to death! You don't want the white slave master to say "I heard that you were there lis-

tening and enjoying the German Nazis or the White Circle leader." What do we care if they are white? If they are speaking the truth for us, what do we care? We'll stand on our heads and applaud![7]

Before leaving for Los Angeles, Rockwell wired the major newspapers and television stations in Southern California to arrange for a press conference upon arrival. He planned on making outrageous statements to create headlines and publicity. However, the Jewish War Veterans (JWV) were one step ahead of him, making preemptive phone calls to the same media organizations requesting suppression of Rockwell's comments. Rockwell took a Continental Airlines jet to Los Angeles, where he was met by Robert Lewton and several other stormtroopers. He gave a brief interview to reporters in the airport waiting room, but there was no media circus as he hoped for. Rockwell took a hotel room in Pomona and borrowed a Walther P-38 pistol from a party member.

In Los Angeles he met with the apostate Jew, organizer and self-appointed Nazi head of the California Nazis since 1960, Leonard Holstein. The two men proceeded to the Los Angeles office of the FBI, where Rockwell introduced himself and Holstein to the Special Agents-in-Charge. He instructed Holstein to cooperate fully with the FBI in every way, including allowing searches without warrants, and to furnish any information concerning the ANP to the FBI. Rockwell told the Bureau agents that he was formally establishing a Western Division and anticipated membership from former Communist Party and Socialist Workers Party members. ANP protocol required these probationary members to visit the FBI office and furnish information concerning their previous subversive activities.

The next day he gave interviews to the media and made phone calls to supporters around the area. Behind the scenes, the JWV was working furiously to get Rockwell's appearance on "The Tom Duggan Show" canceled. Its members contacted the producers of the show but were rebuffed. They asked every post and friendly organization in the area to badger Duggan, the show's sponsors, and the *Los Angeles Times* (owner of KTTV) with angry phone calls and telegrams.

On the evening of March 1, as Rockwell watched "The Tom Duggan Show" from his hotel room, Duggan announced that he had been ordered by network officials to cancel Rockwell's appearance. Rockwell was furious. He wasn't the only one; the station's switchboard lit up.

The following night, instead of appearing on television in front of millions of viewers, he picketed alone in full Nazi uniform in front of the television studio. Simultaneous demonstrations were held in Chicago and Arlington.

The next day Rockwell demonstrated in Pershing Square, Los Angeles's equivalent of New York's Union Square. He had informed the press and television stations of his intentions and brought Leonard Holstein, Bob Lewton, and Dick Anderson as bodyguards. When the four Nazis arrived media people from KTLA were already waiting, along with hundreds of Jewish War Veterans. The moment he started speaking, the mob came to life: shouting, cursing, screaming, spitting at him. When police refused to intercede, the mob's courage increased. They pushed in on Rockwell and his troopers, stretching their arms at his head in a futile attempt to throttle him. A squad of police eventually appeared with bullhorns and made the assembly disperse.[8]

Rockwell's motel room was besieged with calls and wires from the press, radio stations, and colleges. Among them was a phone call from Bill Stout, a liberal commentator and owner of the *Beverly Hills Times.* Stout made arrangements for Rockwell to appear on his program, but once again the JWV applied enough pressure to have Rockwell canceled.[9]

An invitation was tendered by the Committee for Student Action (CSA) at San Diego State College, and Rockwell accepted. Edward Neuner, chairman of the Lectures and Concerts Board (with oversight of the CSA), questioned whether Rockwell's talk would be on an intellectual level or merely propaganda. The university president, Malcolm Love, went out on a limb: "Our students can take care of him. I have more faith in our students than most people."[10]

On the morning of March 8, 1962, Troopers Holstein and Lewton collected Rockwell from his motel and drove him to San Diego. He walked briskly onto the stage of the Little Theater and began his speech in front of three thousand students. He told the audience that he had no intention of causing trouble: "If I had wanted trouble I could have worn my uniform with my Nazi armbands and the whole works. Believe me, I know how to stir people up if I want to."[11]

He called for racial separation and for blacks to unite behind Elijah Muhammad and take pride in their own cultural identity. He also attacked the U.S. government for being weak: "No one is interested in the common interest of this country. They're all in a special interest group fighting each other."[12] He briefly outlined how the Nazi Party would take power. The party's first objective was to become known as a movement, with Rockwell the focal point. It would then dispel the false ideas about itself and tell the American people what it really stood for. Once his followers were organized he could use his popularity to gain power through elections.

He attacked the morals of Americans, declaring that "such garbage as [Henry Miller's] *Tropic of Cancer* should not be sold." (Miller's work had been published in Paris in 1934 but banned in the United States until 1961; its legalization was a sign of the emerging sexual revolution.) Rockwell also made reference to seeing men walking down the streets in Hollywood holding hands: "If there's one thing I'd rather gas than communists, it's queers."[13] As the speech neared thirty minutes, he launched into his "communism is Jewish" canard. A Jewish student in the audience quietly got up from his seat, mounted the stage, and told Rockwell he wanted to speak. He moved toward the microphone, but Rockwell was not about to relinquish the floor and pushed twenty-two-year-old Ed Cherry away. Cherry reacted quickly, striking Rockwell twice in the face, breaking Rockwell's black plastic–framed sunglasses. Rockwell immediately squared off to fight, but Leonard Holstein tackled Cherry and pummeled him until student organizers separated the two men. The remainder of the speech was canceled.

Rockwell proceeded to the office of the student newspaper for an interview. During the long walk to the *Daily Aztec* office, hundreds of students surrounded Rockwell and his men, shouting threats, jostling them about, pelting them with raw eggs. When the student organizers and Nazi entourage finally reached the newspaper office, their clothing was spattered with raw eggs. The students in whom President Love had so much faith had degenerated into an unruly mob.

Rockwell told the journalism students that there was a conspiracy to discourage his speaking invitations; the attack by Cherry was part of a plan to keep other colleges from inviting him. He put the attack in perspective, calling it "a minor skirmish." Such violence hurt his cause in the short run but helped in the long run, "because people finally realize what it is that's running this country—it's terrorism. In other words there is no free speech. For a man who preaches what I do they try to kill you."[14]

A stormtrooper slipped out of the room to fetch their automobile. Rockwell leaned back in a chair, propped up his feet on a desk, and lit a big cigar. Noise from the rampaging students in the hall outside the *Aztec* office and on the lawns outside the building grew ever louder. Several student agitators climbed on the windowsills of the *Aztec* office with anti-Nazi placards. Student organizers and campus officials pleaded with the crowd to disperse for the sake of the professors conducting classes, but the students were belligerent and refused to leave.

As Rockwell got up to leave the *Daily Aztec* office, he handed his shattered sunglasses to John Lowe, a twenty-two-year-old history student, as a souvenir. Rockwell and his lieutenants ran to their car, jumped in, slammed the doors, and locked them. A mob of students surrounded the car, yelling, spitting, throwing rocks, shattering the windshield, kicking in the grill. The Nazis finally got off campus, away from the ruckus, but the harassment was not finished yet. American Airlines received a message from a caller stating a bomb had been placed aboard Rockwell's flight. (It was a hoax.)

Rockwell's attacker, Ed Cherry, told the press he had been incensed by the way Rockwell talked about the Jews, "the way he said the Jews are communists and are the cause of the world's troubles. . . . I went up to the microphone to try to speak. He shoved me away and then I swung at him. It just set off a reaction in me that I couldn't control. . . . I wanted to counteract Rockwell's lies."[15]

Public reaction to Cherry's attack ranged from condemnation to hero worship. Syndicated columnist Inez Robb hailed Cherry as a "genuine folk hero"; she thought Rockwell's dissenters should be "permitted the privilege of a free poke from time to time."[16] Gerald Rife of the *Daily Aztec* took a more constitutional view:

> Our country is built on the principle that every man is entitled to his own opinion and the right to express it. When Rockwell's right was endangered, your right and mine were also endangered. Whether the man is a fascist, a communist, or Satan himself, he has the RIGHT to speak. . . . It is a terrible indictment against the student body of this college that they should stoop to the emotional and degrading level of an ignorant mob.[17]

The next day, March 9, 1962, was Rockwell's forty-fourth birthday. The three members of the Western Division gave Rockwell a small celebration, complete with a swastika-decorated cake. They also presented their commander with a new attaché case. When his scheduled appearance at Pomona College was canceled because of JWV pressure, he took a night flight to Houston and held a press conference in the apartment of reporter Charles Ray. Rockwell told reporters he was in Houston to organize eight card-carrying members and twenty sympathizers into a Texas unit:

> We don't care about the Jews unless they are communist race mixers. . . . Almost all the Jews are for race mixing, most of them are communists, but the ones who are not don't have to worry, we don't want to gas innocent people.[18]

From Houston Rockwell took a plane to Jacksonville, Florida, where he met with Karl Allen, who was trying to organize a Florida unit. Allen arranged an interview for Rockwell at a local television station. Rockwell took a cab to the television station but objected to the $1.45 fare, accusing the cabby of getting lost and taking a circuitous route. He handed the driver a dollar and walked into the studio for the interview. The taxi driver swore out a complaint, and Rockwell was arrested for disorderly conduct and fined twenty-five dollars. The next morning he flew back to Washington, D.C., where he was met by ANP members Bernie Davids, Schuyler Ferris, and Dick Braun. Braun was fresh out of Virginia prison after serving a year on the chain gang for roughing up Ricky Farber.

March 1962 was a busy month for all branches of the ANP. There were numerous protests, beatings, and arrests. On March 17, members of CORE demonstrated against police brutality in front of the Justice Department Building. ANP officers Karl Allen and Bernie Davids received permission from police to counter-demonstrate. Davids carried a placard that read "More Police Brutality for Reds," while Allen dragged a homemade Soviet flag on the ground. The flag caught the attention of authorities, and both men were arrested and convicted for disorderly conduct. Allen appealed the decision in the District Court of Appeals, where the conviction was overturned in February 1963.

Late in the month, the Western Division–ANP staged a protest in front of the Progressive Book Store in Los Angeles. Leonard Holstein commanded three stormtroopers marching in front of the store with placards that read:

Death to the Commie Traitors

Don't Buy Red China's Filth

Without warning, ten men came out of a nearby tavern and attacked the ANP marchers. The outnumbered troopers took a beating; three of the attackers were arrested.[19]

In Chicago, five members of the Chicago unit marched in front of the State-Lake Theater, which was showing the movie *Sergeants Three*, featuring Sammy Davis, Jr. The Nazis carried pickets that read, "Sammy Davis *Jew*nior is a Race-Mixer." Spectators were infuriated. Police arrested the five Nazis on charges of criminal defamation and disorderly conduct.

Another incident occurred at the Vineland Bookstore, the front for ANP-Chicago operations. A telephone installer knocked on the door; when a stormtrooper wearing a khaki uniform, swastika armband, and a holstered .45-caliber automatic pistol opened it, the repairman bolted from the building and notified his superiors at Illinois Bell Telephone. The phone company called police, who raided the Nazi headquarters. Malcolm Lambert and Wayne Mueller were arrested for contributing to the delinquency of a minor, and a sixteen-year-old youth was turned over to juvenile authorities.

The Chicago unit was not deterred. It periodically dispatched storm-troopers to the headquarters of the communist newspaper *The Worker*. One trooper dragged a red flag bearing a hammer and sickle on the ground behind him, while the other marchers carried placards that read:

Communism Must Be Smashed

Communist Meeting Upstairs

Communist Propaganda Mill Upstairs[20]

On April 4, 1962, Rockwell and Karl Allen drove into the District of Columbia to listen to the Senate testimony of ex–Major General Edwin Walker. Walker had accused high-ranking government officials of being members of a "hidden control apparatus" that was coercing the Army and components of the U.S. government to the will of the international-al communist conspiracy. Walker had been relieved of his command in 1961 and admonished for trying to influence men under his command in the 1960 election. Walker told the subcommittee that a "control apparatus" operated in the government "to sell out... our traditions, our Constitution, our sovereignty, our independence."

As the two Nazis descended the heavily carpeted stairs of the gallery, a hush fell over the entire chamber. Spectators and senators watched as Rockwell and Allen were seated. The following day Rockwell attended the hearings again, but this time Capitol police escorted him out of the hearing because of the swastika emblem on his coat lapel: they told Rockwell it was against Senate rules to display placards or signs. Rockwell protested that other people in the audience were wearing emblems on the lapels of their jackets and were not molested, but his plea fell on deaf ears.[21] Both men were escorted from the chamber.

That same month, Christopher Bailey joined the party as a troop leader after being released from active duty in the Marine Corps. Bailey had maintained associate member status for more than a year while a member of the Corps, subscribing to ANP literature, often leaving it around his barracks where other Marines could read it. The more the Corps harassed him about his involvement, the more he committed himself to the party. When Rockwell put out a call for better printing equipment, Bailey responded by purchasing a $3,000 Davidson Model 233 offset-printing press and paper cutter, which he leased to the party for a period of five years at a fee of one dollar per year.[22] The party shipped its old press to the Chicago unit.

Christopher Bailey readies his motorcycle for an "agitation trip" through the District.

Bailey purchased a khaki uniform from a local military surplus store and assumed the responsibility of "duty officer" at headquarters. His job was to meet the public and answer the dozens of crank telephone callers, like the two "Jewish women" who badgered him to identify himself for the ADL files. For all Bailey's monetary contributions, he was never able to attain officer rank: Rockwell was happy to spend his money, but he did not feel he was officer material.[23]

Roger Foss returned to the party in April after a year of self-imposed exile. Rockwell had got word to him that Patler, Burros, and Grandinetti had left. Foss was welcomed back and given the title of assistant national secretary. Rockwell wrote of Foss's return in the *Rockwell Report*, calling him "one of the best Nazis we ever had."

After demonstrations ANP members usually returned to headquarters to watch the evening news on "Jew-vision" to see if their protests would be televised. When the news was over troopers returned to their homes or the barracks, and headquarters would close for the evening. Foss usually slept on the first floor to answer the telephone and repel firebomb attacks. Quite often, unknowing drunks and indigents were given cab fare to Nazi headquarters by enemies of the party; Foss turned away dozens of drunks who stumbled up the steps looking for a place to sleep. Another nuisance was the telephone. It frequently rang all night, tapering off around 3:00 A.M.; it was against party policy to leave the phone off the hook. Most of the callers were hecklers, but sometimes they were homosexuals. One caller made himself a particular nuisance by calling at the same time every night and breathing heavily into the phone. Foss presumed the caller held a night desk job and had nothing else to do; Foss would insult and denigrate the man. The more vicious and ferocious Foss was, the more excited the caller became: the breathing would get heavier, broken with grunting. Foss finally realized the caller was a masochist.[24]

On April 11, Rockwell was scheduled to speak at Hunter College in the Bronx, New York, as one of four speakers appearing at the invitation of a student group called the Competency Party. The other speakers to appear were Gus Hall of the Communist Party, Elijah Muhammad of the Black Muslims, and William Buckley, editor of the *National Review*. The New York City police commissioner received an anonymous letter that read: "IF ROCKWELL COMES TO THIS CITY HE WILL NEVER LEAVE ALIVE." The letter was turned over to the FBI, but no identification was made.[25]

At Hunter, more than 150 policemen were on hand to quell disturbances. Barricades were set up across the street from the entrance of

Gillette Hall, where more than a thousand students marched in protest against Rockwell's appearance. New York City police telephoned Rockwell and told him he would be served with a two-year-old warrant for his arrest if he entered New York City. (The warrant was the result of the near riot in the court rotunda in 1960.) Rockwell decided to skip the speech, sending New Yorker Seth Ryan in his place along with body-guards Roy James and Schuyler Ferris.

Seth Ryan took the stage and told the audience his topic was "Nazism, the Only Alternative to Communism." He told Hunter students that white Americans would never accept African Americans as their equals. He blasted the right wing as "cowards," "creeps," and "political prostitutes."

In May, the Los Angeles County Commission on Human Relations urged the California state attorney general to investigate hate groups in the Los Angeles area. According to the commission's report, "while these organizations do not constitute an immediate threat, more hate is being expressed in this community than ever before."[26] The report considered that it would be inappropriate to characterize the ANP as a "meaningful menace" because "it is small, erratic, and not well disciplined." The commission also recommended that the Board of Supervisors call on the county counsel to investigate the possibility of enacting measures to prohibit the distribution of hate literature and handbills. Another measure was a recommendation that an ordinance be passed prohibiting the wearing in public of any military uniform or insignia not approved by an appropriate agency of the federal or local government.

In mid-June, Rockwell appeared before the Illinois chapter of the National States Rights Party (NSRP) at the LaSalle Hotel in Chicago. He told the audience that Jews were leading "the colored masses" in a revolt, a mutiny against "the maker of civilization"—the white man. He told the audience they could "beat the enemy" with a unified right wing that encompassed not just talkers, not just millionaires, not just fighters, but all of them. He pleaded for them to work together, because activity of the "Ladies Aid Society" type would not succeed.[27]

The Chicago ANP targeted Billy James Hargis for disruption at the annual "We the People" rally in Chicago that summer.[28] Hargis, or "Hoggis" as the ANP referred to him, was perceived as a "kosher-conservative," reaping enormous profit from the Christian conservatives while doing very little to stem the rising tide of Jewish influence across the country. The Chicago unit printed flyers with the same color scheme as the official "We the People" program but titled "Debate of the Century—Is Communism Jewish? Billy James Hargis vs. Surprise Speaker from ANP." The debate was to be a follow-up to the speech by the former governor of Indiana.

On the day of the event, Matt Koehl and three other men distributed flyers under doors in the LaSalle Hotel during the lunch hour. By 2:30 P.M. the phone at the Chicago ANP unit was ringing off the hook. Hargis was so alarmed that he called an emergency meeting with police.

That evening the Nazis rehearsed their disruption tactics, changed into business suits, and drove to the LaSalle. When the elevator doors opened on the nineteenth floor, the Nazis were confronted by dozens of police stationed by the elevator looking for brown shirt stormtroopers. The Nazis walked past the security into the convention area, where things were not going according to plan. The former governor of Indiana had canceled his speaking engagement, creating a gap in the proceedings. A speaker stepped to the podium and announced that Rockwell and thirty stormtroopers had arrived at the airport and had been taken into custody.

Hargis began his talk about the evils of communism, then segued into a pitch for money. His usual tactic was to incorporate his donation line into a prayer and ask for ten thousand dollars; a shill in the audience would pledge the amount. Hargis would play upon guilt in the audience until others donated lesser amounts. Since this was a secular event, however, Hargis was cautious not to turn his talk into a prayer meeting. He asked for ten thousand dollars to "help fight communism," but before his shill in the audience could utter a word, Koehl stood up and shouted, "Reverend Hargis, I'll give you one hundred thousand dollars if you will admit that communism is Jewish."

The convention hall went quiet as Hargis fumbled to respond. Then Nazi Chris Vidnjevich stood and shouted the same thing; then a third. Soon the event was in total disarray. "Tell them, Billy James," screamed Koehl. "Tell them what you told me down in Alabama." Police realized the agitators were Rockwell's men and escorted them from the room into the elevator; they were released in the hotel lobby. Years later, Hargis told Rockwell that the stunt cost him $28,000 in lost donations.[29]

In late June, six ANP members picketed ADL offices in Philadelphia. Occupants in the building opened windows and poured buckets of water on the stormtroopers and pelted them with office supplies, while five hundred Philadelphian bystanders gathered outside police lines, yelling insults at the Nazis. A breach in police lines allowed the mob to swarm through, screaming, "Kill the Nazi bastards!" A riot erupted that left several injured people strewn about the streets in the City of Brotherly Love.[30]

The Virginia House of Delegates passed a bill revoking the charter of the American Nazi Party by a 45–37 vote. The bill banned the use of the word "Nazi" or "National Socialist" in any charter or by any group. ANP Captain Karl Allen appealed to Virginia Governor Albertis Harrison to veto the bill. Allen wrote:

> We cannot believe that the Commonwealth of Virginia sincerely wishes to take stronger action against an organization dedicated to the preservation of the white race and the protection of our constitutional republic than it has against race-mixing agitators and open communists.[31]

On June 28, 1962, Rockwell filed a petition in Arlington Circuit Court to prevent Virginia from revoking the charter. The same day, the federal government placed a lien on Rockwell's property for nonpayment of $192.52 of his 1960 federal income taxes—the first of several Internal Revenue problems. The next day the Virginia state legislature revoked the ANP's corporation charter and passed the ban on the use of "Nazi" and "National Socialist." Rockwell applied for a charter under the name ANP Inc., which was denied on a technicality. He was eventually granted a charter under the name George Lincoln Rockwell Party later that year. The new charter was almost identical to the previous one, with Karl Allen replacing Seth Ryan on the board of directors.[32]

In Miami, Florida, ANP members Roger Foss and Gene Shalander were sentenced for disorderly conduct stemming from a picketing demonstration. Judge Jack Wallace told the men he would reduce their sentences if they agreed to write out in longhand the Declaration of Independence and the U.S. Constitution a hundred times each. The men refused. Foss was sentenced to six months in jail, with sixty additional days for striking a policeman; Shalander received four months.[33]

In early July, the ANP staged an attack against Barry Goldwater, who was appearing at a Human Events convention at the Park-Sheraton

Hotel in Washington. Rockwell learned of the event only the night before; with no time to spare he created a leaflet of "twenty of the most damning facts," entitled "Goldwater is a plant." The morning of the speech the men at headquarters printed two thousand leaflets. Seth Ryan led ten stormtroopers dressed in civilian clothes to the Park-Sheraton to distribute the propaganda.

Rockwell hoped to destroy Goldwater's political career by pointing out his Jewish heritage, his membership in the NAACP, and that as a top member of the Senate Labor Committee he had "railroaded" through the confirmation of a "radical pinko Jew lawyer" named Arthur Goldberg as the secretary of labor. The party newsletter reported, "When Barry Hebewater got up to speak, his welcome was less than enthusiastic. . . . The Jews will have to hunt up a new Kosher leader now." [34]

In late July, Rockwell slipped into Great Britain, which had denied him a visa. Rockwell and Colin Jordan, head of the British National Socialist Movement, had decided to hold a secret formation meeting in England to create the World Union of National Socialists (WUNS). Since 1959, when he had coined the name World Union of Free Enterprise National Socialists, Rockwell had envisioned various international Nazi movements working together under the umbrella of a pan-Aryan organization to implement their racial policies among the world's population to create an Aryan world order.

The first step in the process was getting into England. Secret planning took place between Rockwell and Jordan's deputy, John Tyndall. Rockwell took several security precautions. First and foremost was total secrecy: no one in the party knew of the mission. Second, he would use the Irish airline Aer Lingus, since the airline employees would be less likely to recognize his face or name. On July 28, he flew to Boston and caught a flight to Ireland. No one in Arlington knew of the departure. As the jetliner climbed into the night sky, Rockwell drew a deep breath and a sigh of relief. The weeks of planning, the secrecy, the nervous strain of waiting for six hours in the Boston airport, the passport and ticket checks, had pushed him to exhaustion. He fell into a deep sleep.

When the plane landed in Shannon, the nervous tension reappeared—a lump in the throat, stomach pain, sweaty palms. He was not accustomed to cloak-and-dagger activity. Trying his best to look like just another tourist, he disembarked and walked to the customs shed with the other passengers. As the Irish customs agent reviewed his passport, he steeled himself for rejection and deportation. The customs man asked where he was staying; Rockwell told him he was meeting friends and that they knew the location. The officer slammed his rubber stamp onto the passport and motioned him through the exit gate. It was so easy he wished he had brought his uniform and some party literature, but this was only Ireland; he still had to get to England.

A tall, good-looking man with blond hair approached Rockwell with an outstretched hand and said, "I'm with Mr. Jordan." John Tyndall shook hands with Rockwell and escorted him to a tiny British car containing the leader of the British National Socialist Movement, Colin Jordan. Rockwell and Jordan shook hands as the car sped away from the airport. One of the Englishmen opened a satchel containing several firearms, which they said they were carrying in case they needed to defend themselves from Israeli kidnappers.

Jordan's political development had been similar to Rockwell's. Born in 1923 in Birmingham, England, he had attended Warwick School, where he won a university scholarship in history. With the advent of World War II he had joined the Royal Air Force. While on deferred service awaiting flight training, he declared his opposition to the war and was transferred to the Royal Army Medical Corps for the duration. After demobilization he resumed his studies at Cambridge University, where he organized the Nationalist Club, served on the staff of the school newspaper *Varsity*, and debated with the Union Society. He had graduated in 1949 with honors.

In 1958, Jordan formed the White Defense League, which merged with the British National Party in 1960. From this amalgamation came the British National Socialist Movement (BNSM), under his leadership. Like Rockwell, Jordan had no patience for closet Nazis or right-wingers too cowardly to speak out in public. In early 1962 Jordan led a violent BNSM rally in Trafalgar Square which led not only to his dismissal from his teaching post but also to disqualification as a teacher. At the time of Rockwell's arrival Jordan was being prosecuted for the riotous Trafalgar rally and for taking part in something called the BNSM Defense Corps, an armed unit of the BNSM.

Rockwell, Jordan, and Tyndall traveled north to the border with Ulster, branching off from the main road to a country lane to finalize their plans for a world National Socialist organization, in case Rockwell was apprehended at the border. For more than an hour Rockwell and

Jordan discussed the details of the World Union of National Socialists. They crossed the border with no difficulty and drove to Belfast, where they bought tickets for a steamer that would take them to Heisham, England. That evening they departed, arriving in Heisham at 5 A.M.

The British Nazis took one final security precaution: they placed Rockwell on a train by himself to disembark at the next station and return to Jordan's red MG sports car. They drove into London to photograph Rockwell in front of all the tourist attractions: Big Ben, Trafalgar Square, 10 Downing Street, Scotland Yard. He even posed for photos with London "Bobbies" in front of Buckingham Palace. They planned to sell the photos to English tabloids. The tourist jaunt complete, they drove to the site of the would-be Nazi encampment in Cheltenham, 130 miles to the east of London, where Rockwell checked into an inn as an American writer named George Henderson.

Rockwell was shocked by the miscegenation in England; mixed couples were everywhere. He was enraged at the sight of blacks walking hand in hand with pretty, blond English girls. After Rockwell had been at the inn for three days, Jordan arrived in the MG and drove him to their "secret" camp in Gloucestershire, in the Cotswold Hills. By now the British press knew Rockwell was in the country; so did the Special Branch of Scotland Yard. Knowing Rockwell was "hot," Jordan parked the MG in a wooded area near the camp and escorted him through the pitch-black forest to avoid the press and detectives. They made their way through the forest until they heard the crackling of a fire behind a small wall.

Milling around the campfire were a dozen members of the British National Socialist Movement. Jordan went ahead to check the area, stepped into the light, and announced, "We have a surprise visitor. None other than Lincoln Rockwell." When Rockwell stepped out of the darkness into the campfire light, a roar of cheering went up among the men—so loud that the Special Branch detectives hiding outside the camp wondered what was going on.[35] Rockwell was momentarily stunned, but he regained his composure enough to give a highly charged speech, hailing the miraculous rise of National Socialism, "which alone, stood athwart the path of criminal Jew-communism, race-mixing and subversion."[36] When he was finished speaking, they all shouted, "Heil Hitler!" The World Union of National Socialists was born.

The next morning the British Nazis faced the difficult task of getting

Colin Jordan and Rockwell form the World Union of National Socialists in England's Cotswold Hills in August 1962.

Rockwell away from the encampment. The road adjacent to the camp-site was crawling with newspaper correspondents, curiosity seekers, police, and Scotland Yard detectives. They decided to trick the reporters by using a decoy. They dressed another man in a "B-movie" spy-type outfit—trench coat, dark glasses, woman's scarf—to leave the camp with Jordan in the MG, past the waiting onlookers. The reporters took the bait and followed in hot pursuit.

That evening Rockwell and several women walked arm in arm past the remaining agents and reporters, singing and laughing, pretending they were going to a pub to quaff a few pints. They walked two miles, then Jordan returned in the MG to pick him up. For the next four days Rockwell scurried from place to place, keeping one step ahead of Scotland Yard. Jordan paid for all Rockwell's expenses, obtaining £100 for him from the *London Daily Mirror* as a fee for an exclusive photo-graph of Rockwell at the Cotswold camp.

Back in the forest, more than a hundred vigilantes from the nearby Gloucestershire village of Guiting Power stormed the encampment and routed the remaining Nazis. Led by pub owner Walter Morley and Clement Timms, they punched their way past cudgel-swinging guards. Men rolled in the mud amid the tangle of the fallen tents, and a shotgun blast shredded the swastika flag flying above the camp. Seventy policemen intervened to quell the fighting. The camp was leveled and the Nazis defeated, but Rockwell was nowhere to be found.

Acting on a tip, Scotland Yard sent four detectives into the heart of London, where they spotted Rockwell getting out of a car and placed him in custody. After spending the night in Cannon Row police station, he was escorted by Yard detectives to a Pan American jet bound for Boston. The Metropolitan Police confiscated the £100 to pay for his repatriation. Shortly before takeoff, a bomb threat delayed the flight. When the plane had been thoroughly searched, Rockwell climbed the stairs to the plane, turned at the top of the steps, and raised his right arm in the Nazi salute toward the horde of photographers.[37]

In Boston, dozens of reporters awaited his arrival. He gave a brief press conference before catching a connecting flight to Washington. Awaiting his arrival were six stormtroopers in full Nazi uniform, formed up, three men on each side of the gate. The first man off the plane was Jewish. He stopped at the gate, stupefied by the presence of six stormtroopers shouting "Sieg Heil!" His paralysis was shattered by Rockwell's booming voice behind him, echoing throughout the terminal, turning heads, attracting gawkers. The honor guard escorted Rockwell to a waiting convertible.[38]

Back in Arlington, Rockwell typed a document entitled The Cotswold Agreements, a declaration establishing the World Union of National Socialists (WUNS); he immediately released it to the press. His trip to England had been a huge success. For the cost of a two-hundred-dollar plane ticket he had received enormous worldwide press coverage, including an exclusive with the *London Daily Mirror.*

FBI agents converged on ANP headquarters to determine if Rockwell had violated the Foreign Agents Registration Act of 1938. Rockwell told the FBI agents the "Cotswold Agreements" were phony and that his statement to the press that he had signed an agreement at Cotswold, England, forming an international organization called the WUNS was not true.[39] He had lied to the press. The FBI closely monitored his actions to see if he was "acting within the United States as an agent of a foreign organization."[40]

The Cotswold Agreements purported to forge an alliance between representatives of the British National Socialist Movement, the American Nazi Party, the Belgium National Socialist Movement, the French National Socialists, the First German National Socialist Hundred, and the Austrian National Socialists. Except for Colin Jordan's British National Socialist Movement, the European groups were completely fictitious, invented to make the document look impressive and enhance the ruse. The agreement named Colin Jordan the "International Leader" and England the "International Headquarters." Jordan could tell the English press very little about the terms or conditions of the agreement until Rockwell sent him a copy. Appointing Jordan as leader of WUNS was a surprising act of humility for Rockwell; perhaps he recognized that Jordan's ability and contacts were critical to a successful international movement. Another reason for appointing Jordan was to skirt the Foreign Agents Registration Act.

Whether the agreement was phony or not, small cells from around the world (Chile, France, Japan, South Africa, Australia) wrote ANP headquarters requesting entrance into the World Union of National Socialists. Rockwell granted them memberships, and he recapped international WUNS activities in every issue of the *Stormtrooper.* To the casual observer it appeared that a worldwide Nazi movement was under way, a movement directed by Lincoln Rockwell and Colin Jordan. Before the year was over, Rockwell would succeed Jordan as its leader.

Rockwell's journey to the Cotswold Hills was fortuitous in other ways besides publicity. He made contact with two foreigners who helped complete his political maturation: Savitri Devi and Bruno Ludtke.

Savitri Devi was born in France in 1905. She trained as a chemist, earned a doctorate, and moved to India in 1932 to study ancient Aryan philosophy. She gave up her birth name—Maximiani Portas—adopting Savitri Devi after the Aryan sun goddess. A disciple of Hitler, she wrote several postwar works on Aryan mysticism and National Socialism: *Gold in the Furnace, Defiance, Pilgrimage,* and *The Lightning and the Sun.*

Bruno Ludtke was born in Hamburg in 1926 and joined the German army in 1944. He idolized Hitler and did not let go of this passion at the war's end. From the moment he met Rockwell, he devoted his energies to tutoring Hitler's heir on the subtleties of National Socialism. The two men formed a mutual admiration society, encouraging and inspiring each other when things were not so good. Ludtke became Rockwell's eyes and ears in Europe and the WUNS leader in West Germany. He translated Rockwell's literature into German where it was distributed—at great peril to Ludtke under West German anti-Nazi laws—to secret Nazi contacts throughout the country. He wrote Rockwell that his words were "like the rain going down to the thirsty ground."[41]

In reaction to Rockwell's Cotswold announcement, the Jewish War Veterans, during their sixty-seventh annual convention, sent a telegram to U.S. Attorney General Robert Kennedy asking for immediate steps to have Rockwell registered as a foreign agent: "The announced formation...of an international fascist movement makes it imperative that these lice be under perpetual surveillance as an arm of an alien philosophy."[42] The next year, at the sixty-eighth annual convention, the Jewish War Veterans adopted two official resolutions regarding Rockwell. One resolution asked for the government to require Rockwell to register as a foreign agent; the other contained four points:

1. The attorney general to place the ANP on the subversives list.
2. The postmaster general and Justice Department to "enforce federal laws governing the use of the mails which prohibit the mailing of material...in the name of the American Nazi Party."
3. State authorities to enforce laws for inciting riot, disorder, and breaches of peace.
4. Federal and state agencies to weed out Rockwell followers in their ranks.[43]

Rockwell was always leery of the Jewish War Veterans: "I fear the Jewish War Veterans. I don't blame them though, they're fighting for their side, I'm fighting for mine."[44]

The animosity between Rockwell and the National States Rights Party came to a head in August. NSRP leaders J. B. Stoner and Ed Fields were tired of losing not only manpower but *Thunderbolt* subscribers to the ANP. Fields had never felt the two groups were either in competition or closely related: the NSRP was predominately localized in the Deep South, segregationist, and had no activity in Virginia. Fields wanted none of Rockwell's "shoulder-to-shoulder" alliance; he believed the masses would simply reject Nazism as a foreign operation. He also thought any NSRP-ANP alliance would alienate the man on the street from the NSRP, because unlike the Nazis, the NSRP was not a radical organization. Fields saw it as simply one of many segregationist groups in the South.

Their differences came to a head at a meeting in Louisville, Kentucky. Fields went to Rockwell's hotel room to discuss the agent provocateur who had apparently infiltrated the right wing and was moving from group to group, spying. Upon Fields's warning, Rockwell picked up the telephone and called the FBI, while he was still in the room. To Fields it was evident that Rockwell could not be trusted.[45]

Fields held a deep distrust for the FBI, whereas Rockwell had a fanatical devotion to Hoover's Bureau. Rockwell saw Hoover as a strident anticommunist, practically the only government official doing anything to thwart communism. Rockwell was always very forthright in his dealings with the FBI, which did not go unnoticed at the Bureau. Their internal memorandums referred to him as "very cooperative with Agents."

Rockwell hoped Hoover and his men secretly admired the ANP and its endeavors, but there was no mutual admiration society. The FBI distributed an unflattering monograph on Rockwell to field offices. It described Rockwell as "a professional bigot, a 'con' man, a malcontent, and a chronic failure, who will stop at nothing to gain notoriety and even power.... He is a man whose tongue and pen are jagged weapons of slow destruction...a shrewd small mind inflated into a national nuisance by undeserved publicity. He is a braggart and bully, who tries to delude his maladjusted followers into believing they are crusaders."

Despite Rockwell's failings, the Bureau saw the ANP as a threat:

> Though small in numbers and influence, the ANP is a dangerous organization of misfits who are psychologically and physically capable of perpetrating acts of violence.... If this organization is ever in a position to do so, these American Nazis—like the Nazis of Hitler's Germany—will follow through with their obnoxious objectives of liquidating all whom they consider inferior. It is well to remember that in his early days Adolph [*sic*] Hitler, like Rockwell, was ridiculed and scorned.... We would do well to heed the American Nazi Party and to remember that history is replete with incidents where a nucleus of an organization and the "right" conditions merged to shake the foundations of the world.[46]

The August issue of the *Thunderbolt* accused Rockwell of accepting money from Jewish interests, being an FBI collaborator, a phony patriot, and a communist. It was no secret that Rockwell turned over names of members to the FBI or that he accepted money from anyone who was willing to donate, but it is highly unlikely that he was on a Jewish payroll. Proponents of the "Jewish financing" theory believe Rockwell served a vital interest for the Jewish community by representing a constant threat to their well-being, a constant insecurity for the Jewish psyche. Rockwell's activities enabled various Jewish organizations to appeal for funds to "fight the Nazis" and thereby keep their coffers full.

Rockwell, who referred to the NSRP as the "Nazi Sneaks & Rats Party," always felt it was a Nazi group in disguise. Its "Twenty-five Points" was a carbon copy of Hitler's, and its lightning bolt emblem was a stylized swastika. Rockwell demanded a retraction of the charges, but Fields refused, and the battle lines were drawn. The two traded barbs and accusations for several years. Rockwell eventually filed a $550,000 libel suit in federal court in Alabama claiming Fields was engaged in a conspiracy to ruin him.[47]

Their feud ended in 1965 with an out-of-court settlement in Rockwell's favor. Most of the depositions supported Rockwell's position, and the turning point came when Rockwell learned that Fields (who was married) was allegedly seeing a young woman. When Rockwell threatened to reveal the tryst in the *Rockwell Report*, Fields decided to settle. He paid Rockwell $1,000 and printed a retraction in the *Thunderbolt*. Rockwell printed Fields's apology in the *Rockwell Report* to "rub it in." Fields maintained that the settlement had been worked out between Jesse Stoner (co-founder of the NSRP) and Rockwell to put an end to the dispute, but Rockwell was not above using dirt on anyone. He would bulldoze opposition without remorse.[48]

After the failed Bay of Pigs invasion in April 1961, student groups around the country continued to stage protests against the U.S. action. On September 22, sixteen members of the Student Peace Union (SPU) marched with placards in front of the White House. In the afternoon, seventy-five members of CORE joined them. At dusk Rockwell and seven stormtroopers dressed in Nazi uniform arrived to counter-picket with a swastika flag and racist placards.

Two couples out for an evening stroll after attending a bar mitzvah passed the Nazis picketing in front of the White House. One of the men, Jack Dubrovsky, became furious when he spotted a stormtrooper carrying the swastika flag. Dubrovsky ran to the Nazi flag bearer and ripped the staff from his hands. The other Nazis closed in on

Dubrovsky and dropped him to the pavement. A police detail of eight men rushed in to stop the fracas; though two patrolmen were injured, they arrested seven Nazis and the assailant Dubrovsky for disorderly conduct. Rockwell had already returned to the barracks and was not at the melee. The SPU and CORE demonstrators continued to march during the fight and took no part in the incident.[49]

Toward the end of the month, Rockwell appeared in District Court to block a television program he feared would damage his reputation. Acting as his own attorney, he asked Judge John Sirica to block an upcoming episode of *The Defenders* that depicted the trial of a "teenage American Nazi" accused of first-degree murder. CBS attorney Percy Shay told Sirica the program was to be about a youth who paints a swastika on a Jewish temple and who, given full benefit of the law, is found not guilty of a murder charge despite community sentiment against him. Shay said the program did not refer to the Nazi Party but did depict the "dastardly" act of a teenage boy who engages in "Nazi-like" activities. The network demanded a million-dollar bond to suspend the episode. Judge Sirica told Rockwell he would have an adequate remedy at law in a suit for damages after the program was shown if he felt he had been injured.[50]

When the show was televised the Nazis were glued to their sets. Rockwell described the episode:

> The Jews put on a one-hour TV show, blasting us again. . . . The vicious Nazi hate-mongers were actually shown with copies of our *Stormtrooper,* etc.! All through the damned thing, we all groaned and roared with agony and anger as the Jew misrepresentations got worse and worse. After the Kikes got the thing built up to a peak, they had the inevitable rotten-looking old Kike jump up in the court room showing his tattoos, believe it or not, and start screaming:
>
> > You'd better stop these Nazis now, before it's too late! My whole family was gassed in Germany and I know just how it started there. Oi!
>
> —and then this vile Hebrew saves the life of the vicious, snarling Nazi stormtrooper who is accused of murder![51]

Rockwell never pursued a lawsuit. He could see that the network's use of a neo-Nazi theme did not impugn his character in the least. If anything, he enjoyed the publicity of the casual association created by the program.

On September 28, Martin Luther King, Jr., was speaking at the closing session of the sixth annual national convention of the Southern

Christian Leadership Conference (SCLC) in Birmingham, Alabama. As he neared the end of his speech, King reminded the audience that Sammy Davis, Jr., would perform a fund-raising show for SCLC in New York. Six rows back ANP officer Roy James got up from his aisle seat, leaped onto the stage and threw a right cross that made a loud "pop" when it smashed into King's left cheek. A stillness fell over the crowd. King made no attempt at defense or retaliation. He staggered back, and James kept coming, slamming King with a left to the side of the head and two kidney punches to the back.

The audience surged collectively toward the stage. James, sensing the crowd coming to life, slowed his pace and struck King's trunk as hard as he could. King was knocked backward but turned to face James, dropping his hands in non-violence.[52] James was shocked by King's action and hesitated, giving Wyatt Walker and Ralph Abernathy the opportunity to restrain him. The audience broke into a song while King and his colleagues spoke with James. King returned to the podium and told the audience that James was a member of the American Nazi Party.[53]

James, who had arrived in Birmingham earlier in the week, claimed he had not known King was scheduled to speak in the city. On a whim, he had decided to go to the SCLC meeting. He was angered by King's reference to Sammy Davis, Jr., because Davis was married to a Caucasian actress, Mae Britt. After the incident, Judge Charles Brown held a fifteen-minute hearing. King testified that he had never seen James before and said, "In all conscience, I do not want to press charges against this man."

"That's impossible," Judge Brown yelled, describing James's act as an "uncalled for, unprovoked assault." James pled guilty to assault, and Brown sentenced him to thirty days in jail and a fine of twenty-five dollars. The mayor of Birmingham, Art Hanes, approached James after the sentencing, pointed a finger at him, and shouted, "I'm telling you right now, we don't want you to come back to Birmingham. We're not going to put up with rabble-rousers."[54] James sat stone-faced.

Rockwell wrote a letter to James congratulating him for his actions:

> While I must say that what you did was a violation of Party orders and policy, I can also tell you that your heroic deed has put new heart into hundreds of people who have called, written, and even come here to say how grateful they are that our side has struck a blow at last....
>
> I, personally, think of you many times every hour and fully appreciate the sacrifices you have made for your race and nation.[55]

The ANP published a "blow by blow" account (as James saw it) in the November issue of the *Rockwell Report* titled "How I Bashed Nigger King."

The American Nazi Party's Lt. Roy James, the Nazi who bashed Martin Luther King in Birmingham, Alabama, has just returned from serving a 30-day sentence for the "crime." Although what he did was actually a violation of Party regulations, which forbid law-breaking, the sensational nature of Roy's deed prompts us to give our readers a blow by blow account.

This is in response to hundreds of letters, wires, calls, and other inquiries from people all over the world. Here then is a blow by blow account of the bashing, in question and answer form, as Roy told it to us.

Q. HOW DID IT FEEL TO BASH MARTIN LUTHER KING?

A. Well, although I lost my temper, mentally it felt like striking out against everything that was evil and vile. Physically, it felt like smashing your fist through the crust of a pumpkin.

Q. WHAT BROUGHT YOU TO BIRMINGHAM?

A. I was passing through on Party business. I had some time to kill, heard King was in town, so I went out to hear the rat speak.

Q. DID YOU PLAN ON BEATING THE DAYLIGHTS OUT OF KING?

A. No. Actually, I violated Party regulations. It was a spontaneous reaction—the kind of thing you'd get if you saw a savage black ape, drunk on Jew booze, attacking a young White girl.

Q. WHAT DID KING SAY THAT SO ENRAGED YOU?

A. He began exalting Sammy Davis, Jr., and holding him up as an example of "Americanism." I couldn't stand it anymore.

Q. HOW FAR AWAY WERE YOU?

A. I was in the sixth row, but in a flash I was up on the stage, stalking the black beast.

Q. WHAT WAS THE LOOK ON KING'S FACE?

A. It was pure horror, like he knew the moment of truth had arrived, like he knew he was going to pay for all his race-mixing and communism.

Q. DID HE SAY ANYTHING?

A. There wasn't time. His white eyes opened wide and his lips seemed to be forming into the word "No," but then my fist was pummeling his face.

Q. WHAT WERE YOUR THOUGHTS AS YOU STRUCK THE FIRST BLOW?

A. Of administering justice to a vile communist race-mixing nigger agitator.

Q. DID HE BLEED MUCH?

A. Yes, quite a bit. The blood was gushing out all over the place. I think I busted a vein. His face was all cuts, and it began puffing.

Q. DID YOU KNOCK KING OUT?

A. Yes, cold. But several coons caught him as he fell.

Q. WHAT HAPPENED NEXT?

A. All the coons in the audience (there were 500 of them) began yelling and surging forward. I was really mad. I tore off my coat and shouted for them to come on, that I'd take on the whole mob.

Q. THEN WHAT HAPPENED?

A. They seemed stunned and stopped in their tracks. Then the coon ministers restored order. If they ever charged they would have torn me to pieces. But I was not afraid of it at the time.

Q. DID YOU SEE KING AGAIN?

A. Yes. They tried to arrange to get a photo of him talking with me but I warned King to stay away from me.

Q. WHAT DID KING DO THEN?

A. He stayed away.

Q. WHY WERE YOU TRIED SO QUICKLY?

A. The coons and Jews wanted to hush the whole thing up. I pled guilty so it would not look like I was trying to deny it. After the trial they took King to the hospital.

Q. HOW WERE YOU TREATED IN JAIL?

A. Like a conquering hero. All the White prisoners wanted to shake my hand. The guards all congratulated me and gave me cigarettes and candy. I don't smoke so I gave the cigarettes to White prisoners.

Q. WERE THERE ANY CLOSE SHAVES WITH NEGRO PRISONERS?

A. Well, the jail was segregated, but one time, through a mix-up, I ended up in the coon section at chow time. They all stopped eating and stared at me. You could hear a pin drop. I knew if I showed fear I was a goner. So I defiantly stomped up to the coon dishing out chow and demanded a heaping portion.

Q. WHAT HAPPENED NEXT?

A. He seemed awed. But he gave me the heaping portion. The other coons were all stunned. I ate and left when the gate opened.

Q. DID NSRP [National STATES RIGHTS PARTY] PICKET KING AT ALL?

A. No. I guess they were home thinking up more lies about us.

Q. WHAT WERE YOUR THOUGHTS THAT FIRST NIGHT IN JAIL AFTER THE TRIAL?

A. I felt good and proud all over. You do, you know, when you belong to the greatest fighting outfit in the world.[56]

Rockwell traveled to Northfield, Minnesota, on October 9 to give a speech at exclusive Carleton College. His invitation had been tendered by a student group called Challenge. The topic was titled "Nazism: The Only Real Alternative to Communism." John McAuliff, a Challenge board member, explained that Rockwell had been invited because "he represents ideas that twenty years ago produced the most terrible war machine in Western history. These are ideas that students should come up against—from a partisan source—to appreciate their impact upon history."[57]

More than eleven hundred students packed Skinner Memorial Chapel to hear Rockwell give his first unopposed speech. He explained the makeup of a National Socialist:

Every National Socialist believes in idealism. Believes in something that is worth more than his own, one single human life. He's willing to die for something. . . . If you're a fanatic, you'll produce something great, you'll create. Creativity is fanaticism. Every creative genius has had to be a fanatic. We are ideological and idealistic fanatics, just like the communists. . . . In between the Nazis and the communists is the great mass of non-fanatics. The TV watchers and the comic book readers.[58]

He explained the four phases of the party's accession to power and its objectives when it attained power—including legal disenfranchisement and removal of blacks to Africa. When asked what would legally constitute a black, he said, "I would say anybody that's only say, got a thirty-second Negro blood, perhaps this could be overlooked. . . . We certainly don't want to work injustices." When a reporter asked about his own ethnic background, Rockwell, in cocky reply, snapped, "If you're looking for coons in my background there aren't any in the wood pile as far as I know." In the speech and in the press conference that followed he detailed many of his beliefs:

The country:

Our patriotism, our spiritual life is dead. Our young people don't seem to have any aim or purposes, nothing to live for, except booze, TV, cars, and running around. They don't have any aim in life.

About Kennedy's being a "crypto-communist":

I think a crypto-communist is a man who disguises his communist beliefs under a liberal flag.... He's disguising the effort to win the world for communism.

About homosexuality:

I am against homosexuality in any form at all, I think it's degeneracy. No animal except man is degenerate enough to be a homosexual. I think this is horrible.

About materialistic selfishness:

I think materialistic selfishness is one of the plagues of our democracy. There's no spiritual value in our people anymore because they've become too selfish and materialist.

About hypocrisy:

Those who shout the loudest that they are for brotherhood and love of the Negro people...do not mix with the Negro people on a social level and they certainly don't send their children to Negro schools. And I think this is the ultimate and the most disgusting kind of hypocrisy.

About the Black Muslims:

He's [Elijah Muhammad] a black supremacist and I'm a white supremacist, that doesn't necessarily mean we gotta kill each other.

About the use of "Nazi":

If I dropped the term Nazi, you wouldn't be here and I wouldn't be here. Nobody would be interested....The term Nazi is the closest possible description to our philosophy, but it also serves a very good purpose in agitation business.[59]

The audience was one of the most courteous and respectful he would ever address. There was no heckling, no catcalls, no booing; they even gave a round of applause at the conclusion of the speech—a night-and-day difference from his San Diego State College appearance the previous spring.

On October 12, Bernie Davids led four ANP troopers to Philadelphia to protest communist Gus Hall's appearance at the Adelphia Hotel. Earlier in the week, Seth Ryan went to federal court in Philadelphia asking for a writ of mandamus ordering the police department to uphold their right to picket. The writ was denied on a technicality, but the hearing generated publicity by TV, radio, and newspapers. On the day of the scheduled picket the city called out 150 policemen in riot gear to hold a mob of two thousand at bay. The Nazis drove up in a car with Kentucky plates, but Frank Rizzo's police were looking for a car with Virginia plates. The Nazis drove right up to the intersection near the hotel and jumped out with signs reading:

Karl Marx Was a Crackpot
J. E. Hoover Was Right
Communism Is Treason
Go Home Gus Hall

Police were eventually overwhelmed by the mob, and vicious fighting broke out. The Nazis were hustled into a paddy wagon, which the mob attempted to overturn. Police were swinging nightsticks left and right, striking heads, trying to subdue the mob. The five Nazis were arrested and charged with inciting a riot, disorderly conduct, and breach of peace; their bail was set at $2,500 each. Bernard Davids, Robert Sharp, Bernard Cook, Paul Uhrig, and Ed Kester would languish in Moyamensing Prison for four months before their case was brought to trial.[60]

Rockwell saw the Philadelphia situation as an opportunity to exploit the same federal laws that were permitting integration in the South: a perfect opportunity "to avenge Ole Miss." The University of Mississippi in Oxford had erupted in violence after federal courts ruled that African American James Meredith could attend classes there. Hundreds of U.S. marshals had been sent to escort Meredith to the campus to register as the school's first black student. The massive rioting that took place on the campus had been quelled with the aid of three thousand soldiers and federalized National Guardsmen. Since the ANP writ had been denied on a technicality, Rockwell believed a properly constructed writ would be approved and thereby mandate police, if not federal, enforcement of the ANP's right to peaceful protest:

We can smash the filthy Jew terrorists with the same weapons they have used against white Christians—in Mississippi and elsewhere. . . . We can beat the daylights out of the Jews with the law. The Jews have chosen to make their stand in Philadelphia as the white gentiles did in Mississippi.

Rockwell had grand visions:

> Down the main street of Philadelphia marching legions of armed para-
> troopers prod the hate-crazed mob with steel bayonets. In the center of
> this marching armada, proudly walks a single white American.... The
> lone white, Christian picket marches up and down behind the wall of
> federal marshals and army bayonets, carrying high a sign, "Communism
> and race-mixing are Jewish."

Rockwell asked his supporters for "real" money to avenge Mississippi.
The money never arrived. The party was unable to raise the $2,500 bail
for any of the troopers jailed in Philadelphia.

In England, Colin Jordan, leader of the National Socialist Movement,
was also having legal troubles. Jordan had been convicted of violating
the Public Order Act, "organizing a unit in such a manner that reasonable apprehension was aroused that the unit might be used as a strong
arm force in promoting a political cause."[61] Jordan was brought before
the judge; the packed courtroom fell silent as he turned to speak:

> Nothing will stop us! As long as I live or as long as my opponents allow
> me to do so, I shall fight for what I believe to be right for my race and
> nation. I am guilty of being anti-Jewish because I love my country and
> hate what the Jews have done to it.[62]

Cheers broke out among his supporters in the courtroom. Jordan
was sentenced to ten months in prison, his deputy John Tyndall to six
months, and section leaders Roland Kerr-Ritchie and Dennis Pirie to
three months. One of Jordan's associates declared that the British Nazis
"will take orders from George Lincoln Rockwell, leader of the United
States' National Socialists." Rockwell thus assumed full control and
leadership of the World Union of National Socialists.

The ANP was now directing the World Union of National Socialists
(WUNS), the Fighting American Nationalists (FAN), the White Youth
Corps (WYC), and the Committee to Organize Opposition to Negroes
(COONS). COONS was an ad hoc, internal, front group whose purpose
was to obtain signatures on petitions urging anti-black legislation. The
party used COONS to picket in the District of Columbia against black
activism. Since there was a strong press blackout against the party, front
groups were used to gain publicity.

On October 22, President Kennedy proclaimed a naval quarantine of Cuba after learning that the Soviets were installing medium-range ballistic missiles on Cuban soil. The Soviets were attempting to install clandestinely a massive nuclear strike force that would give them not only military superiority but political leverage of international magnitude. Kennedy publicly warned the Soviets that any attack from Cuban bases would mean U.S. retaliation against the USSR itself. For six days, people around the world braced themselves for a nuclear exchange between the world's two superpowers.

Rockwell believed the Cuban Missile Crisis was a contrived hoax to swing the 1962 congressional elections to the Democrats. Rockwell wrote, "Bases...take months to build! Everybody in America, except our President knew about the missiles for at least three months....The Cuban missile bases were not camouflaged at all. In fact any photo-interpreter can testify that they were obviously set up as ostentatiously as possible with the specific intention of providing 'evidence' of missile bases."

He lamented the outcome: "Precisely as we predicted, all the John Birch Society candidates in the election are whipped....All signs before the Cuban 'crisis' pointed to their victory! What need of a John Birch Society to fight the reds, when our own President has proven himself as the 'fearless fighter' and 'leader' who can whip the devil himself, old Mr. K[hrushchev]."[63]

The next month Rockwell and Gary Smith embarked on a five-thousand-mile tour of the country in a 1953 Cadillac, arranging meetings among supporters and encouraging the formation of headquarters units. There were donations to be solicited and favors to pay back. On their way through Texas they stopped in Houston, where Rockwell telephoned a supporter named Alan Welch, a COBOL computer programmer working on IBM mainframes.

Welch had grown up in east Texas as a political conservative and avid supporter of Robert Taft. In his teens, he became a Revolutionary War buff and fell in love with the Constitution and the idea of liberty. He said that having been raised in the South, he had "an ingrained feeling" about blacks: he didn't hate them, but felt that the white and black races should have their own destinies, separate from each other without rancor or hostility. He knew very little about National Socialism or Adolf Hitler; his only knowledge of Jews was that they owned many department stores and that some people said they were stingy.

In 1960, Welch was working at his first computer-related job in downtown Houston. At lunchtime he made a habit of walking along Texas Avenue. One day he had spied a *Police Gazette* magazine with a huge picture on the front page of "America's Would-be Nazi": the picture was of George Lincoln Rockwell. After reading the article he sent a letter to Arlington. Rockwell responded with a packet of information, and the two men continued to exchange letters over the next two years.

Welch was a bit shocked when Rockwell and Gary Smith telephoned that they were in Houston and wanted to meet him. Welch chauffeured the two men around Houston, showing them the sights, including the zoo, where Welch learned that Rockwell had a tender, respectful regard for animals. The image and the man were completely dichotomous. The media portrayed Rockwell as a ferocious Nazi—Welch saw an exceedingly kind, intelligent man with a sense of humor.

When the tour was over, Welch took the men to his apartment to rest before they left for California. He felt Rockwell and Smith were sizing him up, studying him. When Rockwell and Smith departed, two Houston detectives came to Welch's apartment to see what sort of person Welch was, whether he was a troublemaker or not. The next week Welch was fired from his job. With no job, no money saved, and no prospects, he called the Arlington headquarters; when word of Welch's situation reached Rockwell, he invited Welch to come to Arlington and work for the party. Welch sold his belongings and boarded a Greyhound bus. When he arrived at headquarters he met all his "heroes": Roy James, Karl Allen, Ralph Forbes, Gary Smith, Brent Bell. They set up a cot for him in the basement of the barracks. He happily curled up next to the old oil-burning furnace on that, the first night of his career as a National Socialist.[64]

The party achieved some minor gains during 1962. The FAN unit in Chicago became a full-fledged ANP unit and acquired a headquarters building. The Chicago and West Coast units were in crucial locations for agitating and protesting in the upcoming years of civil unrest.

The establishment of WUNS was another building block set in place for the resurgence of National Socialism. Although a paper organization, WUNS enabled Nazi cells around the world to align themselves with an international organization. Several cells were established around the world. Each unit had total autonomy; it was free to engage in activities that suited its interests.

On one occasion Rockwell attempted to meet with the leaders of an Argentine Nazi group called Tacuara. Tacuara was composed of young men rumored to have the support of extremely conservative and influential members of the Argentine police and armed forces. The Argentine government turned down his request because his presence was "undesirable, as he might promote activities contrary to the feelings of the people of the Argentine republic."[65]

Although the ADL and the Jewish War Veterans continued to sabotage Rockwell's appearances and promote a press blackout of his activities, preventing even wider exposure of his views via television, radio, and college appearances, overall it had been a banner year for ANP publicity. Rockwell received tremendous amounts of media attention for his appearances. The fisticuffs at San Diego State had made syndicated columns around the country. His speech in front of Elijah Muhammad's Black Muslims had made the front page in the Chicago newspapers and had given credence to a Nation of Islam/ANP relationship. The trip to England had provided international exposure for his movement, while Roy James's assault of Martin Luther King had warmed the hearts of racists all over the country. Rockwell had big plans for the future. Earlier in the year, he had explained his political aspirations in a magazine article: "I'm going to become the Governor of Virginia...by 1966 or 1968....We'll be electing Congressmen and Senators from all over America. There are two admitted Birchites sitting in the house right now....With all the support I'm getting, I should be able to run for President in 1972."[66]

8

1963: MARCH ON WASHINGTON

The swastika is the symbol of Aryans, white conquerors. . . .
The Jews confronting the swastika and Nazis become
raging maniacs and I take advantage of that.
— Rockwell, 1963 interview

Rockwell's American Nazi Party was not, of course, the first right-wing extremist organization in the United States. The Ku Klux Klan, for example, had a massive following in the 1920s—nearly four million. The Klan persecuted Catholics, Jews, foreigners, and communists but ultimately went bankrupt after a federal suit for income tax delinquency. It revived in the 1960s as the civil rights movement gathered momentum and the federal government mandated state compliance with the new laws.

Nor was it even the first pro-Nazi group. The German-American Bund had had thousands of members in the 1930s, under the leadership of Fritz Kuhn. Unlike Rockwell's Nazis, many of Kuhn's people were German-Americans or foreign nationals drawn to the Bund for social and cultural reasons. Many had experienced scorn and prejudice from their fellow citizens in World War I and simply wanted to associate with other Germans. The Bund was neither financed nor directed by the Third Reich. Hitler didn't want it perceived as a German attempt to mobilize a fifth column in the United States. Although the Bund stressed its independence from the German government, it did have its stamp of approval.[1]

In 1963, the right wing was on the rise in the United States. George Wallace was sworn in as governor of Alabama, pledging to fight for "segregation now, segregation tomorrow, and segregation forever." In June, Wallace defied presidential orders to allow two black students into the University of Alabama. President Kennedy had to federalize the Alabama National Guard to enforce the school's desegregation. The next day, Medgar Evers, the field secretary of the NAACP and civil rights leader in Jackson, Mississippi, was shot in the back and killed by Byron de la Beckwith. James Meredith, the first black student at the University of Mississippi, announced his intention to withdraw after three hundred students met him in the cafeteria screaming "Go home, you nigger!"[2]

In late January, Rockwell and Roy James traveled to Chicago to give a speech at Northwestern University and straighten out some personnel problems at the Chicago headquarters. The speech at Northwestern was canceled at the last moment by school officials who felt "no good purpose would be served." Rockwell gave Roy James command of the Chicago unit and reassigned Chicago leader Matt Koehl to Arlington as the national organizer. James was ready to leave the party; transferring him to Chicago was a last-ditch effort to retain his service, and Koehl's military-style discipline of his volunteer force was decimating the Chicago unit.

The city of Chicago had cited numerous building code violations against the ANP building, at 2124 Damen Street. Rockwell believed the citations had been trumped up to pressure the owner of the building into evicting the ANP; he conducted legal research into them. He phoned local supporters to solicit donations for repairs, but very little could be done. The building was in a terrible state of disrepair, and the owner refused to bring the property up to code. Rockwell put out the word that the continued existence of the Chicago headquarters was in jeopardy unless additional funds were received; on May 13, 1963, the city's building department obtained a court order to close the ANP's first-floor assembly hall. Party leaders voluntarily abandoned their ramshackle second-floor living quarters.

Roy James went right to work. Martin Luther King was in Chicago, giving a speech at Orchestra Hall. As King looked out into the audience, he was startled to see James sitting near the front, with five other Nazis. The sight of James brought back memories of Birmingham four months earlier, when James had come up onto the stage and punched him. King delivered his speech with no apparent nervousness, but he was wondering if this would be his final talk.[3] The speech ended without incident, and he proceeded to the reception line. He watched nervously as James and his companions approached, then beckoned a policeman to intercede.

"You're the one who attacked me," King cried out at James, robbing him of the initiative. The Nazis quietly withdrew from the room. King was visibly upset and frightened by the encounter.[4]

John Patler's American National Party published its fourth and final issue of *Kill!* magazine in February with the headline: "The American National Party Is Dissolved." The American National Party had lasted just over one year, never gaining more than a handful of followers. *Kill!* magazine had been simply an outlet in which Patler and Burros could trumpet their own exploits and attack other right-wingers, including Rockwell, for hypocrisy. Patler had a change of heart and went to great lengths to make amends with Rockwell. He devoted the entire final issue to the theme "Rockwell Was Right." This "patching up" was his first step in returning to the ANP.

Dan Burros and Patler now had a falling-out, when Burros decided to watch a football game on television rather than picket Eleanor Roosevelt's funeral in November 1962. Patler marched alone with a sign reading "Ship her smelly corpse back to Moscow." He was arrested and sentenced to ninety days in jail; Burros remained in New York, where his destiny awaited.

Rockwell gave a speech at the University of Virginia on February 14. Attired in business suits, Rockwell and three stormtroopers took the stage before a packed house of 1,200 people in Cabell Hall. He drew frequent laughs during his presentation, and a roar when he reminded the audience that he was delivering a "philosophical lecture." He called for stronger national leadership and a new era of "neo-barbarians": "You can't live like beatniks and peace-creeps."[5] He told the audience that the objective of the American Nazi Party was to unite white people. There were no incidents of violence.

Back in Arlington, Rockwell granted an interview to a college student, Mary Blake French, for a story in the *Virginia Gazette.* When she arrived at headquarters she was escorted to the barracks for the interview.[6] It appeared to her that Rockwell did not take himself or the movement seriously; his attitude was "lighter" than most "legitimate" politicians. He explained the party platform:

[Membership] There are three classes of members: stormtroopers, who are willing to lay their lives on the line, associate members, numbering roughly 1,500, subscribers and supporters—people who are friendly to the cause, numbering about 12,000.

[Funds] We require a lot of money but we have damn little. We get it from the little people. We have people doing work all over the place for nothing. Sales of literature help. No Jewish program could exist for one day on what we exist on.

[Anti-Semitism in the Soviet Union] It's the religious Jews that are being discriminated against. Russia is being run by communist Jews. It is as a religion that the Jews are being discriminated against in Russia.

[Good Jews vs. Bad Jews] About 80 percent of adult Jews are accomplices in race-mixing. We have no objection to Jews—just dishonest Jews. So many Jews are race-mixers that we deal with all Jews as if they were. If I find out different I apologize. I'm not after Jews because they are Jewish. I'm after most Jews because they are trying to push communism and race-mixing. I hate Alger Hiss just as much. I have no more respect for him than for the race-mixing Jews.

[Civil Rights Bill] I'm absolutely scared about the whole thing. Either the bill will be passed and it will lead to unprecedented catastrophe or it will not be passed and result in immediate catastrophe. Most Americans who don't live around niggers think that they will help the nigger but when it comes to the point where it affects them directly, you'll find mass uprising.

[Black Muslims] They recognize the truth—that neither group [white or black] likes the other. The only two groups that recognize the truth are the Nazis and the Black Muslims.

[CORE/NAACP] They're run by Jews, all their money comes from Jews, and they're a plain naked communist front.

[Negroes] The whites will never live with the blacks. You can't force it. The blacks will start the revolution and the whites will finish it. The blacks are biologically inferior human beings—based on their record in civilization.

[Right-Wing Groups] They're cowards.... At least the liberals will fight. Most of the right wing are despicable and cowardly.... The Ku Klux Klan is anti-Catholic and I won't tolerate that kind of religious bigotry.

[Zionists] Zionists openly say they are not loyal to America but they are loyal to Israel. That's treason to this country.[7]

[Why "Nazi" Party] When I began there was no right wing. Nobody paid any attention to a rightist. If I said I was a Nazi I'd get attention. It appeals to the young too. I repel cowards. The swastika is the symbol of Aryans, white conquerors.... The Jews confronting the swastika and Nazis become raging maniacs and I take advantage of that.[8]

Amid bomb threats and disorderly conduct arrests, Rockwell spoke at the University of Chicago on February 25. Sixty policemen were on hand as Rockwell delivered a two-hour speech in Breasted Hall to a mere 275 students. University officials had changed the location of the speech from the spacious Mandel Hall to the smaller Breasted Hall after receiving a bomb threat. Police arrested two men outside the hall for disorderly conduct when they shouted insults at Rockwell. One of the men, Bolek Stelzer, told reporters his grandparents, parents, brother, and sister had been killed by Nazis in the Bergen-Belsen concentration camp. The other man, Benjamin Baran, claimed his parents, three brothers, and sister had also died at Bergen-Belsen.

Wearing a blue suit, Rockwell stepped to the podium and told the small audience he had gone broke as a conservative, had become a radical, and now spoke all over the United States. At one point in the talk Rockwell became so animated that he accidentally kicked his attaché case to the floor in front of the audience, spilling papers, news clippings, and a corn cob pipe. Students snickered and laughed as Rockwell tried to portray himself as "just a boy from Illinois . . . trying to save my country and the white race."[9] More than eight hundred protesters braved freezing cold weather outside the hall in order to heckle Rockwell when he left the auditorium, but police foiled them by whisking him out through an adjacent building.

The next day, in Miami, ANP member David Petersen hopped out of a car with a placard to picket the Seybold Building, home of the local ADL office. His red-lettered placard read:

Communism Is Jewish
ADL Is Jews' Secret Police

He told reporters, "I'm here to protest Jew tyranny. I belong to the American Nazi Party. We're going to open a party headquarters here in a few weeks." After he had marched up and down the sidewalk for only three minutes, an angry crowd converged around him. "All right," said a man in the crowd, "if the cops aren't going to do anything, we can.

Let's get him!"[10] At that point several plainclothes police officers attempted to place Petersen under protective custody. When Petersen struggled, four uniformed officers grabbed his limbs and carried him off to a waiting paddy wagon. He was not arrested.

A few weeks later Petersen and John McClure were assaulted by three men in front of the Fontainebleau Hotel in Miami, where they were protesting a fifteenth-anniversary celebration of Israeli independence. The VIP event, attended by former United Nations Secretary-General Trygve Lie and Senator Hubert H. Humphrey, was to launch the 1963 campaign to raise $75 million for Israel through the sale of bonds. Both Nazis wore khaki uniforms and swastika armbands, and they carried placards:

Buy U.S. Bonds, Not Israeli Bonds
Death to Traitors
Zionism Is Treason
Forget Israel, Free Cuba

They marched a few minutes before a dozen cabdrivers, a hotel valet, and a former president of the Jewish War Veterans attacked them. The fighting was vicious, but police broke it up and made no arrests. The next day Miami City Attorney Robert Zahner ordered a raid on the Nazi headquarters, located in the Pacific Building. He had a copy of the lease issued to ANP Deputy District Commander John McClure allowing McClure to operate a political office in his name. Zahner attempted to get the lease canceled.

McClure, sporting a cut above one eye and packing a .45-caliber pistol, told reporters he had no intention of being forced out of Miami. But a few weeks later McClure was arrested for carrying the pistol. McClure claimed his arrest was entrapment, that the Florida constitution gave him the right to bear arms.

Judge Ben Willard told him, "You may have a legal point, but I don't agree with you, and unfortunately for you, I am the judge."[11] Willard permitted McClure to leave the county; if McClure ever appeared in Dade County again, Judge Willard promised to impose a jail sentence. In effect, McClure had been thrown out of Dade County.

The next week Claude Pepper, a Democrat from Florida, introduced a bill in the House of Representatives to outlaw the display of the Nazi swastika and the Soviet hammer and sickle. The Miami Beach Council also banned all swastika and hammer and sickle signs, by a vote of 4–2. Opposition to the ordinance was led by Howard Dixon, attorney for the Florida Civil Liberties Union, and Harold Kramer, executive director of the Miami office of the American Jewish Congress—who stated, "However well intended this ordinance is meant, it will not harm the Nazis and may very well aid them."[12]

Meanwhile, the party was concerned about the five troopers sitting in Moyamensing Prison in Philadelphia. All attempts either to make bail or bring the case to trial had failed. City officials refused to accept any writs or legal documents from ANP representatives. Karl Allen went to federal court in Philadelphia for a writ of habeas corpus to force the city officials to accept their legal requests and commence proceedings against the accused. Having no choice, the city accepted the documents but refused to grant a speedy trial. The party retaliated by printing a leaflet for mass distribution entitled "Must Men Starve to Get Justice in Philadelphia?" The tract, printed on a superimposed image of the Liberty Bell, alleged gross infringement of civil liberties by the city, equating it to political persecution. Allen led a contingent of Nazis to Philadelphia and plastered the city with the leaflets.

It worked. The ACLU contacted the ANP and arranged for a gentile lawyer to represent the five jailed Nazis. A top-shelf lawyer brought the case to trial and made short work of the district attorney. The jury came back in twelve minutes with a "not guilty" verdict. After more than four months of imprisonment for demonstrating against Gus Hall, the Nazis were set free. Davids remembered the confinement as having been extremely trying during the Cuban Missile Crisis; they had not wanted to be sitting in jail when the nuclear weapons struck.[13]

After continual prodding by Floyd Fleming, Rockwell offered Karl Allen the position of deputy commander. Allen accepted on the condition that J. V. Morgan, the current deputy commander, was in agreement. Morgan had no problem with the change; Allen was a full-time officer, and he was not. Rockwell graciously bestowed a newly created title of "party adjutant" on Morgan, to rank directly under Karl Allen as the number-three man in the organization.

Allen's stature within the party had increased dramatically. He was so valued as the party administrator that Rockwell prohibited him from undertaking missions; he did not want Allen to spend time in jail. Allen was the man who got people out of jail; he was looked upon as the party "guardian." Although it pained him, Rockwell displayed total indifference toward jailed troopers; he felt powerless to help, since the party had no bail money "slush-fund." Allen took it upon himself to extract bail money from sympathizers.

There were other personnel changes as well that spring. Roy James was promoted to captain, and Alan Welch was awarded the Medal of Merit for six months' work keeping the party's financial records.

In early March, the party staged a publicity stunt in Lafayette Park in Washington, D.C. Stormtrooper Andrew Chappell was known among the other party members as a "beefsteak" Nazi: Nazi brown on the outside and "Red" on the inside. Chappell knew the *Communist Manifesto* forwards and backwards but like many of Hitler's stormtroopers had converted to National Socialism. Chappell was also an ex-convict, a man almost totally devoid of emotion; he could picket all day in cold, rainy weather and run long distances by the hour.[14] His stunt was to run one hundred laps around the park "for the white race." The party took photos of the event for the *Stormtrooper,* telling reporters the fifty-mile run was dedicated to the white race, to demonstrate the superiority of Nazis over liberals, Jews, and "peace creeps." It took seven hours and twenty-three minutes to complete.[15] Rockwell boasted that Chappell would soon be running from the ANP headquarters to Richmond (110 miles) with the party's application for a new corporate charter.

On April 20 the party celebrated Hitler's birthday with a rally outside the barracks. Rockwell flew in from Chicago in the late afternoon to host the event. There were speeches by Rockwell and Emory Burke (his friend and a right-wing leader from Montgomery), songs, and a giant swastika-decorated cake, and a few beers were consumed around a huge campfire. National Socialism was alive and well in Arlington, Virginia.

Soon after the Hitler celebration, John Patler arrived in Arlington, hat in hand, eager to rejoin the party. Rockwell had been secretly negotiating his return. He had worked out a way to bring Patler back, but he was worried that it might cause defections. Roger Foss, Seth Ryan, and Ralph Forbes were adamant about blocking Patler's return.

The men gathered for a meeting in which Patler admitted his previous errors and asked for a second chance. He confessed that his charges against Roger Foss for "viciously beating a fellow party member" had been false. Rockwell argued that Patler's courage and artistic ability outweighed his hot temper and clique-forming habits.

Rockwell persuaded the newer party officers, Karl Allen, Matt Koehl, and Alan Welch—men unfamiliar with Patler—to vote for his reinstatement.[16] A vote was taken, and Patler was accepted, but not without cost: Roger Foss, incensed by the readmission of a traitor, screamed at Rockwell, "Who's fucking who?" In the heat of anger, Foss accused Rockwell of treachery and demanded a court-martial, but Rockwell insisted he was immune from such charges.[17] Foss and Forbes resigned on the spot. Rockwell tried to persuade them to stay on, but it was no use.

In California, Leonard Holstein led four members of the Western Division–ANP on a picket of the fifteenth anniversary of Israeli independence celebration and fund-raiser at the Shrine Auditorium in Los Angeles. The Nazis wore steel helmets and carried placards with anti-Israel slogans. When a fight erupted between Nazis and Jews, the Nazis used the wooden placard handles to club the attackers. The fight lasted ten minutes; four Nazis, four Jews, and four policemen were injured. The ANP members were arraigned on charges of conspiracy and assault with deadly weapons and were held on $5,000 bond.

Rockwell seized the opportunity to replace Holstein with Ralph Forbes. Forbes jumped at the chance, quickly making arrangements to move his family west. Rockwell also tried to coax Foss back. He put out the word that Roger Foss, "one of the most able bodied and well-liked Nazis," had resigned in disagreement over Patler's return. He urged Foss to "put aside his personal animosities and return to the Cause he has served so well."[18] Foss would have none of it; by year's end he was making a living as a scuba diver in Honduras.

On May 2, 1963, Ralph Forbes held a press conference in Los Angeles to announce his transfer to the Western Division. He lamented Holstein's incarceration and predicted Holstein would receive the "Order of Adolf Hitler" medal for leading the demonstration against the Israeli bond drive. Rockwell arrived in Los Angeles on May 6 to attend Holstein's trial. He announced that Leonard Holstein was being removed as the leader of the Los Angeles unit because he was "too impulsive."[19]

In early May, Rockwell attended the trial of the fourteen Black Muslims accused of rioting outside Los Angeles Mosque No. 27 on April 27, 1962. During the melee, police had opened fire on the Muslims, killing one man and wounding six, paralyzing one man for life. Black Muslims were enraged by the shooting. The trial garnered major headlines in newspapers across the country, and Rockwell sensed an opportunity for publicity.

Rockwell entered the courthouse, greeted Muslim leaders, and offered his support. He turned to reporters:

> The Muslims are being persecuted just as the Nazis are being persecuted. They are dedicated to the same ideals as the Nazi Party—the separation of the black and white races—and we work together in many things. The fact is that most of the Negro people in this country are in complete agreement with the Muslims and their ideals just as most of the white people in this country are in agreement with the Nazis.

Rockwell predicted the fourteen Muslims would not get a fair trial, that they would be "railroaded for crimes they did not commit, just as my own boys are being railroaded over the trouble at the Israel rally." [20] On June 14, an all-white jury found eleven Muslims guilty.

Rockwell believed millions of blacks were fast becoming anti-Semitic due to the influence of the Nation of Islam. Unlike white anti-Semites, who Rockwell believed were either "bought off or terrified of a Jewish-press smear," blacks, who were already on the bottom of the economic rung, had nothing to lose by fighting the Jews. Rockwell wrote, "In every black ghetto in America, the owners of the roach and rat-infested tenements who gyp the Negro occupants out of relatively fantastic rents are Jews. The ruthless dealers in vice, who sell the Negro liquor, dope, gambling equipment, and other marks of Negro degradation are more Jews.... The Honorable Elijah Muhammad, Malcolm X and other Muslim leaders have been tirelessly blasting these Jew liars and exploiters all over America." [21]

On his return trip from the West Coast, Rockwell made a whistle-stop in Boulder, Colorado, to address an audience of three thousand students at the University of Colorado. The speech had been arranged only fourteen hours in advance by the student newspaper, the *Colorado Daily*, and the Associated Students of the University of Colorado. The *Colorado Daily* ran a large headline and picture of Rockwell on the front page, urging students to attend the speech in Mackey Auditorium by the "Enemy of Democracy."

When opposition groups learned of the forthcoming speech it was too late to mount any serious protest. The Young Socialist League was the only group to picket. Its placards read:

Remember Auschwitz

Stay Away

A few days after the speech the weekly *Intermountain Jewish News* ran a headline that read, "ADL Asks C.U. to Explain Rockwell Appearance before 3,000." The essence of the article was that Colorado University had not provided students with sufficient background information about Rockwell's intention to exterminate Jews and deport blacks. The next issue of the *Rockwell Report* reprinted the article and published an editorial by Rockwell:

> The students have been told by the Jews and liberals that it is their sacred duty to hear everybody and everything, even COMMUNISTS, and that it would destroy "academic freedom" to deprive communists of their "right" to spread their treason at every college in the land—as the reds are busy doing RIGHT NOW. Now suddenly, the students . . . are confronted with their liberal friends . . . snarling and demanding an "explanation" for granting "academic freedom" to ROCKWELL! Do the Jews consider the American college student too stupid and foolish to listen to me and evaluate my ideas—or lack of them? If so, then how come they do not squawk about the COMMUNIST speakers? Why no demand for "proper background" of the RED speakers?[22]

With the frequency of Rockwell's college appearances increasing, the ADL redefined its position on Rockwell:

> ADL shall not publicly oppose platform invitations extended by colleges and universities to such persons as Rockwell. ADL should, whenever possible, be certain that college and university groups considering such invitations are fully informed about Rockwell's previous history and record.[23]

Some members wanted to declare that the ADL considered the use of swastikas and Nazi uniforms in public demonstration to be outside the boundaries and protections of the First Amendment, but this was not adopted.

In Arlington, the party had eighteen full-time members living in either the headquarters or barracks. Daily activities for troopers included such physical training as weight lifting, pull-ups, and jogging, but their favorite activity was hitting a punching bag. The majority of the time was spent hanging around the barracks waiting for picketing assignments or distributing leaflets, or printing party publications. The best duty was accompanying the commander somewhere as his bodyguard, but the daily life of a live-in party member consisted mainly of boredom and grinding poverty. The buildings were in need of constant plumbing and electrical repairs, which the men had to perform themselves or do with-out. The water pump at the barracks was constantly breaking down, forcing troopers to ration their water usage. Each day someone from the barracks drove two miles to headquarters in a vehicle filled with water containers. Headquarters was on city water, so there was no pump to worry about, just the bother of filling containers every day. The party had no funds to hire a plumber to fix the dilapidated pump. Eventually J. V. Morgan found the necessary parts and repaired the pump himself.

A mishap caused a fire at headquarters that summer. Karl Allen, Bernie Davids, and Brent Bell were gluing on the covers of the second edition of Rockwell's autobiography. Someone left a hot plate turned on, and the fumes from the rubber cement ignited. A wastebasket caught fire, and then a wall. Gary Smith, the duty officer, ran across the street, with his .45-caliber on his hip, to telephone the fire department. Davids found the fire extinguisher, which someone had moved behind a door, and put the fire out before the firemen arrived. When they did, Rockwell was there to berate them for being so late.[24]

Food had not improved, either; troopers ate whatever they could afford or whatever was donated. The usual staples were canned hash, oatmeal, potatoes, chicken noodle soup, chicken backs, chicken neck soup, cornbread "johnny cake" with beans, day-old doughnuts, and macaroni. The best meal of the day was the thirty-five-cent bacon-and-eggs breakfast at a local diner.[25]

Rockwell's biggest weakness as a leader was his inability to place restrictions upon himself. Although he generally abstained from alco-hol, most every other facet of his life was unrestrained, especially the use of party funds. The party had no cash-flow control at all, no savings account, no slush fund for bail money, no food or utilities budget. Rockwell simply used the finances for whatever he wanted, whenever. When money was scarce, the party did without. Floyd Fleming was always pressing Rockwell for the rent on the headquarters property. He pleaded with Rockwell to let Karl Allen take control of party finances or at least to appoint someone as treasurer. The wiry sixty-year-old—who voiced praise for Father Coughlin (the Catholic priest silenced by the Church for attacking Jews and communists on his radio program in the 1930s)—would shout, rant, and rave, fling his arms in wild gestures and follow Rockwell from room to room. Fleming could not even insure the property because of the ANP occupancy. Rockwell would promise to pay something the next week, then lock himself in his room. Fleming was seldom paid.[26]

Once when a sympathizer from Tennessee stopped by the headquarters to see the commander, Allen telephoned Rockwell at the barracks and related the request, but Rockwell refused—he was "too busy." Allen made an excuse that Rockwell was "indisposed" and politely thanked the supporter for stopping by. Before leaving, the supporter handed Allen an envelope containing $1,800, a windfall for the party. Fleming, who was at headquarters at the time, demanded Allen hold back $600 to pay for 45 rpm records the party was having made. Allen agreed and gave Rockwell the balance. Rockwell was uneasy about Allen withholding money, but he sensed the odds were against him on the issue, since Fleming was involved: better to let Allen hold the $600 in reserve to keep Fleming happy than to make an issue of the matter and jeopardize his support.[27]

Intraparty rivalries developed between the men at headquarters and those in the barracks. The headquarters men stressed the "American" aspect of the American Nazi Party by placing George Washington's portrait to the right of the swastika, the place of honor, and wearing strictly khaki uniforms—no black leather allowed. Gary Smith joked that they were "as American as apple-strudel." The barracks clique emphasized the Germanic version of National Socialism: German uniforms, emblems, slogans, black leather, anything Teutonic. The "American" clique, who referred to themselves as "Spartans," upped the ante by tattooing swastikas on their left arms, just above the T-shirt sleeve so as not to be noticeable in public.[28]

Rockwell had succeeded in gathering a group of men with the same ideology into a unit—men who lived for the party and committed their total efforts to its success. The year 1963 was the high point for the ANP in terms of the quality of its manpower. Now able to shift the day-to-day operational responsibilities to officers, the party was beginning to transform itself from a club-like group into a business organization. Rockwell focused his energy on writing bombastic literature for the *Rockwell Report*, the *Stormtrooper*, and other propaganda. With the artistic talents of Patler and Brent Bell at his disposal, party literature developed a

Rockwell and his stormtroopers give the Nazi salute outside headquarters.

distinctive, lurid look, with eye-catching layouts and provocative head-lines. Rockwell spent long hours alone in his room, listening to the music of J. S. Bach and writing commentaries on the current events around the country.

Of the two official party publications, the *Rockwell Report* had been created as a pseudo-intellectual magazine for middle-class readers. The cover usually displayed a small head-and-shoulder photo of Rockwell wearing a suit, alongside an outrageous headline like "How Can Jew and Nigger-Loving Liberals Be So Stupid?" or "Martin Luther Coon—Black Puppet for Red Jews." In contrast was the *Stormtrooper,* a semimonthly, highly sensationalized booklet packed with photos, racist humor, cartoons, descriptions of violence, insults, and white power slogans, all designed to capture the attention of American philistines. It featured a section called "Combat Reports" that ran cropped photos of Nazi street action around the country. The "International Nazi" section gave updates on Colin Jordan, Bruno Ludtke, and other WUNS movements around the world. *Stormtrooper* typically featured a Nazi crossword puzzle,

"Brotherhood Beauts" (anecdotes about "coons" and "niggers"), and a feature story on a party officer, "Know Your Party Officer."

Street propaganda was created and printed to coincide with current events, like the "Goods on Goldwater," a listing of "facts" proving Goldwater was a phony from the left wing sent over to lead the opposition. Perhaps the vilest pamphlet ever created by the party was a booklet called "The Diary of Ann Fink." On the cover was a caricature of the cartoon character Alfred E. Neuman (of *Mad* magazine) instead of a girl's face. The sixteen pages contained photos of World War II concentration camp victims with "humorous" captions. One photo was of a male prisoner in striped pajamas, slumped against a barbed-wire concentration camp fence. The caption: "Man-o-Manischewitz, what a wine!" John Patler eventually suspended printing and distribution of this hate pamphlet; the party was "maturing," rising above the gutter appeal of the early literature.

Rockwell struggled to segregate his writings properly for the *Stormtrooper* and the *Rockwell Reports*. Some of his articles were short and pithy, others long and rambling. Even J. V. Morgan, who rarely commented on such things, pointed out the problems, including Rockwell's use of crude words and gutter slang. Many party members believed that gutter talk should not come from the leader of the organization, that a more intellectual approach would be more effective, but Rockwell continued to use bigot's language in literature and in public, to be "one of the boys."[29] He firmly believed that a successful propaganda machine had to focus its publications at both lower-class and middle-class society. Others believed that his vulgar methods, using the word "nigger" and berating Jews, were those either of a fool or an agent provocateur trying to ruin the movement. But Rockwell felt that elections and donations were not won with Ph.D.-level logic. Like Hitler, he needed to hit the gut-level, populist emotions of the lower class.

The *Stormtrooper* was purposely designed to be brutal and shocking, in order to force attention to it. He needed to instill in the "public mind" the image of his all-out hostility toward Jews and blacks, regardless of the cost in terms of pseudo-intellectual support. Simple propaganda, appealing to "Joe six-packs," was the only way to gain the sheer number of votes needed to sweep him into power. He would worry about the intellectual John Birch tea party types later.

Several party officers wanted to elevate the movement to a higher plane, to raise their version of National Socialism from the juvenile mentality of name-calling and crude words to the status of a respectable political organization, an organization based upon sound business practices, not a dictatorship. But all attempts and suggestions for reform were rebuked by Rockwell. Instead of dealing with intraparty concerns and pressing financial matters, he chose to ignore the issues and deflect the criticism. Dissension festered throughout the summer of 1963.

On June 14, 1963, a large procession of civil rights proponents assembled around the White House for a symbolic march to the Justice Department. The ANP, knowing far in advance about the event, had planned a disruptive counter-demonstration. It painted an entire oil-cloth, three feet wide and fifty feet long, with the slogan "WHITE MAN—FIGHT" proportionately spaced the length of the canvas. The men arrived at the White House and set up their counter-demonstration directly across from the civil rights protesters. The huge banner was lifted into the air on twelve-foot-long poles spaced every twelve feet. The massive banner could be seen and read three blocks away. The remaining troopers carried pickets:

Race-Mixing Stinks

Down with Race-Mixing

Separation Or Death!

They Don't Want Civil Rights; They Want Special Rights

As the civil rights procession assembled and marched down Pennsylvania Avenue toward the District Building, the ANP pickets fell in behind. When the parade arrived at the District Building, Nazis Karl Allen and Dave Petersen—dressed in gorilla costumes—jumped into the front of the civil rights marchers and they led them with a placard reading "Join Our March for Civil Rights." Many of the civil rights marchers were baffled by the appearance of the two "apes" and missed the mockery. The police were not baffled; they quickly arrested the two.[30]

On that same day, Rockwell sent a "cease and desist" letter to Gerald L. K. Smith in reaction to rumors that Smith was calling him a "traitor." This was part of the continuing saga of infighting and backstabbing that plagued the ANP:

I have an international organization and am winning more and more of the "patriots" who begin to see the sense of our fight. With the nigger revolution starting, as we have been predicting, and economic catastrophe around the corner, we will soon be OBVIOUS as the only hope of our Race and Nation. More and more worried Americans are quitting the useless "paper fight" of literature and talk and coming over to our street fight.

Instead of being grateful that a FORCE is arising at last to DO what you have been talking about for so long—and so well—you are now telling people we are "working for the Jews."

I am presently in a position to file suit in Los Angeles against your charges that I get "money from the Jews" but I do not want to do any such thing. The Jews love nothing better than to see us all fighting each other when we should be fighting THEM, the ENEMY. . . .

How about ACTING like a good Christian you so much like to talk about and write about? Good Christians don't bear false witness. Nor do they attack White Men who are hard pressed by the Jews, whom Christ called the very sons of the Devil.[31]

Rockwell's relationship with other political activists was two-dimensional. First, he would offer his "services" as a street fighter and encourage a "unified" front against the enemy. Then, after he had been rejected and all hope of cooperation had been dashed, he would go on the attack. He followed this pattern with Buckley, Hargis, Fields, Smith, Welch, even the Black Muslims. He understood why the ANP was anathema to other right-wingers: association with his group would subject others to harsh criticism and smears by Jews. But he believed right-wingers were being smeared by Jews without his help. Why should they not join together in their fight? The John Birch Society (JBS) was a good example. The JBS leader, Robert Welch, was not a favorite of the Jewish community, but he was not a proven anti-Semite, either. Rockwell believed Welch was being smeared in the press by hostile Jews, but Welch was careful to blame negative press on "Comsymps"—communist sympathizers. Welch wrote in the JBS *Bulletin*, "So long as I am heading The John Birch Society, any of its members who knowingly collaborates in any way with Rockwell or any of his crew will immediately be dropped from our membership."[32]

In early July, Martin Luther King announced plans for a nonviolent civil rights protest on August 28, to be called the "March on Washington for Jobs and Freedom." The march would amalgamate the "big five" civil rights groups—SCLC, CORE, the NAACP, the Urban

League, and the Student Non-Violent Coordinating Committee (SNCC)—in an effort to persuade Congress to support the civil rights legislation President Kennedy had put before it. When the groups promised that no violence or civil disobedience would occur, President Kennedy publicly endorsed the rally.

Rockwell announced his plan for a counter-protest against the March on Washington. The counter-demonstration would be the focus of the ANP for the remainder of the summer. Rockwell planned a whirlwind speaking tour through Virginia to drum up support and solicit volunteers for a "counter march." He gave the press an itinerary listing seventy-three towns and cities he would visit between July 11 and August 25, 1963. He mailed a letter to officials in each of the cities:

> I am making an effort to do everything legal to stop the Communist-Negro Revolution now going on in our Country.... We are almost all veterans who are simply sick and tired of communism and race-mixing—and the gang of Jews who are trying to force these filthy things down America's throat.
>
> Please let me reassure you that we wish only to SPEAK to our fellow Virginians, not to cause any trouble. There will be no uniforms or insignia of any kind, and we will obey the letter of the law, plus all reasonable requests of your department.[33]

In addition to the counter-march, Rockwell decided to conduct the first American Nazi Party national convention the same weekend. A party convention had been slated for Chicago in November, but the Chicago unit was without a building. The extra party members would also bolster the procession of men in the counter-march. The party also scheduled a three-day leadership training course at headquarters for the Labor Day weekend, August 30 through September 1, immediately following the national convention. The party urged all members to attend, especially those planning any serious political activity in their communities. Party officers would teach every aspect of National Socialism as well as ANP picketing and agitation techniques; the registration fee was five dollars.[34]

Rockwell's speaking tour of Virginia received better-than-expected results. He drew big crowds, and much press coverage, and people actually cheered—which amazed him.[35] There was a huge crowd in Culpeper, and in Norfolk he filled the civic auditorium.

However, on July 19, trouble erupted in Emporia, Virginia. The mayor and police chief purportedly told Rockwell that "niggers" constituted 65 percent of the population and that the city fathers would have a serious problem if he spoke. Rockwell sympathized with them but insisted on speaking; otherwise it would set a precedent that could be exploited by other cities wanting to avoid trouble. He offered to speak in some inaccessible location, like the basement of the police station or even the garbage dump, so he could truthfully say he had spoken in Emporia, but city officials declined his proposition.

Ever persistent, Rockwell, Roy James, and "Chaplain" Don Wiley drove to a parking lot adjacent to the municipal building, where they were joined by Deputy Commander Karl Allen and stormtrooper Chris Bailey. As Rockwell prepared to deliver his speech, Police Chief Herman Weaver and five Emporia police officers hurried out of police headquarters to confront Rockwell. Chief Weaver asked, "Are you still going to try and make that speech?"

"Yes, sir," replied Rockwell. "I intend to make an attempt so that you will have enough to stop me for legal purposes." Chief Weaver dug into his jacket pocket and waved a warrant in front of Rockwell. "I already have enough to stop you," he said. The warrant charged Rockwell, Wiley, and James with "unlawfully and feloniously inciting the white population of Virginia to acts of violence and war against the colored population." Their bond was set at $1,500 each. The next day, July 20, Karl Allen brought a bondsman from Suffolk to bail the men out. Rockwell was released on bond, but Wiley and James remained in jail for lack of $360 bail money.

Immediately after Rockwell's release from jail, Karl Allen and Chris Bailey drove him eighty miles to Norfolk for an important appearance. Twenty troopers had worked the entire day in wretched heat to distribute thousands of advance circulars and posters promoting the event. Rockwell stepped to the podium and delivered a compelling speech, drawing applause and cheers from the audience. These were the moments he craved, chances to display his charisma and present his ideas to hundreds of people.[36]

On July 23, Rockwell filed a detailed civil rights complaint against the city officials of Emporia, Virginia, for "conspiring to deprive him the right to speak from public property." As with Rockwell's previous complaints of this nature, the Justice Department failed to act on his

A cartoon by John Patler about "the black revolution."

behalf, but Emporia in late November dropped all charges against Rockwell, Wiley, and James due to "insufficient evidence to prove that they had committed the acts for which they were charged."[37]

The ANP's application for a Washington parade permit for August 28 was refused by the Metropolitan Police Department, with the explanation that "such a permit would only be issued to 'Negro rights' demonstrators," who would be given preferred treatment that day. ANP captain Alan Welch told reporters the ANP would parade in the District of Columbia irrespective of whether they were granted a permit. Rockwell stated, "The white man is not going to be run off the streets of the nation's capital on the 28th day of August, 1963. Ten thousand angry white men cannot be stopped from marching."[38]

The Peace Action Center (PAC), a pacifist group composed of various religious groups from around the country, filed a protest in support of the American Nazi Party's request to parade in a counter-demonstration to the civil rights march. Florence Carpenter, acting director of the PAC, wrote a letter to Metropolitan Police Chief Robert Murray:

> It has been said of many demonstrations for unpopular causes that they constituted incitement to violence, but it is the right to demonstrate for an unpopular cause which is most in need of protection. Denial of Rockwell's request to parade peacefully is to open the door to denial of such a request to anyone, including the civil rights movement.[39]

The Nazis were spreading the word that the "March" had been scheduled for a Wednesday so "four million Negroes on relief could be recruited by the "Jews and Communist agitators" to threaten Congress while the white man was at work. Rockwell believed communists were

Author's collection

Nazis protest Bayard Rustin, lead organizer of Martin Luther King's 1963 March on Washington.

orchestrating King's every move. (In fact, King was privately warned by President John F. Kennedy to break formal ties with two of his closest advisors, Stanley Levinson and Jack O'Dell, who Kennedy believed were communists. Kennedy feared that a public revelation of their backgrounds would harm not only King and his movement but also Kennedy's civil rights bill.)[40] The ANP also tried to draw attention to the deputy director of the march, Bayard Rustin. Rustin's checkered past included time in prison for draft evasion, conviction for homosexual activity, and membership in the Young Communist League.[41]

As the day of the massive civil rights march approached, Rockwell boasted that he had received twelve thousand pledges from supporters, though he predicted that only two thousand would actually show up for the march. Anything near two thousand would have been an enormous victory for the party, in terms of visible representation at the event and financially as well. Donations would swell the party treasury, further increasing the scope of its activities. Privately, Rockwell was concerned that the counter-march would be a failure and an embarrassment to his movement. He tried to get King's permit canceled by appealing to several powerful segregationist congressmen (John McMillan, Watkins Abbott, Charles Bennett, and Joe Waggoner), but his letters and visits went for naught. They wanted nothing to do with him. In desperation, he wrote Alabama governor George Wallace and

Mississippi governor Ross Barnett, pleading with them to speak at his counter-demonstration. Neither responded.

In California, Ralph Forbes led a small disruption campaign against CORE. As actor Marlon Brando led a small procession of CORE marchers, Forbes jumped into his way with a sign reading "Marlon Brando Is a Nigger-Loving Creep."[42] Brando made no reaction to the sign. He would get the last word with his Emmy-winning portrayal of Rockwell in the television adaptation of Alex Haley's book *Roots*.

The California Superior Court issued an injunction prohibiting the city of Redondo Beach from stopping the ANP from holding public meetings. The ANP had been represented by the ACLU in this groundbreaking ruling, which opened the way for rallies on public property. Ralph Forbes told the press that counter-demonstrations against the civil rights march of August 28 in Washington would be held in Burbank, Hermosa Beach, and Los Alamitos; they would be attended by not only ANP members but the Fighting American Nationalists, the Keep America White Committee, and the Nazi Party Women's Auxiliary.

August 28, 1963, finally arrived. Troopers and supporters awoke at 5:00 A.M. to the reveille bell outside the barracks. Eighty sympathizers from all over the country had arrived that week from Washington State, Oregon, California, Florida, Louisiana, Colorado, Michigan, Illinois, Wisconsin, Minnesota, even Canada. Rockwell gathered the men for a final briefing in an atmosphere charged with excitement and anticipation. No one spoke; all eyes were glued to the commander as he instructed them to keep iron discipline and to be 100 percent legal. Some of the men were seated, others were standing, sipping coffee. No one knew what the day's events would bring. Many wondered if open race war would erupt, ending in death and maiming in their ranks. Would the federal government arrest them if fights broke out, or simply shoot them in panic?

J. V. Morgan gave vehicle assignments, and the men proceeded to the cars. The silent caravan departed down the long barracks driveway, leaving behind a skeleton crew of four men to guard the site. The procession made its way out of Virginia and across the Potomac just as the first rays of sunshine burst over the horizon to the east. The cars pulled up at the Washington Monument grounds and waited for Rockwell to disembark; as a matter of symbolism, the first foot to touch the grounds that historic day was to be George Lincoln Rockwell's. The men followed their commander to the monument, and the cars returned to Virginia.

The Nazis wore civilian clothing. The police had prohibited uniforms, insignias, or any type of symbols. They could not demonstrate, give speeches, sing, or perform in any way; in short, they could do nothing but "stand fast as the lone protectors of the white race." Police escorted them away from the Washington Monument to a section of the Mall between Fourteenth and Fifteenth Streets, where they remained under heavy guard. Two hundred military police kept them virtually out of sight by forming a perimeter around them fifty yards on a side. The militia also prevented any latecomers from joining them: no one was allowed to come through the armed perimeter. The ANP members could only speculate how many sympathizers were turned away.[43]

At 11:15, as hundreds of thousands of civil rights marchers swarmed over the Mall, Karl Allen, ignoring two police warnings, made a short speech before being arrested: "We are here to protest by as peaceful means as possible the occupation of Washington by forces deadly to the welfare of our country."[44] Allen's was the first of only three arrests that entire day.

Rockwell assembled the "Valiant 87" supporters in single file and led the procession across the Fourteenth Street bridge into Arlington. Asked about the failure of his extensive speaking tour through Virginia to attract sympathizers, Rockwell said, "The right wing, I'm sorry to say, is the most cowardly thing in the world. The Negroes are brave enough to go out and be arrested by the thousands. But the white man is a coward at this point. I'm ashamed of my race."[45]

In the District jail, Allen was surprised to find himself the only prisoner; all others had been temporarily removed to Reston, Virginia, in anticipation of mass arrests. Allen's lawyer had him released in fifteen minutes on a $300 bond. Rockwell was amazed to see Allen back at headquarters so soon.[46] Allen was convicted of making a speech without a permit and sentenced to ten days in jail or a fifty-dollar fine; he appealed to the District Court of Appeals and won a reversal, because the government had failed to prove that his speech had been given on the Washington Monument grounds.

In California, the Western Division was having a tough time of its own. Ralph Forbes had arrived in Burbank to give a speech in McCambridge Park. Flanked by two stormtroopers, Forbes walked

Author's collection

Rockwell and his counter-demonstrators during the 1963
March on Washington.

stiffly to the center of the park, where he was immediately encircled by
reporters, television cameramen, and agitators. He stood quietly amidst
the throng, his hands clenched at his sides. When the angry crowd
began to quiet down, Forbes grabbed a clipboard that held his text and
began to speak: "Fellow Americans."

The crowd, almost in one voice, began shouting, drowning him out.
There were angry shouts and threats from the crowd, but a contingent
of thirty policemen discouraged the agitators from becoming violent.
Instead, the hecklers derided Forbes, yelling "Why don't you go home?"
and "Nazi rat, you're as bad as communists." Forbes raised his voice
and tried speaking again: "The civil rights march today in Washington
is a communist-led march." The crowd booed and catcalled throughout
his talk, but Forbes shouted through the turmoil. He ended his short
speech, calmly picked up his briefcase, and returned to his car, looking
straight ahead, his jaw tightly clenched.

To most observers, the March on Washington was a tremendous success for the civil rights movement and the Kennedy administration.
There was no violence, King made his famous "I have a dream" speech,
and Congress witnessed firsthand the widespread support for the movement: more than 25 percent of the marchers were white. But the march
also marked the end of the nonviolent civil rights movement. Many of
the country's poor blacks who listened to the event on radio or watched

it on television believed that Malcolm X had the answer, that blacks should claim equal rights "by any means necessary." Malcolm X called the march the "Farce on Washington."[47] The SNCC hierarchy of James Forman and John Lewis now decided that the march had been a "sham perpetrated by the liberal-labor coalition of Rustin, Roy Wilkins [of the NAACP], Walter Reuther [United Auto Workers], King, and the Catholic and Protestant hierarchies." Forman believed that the Kennedy administration had used "white liberals and sell-out Toms to create a base of support for the civil rights bill . . . to stifle manifestations of serious dissent and to take the steam out of the black anger . . . to psych-off local protest and make people feel they had accomplished something, changed something, somehow—when, in fact, nothing had been changed."[48]

On September 15, just eighteen days after the march, a bomb exploded during Sunday school at a Baptist church in Birmingham, Alabama, killing four young black girls and injuring twenty other children. Much of the nation expressed outrage and grief over the cowardly act. Many blacks around the country stepped up the tempo and degree of their protests, inching farther and father away from the doctrine of nonviolence.[49]

When the post-march euphoria subsided, party operations returned to normal. The party mascot, Gas Chamber, got loose from headquarters and was killed by a truck. The party memorialized the veteran of many pickets with a bit of party-style humor:

> The Party dog, "Gas Chamber" apparently got fed up with the chow around here. He has been running around Northern Virginia siring dozens of little "Hate-dogs" unbeknownst to the owners. . . . In the process, he found a liberal family where they kept feeding him a lot better than we could. . . . The result is a Jew-loving, race-mixing liberal family which now has a nigger-hating, anti-communist "hate-dog" named "Gas Chamber."

ANP "chaplain" Don Wiley was dishonorably discharged from the party after being arrested for stealing an ambulance. Wiley had stolen the ambulance, turned on the flashing lights, and raced at ninety miles an hour down the streets of Arlington before being caught. Rockwell had utilized Wiley—a former Bible college student from Kentucky—as a "chaplain" to open each counter-march rally with a blessing. Rockwell felt the "blessing" would appeal to the underlying religious instincts of the populace in Virginia and set a stately tone for each rally. After Wiley was arrested by police, the party discovered a briefcase full of ANP documents

Wiley had been going to release as well as a diary of his "spy" activities.[50]

World-renowned photographer Richard Avedon, traveled from New York to conduct a photo shoot of Rockwell at the barracks on October 8. Avedon and a female assistant spent several hours shooting pictures of Rockwell around the barracks. Avedon wanted Rockwell's picture for a book of American personalities to be called *Nothing Personal*.[51] Rockwell's notoriety was increasing.

On October 10, the ANP executed a carefully planned disruption of a discussion panel titled "Civil Rights and Civil Liberties" at American University in the District of Columbia. The action was the brainchild of Brent Bell and Seth Ryan. Their plan was to infiltrate Leonard Gymnasium with every available ANP member—except Rockwell, because he would be recognized—to disrupt both the speakers and the audience. A rumor swept the campus earlier in the day that Rockwell and stormtroopers would attend the meeting; a large contingent of muscular athletes waited outside the auditorium for his arrival.

The first speaker—the ANP's primary target—was Aubrey Williams. Williams was president of the Southern Conference Education Fund, which Rockwell believed was a front group for communist activity in the South. Williams and King had sat side by side at the Highlander Folk School in Monteagle, Tennessee, in the 1950s. Rockwell and many others believed Highlander was nothing more than a communist training school for insurrection, because Rosa Parks, John Lewis, Marion Barry, and many others in the civil rights movement had trained there.

Williams stepped up to the podium to begin his talk, but each time Trooper Gary Smith started coughing. Audience members pointed out the agitator to the two District policemen walking up the aisle. Police asked Smith to leave with them, but he refused. They tried to seize Smith, but he pushed them back, ran for the stage, and attempted to climb up, all the while shouting, "This is a communist meeting!" A policeman caught up with him and whacked him across the skull with a nightstick so hard that a "crack" could be heard at the rear of the gym. He was dragged from the gym, taken to District General Hospital for eight stitches in his scalp, and charged with disorderly conduct.

When the crowd settled down, Williams started speaking once again, but now a different Nazi heckler disrupted him. He finally gave up when a third heckler broke his concentration. The hecklers were removed from the gymnasium, shouting "Heil Hitler!" and other Nazi slogans, but the ANP had succeeded in driving Williams off the stage.

The next speaker, Frank Wilkinson, executive director of the National Committee to Abolish the House Un-American Activities Committee, took the stage with a sigh of relief that the Nazis had been removed. He had said only a few words when a blond girl in a red dress rushed onto the stage and attacked him with clawing fingernails, shouting, "You race-mixing swine!" A policeman restrained her with a full-Nelson wrestling grip and pulled her from the stage. When Wilkinson resumed talking, Alan Welch disrupted him. Welch was grabbed by four men and dragged from the building. The men turned him upside down, preparing to pile-drive his skull into the sidewalk, but a District policeman appeared at the critical moment and put a halt to their effort. There were many more Nazis seated in the audience, and they

Nazi sympathizer Eva Hoff attacks civil rights activist Frank Wilkinson at American University.

too began heckling Wilkinson until removed by police. All told, fourteen hecklers were arrested for disorderly conduct, including Brent Bell's girlfriend, Eva Hoff.[52]

In mid-October President Kennedy extended "a hundred thousand welcomes" to the Irish prime minister, Sean Lemass, in a ceremony on the south lawn of the White House. Afterward, Kennedy and Lemass led a parade through downtown Washington. Crowds along the way applauded as the men passed by in the open limousine. When they reached the District Building, Washington's city hall, Rockwell and seven stormtroopers appeared in full uniform, waving placards. One placard read, "The great Joe McCarthy was Irish" and another "85% of our Nazis are Irish." Rockwell had managed the stunt by assembling his men ten minutes before the presidential limousine's arrival.[53]

In California, on October 24, the trial for the five Western Division–ANP members arrested for inciting a riot outside the Shrine Auditorium went into a fourth day. The trial proceeded smoothly until a mental patient, Solomon Levine, in a locked security room adjacent to the courtroom, screamed through the little wire window, "I'll kill those Nazis! You better convict them. Those Nazi rats!" Judge Herbert Walker ordered bailiffs to move Levine back to his jail cell and told the jury to retire until order was restored, but as Levine was being led from the area he yelled at the jury that they had to find the Nazis guilty. Judge Walker was forced to declare a mistrial. He ordered the Nazis to return to court the next day for a new jury selection.[54] On November 11, the five ANP members were found guilty of assault and conspiracy.

Martin Luther King entered Danville, Virginia, on November 15 to conduct "Operation Dialogue," an effort to confront Danville whites with the immorality of racism. Danville had no black elected officials, very few black registered voters, and few black clerks in the downtown business establishments. If the operation was unsuccessful, King threatened, there would be demonstration marches, boycotts, and pray-ins. Danville had experienced several flashes of racial violence that summer. In June, firemen had turned their hoses on demonstrators while nightstick-wielding policemen and deputized garbage men clubbed protesters.

Rockwell believed Virginia was his exclusive domain. He told the press he would set up a command post in Danville to drive King from Virginia. The plan consisted of countering King's every move with a like attack: "If King speaks, I will make a counter-speech. If he holds a rally, I will hold a counter-rally. If he leads demonstrations, I will lead a counter-demonstration. And if King doesn't return to Danville, we'll pull out and go about our business."[55] Rockwell gave Karl Allen and David Petersen the mission of going there to stir things up. Allen was anxious for some street action; he was feeling frustrated and cooped up at headquarters.

On November 15, King was preparing to speak at the High Street Baptist Church in Danville. He was introduced by Reverend L. W. Chase as "the living symbol of man's struggle." Before Chase was finished, Karl Allen, dressed in street clothes, approached the pulpit and told Chase he wanted to speak. Burly SNCC guards, dressed in overalls to present the image of "field hands," grabbed Allen and prepared to drag him out, but Chase and King persuaded them to listen to Allen.

Allen mounted the stage and looked out at the sea of black faces in the church pews. He identified himself as deputy commander of the ANP and said, "I'm here to tell you I am [as] opposed to this man [pointing to King] as any man can be." He noted that Chase had referred to King as a "symbol"; who, he asked, had made him a symbol? He pointed to the CBS television cameras and said that King had been made a symbol "by the same gadget you see here in the middle of this holy temple." He told the audience King had been selected as their leader because he had been trained at the Highlander Folk School and that "Jews in New York are backing King's organization."[56] When he had finished, local police escorted Allen and Petersen to the bus depot.[57]

Rockwell wanted to assign a few men to stay with Karl Allen in Danville and establish a semipermanent outpost to harass King's operation in southern Virginia, but the plan never got off the ground. On Friday, November 22, television anchorman Walter Cronkite disrupted the soap opera *As the World Turns* to inform the nation that President Kennedy had been shot in Dallas. For the next three days, every moment of the agony and anguish of the president's family was displayed in living rooms and dens across the nation. The entire population of the United States tried to make sense of the brutal event.

Some political theorists believe the game of politics is played between the left and the right, above the heads of the middle. Extremists viewed the killing of the president with detachment, as something similar to losing a piece on a chessboard. Malcolm X called the killing a case of "the chickens coming home to roost." Rockwell, however, sensed the anger of the American public toward political extremism and decided to lower his profile and "circle his wagons" for the time being. It was possible that the right wing—possibly his American Nazis—would be blamed for the killing. He directed Allen to abandon the "mission to Danville" and return to Arlington. King also withdrew.

In the fall of 1963, the National Students Association (NSA) of Hofstra University in Hempstead, New York, sent letters of inquiry to fifty potential speakers, including Rockwell. Someone leaked the information to a *Newsday* reporter, who exposed Rockwell's invitation. Robert Van Lierop, president of the Student Council, was called to the dean's office to see the dozens of protest letters sent in by the public. Later in the day the Student Council voted on a motion requesting a student referendum. It was defeated 2–10; a motion to withdraw Rockwell's invitation was defeated by a narrow margin, 5–6. The Student Council held its ground, determined to exercise the rights granted it by the university. Its members drafted a letter to Rockwell outlining the dates and conditions of the speech.

On December 1, Rockwell's acceptance letter was received by Van Lierop. School administrators washed their hands of the event by passing a resolution condemning Rockwell while defending the right of Hofstra students to examine issues, questions, persons, or problems with which they were concerned. By mid-December more than 100 letters and 150 phone calls had been received by the university regarding the invitation, most in protest of it.

On December 8, Karl Allen, deputy commander of the American Nazi Party, resigned. Allen had reached his limit of tolerance for Rockwell's style of leadership. Allen envisioned a self-perpetuating party that had bylaws and a functioning, not figurative, board of directors that could sustain the party through years of personnel changes. Such a board could create policies and procedures for running the organization while attracting funding on a greater scale than could the shock methods Rockwell employed. Allen felt Rockwell's abilities as a writer, speaker, and leader were undermined by his failure to organize the party on a businesslike basis. Without bylaws and operating procedures the party would never be more than a cult of personality. The present hand-to-mouth existence was simply too trying; a nation cannot be kept at war for too long—its morale wears down. The monastic existence required of ANP members had no upside, no compensation: bad food, no pay, no liquor, few women, getting beaten and arrested, having to listen to idiots spout off and see leeches hang around doing nothing.

Allen wrote an official statement of resignation, specifying that he was leaving for personal reasons. He explained to the men under him at headquarters—Harry Blair, his protégé Robert Lloyd, Gary Smith, David Petersen—that he was leaving for personal reasons and they should stay on and give their loyalty to the next deputy commander. Rockwell posted Allen's resignation on the bulletin board at the barracks. He emphasized to the men that Allen was leaving on good terms and could be reinstated any time he desired.

Allen's resignation had caught Rockwell by surprise. The festivities of the summer's national convention and counter-march on Washington had been the high point of the year. Now he had lost his best-educated, highest-ranking officer, and there was grumbling from the other men. To make matters worse the Internal Revenue Service now filed a tax lien against him for $264.

Not willing to accept the fact that his men were dissatisfied with his leadership, Rockwell chose to believe they were suffering from a lack of ego gratification. Since he was always in the spotlight, always the center of attention, he surmised, his men needed some "building up" in recognition of their dedication, loyalty, and valor. He dedicated the December issue of the *Rockwell Report* to his men, with the large, bold headline "A TIME FOR HEROES!" Each man's photo was included, with a brief recital of his completed missions and decorations. But it was too late.

By the end of December a mass exodus of party members was under way. Long-standing members, loyal to Rockwell for years, decided the party had stagnated under Rockwell's self-serving leadership. By Christmas, twenty of twenty-six active members quit the party, including long-time supporters Karl Allen, J. V. Morgan, Seth Ryan, Brent Bell, Roy James, and Bernie Davids.

Fleming and some others approached Karl Allen, now living in the District of Columbia, about specifying to Rockwell the terms and conditions under which they would return. The men held several meetings and drew up a list of grievances emphasizing Rockwell's inability to "refrain from inserting his personality and judgment into every minute part of the Party's operation."

> All efforts to remedy this situation voluntarily and by verbal agreements have failed. The Commander seems to feel that the abdication of the slightest prerogative or privilege, even to men of proven ability and faithfulness, is a direct threat to his leadership of the Party. To the contrary, it is the only way the Party will ever grow and become more than a one-man show. . . .
>
> We did not come to advance a man but a cause; not to save an image, but a nation; not to preserve a memory, but a race. It is for this and this alone that we have suffered, starved, and froze [*sic*]. It was not for George Washington that the men at Valley Forge endured, but for the United States of America. Nor was it for George Lincoln Rockwell alone that we have so long suffered and fought, but for our race and nation.[58]

The paper demanded several operational changes. Rockwell was to relinquish administration of finances to a qualified man of his choosing; form a Promotion Board to oversee the just and proper advancement of men within the organization; adopt a hierarchical structure with appropriate ranks and structure, and also a bill of rights allowing party members to petition grievances and specifying procedures to be followed.

The most controversial and divisive clause was the demand for alteration of the corporate bylaws on the appointment of the board of directors. They requested a four-fifths vote, rather than appointment or removal at Rockwell's discretion. This was the ultimate stumbling block for Rockwell; he believed a "four-fifths clause" would enable outside forces to take control of the party through the board. Rather than negotiate this clause with the disaffected men, Rockwell ignored the document and closed the men out. Thereafter he would refer to the mass exodus as "the mutiny."

It had been another tumultuous year for the American Nazi Party. Rockwell had started 1963 with several prestigious university appearances while continuing to develop techniques of street agitation and enemy disruption. The ANP had lost its Chicago facility because of building code violations, but the men of that unit remained active.

There had been more major personnel shifts. John Patler was reinstated, Roger Foss quit, and Ralph Forbes was transferred to the leadership position of the Western Division to keep him from breaking ranks. By the end of the year, Rockwell's dictatorial leadership had caused massive desertions.

But Kennedy's assassination fueled Rockwell's outlook that the country was being attacked by communists both internally and externally. The greater the chaos, the more likely the common man would vote a "strong man" into power to restore law and order.

9

1964: AMERICA FOR WHITES

Two bullets should not make a saint out of a
bad president.
— Rockwell, Hofstra University, 1964

The party began 1964 reeling from the "mutiny" of 1963. Not only was the manpower shortage restricting party activity, but donations from sympathizers had dropped off too. Faced with the task of rebuilding the officer corps of the party, Rockwell promoted his remaining men. Alan Welch took over as the deputy commander, Matt Koehl became the national secretary, Robert Lloyd became the security officer, and John Patler took over editorial duties of the *Stormtrooper*. The "mutiny" presented a golden opportunity for Patler to regain his stature and exert his personality within the party.

On February 3, 1964, Rockwell drove to Hempstead, New York, to speak at Hofstra University. Two hundred law enforcement officers awaited his arrival, stationed along a special motor route that had been cleared of students. On the Friday before his speech someone had raised a homemade Nazi flag atop the school's flagpole; the administration was not amused. Tickets for the speech were issued to students by row and seat number on a "first come, first served" basis; tickets had been shuffled prior to distribution to avoid concentrated demonstrations and prevent students from obtaining blocks of seats. Each student was required to show a valid Hofstra identification card and sign a seating register for the seat number assigned by his or her ticket. Every person entering the Playhouse Theater was searched, and all packages were checked at the door.

Morton Blender

The promotion ceremony for Robert Lloyd.

The New York City Police Department bomb squad and the Nassau County Police Department were consulted about the most effective way of dealing with bombs and bomb threats. As a result, the Playhouse was sealed off from the rest of the Hofstra campus at 8:30 A.M. the morning of Rockwell's visit, and the building was thoroughly searched. Three false bomb threats were received.

Rockwell arrived at the rear of Weller Hall, where he was met by two Nazis, student leader Robert Van Lierop, and university security guards, who escorted him through the rear entrance of the Playhouse into the rehearsal room for a press conference. He stunned newsmen with a comment on the recent Kennedy assassination: "Two bullets should not make a saint out of a bad president." [1]

Robert Van Lierop introduced Rockwell to the vast student audience: "This is an attempt to bring into proper focus, before our student body, the issues of contemporary America so that we might decide for ourselves the moral value of certain views and certain organizations." [2] A hush fell over the 1,650 people in the audience as Rockwell stepped to the podium, where the Hofstra seal was conspicuously missing. "This is probably one of the most liberal, leftist and Jewish universities in the country.

I've got to give you credit for inviting me here."[3] He predicted that his visit to Hofstra would cost him an arrest. (It almost did. The New York City Police Department's Bureau of Special Services had a warrant for his arrest, valid anywhere in the state of New York. Nassau County police officials were ready to enforce it at Hofstra if the warrant was turned over to them, but New York City authorities decided to save the warrant for themselves to prevent Rockwell from speaking in New York City.)

One of the topics he discussed was "biological hierarchy." He told the audience that humans belong to the animal world and that science has no differentiation between the animal world and humans, simply a "biological hierarchy" based on intelligence. Different breeds of humans are categorized into races, and some races are more intelligent and therefore superior on the hierarchy tree. Van Lierop moderated the question-and-answer session after the speech. Among the questions was a hypothetical situation: If he [Rockwell] were shot and rushed to an all-Negro hospital, would he accept transfusion of Negro blood? Rockwell replied, "I'm one hundred percent realist. I'd accept blood from Sammy Davis, Jr."[4] The audience roared with laughter.

On February 19, Rockwell traveled to Colorado State University in Fort Collins, where he spoke to a crowd of a thousand CSU students and faculty on the topic "National Socialism: The only alternative to Communism." He digressed from the topic immediately, choosing instead to discuss racial differences: "Some dogs are smarter and better than other dogs. There are better breeds in all animals. Yet there is a religion that says that all apes on two legs are equal and there is nothing scientific to prove this."[5] He bemoaned the inaccessibility of television broadcasting—"Freedom of speech is only for the rich." A Rockwell government would allow any person who petitioned to have an hour on television, "rather than only the millionaires."[6]

He commented that party membership was going down but the quality was going up. Nazism gave his young men something to believe in: "Most of my guys are ex–juvenile delinquents and I'm proud of it." He berated Governor George Wallace of Alabama and Governor Ross Barnett of Mississippi for not "stick[ing] up for what they believe. I would go to jail any time for my beliefs."

During the question-and-answer session after the speech, he explained his solution to the tense racial situation:

Give the Negroes their money and let them establish their own state in Africa. . . . Colored people are still eating each other in some parts of the world. I do not hate the colored man. Personally I admire Malcolm X. I simply say the black man hasn't had biological time to mature like the white man has. . . .

People who are pushing for civil rights are using the Negroes. Every single Negro organization except the Black Muslims is led by New York Jews. . . . Jews are a race. You can recognize them. Some people say they are only members of a religion but you don't grow a long nose by going to church. . . .

All I want to do is exterminate communist traitors. Whether they're Jews or not is immaterial to me, but I believe a large proportion will be Jews. . . .

Sure I'm a hate-monger. I think we ought to hate bad things. I'm not the least bit ashamed to hate communists and traitors. . . . Our president wouldn't have been shot had we been in power because Mr. Oswald would have been buried. Oswald should have been shot the day he left for Russia.[7]

Rockwell departed Colorado for the University of Kansas in Lawrence. Before the speech he gave a forty-five-minute press conference:

My major activity, I'm an agitator. The right wing has got plenty of talkers and plenty of writers and pamphlet passers and rally holders. But there's almost nobody else in the right wing who'll go out amongst the enemy and get out there in the street where you get arrested and where you get attacked. And this, I think, is our function.

Asked about the party's effect on the general public, Rockwell said:

It has exactly the psychological effect I want. I am not rich like Robert Welch, I have no way at all of reaching the masses of people, except my own wits. And I have used my wits and the Nazi-dramatic approach to be able to become known well enough to begin to reach people. . . . I have built an image in the American public mind. Whereas I don't think there's any image of a guy like Robert Welch or any of these other people. They're just like cream puffs, they don't amount to anything.

A reporter asked if his party was reaching the masses:

Not yet . . . when there is economic catastrophe, which I think is ahead. As along as people have two cars and electric toilet seats warmed up for them . . . as long as people have that kind of luxury, they're not going to do anything politically radical. When the communists have precipitated race and economic chaos, then, like the hungry wolf, they'll be ready to do something.

He discussed Nazi Party protests and agitation methods:

We're a political guerrilla warfare band. And wherever the enemy is doing something that I feel we can effectively attack, I try to concentrate my maximum strength at their weakest point. When Gus Hall is preaching race mixing, for instance, I feel this is an excellent thing for me to picket because this drives into the public mind that race mixing is a communist project....

The March on Washington, I think the great vast majority of white Christian ordinary people in this country despised that March. All the rest of the right wing chickened out except us. We were there on the spot...and the fact that we were there built up a reservoir of good will in the hearts of the American people towards us....Anytime liberals start telling me how great Negroes are and how we ought to mix, I like to ask them if they would care to accompany me on a walk through the nation's capital some evening. And if they came out at all on the other side, they'd be hate-mongers like me, if they made it.

Asked about "the inferiority of Negroes and Jews":

The way you decide is on their record. On the record, the Negroes are an inferior race. The product of the Negro people is cannibalism, chaos, savagery, and what you see in Central Africa where pure Negroes have not been disturbed for thousands of years. And their record is absolutely abominable, they're a bunch of inferior...close to animals. On the other hand the Jewish race has a record not of great production, but certainly of great agitation. They're a brilliant race. I think perhaps on the basis of pure brain power they are superior. I think the Jewish race lacks moral principle.

About the Black Muslims:

I used to have the highest opinion of them. I still have the highest opinion of Malcolm X....Muhammad, I think is becoming senile and his sons...have taken over, and I think they are communistic. They are following the communist line right down the alley....

I think what's happening is Malcolm X is going to split off with the nationalistic right-wing nigger movement and I will back him 100 percent, I admire him. I tell you, I admire him more than I admire most Americans, white Americans. He's a great man, I think he's better than most white men....

Asked to explain the photographs of World War II concentration camps where Hitler killed six million Jews, he responded:

In 1957 I sat down and wrote the most atrocious bunch of lies I could concoct about Nazi medical experiments. I just made them up....I sent it into *Sir!* magazine, a Jewish magazine in New York and I sold it for 75 dollars.[8] And they printed it with a whole bunch of photographs that I had never seen in my life before, which they said were photographs of the events in my story... by Master Sergeant Lew Cor, which is Rockwell spelled backwards.

His definition of a Jew:

Well, there's several different kinds of Jews. One of them is Marilyn Monroe, that's a pretty nice type of Jew. And there's also Jews who are religious Jews; Zionists, people who are devoutly religious and believe in God. And then there are people like the Rosenbergs, Greenglass, Weinbaum, Moscowitz, Harry Gold.... These people are atheists. It's quite impossible to be a communist and to be a religious Jew.... Therefore, if a person like the Rosenbergs or Soblem are Jews and they are recognized and admitted as Jews, then they're atheists; Jews are not a religion, Jews are a breed of people that you can recognize.[9]

When the press conference concluded he was escorted to the Kansas Student Union Ballroom, where 1,900 people awaited his speech. Like most college audiences, the Kansans expected to see a shrieking uniformed Nazi spewing diatribes; they were disappointed to see a conservatively dressed, well-mannered speaker. Instead of preaching Nazi doctrine Rockwell spoke about the party's daring street actions, protests, and the new censorship going on in the country. He also appealed for the students to become fanatics:

Those of you who will accomplish anything... will be fanatics on their subjects, whatever it is. They'll drive and they'll push until they excel. The extremist will win. Those of you who are moderates and just dabble a little bit in your subject, you'll disappear and be brushed aside. The age of extremism has not passed, the world has always been an age of extremism. The successful people are the extremists, the unsuccessful people are the moderates.[10]

Rockwell delivered what he considered to be his best college speech to date. Afterwards the student sponsors treated him to a sumptuous dinner before taking him to a motel for the night. A school newspaper editorial summed up his appearance:

There is no doubt about it, he [Rockwell] knows how to get the most out of a speaking situation. A random sample of student opinion afterward found no one really very much against Rockwell, but no one very much for him either.... The seed of doubt was planted. The idea that maybe he isn't so bad after all began to grow. His purpose was accomplished. He whitewashed a bad image.[11]

The University of Kansas appearance established several ideological benchmarks. The tenets expressed are worth looking at, for they reveal much about Rockwell's worldview. He admits his primary purpose is agitation: to go out in the streets, where other right-wingers are afraid to go, and fight "the enemy." He dismisses Robert Welch—"Rabbit Welch," as he called him—as ineffectual because the John Birch Society will not take its message to the street in public demonstrations where direct face-to-face confrontations with "communists" occur. With the exception of the Ku Klux Klan, Rockwell lumps all other right-wingers into this mold as well.

He defines his use of Nazism as a "dramatic approach" for being noticed by the masses. He describes his party as a "guerrilla warfare band" with a strategy of focusing its limited resources on the enemy's weakest point. It is crucial for the ANP to counter-picket, if not attack, leftist events so the public will think of the ANP as the only opposition to the counter-culture demonstrations that are then becoming more and more pervasive around the country. He is realistic enough to recognize that the public will never accept his methodology as long as people live lives of comfort, but he is convinced that racial discord and economic catastrophe will eventually destroy the country. The masses will then look for a leader with his type of solutions to restore law and order.

Rockwell bases his racial theories on his own sweeping and undocumented generalizations of "performance." Blacks, judged by their record of achievement in Africa, are inferior humans. According to Rockwell, they had never invented a wheel or a sail or domesticated animals. He is quick to point out instances of savagery and cannibalism of central Africa and to say that most slaves were children sold to Arab traders by their parents.

He credits the "Jewish race" for its brilliance, calling Jews "superior" but lacking in moral principle. He also tries to differentiate religious Jews from the atheist Jews who "were communists." By breaking Jews into two camps, he can generalize and use the crimes of the Rosenbergs, of Greenglass and Weinbaum (convicted of espionage for passing atomic secrets to the Soviets), as examples of the "typical activities" of atheist Jews. Holocaust denial was also addressed (though Rockwell would change his view on this in later years). Once again, he used one example *(Sir!)* to imply sweeping generalizations on an entire issue.

The next day, Rockwell traveled to Billings, Montana, to deliver a speech at Rocky Mountain State College. There had been a mix-up in arrangements, and he arrived just minutes before his scheduled talk. Student sponsors picked him up at the airport and rushed him to the auditorium. The speech itself was uneventful, but the follow-up question-and-answer session was a ruckus. First a Chinese professor charged down the aisle screaming in Mandarin. Then a black in the balcony shouted for Rockwell's deportation to Germany.

From the auditorium he was taken to the student union building for a regular supper with the students. While he was eating, a beautiful blond coed at a nearby table was approached and touched by an African-American male in a "most familiar and improper manner." Flaunting their race mixing in his face as they were, as a guest he had little choice but to look away in disgust. He was astounded that the student body, which he expected to be mainly white and conservative, was full of "Negroes, Jews with beards and beanies, Chinamen . . . the most nigger-loving group of students I have ever encountered at any except the big city schools."[12]

He participated in an informal seminar with staff of the RMC student newspaper, the *Echo*. He was astounded to find the students were "not half so much communists as nigger-lovers." They were passionate about black equality: "They are totally and blindly convinced that Negroes are simply white people with dark skin." He was convinced that the only way to educate, "to unbrainwash these blind and foolish kids . . . to let them experience nigger equality at first hand," was to send them on a trip through the middle of Washington, D.C., on a summer night.[13]

On February 26, a play entitled *The Deputy* opened in New York amid protests and violence. By German playwright Rolf Hochhuth, it attacked Pope Pius XII for his failure to condemn Adolf Hitler during World War II. Outside the Brooks Atkinson Theater, where the play was being produced, more than 150 marchers gathered in protest, including the Veterans of Foreign Wars, the Committee to Protest *The Deputy*, Citizens for Mutual Respect, and the American Nazi Party. Captain Matt Koehl led a squad of four Nazis with signs:

Deputy Is Hate
This Is a Hate Play

This Play Is Anti-Catholic
Jews Mock Pius XII

New York police were prepared for violence because the European premieres had been riotous. One bystander bolted through the crowd toward the Nazis but was beaten to the ground by police with billy clubs.[14]

The party finances were so low that Rockwell had to borrow air fare from a supporter to get to Minneapolis, Minnesota, for a speech at the University of Minnesota on March 6, 1964. The appearance had almost been canceled when the sponsoring student group, the Young Democrats Farm Labor (YDFL), were bluffed into rescinding the invitation. The YDFL faculty advisor, Arnold Rose, professor of sociology, had threatened the club with disestablishment, though he had no authority from the State Central Committee to do so. Rose had taken it upon himself to "coerce the YDFL, through a queer assortment of bluff and academic legerdemain, to take a position for which he could not present an adequate case."[15]

Denis Wadley, the vice-president of YDFL, had spoken in favor of Rockwell's appearance:

> YDFL is not sponsoring this program simply for novelty. The club has been on record in support of academic freedom for a long time, and we think this belief applies to the right as well as to the left.... We think people have a right to hear people of all beliefs, no matter how radical or unacceptable, and make up their own minds about them. Anything short of that is censorship.[16]

When YDFL decided to drop the invitation, the Union Board of Governors had extended the offer.

When Rockwell's airplane landed at Twin Cities International Airport, a large contingent of reporters, photographers, and television cameramen was waiting for his arrival. In the Union Ballroom he took the stage in front of blinding television lights and told the audience of 1,200 people:

> Americans are spiritually empty; National Socialism provides them with something to believe in and to die for if necessary.... The American people want another Hitler. You don't believe it here in college, but they're saying it out in the bars. The masses hate communism and race-mixing and if they find a man to lead them, they'll vote for him....
>
> I am out to do something concrete; I am a counter-revolutionary. After eight years as a conservative I realized that we are not fighting an idea, but

a revolution that has already taken place. We have a Marxist social democracy here.[17]

Outside the building twenty-five protesters braved sub-zero temperatures to picket his appearance. Many of the two thousand students who failed to get seats listened to the speech outside on a public-address system.

On his return plane ride to Arlington, Rockwell wrote an urgent plea in the party's *Confidential Newsletter* (sent to ANP members only) asking for donations toward a pickup truck camper that Alan Welch had located in Amarillo for $1,500. Such a vehicle would cut down on the exorbitant airline expenses and enable several stormtroopers to accompany him on every trip. Since they could cook and sleep in the camper, they would save money on motel and restaurant expenses.

By late March of 1964, the lack of manpower in Arlington was so severe that nearly all picketing and public demonstrations had stopped. It was taking every man available just to keep up with party business and correspondence. Rockwell asked members from around the country to report to national headquarters for stormtrooper duty. Several other party policies went into effect: the minimum probationary period for incoming personnel was increased from thirty to sixty days; only official, card-carrying stormtroopers could refer to themselves in public as "stormtroopers" or wear the appropriate uniforms; no member was allowed to represent himself as an officer or agent of the party unless commissioned by the commander or appointed by the party.

"Members" were defined as dues-paying sympathizers living outside the barracks. "Stormtroopers" were those who lived in the barracks. However, in public rallies, Rockwell referred to the men in his ranks as stormtroopers regardless of whether they lived in the Arlington barracks or had served out the probationary period.

The FBI tallied national ANP membership in 1964 at just less than one hundred. Stormtrooper strength never exceeded thirty-five nationwide. In his college speeches, Rockwell claimed hundreds of members, but this was not factual. He was probably claiming the writers of the hundreds of letters he received with donations of a dollar or two as members, to bolster the ANP image.

Barbara von Goetz, Rockwell's secretary, continued her diligent service to the party. She had met Rockwell in 1960; she had just returned from a vacation in Germany and invited Rockwell to dine with her family and watch slides from her journey. Her family had always been pro–National Socialist, never failing to celebrate Hitler's birthday on April 20 with a chocolate cake. She had started attending ANP rallies in Judiciary Square and the weekly meetings at headquarters. Before long she had put her formidable secretarial skills to work for the party.

On one occasion, Rockwell's mother came to visit him in Arlington, and the three of them went to a German restaurant called Old Europe, on Wisconsin Avenue in the District of Columbia. After they had waited more than an hour for service, the waitress informed them they would not be served, the Jewish owner having decided against it. Rockwell was shocked and embarrassed; he was not in uniform or wearing any swastikas. To make matters worse, when they left the restaurant police swarmed and interrogated him in front of his mother. The evening was a disaster.

On another occasion a supporter gave Rockwell a malamute puppy, Wolf; Rockwell and von Goetz took it to the barracks. Just inside Rockwell's room was an Israeli flag that everyone stepped on when entering. Little Wolf was no exception. Von Goetz recalls that Wolf "knew just what to do. It was the cutest sight as he carefully lifted his little leg to initiate the rag. After that we always felt a special fondness for him."[18]

Rockwell flew to Tallahassee, Florida, in late March to oppose the civil rights "March on Tallahassee" then taking place. Due to the Easter weekend rush he was unable to get a flight early enough to stage a counter-demonstration, but the march failed on its own accord. Police were expecting between three thousand and ten thousand marchers, but only 1,500 showed up, because of a dispute between the CORE and NAACP leaderships. Most of the NAACP marchers withdrew from the march, calling it "second class."[19]

From Tallahassee Rockwell proceeded to Jacksonville, where he addressed a small gathering of thirty people on the "Jewish and communist conspiracy." He explained that the "conspiracy" as well as the "Negro Revolution" could be stopped without violence if white men would go out in mass to stand in the way of black protesters. If the blacks tried to force their way, the whites could "defend themselves." He told of an NAACP convention in Atlanta that convened on the same evening that ten thousand Klansmen gathered across town. The Klansmen could have surrounded the meeting hall to prevent the blacks from entering. He emphasized that nothing could be accomplished by violence. If he thought violence would work, he would take up arms and destroy the "Jewish-communist conspiracy," but the federal government was too strong for such action—he could not fight an army.[20]

Rockwell's relationship with William Buckley, Jr., took a strange twist that spring. Rockwell had always acknowledged Buckley's dedication and intellectualism but despised what he considered Buckley's pseudo-conservative tactics and tea-party meetings. The *Rockwell Report* directed frequent barbs at him. When Buckley lambasted Rockwell in the *National Review*, calling him a "moral maniac," Rockwell wrote Buckley:

> I would be most grateful if you would take the time to send me a reasoned statement showing that what I preach and have fought so hard for and have sacrificed so much for is a "mania." I can assure you that I will not expose or print any such letter. [If you convince me,] I will not only quit, but I will go to work to repair such damage as I have caused by my political efforts.... If you can do this much for me, Bill, for God's sake please do it.[21]

Buckley was moved by the letter, interpreting it as a "cry for help." He later wrote, "The non-totalist tone suggested the barest possibility of that revival of spiritual modesty which necessarily precedes conversion." Still, Buckley felt unqualified to communicate the theological teachings necessary to direct a conversion, so he asked Rockwell if he would agree to confer with a young priest whom Buckley described as "brilliantly learned and persuasive and adamantly anti-liberal—so as to ensure at least one common denominator."

To Buckley's surprise, Rockwell agreed to meet with the priest. Rockwell's true arrogance and conceit, however, revealed itself in his letter to the priest:

> You are accepting a challenge which no other man before you has attempted. No matter what you think now, I am not an evil person, and am as sincere in my beliefs as any human being who ever walked the earth. I cannot help feel that you will be hurt if you are unsuccessful in demonstrating error in our factual beliefs or reasoning.[22]

Their evening meeting took place in the rectory of St. Matthew's Cathedral in Washington. They discussed basic spiritual concepts and the effects of Christianity on mankind. After a short time Rockwell changed subjects, revealing his duplicitous intentions for the meeting. He told the priest, in so many words, that he wanted to offer his party's services, as the "street fighters of the American conservative movement," to Mr. Buckley. The priest heard Rockwell out, hoping the conversation would return to things spiritual. It did not. The priest observed that Rockwell's convictions seemed to be based on passion rather than logic, his goal, attainment of power, with no regard to the means. He was ruthless; his drive for political power would not be slowed by morality.[23]

The priest wrote Buckley that Rockwell's mind was a disaster area: he was a Nazi of the 1937 variety. Neither the priest nor Buckley ever heard from Rockwell again. Buckley lamented that the episode revealed a "glimmer of a conscience, and sometimes that conscience stirred like a three-month fetus."[24]

Rockwell's use of the slogan "white Christian America" caused some consternation among his followers. Matt Koehl explained that Rockwell was agnostic in the sense that he did not presume to fathom—and could not prove in rational terms—the ultimate reality of the Almighty. On the other hand, Rockwell spoke of a "Providence" which had sent Adolf Hitler, just as he frequently alluded to—and came to believe devoutly in—a mysterious "destiny" that he sensed was guiding him and the fortunes of the movement.

His use of the term "white Christian" was an expedient for reaching people whose sympathy and support he hoped to enlist. He regarded it as preferable to other descriptive labels, such as "white non-Jewish" (too clumsy and unwieldy), "Aryan" (unfamiliar or otherwise thought by many to mean only blond, blue-eyed Nordics), or "white" (within which most would lump Jews). He was trying to appeal to the American majority population, specifically excluding Jews, in terms that they could easily understand and with which they could identify. Moreover, the appeal to "white Christian" folk enabled Rockwell to siphon off some of the financial support that had been going to "Christian pay-triot" profiteers.[25]

Rockwell did not believe in miracles or the supernatural, but he did believe that a "power beyond us" was at work. He equated the swastika with the Cross; his Nazis were like the early Christians in the catacombs. He considered the ANP a religious movement, that every member was full of religion: "My guys are like Monks, this is almost like a monastery, a hate monastery."[26]

Rockwell was secretly formulating a plan to blend National Socialism with a pseudo-Christian front group. The use of a Christian front group was strictly tactical. Hitler was still Rockwell's religion. He toyed with the name Christian Naturalist Church. Colin Jordan chafed at the idea of using religion to further the cause, but Bruno Ludtke believed Rockwell could manipulate America's intrinsic "religious fury" to seize political power.[27]

In the summer of 1964, Rockwell met with Wesley Swift, the leader of the Christian Identity Church. Identity members believe that Jews are not actual descendants of the biblical Israelites, but merely imposters. They believe that Aryans are the true Israelites, God's chosen people. Identity followers believe they are locked in mortal conflict against Jews and the dark-skinned of the earth, whom they call "mud people."

Swift created Identity congregations throughout the country, but his power base was California. The meeting between Rockwell and Swift was a preamble to a fruitful relationship between the two groups. By 1965, Rockwell would appoint Ralph Forbes, the leader of the California Nazis, as the party's own Christian Identity minister.

On April 11, the White Party of America (WPA), led by Karl Allen, was officially launched. Its first activity was a simultaneous picket in Washington, Richmond, and Baltimore in opposition to the civil rights legislation before Congress. The group sporadically published a newsletter called *The White Letter*. The White Party leadership comprised ex-ANP men like Allen, Bernie Davids, Seth Ryan, and Chris Bailey. The group created somewhat of a rivalry in the local area, since they were located in Alexandria, just a few miles from Arlington and ANP headquarters. White Party membership was at times greater than the ANP's, but the national press had no interest in the group—proving Rockwell's axiom that "without the name Nazi" no one in the media cared.

In mid-April, three religious students—one Catholic, one Protestant, one Jew—began a vigil at the Lincoln Memorial, praying around the clock in shifts, until the civil rights bill (then undergoing its eighth week of filibuster in the Senate) was passed. Rockwell and five ANP members went to the Lincoln Memorial to observe the demonstration. They devised a strategy for conducting their own twenty-four-hour vigil at the Lincoln Memorial—against the passage of the bill. On April 28, having secured permission from the government to conduct a silent protest, Rockwell and five troopers began their demonstration with a placard reading "American Nazi Party Vigil on Behalf of America's White Majority Against the Civil Rights Bill." Twenty-three members took turns keeping the vigil for twenty-one days and nights.

Since the Democrats controlled both houses of Congress, the bill finally sailed through the House, 290–130, and through the Senate, on

June 19, 73–27. Strom Thurmond, a senator from South Carolina, called it "a sad day for America," while Jacob Javits, Thurmond's counterpart from New York, called it "one of the Senate's finest hours."[28] Two days later, three CORE voter registration workers were murdered in Mississippi.

On May 14, Rockwell addressed two thousand students in the Bowen Field House at Eastern Michigan University. He outlined his program to the students amid boos, hisses, and laughter, but there were no protests or opposition groups.[29] From Michigan he proceeded to Greeley, Colorado, to speak before nine hundred students at Colorado State College. Outside Gunter Hall a large group of students picketed his appearance with placards reading:

There Is No Race But the Human Race
Rockwell—Genocide
Hitler, Mussolini, Rockwell—The World Is Sick of Dictators

Inside the hall, Rockwell shook his fist in fury, screaming:

You have been brainwashed by the liberals, the peace creeps, you must hear both sides of the story. You do not hear both sides, look at radio and TV—they are completely owned by three companies—ABC, CBS, and NBC. This wouldn't be so bad, but these companies are controlled to the man, by Russian Jews.

Many of his comments drew boos and laughter, but he eventually silenced these:

Strong civilizations are characterized by wholesomeness, patriotism, and self-sacrifice. Weak civilizations, like ours, are characterized by unwholesomeness, love of money, and love of luxury.... We are like the Roman Empire in the days when the savages were taking them over.[30]

After the speech he collected his $160 honorarium and checked into a motel for the night before proceeding to Washington State the next day.

On May 22, the Western Division leader, Captain Ralph Forbes, gave a speech to a capacity crowd of 6,500 in the Harmon Gymnasium at the University of California at Berkeley. The large audience was better suited for Rockwell, but he had been unable to attend. Forbes groped for words as he tried to explain the superiority of the white race to the massive audience of belligerent, heckling students.[31]

On May 29, 1964, Rockwell gave an afternoon speech at the University of Washington in Seattle. He was the first controversial speaker to appear there since a "speaker ban" had been lifted, and students were extremely excited about his appearance. The school paper had hyped the event, printing some of Rockwell's more scandalous statements about blacks:

> They will be just like the Indians on the reservations. And they won't get off the reservations, except with a pass. We're going to see to it that there is no mixing. The only way my grandchildren are going to be able to see a nigger is to go to the zoo. . . .
>
> Malcolm X will win the black people, and I will win the white people. He wants to go to Africa and I want to help him and give him a fair shake. And the only way he can do it is with our help and we'll give it to him. He'll work for it and the Negroes will vote for us so they can get out of here. . . . Malcolm X can believe in Negro supremacy until he's blue in the face—over in Africa. I don't care how superior he thinks he is to me, as long as he gets out of here. . . . [32]

When Meany Hall filled to capacity hundreds more students listened to his address via loudspeaker in Architecture Auditorium—more than four thousand students and faculty heard his speech. Rockwell told the audience the television networks were controlled by Russian Jews: "You will never see a Jewish or Commie criminal on TV." He divided Jews into two groups: "Religious Jews wear those little black beanies while atheistic Jews are communists." As an example of "atheistic Jews" Rockwell cited Picasso (his "modern sculpture looks like something shoveled from a cow pasture"), Gertrude Stein (a "queer Jewess" and mastermind behind the degradation of poetry), and Jacob Epstein (another mastermind of modern sculpture); all three were promoting decay in America.

He predicted a split between the major ideologies in the world because of racial differences, the Sino-Soviet split being an example of "white and dark communists" separating because of race: "The day may come when the Russian Reds and the West will stand shoulder to shoulder to fight the dark people who are rising." [33]

Rockwell believed this Battle of Armageddon would not be fought over ideological, economic, or philosophical issues. Instead, it would be a battle between "colored" people and white people. Since white people were outnumbered on earth seven to one, Rockwell believed it was imperative that white people unite first. If China developed a hydrogen bomb, it would lead the world's colored races against the world's white people. [34]

By June, manpower at ANP headquarters was once again at full strength. Rockwell had been successful in getting supporters from around the country to move to Arlington for the summer. With manpower at his disposal Rockwell launched a series of harassment and publicity stunts against leftists and political opponents. The free publicity attracted more donations; sympathizers could see their money at work. Such ANP "guerrilla warfare" was intended to put fear into the "enemies" of the party, fear that the ANP was always nearby and could descend with seeming impunity at any time. Not only did the attacks provide great exposé copy for *Stormtrooper* magazine, but the daring exploits gave the men a sense of mission, importance, and camaraderie, and kept them from fighting each other.

The first attack took place on June 8 in the National Theater, where civil rights workers were giving testimony on the violence and intimidation used by Mississippi law enforcement officials. The meeting, sponsored by the Council of Federated Organizations, was crucial in planning, staffing, and supervising the voter registration and civil rights agendas throughout Mississippi.

The meeting was under way less than five minutes when ANP Captain John Patler got up from his fourth-row seat and jumped onto the stage, shouting "OK, let's stop this show." He told the audience he would "stand here all day" in opposition, calling them "a bunch of filthy swine." Patler continued insulting the audience until it erupted with angry shouts; he merely cracked a grin and laughed. The audience tried singing "We Shall Overcome" in an attempt to intimidate Patler, but the attempt backfired; the Nazi joined in the singing, substituting his own words about "niggers" and Jews. When a policeman finally arrived and ordered Patler off the stage he sat down in "civil disobedience," forcing the officer to drag him off by the arm. Patler was charged with disorderly conduct.[35]

A few days later another ANP attack took place when West German Chancellor Ludwig Erhard emerged from the State Department in Washington. Nazi Jerry Cochran rushed Erhard with a big sign reading "Free Bruno Ludtke," referring to the WUNS leader in Germany who was recently arrested for promoting Nazism. Erhard and Secret Service agents were stunned by Cochran's bold demonstration; he was stopped only four feet from the chancellor, close enough for assassination.

The next week NAACP leaders from across the nation descended on Washington for a national convention. Outside the convention center, a block-long line of uniformed Nazis carried pickets each day. The signs read:

Down with the NAACP
Integration Stinks
Who Needs Niggers?
N.Y. Jew Heads NAACP

During one of the NAACP banquets, ANP Captain Robert Lloyd infiltrated the dinner party disguised in red hair and beatnik clothes. He walked up the aisle, mounted the stage, stood at the podium, and announced into the microphone that the audience would all have to return to Africa. He threw handfuls of Nazi-printed, one-way "boat tickets" into the predominantly black audience. While police scrambled to pull Lloyd from the podium, another ANP member who had infiltrated the event released a box full of mice. Shrieks and yelling erupted throughout the banquet room, thoroughly disrupting the event. The next night, the finale of the convention, Nazi stormtrooper Jerry Lynne, done up in blackface and stovepipe hat, charged into the ballroom of the Statler-Hilton shouting, "Ah's your Uncle Remus and Ah's come to take you niggers back to Africa."[36] Lynne was quickly thrown out of the ballroom and arrested.

A few days later ANP member Jerry Cochran sat in the Senate gallery listening to the debate on the civil rights bill. Cochran took out a flag bearing the swastika, jumped up and waved it above his head, yelling, "The only hope is Rockwell. . . . You can't pass the civil rights bill!" He was immediately subdued by Capitol Police, taken into custody, then shipped to the District of Columbia General Hospital for mental observation.

President Johnson signed the Civil Rights Act on July 2, calling for Americans "to join in this effort to bring justice and hope to all our people and peace to our land."[37] A media blitz ensued. Publishing houses cranked out books on African Americans and the race issue at a rate of nine new titles a week—most with a liberal bias. Television and radio were also thoroughly sympathetic to the civil rights situation. Racial prejudice was now an unquestioned evil—like pollution or drunk driving. A heterogeneous journalistic movement in support of civil rights was undertaken by not only the magazines of mass circulation, like *Time*, *Newsweek*, *Life*, and *Look*, but also by the *Wall Street Journal*, the *New Yorker*, and *Esquire*.

On Sunday, July 5, of the Independence Day holiday weekend, an anti–civil rights protest was scheduled to take place on the grounds of the Washington Monument to pressure Congress to repeal the Civil Rights Act. Organized under the auspices of the Committee of One Million Caucasians, the rally was planned and sponsored by a group of Klansmen under the direction of the United Klans of America.

It was Rockwell's fondest desire to establish white racial unity as a basis of political action, and he made overtures to a wide spectrum of racist organizations to promote this end, including the various Klan groups. Most of these groups were afraid of being tarred with the "Nazi" stigma and turned him down outright—like Robert Shelton of the United Klans of America, who went to great lengths to establish his anti-Nazi credentials. Rockwell felt indebted to the Klan for "saving the South" after the Civil War, but he believed its tactics were wrong. Terrorism on a small scale would not work—it only made martyrs, which inflamed the passion of the masses. Second, he saw the Klan as deploying itself in terms of retreat and defense rather than attack—which was the only way to win a war.

Some Klan groups were inclined to cooperate. James Venable, leader of the Klan sponsoring the Committee of One Million Caucasians, exchanged communiqués with Rockwell on the event. Klan sponsors were hoping for two hundred thousand supporters at the event, but only three hundred showed up. When Venable failed to appear at a press conference and later the rally itself, Rockwell took control of the demonstration and blasted the right-wing leadership:

> Not one of them [the no-shows] will stand up here and the liberals can have a big laugh about it. We have nothing but shame. . . . You know why? Because our people are cowards. They're yellow. The civil rights workers in Mississippi at least have guts and are willing to die for their cause. That's what the conservatives need.[38]

During the meeting the crowd was given reports on the progress of Nazi Andy Chappell, who was supposedly running the 110 miles from Richmond with a petition to repeal the Civil Rights Act. Hours later, a panting Chappell arrived, wearing an American flag on his front and a Confederate flag on his back. Virginia state police had no report of anyone running from Richmond, but it was a nice bit of showboating for the ANP.

The Klan leadership's failure to follow through was an important lesson. The ANP came to rely solely on its own resources in achieving its goals and furthering Rockwell's motto, "White Man, stand with us and fight, or stand out of our way!"[39]

In July, Barry Goldwater accepted the Republican presidential nomination, criticizing the Democrats as soft on communism and failing to maintain America's security and moral order. He told the convention, "extremism in the defense of liberty is no vice." A few weeks later the ANP executed a well-planned disruption of Goldwater's arrival at Washington National Airport. Rockwell didn't like Goldwater for a variety of reasons. First and foremost, of course, was his Jewish heritage. He also didn't like the "leftist" track record Goldwater left behind in the Senate. He called him "Goldfink" and promoted the idea that Goldwater was "sent over" by the Left to take over the conservative movement.

A two-pronged disruption plan was devised. A dozen troopers in street clothes rode buses made available to the public by Goldwaterites to Washington National Airport early in the day to secure the best positions near the speaking podium. Their assignment was to create a diversion by yelling and shouting while one of the troopers rushed Goldwater to get the attention of security forces and loyalists. After a lengthy wait, Goldwater arrived and stepped to the podium. Before he could utter two words he was drowned out by stormtroopers yelling "We want Rockwell!" over and over; stormtrooper Louis Mostaccio charged the podium. While security forces concentrated on these storm troopers in mufti, eight other troopers doffed their overcoats, exposing their Nazi uniforms and anti-Goldwater placards. Goldwater was whisked from the podium by Senator Everett Dirksen and into a waiting limousine.[40] The media turned their cameras on the stormtroopers for the evening news. A glorious welcome by supporters had been marred by the incursion of Nazis.[41]

The Nazis were not the only group attacking Goldwater. The Democratic propaganda machine was castigating him with television commercials. Its ads depicted Goldwater as a moss-backed warmonger ready to attack the Soviet Union, sell the Tennessee Valley Authority, and abolish Social Security. The masterpiece of the campaign was the notorious "Girl with Daisies" commercial, depicting a lovely, innocent little girl, picking wildflowers in a field, suddenly being blown up by a thermonuclear blast. Viewers were urged to vote Democratic to prevent such an event.[42]

On September 3, the House Committee on Un-American Activities held a hearing on the illegal travel of American students to Cuba. The final witness of the day was Morton Slater of New York, who told the committee that the hearing was a "farce" with no legitimate purpose. Capitol Police, having been alerted to the presence of three ANP members in the audience, strategically positioned themselves in the aisles adjacent to them. Unnoticed, a man from a different section of the audience got up from his seat and quietly walked up the center aisle. No one took a second look at Lon Dunaway, except those who noticed the swastika armband on his left arm.

When Dunaway neared the front row he charged over the seated police and onto the table at which Slater was testifying. Shouting "Down with Castro!" he lunged at Slater, driving him from his chair to the floor. It took eight Capitol policemen to subdue and carry Dunaway out of the hearing room, holding both arms and legs; one officer kept his hands clamped over Dunaway's mouth to cut off his continual scream, "Down with Castro! Long live Rockwell!" When the melee erupted, the three other Nazis had merely stood and photographed the event for the next issue of the *Stormtrooper*. Dunaway was sentenced to six months in jail.[43] The attack had been carefully orchestrated by the ANP. The "high-profile" Nazis had been used as decoys to distract security forces from the real attack. The guards had been so focused on the three known Nazis that they had neglected to watch the rest of the crowd.

On October 3, the Nazis held a protest outside the Hollywood Bowl, where a "Night of the Stars" event was taking place. A bystander watching the Nazis jumped out from the crowd and without warning punched stormtrooper Ken Taylor in the jaw so hard that his jawbone shattered in several places. Taylor spent more than a week in the hospital with his jaw wired shut; the attacker, Terry Medway of Great Britain, was convicted of disturbing the peace and fined fifty dollars.[44]

Rockwell's next speech was at the University of Michigan on October 13. The invitation caused quite a stir on campus and in the community. The *Michigan Daily* was bombarded with letters to the editor: "If the [Michigan] Union persists in inviting men like Rockwell . . . it is time we re-evaluated the appropriateness of providing the Union with twelve dollars out of every man's tuition."[45] Another letter, this one from an associate professor, read, "Fascists and Communists may speak here, yes, and all those who do not cross the line into cultural bestiality. But a Nazi must not enter this house."

A distraught Jew wrote,

> As a member of the religious and ethnic group of which his liking [*sic*] exterminated six million, I demand that the Union abrogate, absolve and withdraw their invitation to this creature.[46]

The invitation stood. Rockwell told the audience of 4,100 people in Hill Auditorium that he used the word "Nazi" as a mere publicity device: "One needs to get attention somehow for his political beliefs. This is merely my way of getting my views aired and ensuring myself a large, if hostile, audience." He explained that he won people over by using a logical approach to convert intellectual audiences, and a racist method on the working class:

> The racist approach plays upon the natural racist inclinations of the working class and upon their tendency to see things as two extremes rather than accepting parts of both points of view as the educated classes have learned to do.[47]

The following day, a student editorial in the *Michigan Daily* grasped the essence of Rockwell's political aspirations:

> Anyone who dismisses George Lincoln Rockwell as a man who wants to kill Jews is missing the boat....Although Rockwell rejects Goldwater, enough of his beliefs are sufficiently similar to attract essentially the same kind of people....If Goldwater can come in reach of the American Presidency, it is conceivable that Rockwell might, because many of his non-racial beliefs are only a step further than Goldwater's....That is why Rockwell is potentially dangerous. Fascism can, possibly, arise here, and those who dismiss Rockwell as nothing but an anti-Semitic hate-monger are missing the point.[48]

His next speech was at the John F. Kennedy Theater at the University of Hawaii on October 20. Adorned with a lei around his neck, he told the 350 students, "I think you're developing a new society here, one that is racially homogeneous and will be peaceful...and I have no objection to that here in Hawaii. I don't know any Japanese who has formed an NAACP and tried to push himself in like [the blacks] has on the Mainland."

He told the audience the American government "reached its golden mean—a perfect balance between tyranny and anarchy" in 1786. This continued for fifty years, he said, "but as humanity always does, it made evil out of the correction. It kept moving left and the people who call themselves moderates now would have been stoned by our grandfathers.... Uncle Sam is crawling toward a bomb of anarchy and the bomb is exploding in the streets."

On the topic of race, Rockwell said the white race was supreme because it had proved to be a superior performer, "although we're on the way down fast.... Everything that is contributing to natural order is being destroyed." He referred to the "black race" as "the only one I say doesn't fit in America.... They have produced nothing. They're still eating each other." The government "ought to take ten million a year and build them a decent place of their own in Africa.... We owe the Negroes something... but we do not owe them the right to push us out of our own places, our own private businesses, our own private homes."

He praised the reception he received in Hawaii. "I'm usually ducking rocks and eggs," he said. "This is so much different that I think I'll move to Hawaii." He also praised the Honolulu newspaper. "This morning I had the great pleasure of reading the first really completely honest article I have ever read about myself in newspapers. I have not seen that in six years on the Mainland."

At his second speech of the day, in front of four thousand listeners in the Andrews Outdoor Theater, a small group of Young Republicans carried picket signs into the hall reading:

Young Republicans Against Anti-Semitism

Young Republicans Against Nazis

Nazis Are Un-American

Young Republicans Hate Tyranny

Rockwell blasted Gus Hall of the Communist Party, who was scheduled to speak later that week: "When that communist Gus Hall gets here I challenge him to a debate. And if I can't nail his hide to my wall I'll join up with Martin Luther Coon."

When asked in an earlier press conference in Hemenway Hall for his views on interracial marriage, he had stated, "I think that racial mixing is a sin against nature. That's not hatred. It's a matter of fact. I propose that we take the money we've been spending on foreign aid to communist countries and send our Negroes to Africa... or to Coney Island.

We could put the Jews there too and they could all live together." He also continued his never-ending attack on the television industry:

> Why now they've got colored gunmen on TV. In the old West if a colored man ever showed up wearing guns, that colored gunman wouldn't stay alive very long. Now they've got Sammy Davis, Jr., wearing guns and all the white men run! Have you ever seen a Negro villain on TV? Or a Jewish villain, a Jew with a real long nose? On TV when they show a Jew running a pawn shop he's always giving away money! And he very seldom looks Jewish. He's handsome!

A reporter asked about audience laughter:

> Oh yes, I know exactly where they'll laugh. They always do.... I always get a laugh when I use that Martin Luther "Coon" expression. Once we dressed up a fellow in a monkey costume and rode through Harlem with him as an example of how Negroes and whites get along. People were holding their sides.[49]

After the speech Rockwell was challenged to a debate by a Hawaiian citizen and NAACP member, Tony Todaro. Rockwell accepted, and the debate was televised on KTJR-TV, Channel 13, as the "Special of the Week."

Todaro opened the debate, hammering Rockwell on the "Negro inferiority" question. Todaro returned again and again to this topic in an attempt to pin Rockwell down. Todaro worked himself into an emotional frenzy, raising his voice and abandoning protocol, but Rockwell remained calm and collected, allowing Todaro to embarrass himself. Neither man argued very effectively, and the event became a squabbling match, but for Rockwell it was glorious. He was on television.

A few days later Rockwell again appeared on television, this time in Canada, on the controversial program *This Hour Has Seven Days.* Rockwell's twelve-minute interview was taped in the Channel 4 studio in Washington for the government-funded Canadian Broadcasting Corporation (CBC). The CBC came under severe attack for the appearance. Marcel Lambert, a Progressive-Conservative member from Edmonton, accused the CBC of catering to "nonconformist odd-balls." The Canadian government resisted demands for a committee to oversee CBC operations, fearing such a committee would lead to government censorship.[50]

Wearing khaki clothing and a swastika armband, Rockwell was seated in front of nine stormtroopers at attention. With a large swastika flag hanging in full view of the camera, Rockwell took a few deep puffs on his corncob pipe and told the two interviewers:

> My objective is to carry out what Hitler started, not model my own person on Hitler because this is impossible.... I don't use the word Fuehrer, I'm not a German, I'm an American as you're a Canadian. I consider myself, in terms of Bolshevism—I would be the Lenin to Marx; in terms of Christianity—I'm the Saint Paul.... In other words, I am the spreader, the world spreader of a doctrine which Hitler originated and it was crucified, dead, and buried and it is now rising.

The two interviewers moved quickly to explore Rockwell's belief in holocaust denial.[51] One of the commentators asked, "Do you accept that six million Jews were exterminated by Hitler?" Rockwell smirked, performed a brief violin-playing impression with his hands, and said, "Are you ready to get the violin out now and play me about the six million dead Jews?"

"Do you or do you not—" asked the commentator. "Of course not!" Rockwell snapped. "I have incontrovertible, documentary proof that that's not true. I don't know how many Jews there were in Germany—I heard there were six hundred thousand—and if the percentage is anything like it is over here, I don't think they were exterminated. I would imagine that probably as many as five hundred thousand probably had to be dealt with as traitors, according to law, as they will be here."

The Canadian commentator pressed on: "Do you disbelieve in the evidence accumulated by your own government of the United States and by the government of Britain?"

"I believe in what the FBI accumulates," barked Rockwell, "but the FBI has not accumulated that. The people that accumulated that so-called evidence were mostly Jewish Army officers who I believe were not working for the United States. They were working for Israel and Russia." The Canadian commentator asked, "Commander, how do you feel about the allegations that the American Nazi Party has strong homosexual tendencies?"[52]

> I will say this. In my organization I have men who were homosexuals. They were sucked into that filth—just like drunkards and dope fiends—and I have been able to rescue them. And I'm not a bit ashamed of that, I'll stand shoulder to shoulder with any one of them any day. The only

thing I will not tolerate is a homosexual who is a homosexual. . . . That's one of the biggest enemies.[53] I'd rather gas queers than anyone else."[54]

On October 29, Rockwell spoke in front of 750 students at San Francisco State College. Students used on Rockwell a silent treatment they called "organized nothing" to disturb his presentation. There were no pickets, no protests, and very little heckling from the audience. An Israeli organization on campus passed out yellow Star of David armbands to students as they entered the auditorium. Dressed in suit and tie, Rockwell told the crowd, "I am here to present you some of the thousands of facts you have been denied. . . . If I am lying in my facts I'll go to work for nothing for Martin Luther Coon and B'nai B'rith." Laying the groundwork for his "communism is Jewish" thesis, he quoted from an article allegedly written by Winston Churchill that appeared in the *London Illustrated Sunday Herald*, on February 8, 1920. The article stated that "atheistic, Bolshevik Jews took over Russia during the revolution." He predicted that National Socialism would take over the United States by 1972:

> America is moving to the left. And anarchy will result with a tyrant rising later to control all liberties. Moderates are now somewhere near Gus Hall. . . .
> I am a radical rightist. And we are a counter-revolutionary organization. We will win over the mobs with discipline and a return to law and order.[55]

Rockwell had begun using a new method in his college appearances, telling the students about "facts you have been denied." He used this method for the remainder of his life, attempting to show the existence of a broad conspiracy at work in the United States to keep certain incriminating information from the general public. If he could show government documents from World War I that depicted Jews as instigators in the Russian Revolution, the students might connect the dots and arrive at his conclusion that "communism was Jewish." If he could show that the television networks ABC, NBC, and CBS were headed by Jews of Russian descent, students would realize that television programming was actually furthering the political agenda of the network leadership.

In early November, Rockwell gave a speech in front of 1,300 students in Memorial Auditorium at Stanford University. Hundreds wore Star of David armbands in protest, and the Stanford Peace Caucus and the Stanford Socialist Caucus marched outside the auditorium. Rockwell's flamboyant gestures and statements soon had the crowd howling with laughter.

He predicted that Barry Goldwater would be elected president in 1968 and would "betray" the American people with "race mixing" in 1969. The result would be a race war in which Americans would look for a strong leader to guard them from the "wild revolutionary black extremist." Once this scenario of civil strife played out, Rockwell believed, he would be elected president of the United States in 1972. He said he did not hate Jews who are loyal to the country, or blacks per se, but "Jews are behind communism and race-mixing and I don't think black men are our equals biologically. That doesn't mean I hate them. I don't hate monkeys or gorillas."[56]

In the weeks following the speech the *Stanford Daily* was besieged with letters both condemning and justifying Rockwell's appearance. European-born Professor Anatole Mazour wrote:

> It so happened that I personally witnessed a similar clown in politics, Herr Adolf Hitler, who came to "entertain" the German people. The end proved far from humorous. It proved tragic not only for the German people but for entire humanity and above all for Christendom. The sorrowful legacy of this period is with us—a profound de-Christianization, dehumanization of Western society.[57]

Student David Steingart wrote:

> It is possible to conceive of a situation not far off when we may see the United States playing the roll [sic] of Nazi Germany. Perhaps there will not be enough Jews to persecute—but there will be Negroes. Perhaps Rockwell will propose a Final Solution to the race riots and civil rights disorders. If riots get much bloodier this Final Solution may begin to appeal to the White majority—the backlash . . . the loss in civil liberties for the Nazis is a very small price to pay for the possible prevention of a recurrence of World War II. . . .
>
> I don't expect that more than a few actually sympathize with Rockwell's ideas now. However, everyone who has been subjected to Rockwell's ideas may at some future time (when social conditions are different) look back and say, "Maybe he was right; maybe we should have taken him seriously then." And therein lies the danger.[58]

The *Stanford Daily* editor, Bob Nayor, concurred:

> Many fail to realize, however, that there are practical limits to this freedom [of speech]. For there are times, especially times of crisis, when certain

individuals or ideas are so threatening to the public order that they cannot be safely tolerated.

This is especially true in the case of demagogues such as Rockwell.... If an individual presents a clear danger, his "rights" should not be enforced at the expense of the community as a whole.[59]

On the other side of the fence was Bill Berkowitz, who took Nayor to task:

I find [Nayor's] sentiments ... far more disturbing than Mr. Rockwell's past presence on campus. It is as if the extremist can have nothing to say, or that the consensus in the middle holds a natural monopoly on truth. We should not need reminding that the major contributors to human thought and welfare have been extremists par excellence.

I think visits by holders of minority opinions are precisely those which should be encouraged and solicited at a university. Freedom of speech is a hollow, meaningless right if one cannot speak here, here, or here.[60]

Carrol Blend, another student, concurred:

It is the student body's responsibility to listen with open minds to what he has to say, then judge what he has said in the light of their education and experience. It is neither the responsibility of this university to show sympathy nor express disgust at Mr. Rockwell's antics.... We must make it our sad task to listen to the totalitarian attitude which admits only its own news and seeks to suppress all others so that we may understand and avoid it whatever symbols it uses—swastika or Star of David.[61]

On November 23, Rockwell was in Dallas to announce the opening of the local ANP unit, composed of "forty-seven tough young men in the Dallas area [who] swore to fight communism and race-mixing to the death." Robert Surrey and his wife, Mary, were the driving force behind the unit, which was separated into two distinct groups. The "social group," of twenty to twenty-five people, met at Surrey's residence, while the stormtrooper section, led by Jerald Walraven, met at ANP Dallas headquarters. The segregation of the two groups was necessary to protect the wealthier supporters, who could not risk exposure by taking part in "street action" but whose funds provided the necessary bail money for the stormtroopers, who were willing to be thrown into jail for the cause.[62]

Rockwell flew to Vancouver to deliver a speech at the University of British Columbia in late November, but his speech was canceled at the last minute because of his status as a "prohibited person" under Canadian law. Immigration officials were perplexed how he had gained entry to Canada. Rockwell told officials he had entered Canada at Windsor, Ontario, disguised as a bearded rabbi and flown to Vancouver on Air Canada.

From Vancouver, Rockwell traveled to San Jose, California, to speak at San Jose City College. At a press conference before his speech, Rockwell jammed his corncob pipe in his large yellow teeth and discussed his aims: "I will be successful if I can sow a seed of doubt in some of their minds. Eight years ago nobody ever heard of the right wing. Now look at us." By pre-arrangement, student groups did not demonstrate. A coalition of seventeen student groups from San Jose State College, Foothill College, and City College collaborated on handbills, which were passed out at the door. The thrust of the tract was "Don't react."

Rockwell began by damning Henry Miller's *Tropic of Cancer*, then took credit for the rise of the right wing. He told the students that the American news media had been captured by Jews and that as a consequence the "white Western Christian civilization is...being poisoned and becoming degenerate." He ended his speech by triumphantly shouting, "Not red, not dead, but dead reds!" While he was being ushered out the back door he paused before a wall for newspaper photographers. Somebody yelled, "He's against the wall, shoot him." Nobody laughed.[63]

In 1964 the ANP came under the purview of the FBI's controversial COINTELPRO—Counterintelligence Program. The purpose of COINTELPRO was to "expose, disrupt and otherwise neutralize the activities of the various Klans and hate organizations, their leadership and adherents." The mandate stated:

> The devious maneuvers and duplicity of these groups must be exposed to public scrutiny through the cooperation of reliable news media sources, both locally and at the Seat of Government. We must frustrate any effort of the groups to consolidate their forces or to recruit new or youthful adherents. In every instance, consideration should be given to disrupting the organized activity of these groups and no opportunity should be missed to capitalize upon organizational and personal conflicts of their leadership.[64]

COINTELPRO would be used against the ANP on numerous occasions in the next four years.

The FBI's Richmond field office generated a COINTELPRO action against the party. Its target was National Secretary Matt Koehl. The field office proposed sending the following letter to Rockwell, signed by an anonymous sympathizer:

Dear Commander:

I am going to remain anonymous because this letter may get into the wrong hands.

I took part in the August 28th March on the niggers in Washington last year and was surprised when I first saw Matt Koehl. I thought I knew him then. When I was traveling in the Chicago area, I started to check around. I found that Matt Koehl, your second in command, is part Jewish. His mother's name was Birstein.[65]

I'll bet that this was never told to you and I bet that if you watch Koehl closely you will find that he will meet with some member of the ADL at least once every two weeks.

Yours for future victory
Heil Hitler
A Friend

The Bureau rejected the Richmond field office request to target Koehl.[66]

In the fall of 1964, several cartons of 45 rpm "hatenanny" records arrived at headquarters. The ANP hatenanny was a parody of the "hootenanny" records that were the rage of folk singers in the 1950s and early 1960s. Odis Cochran, father of ANP member Jerry Cochran, could strum on his guitar and sing country-style songs. Rockwell got the idea of recording a record with racist lyrics. Cochran, his son Jerry, and J. V. Morgan recorded two songs in a disused bathroom at the barracks. Side One contained the song "Ship Those Niggers Back!"

Ring that bell. Shout for joy
White Man's day is here.
Gather all those "equals" up
Herd them on the pier.

CHORUS:

AMERICA FOR WHITE
AFRICA FOR BLACK.
Send those apes back to the trees
Ship those niggers back.

Ring that bell. Shout for joy
White Man's day is here.
Twenty million ugly coons
Are ready on the pier.

Ring that bell. Shout for joy
White Man's day is here.

Hand that chimp his "ugly stick"
Hand that buck his spear.

Ring that bell. Shout for joy
White Man's day is here.
Twenty million jigaboos
To Africa will steer.

Ring that bell. Shout for joy
White Man's day is here.
There they go far out to sea
See them disappear.

Ring that bell. Shout for joy
White Man's day is here.
Those boats are leaking badly now
They'll sink, we sadly fear.

Ring that bell. Shout for joy
White Man's day is here.
No more nigger "civil rights"
Led by a nigger queer.

Ring that bell. Shout for joy
White Man's day is here.
Our homes and schools and city streets
Of niggers will be clear.

Ring that bell. Shout for joy
White Man's day is here.
America will be ALL WHITE
The land we love so dear.

Side Two contained "We's Non-Violent Niggers!"

We is de coons of CORE,
An' we done declared a War
To sit-in, crawl-in and de rest,
Until dey sees dat we's de best.

CHORUS:

We's non-violent niggers,
peace-loving brothers.
De White folks better love us
or we's gonna kill them rotten mothers.

We lays in at de door,
We messes on de floor,
We pees on tables and de chairs,
And throws our garbage on de stairs.

Ah is Martin Luther Coon,
Ah is de head baboon.
When I bows mah head and prays a prayer,
Riots and bloodshed fill de air.

Ah's dat Sammy Davis Cat,
Ah's a coon Aristocrat.

Ah ain't no common jigaboo,
Ah's a kosher, nigger Jew.

We's from de N-double-ACP,
We's for human dignity.
We marches, pickets an' we chants,
We rolls our tails up in our pants.

The cover of the hatenanny record depicted a sinking vessel named "USS *Cadillac*," filled to the gunwales with blacks, and President Johnson crunched in the middle.

On December 2, 1964, Rockwell held a press conference to announce the relocation of the Western Division headquarters to Glendale, California: "After four years of effort, we have secured a headquarters, a center of resistance to communism, Zionism, and race mixing. It's a white man's town. It's the best for us." Glendale officials and local churches were furious about the announcement. City Manager C. E. Perkins said, "We feel, and I'm sure everyone else in Glendale believes, they do not belong here. The resentment being expressed indicates a total city feeling against them. We are hoping they don't make a serious effort to locate here."

Ralph Forbes vowed to fight efforts to evict him from the newly leased headquarters at 823 Colorado Street: "I intend to use the house as a center of resistance for the white man to fight communism. I'll fight and we will survive. We will not be driven out." The city refused to turn on electricity until Forbes signed an affidavit promising the house would be used as a residence, not for Nazi activities. "I'll not sign affidavits," Forbes retorted. "I think that's persecution."

Landlord Dom Razzano filed a thirty-day notice of eviction on the basis that his property was jeopardized by the Nazi occupation. Razzano complained that Forbes had failed to mention the house would be used as a Nazi headquarters when he took the lease. Forbes argued that the lease allowed him to use the property both as a dwelling and for political operations. Razzano had thought Forbes was associated with either the Democratic or Republican Party.[67]

The city of Glendale filed papers in Municipal Court against Forbes for operating a meeting hall in a single-family dwelling without a permit. Los Angeles County also got into the dispute; the Board of Supervisors proposed amendments to upcoming legislation to limit the activities of subversive organizations. The supervisors instructed county counsel to draft an amendment to the subversive organization registration law (enacted in 1941 to control the German-American Bund) to encompass the ANP. County Supervisor Ernest Debs warned that the ANP headquarters in Glendale "will have an unhealthy effect on the entire Los Angeles area.... It is bad enough that the Nazi party continues to exist in our great society as an affront to decent patriotic Americans, but it is infinitely worse to have its headquarters in our very midst, sowing seeds of dissension."[68]

In early December, the Chicago unit of the ANP also opened new headquarters, at 1314 West Ohio Street. The dilapidated, three-story brick building had a boarded-up storefront that the Nazis divided into a meeting hall and print shop, while the second and third floors each contained two apartments. The apartments were in shambles: the plaster walls had been cracked, patched, and patched again so that the finish appeared to be stucco; the electrical wiring was in disrepair, and the overhead lighting in each room consisted of a bare bulb hung from a cord. None of the bathrooms had sinks, and the main waste pipe leaked. With broken windows, dirty floors, and musty odors, the building was unfit for habitation but perfect for the American Nazi Party.[69]

After a shaky beginning, the party had ended the year 1964 on a solid footing. The officer corps had been realigned and the stormtrooper ranks replenished. The party had opened new headquarters units in Dallas, Glendale, and Chicago. Rockwell had become a hot item on the college speaking tour. His campus appearances generated considerable publicity, donations, and exposure to mass audiences.

As a political guerrilla unit, the ANP had staged numerous attacks on civil rights groups, political opponents, and Congress, repeatedly gaining national media attention with its daring hit-and-run tactics. Rockwell had also gone public on television and campuses with his Holocaust-denial theories. The party was also targeted for FBI COINTELPRO subterfuge. FBI harassment would increase over the coming years, crippling the party financially and spreading disinformation and paranoia.

10

1965: ROCKWELL FOR GOVERNOR

When I was a young man . . . I never heard of queers; I never heard of people going out and shooting people in the street as a regular thing, there were no vandals in the parks, white people could walk along the streets without being raped and robbed. This is a new development . . . a direct result of the anarchy preached by the Jews.
— Rockwell, radio interview, 1965

The U.S. involvement in Vietnam escalated in 1965, precipitated by Vietcong attacks on a U.S. base in Pleiku, resulting in hundreds of casualties. In reprisal, President Johnson sent 160 planes to bomb North Vietnam. It was the largest air strike of the war to date. In March, the United States began a massive bombing campaign called "Rolling Thunder," and Johnson sent 3,500 Marines—the first official U.S. combat troops in Vietnam—to protect the air base at Danang. By summer, Johnson had increased manpower in Vietnam to 125,000 and had doubled the draft from 17,000 to 35,000 a month to support the war effort

Urban rioting flared several times during the year, causing dozens of deaths and millions of dollars in damage—the most destructive being in the Watts area of Los Angeles. The country was getting a taste of the civil unrest that would follow. The urban violence and the escalation of war in Vietnam played right into Rockwell's hands. His new theme was condemnation of the "phony" war in Vietnam, perpetuated by Johnson to keep the economy moving forward. Rockwell believed Johnson was fighting to lose, as he felt Truman had during the Korean conflict. Fighting communism was righteous, but it necessitated total war to prevent the excessive deaths of American soldiers.

The urban riots reinforced his belief that the black civil rights movement was led by communist agitators, who were inspiring and instigating, if not coordinating, urban destruction and insurrection. The greater the rioting and civil unrest, the better Rockwell's chances of being elected to office. In March he announced his intention to run for the governorship of Virginia as his first step up the ladder to the White House.[1] As he continued his anti-Semitic activities, Rockwell failed to notice—or overlooked—the decree by Pope Paul VI declaring that the Jewish people were not responsible for the death of Christ and had been unjustly persecuted for two thousand years.

On Monday, January 4, 1965, members of the House of Representatives prepared to take a roll call for the opening session of Congress. The pending roll call had been in the news for some time. The Mississippi Freedom Democrat Party (MFDP) was going to attempt to seat three black women, elected in an unofficial ballot among Mississippi African Americans, instead of the white "elected" officials.

The previous summer the MFDP had conducted a four-day mock election under the pretext that the 450,000 African-American citizens of Mississippi were "systematically and deliberately prevented from voting" in the regular election. They had put ballot boxes in barbershops, restaurants, Laundromats, churches, wherever blacks congregated. When the ballots were counted, Aaron Henry, president of the Mississippi NAACP, Mrs. Fannie Lou Hamer, Mrs. Ann Devine, and Mrs. Virginia Gray had been elected. When Aaron declined to travel to Washington, the three women set out. They were quietly turned away from the House chamber and the regular delegation was seated.

The ANP devised a plan to ridicule the Mississippi Freedom Democrats and gain national publicity at the same time. ANP officers Robert Lloyd and John Patler entered the Capitol in street clothes, carrying attaché cases containing makeup and a disguise for Lloyd. Patler found a vacant room near the stairway leading to the House chambers to use as a changing room. Lloyd removed his trousers, exposing black tights underneath. From the attaché cases he took out black face paint and a black, fur-like loincloth to wrap around his crotch and waist. The other attaché case contained a compressed stovepipe hat, which he extended to full height. He repackaged his street clothes into the attaché cases and handed them to Patler. Patler checked the hallway and gave the "all clear" signal to Lloyd.

Lloyd raced out of the room and down the hall to the exclusive stairway that only members of Congress use. He bolted up the stairs to the lobby level, past two slouching policemen. As he neared the chamber entrance a black doorkeeper spotted him and moved to block his path, but Lloyd, running at top speed, slammed a shoulder into the man, went through the door, and jumped into the well of the House. Donning his stovepipe hat, he yelled, "I'se the Mississippi delegation. I demand to be seated."[2]

Members of the House were stunned by the intrusion; total silence filled the room as Lloyd danced and jumped, making unintelligible monkey noises. It was quite a coup for the party—the only time that anyone had ever succeeded in getting onto the floor of Congress to demonstrate.[3] Not since Puerto Rican fanatics had fired weapons in the chamber in 1954 had there been such a ruckus. It took a few moments for the House members and guards to regain their senses, but then one of the members shouted "Throw him out," and police rushed in. The presiding clerk banged his gavel repeatedly to restore order. All eyes, including the ANP cameramen in the balcony, were affixed on Lloyd as he was dragged from the chamber yelling "God bless America. Long live Rockwell!" Lloyd was charged with disorderly conduct and fined twenty dollars.

New Jersey Democrat Charles Joelson was so angered by the incident that he wrote the chairman of the House Un-American Activities Committee demanding an investigation of the ANP. He implored U.S. Attorney David Acheson to prosecute the ANP for conspiracy to commit breach of peace. Joelson was horrified when he learned that Lloyd had been permitted to forfeit twenty dollars bail for his romp around the House floor. He called District Corporation Counsel Chester Gray, demanding Lloyd be apprehended and "tried on the charge pending." Gray was easily convinced and issued a warrant for Lloyd's arrest on misdemeanor charges that carried a maximum punishment of ninety days in jail and a three-hundred-dollar fine.

At 5:00 A.M. on January 15, 1965, the radio beside Rockwell's bed clicked on with the morning news. The broadcaster reported that Martin Luther King would lead a voter-registration drive in Selma, Alabama. The cobwebs in Rockwell's head suddenly cleared; he envisioned King leading a "vicious crew of niggers, beatniks, Jews, and communist-agitators into every tiny restaurant, hotel, and soda fountain in Selma, while television cameras captured his every move, publicly humiliating Selma to the nation." He sprang from bed and devised a plan to offer his "services" to the good citizens of Selma. He caught a plane to Birmingham and a ride to the Albert Hotel in downtown Selma, where he held a press conference. He told the press he had come to Selma to "cause agitation and run Mr. Coon out of town. . . . Mr. Coon is a pro . . . and I ran him out of Danville, Virginia, and I believe I can run him out of Selma. The only technique is to show these communist-type agitators how ridiculous they are." Rockwell promised "to do my very best to stand up for the white people of Selma and Alabama."[4]

With the help of local supporters, Rockwell outlined his plan to ruin King's voter-registration drive scheduled for Monday, January 18. The first order of business was to try to convince the city fathers to designate Monday the eighteenth as "Nigger Day" and string banners across the main entrances of the town: "Welcome NIGGERS to COON DAY IN SELMA." When this idea found no support among the locals, Rockwell tried again. He suggested writing a special "Coon Day in Selma Menu" for restaurants to hand to the "jig integrators" when they demanded service. Rockwell typed up the special "menu."

> The restaurants of this city extend a warm welcome to all coons, jigs, niggers, apes, baboons, and any other jungle life seeking to enjoy communist race-mixing benefits promised by Martin Luther Coon. In honor of the occasion, our chef has lovingly prepared a special menu of the favorite nigger foods. We ask only that our coon guests refrain from snapping at waiters or nibbling on other guests while waiting for service.

The menu included:

Hot, stuffed, deviled Jew
Sammy-Davis Jr. Special (single eyeball on matzoth)
Kosher corned coon and cabbage

Rockwell convinced some locals to donate enough money to buy a plane ticket for Robert Lloyd to fly in from Arlington with his monkey suit. Local print shops were asked to donate their services to print posters with the message the banners would have carried. Rockwell envisioned signs in the windows of every establishment. He also gave away dozens of the ANP hatenanny records containing the songs "Ship Those Niggers Back" and "We's Non-Violent Niggers" to establishments with jukeboxes.

All his efforts were for naught. On Monday, when King arrived, none of the previously eager supporters could be found. Rockwell had no signs, no banners, no music, no car, just Robert Lloyd and his ape suit. He would have to sic ape-suited Lloyd on King when there were television cameras or reporters around. The proper deployment of Lloyd was crucial; if Lloyd were spotted by police too early he would surely be arrested.

At noon Rockwell received word of King's whereabouts. Lloyd changed into the ape costume and went into the street but was noticed by police and arrested as a "suspicious person" before he could get near King. Rockwell went to the courthouse to bail Lloyd out and bumped into King, who was attempting to register blacks to vote. Now irate, Rockwell blasted King with all the venom he could muster. He poked the stem of his corncob pipe at King's face and asked him if he was man enough to stand up "non-violently" and debate him so he could prove to the world that King was "using the local niggers, not helping them."

Under the pressure of the media cameras and microphones, King agreed: "You can speak at our meeting tonight." Rockwell accepted, promising to thrash him good. A heckler yelled that Rockwell was working for the Jews and the FBI. Rockwell turned to confront him; it was James Robinson, with a brass thunderbolt insignia of the National States Rights Party on his lapel. Robinson yelled again, "Let's have some

Rockwell confronts Martin Luther King, Jr., in Selma, Alabama, in January 1964.

vaudeville, Rockwell." Seething with rage, Rockwell walked away from Robinson to avoid a fistfight; he could not jeopardize his golden opportunity to debate King publicly. Once again his best-made plans were being laid waste by fellow white men. He could not understand such treachery.

After waiting outside the courthouse for several hours (no blacks were allowed to register), King and associates walked to the Albert Hotel to register as its first black guests. As King stood at the hotel desk he was suddenly attacked by Rockwell's heckler, James Robinson.[5] Robinson struck King twice on the head before he was pulled away and arrested. King was not injured but decided to rescind Rockwell's invitation to speak. That evening Rockwell was turned away at the church. He could not believe King would renege on the invitation. When he demanded entrance he was arrested for disorderly conduct. Although the ANP "mission to Selma" was less than a complete success, Rockwell's brief confrontation with King was photographed and picked up over the newswires.

Selma officials had their own way of dealing with civil rights protesters, a method quite different from Rockwell's "ridicule" techniques. On March 7, Hosea Williams and John Lewis attempted to lead black marchers to the state capitol in Montgomery, some fifty miles east of Selma, to protest to Governor George Wallace. A problem for the marchers was that Wallace had banned the march and had mustered state troopers to stop it, authorizing the use of "whatever force was necessary."

Groups of marchers departed from Brown's Chapel Methodist Church in Selma for the long journey to Montgomery. Fifty state troopers armed with clubs, whips, and tear gas waited on the opposite side of the Edmund Pettus Bridge, less than a mile from Selma. Behind the troopers were three dozen volunteer "possemen" recruited by Dallas County Sheriff Jim Clark. The marchers were stopped by the troopers and given two minutes to return to Selma. The time expired, and the troopers advanced. The marchers were clubbed and beaten; people screamed and cried. Tear gas was pitched into the crowd until it covered the highway like fog. The marchers retreated across the bridge, back to Selma. The brutal scene was witnessed on television by millions across the country and around the world. In reaction, President Johnson federalized the Alabama National Guard and ordered regular troops to Alabama to protect the Selma-to-Montgomery marchers.

The next week, at a Harlem rally of the Organization of Afro-American Unity, Malcolm X told listeners he had seen Martin Luther King knocked down by a racist and that if he had been there he would have gone to King's aid. He read aloud the text of a telegram he sent to Rockwell:

> This is to warn you that I am no longer held in check from fighting white supremacists by Elijah Muhammad's separatist Black Muslim movement, and that if your present racist agitation against our people there in Alabama causes physical harm to Reverend King or any other black Americans who are only attempting to enjoy their rights as free human beings, that you and your Ku Klux Klan friends will be met with maximum physical retaliation from those of us who are not handcuffed by the disarming philosophy of nonviolence, and who believe in asserting our right to self-defense—by any means necessary.[6]

Malcolm's transition from cordial minister of the Nation of Islam to confrontational advocate of violence in self-defense took Rockwell by surprise. He rationalized that the NOI was becoming communist (Elijah Muhammad was a strident anti-communist) and so Malcolm had quit to lead the black revolution: "One day Malcolm and I or some of my followers will meet in the street and somebody is going to get killed."[7]

On January 19, Western Division leader Ralph Forbes, his pregnant wife, Karen, and their two children took a mattress, blankets, and pillows into the lobby of the Glendale City Hall to protest a city-ordered shutdown of electricity to their home (because of their occupancy, not payment issues). While four stormtroopers marched on the steps outside the building, Mrs. Forbes held a sign that read "I'll have my baby here—there is electricity." She was arrested for "obstruction of city business" and released on her own recognizance (the baby arrived only three days later). The next day Ralph Forbes filed suit to force the Glendale Municipal Light and Power Company to turn on electrical service to his home. He had grown weary of using camping equipment for lighting and cooking.

On January 27, Forbes, Robert Giles, and Alan Vincent went on trial for converting a house into an assembly building without a permit. The three Nazis defended themselves with the help of A. L. Wirin, chief counsel for the American Civil Liberties Union, who entered the case as a friend of the court. Wirin stated, "The ordinance under which the defendants are being prosecuted violates the First Amendment to the Constitution. It makes a crime of all meetings held in private homes, those of the Brownies as well as the American Nazis."[8]

In early February the city of Glendale turned on the power at Forbes's home. The city manager, C. E. Perkins, stated, "Ralph Forbes has met our utility requirements by making application for electric service on a non-domestic basis on the commercial rate and by making the usual cash deposit to guarantee payment for this service."[9] Forbes was eventually convicted of violating the Glendale building code, but the conviction was overturned by the Appellate Court later in the year.

When the Western Division–ANP opened a unit in San Francisco, Forbes held a press conference to introduce the leaders of the new unit, Clyde Irwin and Robert Martell, and made some brief comments on the racial unrest in America:

> If I thought killing Martin Luther King would solve the nigger problem I wouldn't hesitate to do it—or at least try—but I don't think it would accomplish anything but make a martyr out of him. Violence isn't the solution today. The solution is to ship all the niggers back to Africa.

Rockwell praised Irwin, the official spokesman for the San Francisco unit: "I consider him one of the most valuable men in the Nazi movement anywhere in America. He's got a brilliant mind and an articulate tongue. Irwin's an exception among all those niggers and Jews and Commies and sex perverts that have taken over the University of California campus."[10]

Irwin's background was certainly unusual. He claimed to have a 145-plus IQ; he had not completed high school, but he had taught himself enough to pass the entrance exams for college and boasted of mastering ten languages—including Japanese and a rare Hindu dialect—along with the most difficult mathematics, chemistry, and science courses the University of California had to offer. He would not discuss his personal life at the time of his ANP affiliation but did say he "loved to pursue new ventures . . . new experiences . . . things that most people would be too timid to try. . . . That is why I am not ashamed or afraid to be a Nazi."[11]

In early February the party traded in its old printing press, which was in complete disrepair, held together with rubber bands and coathanger wire, for a new press capable of producing eight thousand newspapers per hour. ANP supporter George Ware put up stock certificates as collateral and borrowed $10,000 from his local bank to finance the press. Ware and Rockwell had the foresight to strike an agreement whereby Ware would retain ownership of the printing press and rent it to the party, making the expensive press immune from legal seizure. They had a legal agreement drawn up, notarized, and deposited in Ware's safety deposit box. The yearly rent for the unit was five hundred dollars, but Ware never expected or received one penny.[12]

About this time, *Playboy* magazine contacted Rockwell about doing a feature interview. Rockwell was intrigued by the offer. Although he did not consider *Playboy* to be a smut magazine, he feared such an interview might reek of hypocrisy, since he was always slamming pornography as Jewish-run degeneracy. Could he trust the interviewer to interpret his words accurately? He decided it was worth the risk. The publicity and exposure would be enormous; thousands of dollars in donations could roll into the party treasury from sympathetic white men. And more important, he could get his message out.

Playboy assigned journalist Alex Haley, already writing *The Autobiography of Malcolm X*, to conduct the interview. Haley telephoned ANP headquarters to assure Rockwell he was not Jewish and to set a date for the interview; he neglected to tell Rockwell, however, that he was an African American. A few days later Haley stepped out of a taxi in front of ANP headquarters. Harry Blair, the khaki-clad duty officer, ushered him into the small shrine room to wait.

Haley peered about the black-walled chamber, illuminated by red candles and a red ceiling-hung spotlight focused on the swastika flag. To the right of the swastika flag was a portrait of George Washington, to the left was a portrait of Hitler. Haley noticed a .45 automatic on Blair's hip. After a few minutes, Alan Welch came into the shrine room and told Haley the interview would take place at the ANP barracks. Welch drove Haley to the sixteen-room mansion on Upton Hill. The car turned up the long, tree-lined driveway, past the No Trespassing sign and several stormtroopers. Haley was searched for weapons and escorted down a hallway to Rockwell's room. He noticed a wooden rack containing short, combat-length steel pipes.

The guard opened Rockwell's door and directed Haley inside. Across the room Rockwell stood (beneath a portrait of Hitler for dramatic effect) without acknowledging Haley's presence. Haley took a chair and set up his tape recorder; Rockwell already had one positioned. Rockwell then sat down at the desk opposite Haley, removed a pearl-handled revolver from the desk and set it on the arm of the chair, and said, "I'm ready when you are." Haley started by asking Rockwell about the handgun. Rockwell told Haley he'd been "attacked too many times to take any chances." Before long they shifted into the subjects of black inferiority, Jewish treason, the black revolution, and Rockwell's four-point plan to achieve power. Rockwell was unable to evoke any emotional response from Haley.

Four interviews took place over the next twelve months, until *Playboy's* editors were satisfied with the information Haley had devel-

UPI/Bettmann

Rockwell in the ANP's Arlington, Virginia, barracks.

oped. The two men continued thereafter to correspond with each other. Haley wrote Rockwell from far-off countries like Senegal or Monaco; Rockwell wrote back long, emotional letters detailing his own aspirations, always addressing the envelopes to Haley with the initials "V.I.N."—Very Important Nigger.

Rockwell's interview was not published until 1966.[13] Despite what Rockwell considered a number of "distortions" and "reshaping" by a rewrite man he believed to be Jewish, it was a breakthrough in reaching a mass audience of three million readers. Not only did interest in the party and monetary income increase after its publication, but it established Rockwell as one of the most sought-after speakers on the college lecture circuit.

In February, Rockwell discussed "managed news" with six hundred students in the Wadsworth Auditorium at the State University at Geneseo, New York. Using an analogy, Rockwell told the students a computer would come up with a wrong answer if it were fed incorrect data. This, Rockwell believed, was happening to Americans across the country: news services were funneling only the news items crucial to their agenda instead of the total picture—hence "managed news." The reason was simple: the heads of all three television networks were Russian Jews: at NBC Sarnoff, at ABC Goldenson, and at CBS Paley. In addition to the television networks, Rockwell lumped in Hollywood and the major newspaper chains as well.

Outside Wadsworth Auditorium more than thirty protesters braved five-degree temperature to picket his appearance. Their placards read:

Does Geneseo Need Sick Minds?
Genocide Go Home
Peddler of Murder and Hate

Most of the protesters were faculty members who objected to Rockwell's honorarium of $125, but local units of the American Legion and the Veterans of Foreign Wars were also represented.[14] When the speech was over Rockwell and ANP officers Welch and Patler drove to the State University at Brockport, New York, for a second speech. A crowd of 650 people jammed into Brockport Auditorium while 300 more watched on closed-circuit television. A fierce crowd of hecklers tried again and again to disrupt his concentration. Rockwell's nerves were finally rattled by sporadic laughing that did not coincide with his dialogue. For no apparent reason, the students were laughing; Rockwell was perplexed until he discovered that two school administrators seated behind him were making faces at the audience. He ended his speech by shouting, "Not better Red than dead; not better dead than Red; but dead Reds!"

As Rockwell and his entourage departed the auditorium an ad hoc group called Youth Against War and Fascism waited outside the building chanting "Nazi pig, Nazi pig." One of the protesters, eighteen-year-old Ann Sterling, made a dash for Rockwell and tried to punch him. Rockwell saw the attack, blocked her jab and punched her in the stomach. As she fell to the ground other protesters jumped into the skirmish. ANP officers Alan Welch and John Patler came to life and held the other attackers at bay until campus security forces intervened. No arrests were made.[15]

On February 21, while delivering a speech in New York City, Malcolm X was shot to death by Black Muslim assassins. Throughout the years Rockwell had praised the work of the Black Muslims, but even more so for Malcolm X, often stating that if he had been born black, he would have been like Malcolm X. He had also predicted that Malcolm would split with the Nation of Islam to lead a separate movement. Malcolm had indeed left the Black Muslims in 1963, made a pilgrimage to Mecca in 1964, and converted to orthodox Muslim faith, while developing a more optimistic view regarding relations between the races.

Although Malcolm was no longer a separatist, Rockwell maintained his admiration for the man who was the very antithesis of Martin King. Malcolm was tall, lean, with fiery eyes; King was short, pudgy, with dreamy eyes. The philosophical overlap of the Nation of Islam and the American Nazis—each demanded separation of the races—caused Malcolm problems at times. On one occasion James Farmer of CORE nearly exposed the Black Muslim–ANP association in a public debate with Malcolm at Cornell University. After the debate, Farmer shared his ace in the hole with Malcolm. Malcolm thanked Farmer for not bringing up the embarrassing topic in public. A week later an ANP member called Malcolm asking him to join an ANP picket of CORE because Farmer was married to a white woman and Malcolm was then against race mixing. Malcolm declined the invitation, then called Farmer to warn him of the impending spectacle.

Rockwell's eulogy in the *Rockwell Report* was bitter. He wrote:

I will close this section on Malcolm, pausing to wipe away the tears as I think how he was cut down in the very flower of his nigger youth, by pointing out that Malcolm always preached "Back to Africa" until he went over there to visit his progenitors.[16]

Rockwell refused to believe that Muslims were solely responsible for Malcolm's death. He believed Malcolm had been killed by a conglomeration of communists. The "Red Muslims," the Fair-Play-for-Cuba followers, and Castroites were behind the killing, because Malcolm had been inciting blacks to violence and ruining the communist non-violent approach King was using.[17]

About this time, the FBI COINTELPRO targeted the ANP Chicago unit with a two-pronged attack: ruin the Chicago unit financially and disrupt its leadership. The FBI Chicago field office wanted to expose the unit's building code violations to either the local ADL or the Jewish War Veterans of Chicago, in hopes that one of these organizations would badger the city to assess fines against the ANP. If neither organization would cooperate, the Bureau would itself make the information available to city officials. Exposing the building code violations would financially cripple the unit; repairs and fines would severely restrict its operations, because the bulk of its resources went for the $110 mortgage payment and basic maintenance of the dilapidated building at 1314 West Ohio Street. Any additional financial burden would limit literature creation and distribution, ruin morale, create dissatisfaction among the ranks, and discourage new recruits.[18]

The second prong of the COINTELPRO attack was to disrupt the leadership of the local organization. False expressions of discontent would be directed at Rockwell by letters, either anonymous or signed with the name of a local Chicago member known to be dissatisfied. Such attacks would divide the loyalty of the organization and cause national headquarters to question the capability of the Chicago leadership. The Bureau also considered sabotage by an agent provocateur.[19]

A sympathetic ADL member was recruited in Chicago to act on behalf of the FBI to report the building code violations of the ANP Chicago unit, thus precluding direct contact by Bureau agents with city officials. The FBI also wanted to bait the Jewish War Veterans to action against the Chicago unit; JWV criticism of the ANP was almost non-existent. On February 26, 1965, the Bureau sent an anonymous letter to provoke them:

Jewish War Veterans of the United States
Chicago, Illinois

Gentlemen:

Recently my wife had occasion to ride in a Checker Cab in Chicago with a most outspoken young driver. Immediately after setting out for our home the driver engaged my wife in conversation denouncing the "dirty Jews and Niggers" in Chicago. He proceeded to blame every ill we face today on the Negro and Jew. When my wife cautioned him that he was then speaking with a Jew, he told her in so many words that he couldn't care less. He praised the Nazi Rockwell and mentioned what appeared to be his association with Rockwell's Nazi Party. He was even so bold as to mention their headquarters at 1314 West Ohio Street.

When my wife told me of this incident I took it upon myself to look over this stronghold of Nazism in Chicago. Gentlemen, this is an unimpressive building which could best be described as a firetrap. The thing that does impress me, however, is that the youth of today in this country could at all be taken with a philosophy you and I know should be dreaded. If this young man is typical of the attitude of Rockwell's followers then we must take action.

Though a Jew myself I am not a member of your organization. You have, however, in the past well represented the things that all Americans, no matter their creed or color, hold so dear. Now gentlemen, I fear I must chastise you. I know that you have been vocal in your protests of the Nazis in Chicago in the past. An organization like yours can do little else but fight such a disease as this. Why then in recent months have we heard nothing from you in this regard?

Please, gentlemen, go see for yourselves this headquarters of the Nazis. Do what you can, and now, to put them out of business. Don't fail us now. All Americans need groups like yours, not only the Jew and the Negro. I am sorry, I lack the courage to identify myself. This is even further reason why you must, must speak for me.[20]

As a direct result of COINTELPRO actions, the city of Chicago took action against the Nazis in the form of fines and of pressure to correct the building violations under threat of forced eviction. Chris Vidnjevich, the "officer in charge" of the Chicago Nazis, complained to the local FBI office that statutes were not being uniformly enforced and that his civil rights were being denied in that he was not being allowed to choose his residence and place of assembly. It was ironic that the Nazis had turned for help regarding their constitutional rights to the very organ of the federal government directing political persecution against them. The Chicago unit maintained a small cadre of from ten to twelve members who continued to meet Sunday evenings for "bull sessions."

In early March, Rockwell announced his intention to run for governor of Virginia that November. He boasted that no Southern governor had ever really used the power of office for the Christian people against the "communist-Jew agitators and subverters." Rockwell promised to be different. For starters, he promised to arrest Martin Luther King and other "nigger agitators" for "conspiring to provoke riots and civil disorder." Ten years in jail and a $5,000 fine would surely slow the civil rights movement. After throwing King and others into jail, he would pardon persons convicted of having shot agitators in the past. His next act as governor would be a massive "fire-your-nigger" plan, pursued until all the blacks in Virginia moved out of the state—preferably to Miami Beach or Brooklyn—or started acting like "decent, old-fashioned niggers." All "white scum" and every "coon" who continued to conspire against the state would be publicly identified.

His plan for school integration was to alienate African-American students to such a degree that they would voluntarily withdraw from the integrated schools. Since the federal government could not dictate what was taught in Virginia schools, Rockwell planned to institute daily instruction on racial development. The white race would be championed as the author of everything great and noble in the world; the black race would be "exposed" as inferior and worthless in every way. Black parents would not want their children taught such a curriculum and would pull their children out of these "Rockwellized" schools.

There were several other schemes as well. He promised to enforce welfare regulations to the letter, eliminating benefits for the "lazy, black bums who go out and agitate all day while the white man works to pay black welfare." He pledged nonextradition of white criminals who flee from "nigger loving" states; a race research laboratory through which anthropologists could publish honest statistics on Negro inferiority; and tax suits against the federal government for using Virginia tax money to support "lazy, criminal niggers, and foreign niggers in Africa."[21]

Rockwell codified his black inferiority theory with an article in the *Rockwell Report*, "Alloys vs. Elements." Using photos of Edward Brooke, the attorney general of Massachusetts, and Adam Clayton Powell, the corrupt playboy-congressman from New York, Rockwell attempted to illustrate that any prominent black leader active in the United States was actually more racially white than black.

> Brooke has the features of a White man. So does Adam Clayton Powell. And so does Elijah Muhammad and Harry Belafonte; and so do almost all of the "clever" niggers who are paraded before us to "prove" that niggers are "equal." Whenever some nigger girl wins a beauty contest, it is never, never a "Ubangi" type jig with Negro features—gorilla nostrils, wool instead of hair, monstrous, swollen lips and murky African eyes. In short, these "equal" niggers they always cram in our faces to prove racism is wrong, are not niggers. They are white people with some nigger blood.[22]

As an example of his "darker-the-dumber" theory, Rockwell liked to ridicule dark-skinned John Lewis of SNCC as "Liver-lips" and an "outright idiot" for nearly ruining the March on Washington with his ridiculous "scorched earth" speech. Rockwell believed blacks were instinctively drawn to "white blood" by race mixing. He liked to point out that even Malcolm X acknowledged that lighter-skinned blacks were favored in the African-American community.

On March 11, the ANP staged a picket in front of the White House. Metropolitan Police received a threat that a bomb or hand grenade would be thrown at the marchers. The Secret Service was notified, but no incident occurred.[23] A few days later John Patler was arrested for disorderly conduct when he marched alongside civil rights protesters holding a sign, "America for Whites." He was arrested for attempting to incite a breach of the peace but was later acquitted by Judge John Malloy, who believed that Patler had not been actually trying to incite the civil rights marchers to attack him.[24]

On April 2, Rockwell flew to Dallas for a rally, but the contract for the meeting hall was rescinded by the proprietor. His Dallas men quickly arranged an outdoor rally in Ferris Plaza. Rockwell told the crowd of two hundred that he had recruited "a group of fighting men ready to fight and die if need be to make this a Christian nation." There was considerable opposition to his speech. Many anti-Nazi pickets were on hand with signs reading:

America Yes, Hitler No

Would You Trust Your Daughter to Marry a Stormtrooper?

From Dallas he went to the University of Colorado at Boulder to look into the death of ANP sympathizer James Pearson. Pearson, an engineering student, had been gunned down as part of a bizarre lover's triangle. Rockwell also held a brief question-and-answer session with students in Libby Hall. A black student approached him and asked him for a "boat ticket" back to Africa and then kissed him on the top of the head as cameras flashed. Rockwell remained calm and continued to answer questions. When asked why students joined the ANP, Rockwell said, "Young kids like to do naughty and bad things to displease their parents. And there is nothing more naughty or bad than the American Nazi Party. The old iconoclasm used to be communism, now it's Nazism."[25]

The second week in April, Rockwell spoke at Ohio University in Athens to a students-only audience of 2,800 in Memorial Auditorium. As he stepped out on the stage and looked out at the sea of students he was stunned by a sight he had never experienced before—the two thousand-plus students were all wearing white shirts. He was taken aback; the usual protest symbol was the yellow, six-pointed star worn as a button or armband. He quickly regained his composure and turned the crowd's hatred to laughter: "I see you all wearing white here tonight. What is this, a college full of virgins? You guys too? You all virgins?"[26] The students roared with laughter and melted in his hands. For the rest of the evening he played the crowd like a well-tuned banjo, evoking laughter time and time again. But when he announced that he was running for the governorship of Virginia, the students also burst out laughing. Rockwell shouted back, "Don't laugh now at my running for governor because on November third you may be laughing out of the other side of your face." The speech ended without incident. A student editorial summed up the event:

> Rockwell is a great public speaker. He lowered his level to that of the audience to facilitate a maximum flow of ideas. . . . In short, the intellectual level of Rockwell's performance was lowered to childishness and absurdity. Yet the audience responded favorably, giving him positive feedback. It is both surprising and disappointing that the students of Ohio University fell game to such a performance. But Rockwell had us completely "psyched" when he addressed us as "boys and girls."[27]

Rockwell filed for governor of Virginia on April 20, telling reporters the election would be the last chance for the state's white population to maintain supremacy over the blacks:

By 1968 the elections will be dominated by Negroes as they are in many other parts of America. It will be impossible for white people ever again to regain the strength and unity to stop black domination of Virginia if we don't do it now.[28]

Rockwell decided to run as an independent, representing the White Majority Party instead of the American Nazi Party. He felt the name would help broaden his base of support in Virginia; it was simply more palatable to the average voter than "Nazi." He also knew that once he delivered the required signatures to get on the ballot, television and radio stations would, by law, have to accept his advertisements.

Alan Welch described the gubernatorial campaign's significance. First, it was a different type of activity (not agitation) for the party, and as such it pleased many of Rockwell's supporters because of its familiarity—a good old American election. It also gave Rockwell credibility in the eyes of some, who now poured forth their energy and money to help the campaign. Second, the campaign gave Rockwell a chance to stand up in front of Virginians and exhibit his real personality, in contrast to the media portrayal of his person. People could see and listen to him in person, like every other candidate, and judge for themselves. Third, lightning might strike. He did not really think he had a chance to win, but still, the possibility was there. Something might get started and snowball; there was nothing to lose.

Ralph Plofsky, the national commander of the Jewish War Veterans, urged the State Board of Elections to refuse to certify Rockwell's gubernatorial candidacy: "The candidacy of Rockwell, given legal status by the state, would mock the sacrifices of the many brave Virginians who died in war against Nazism."[29]

John Patler, referring to himself as the party's director of propaganda, issued a change in policy in the intra-party newsletter. The time had come for the party to "grow up" and eliminate the "sick humor" and frivolous propaganda, to concentrate on positive propaganda, to reveal the "true image" of the party and its goals. "Our fight is no joke," said Patler. "It's time to get serious and start our driving march to political victory."[30] Patler asked all units to suspend distribution of the "Diary of Ann Fink," "Eichmann Speaks," "Jew-Traitor Surrender Pass," "Brotherhood Dictionary," "A Plea to the Jews," and "Niggers! You Too Can Be a Jew!"

Between April and June 1965, the FBI interviewed ex-ANP members and law enforcement officials for their opinions of Rockwell's aims,

A Rockwell-for-governor handbill.

purposes, and goals. Assistant Attorney General J. Walter Yeagley had requested the investigation to determine

> if there is evidence that instructions were given or suggestions made at American Nazi Party Headquarters to show that the published aims of the organization are not the true aims of the American Nazi Party and that the organization has adopted a policy of advocating the commission

of acts of force or violence to deny others their rights under the constitution of the United States.

The first interviewee was Raymond Cole, of the Arlington County Police Department. Cole testified to innumerable contacts with Rockwell and interviews with nearly a hundred American Nazi Party members since the party's inception in 1959. Cole was convinced that Rockwell was a "physical coward" and would not attempt or advocate violence or illegal activities to overthrow the government. He characterized Rockwell as a "loudmouth" who did not want to work for a living, whose only purpose was to "disrupt and antagonize." The Bureau conducted dozens of interviews with ex-Nazis, none of which supported the premise that Rockwell's true intentions were to use violence to achieve his objectives.[31]

Rockwell flew to California and brought the Western Division up to speed on his election activities in Virginia. He told the men at the Glendale headquarters that once he was elected he would initiate several radical changes in state government:

1. Issue an order that all public schools teach white supremacy for one hour every day.
2. Deputize all white men in Virginia so they could carry guns. "If any nigger gets smart, he'll get shot." If a white man was tried and convicted, Rockwell would grant a pardon.
3. Outlaw the federal income tax. Rockwell claimed he had found a loophole in the law such that if a filer wrote "I take the Fifth Amendment" across his income tax return, the IRS would be powerless to collect monies.
4. Push legislation to outlaw the ADL and NAACP.[32]

On April 27, Rockwell appeared on the *Michael Jackson Program* on radio station KNX-CBS Los Angeles. The fifty-thousand-watt station aired the entire Rockwell-Jackson dialogue as well as callers' questions for more than three hours that evening. The two men maintained a verbal joust throughout the interview; at times their exchanges were so heated that Jackson bolted from his chair in anger, twice threatening to end the interview after Rockwell uttered "Martin Luther Coon." Rockwell apologized for the slips, and the interview continued.

One of Jackson's primary questions to Rockwell was "Why does America tolerate you?" Rockwell replied,

I don't think America tolerates me, I think the majority of Americans think the same way I do, most of them don't care to say so. Most of them are fed up with Negro pushing, they're fed up with the Jewish-communists who have been time and again exposed as selling us out to the Soviet Union; they're fed up with the cowardice of our administration. I think they're grateful that we're finally fighting in Viet Nam, but...I think we'll lay down like we did in Korea and quit. In other words, I think the people are with me....They don't like the name [Nazi] but they believe what I believe.

During the course of the interview, Jackson described himself as a "peace-creep," a "love-monger," and a Jew. Most callers expressed anger at Rockwell; some admitted to being Jewish or black. Several callers praised Rockwell, one going so far as to say, "I'm sure God is on his side." By the end of the show both men were thoroughly exhausted from verbal battling. Protests against the station were immediately lodged with the FCC by several listeners.[33]

On April 30, Ralph Forbes was convicted of violating the Glendale Building Code and sentenced to five days in jail and a $550 fine. Forbes was booked and released on bail, pending appeal. The next week, in a separate case, Forbes won the right to remain in his house until the lease expired on November 30. His landlord was ordered to pay for the court costs of the eviction proceedings.[34] The Western Division had twenty-five members who attended meetings and contributed funds. Forbes allowed visitors to attend three meetings as an observer; after that the person had to request membership or be prohibited from attending.

On May 15, three Western Division–ANP troopers were arrested in front of a Glendale supermarket. Walter Gould, Fred Harry, and Robert Giles were staging a counter-picket of CORE, attired in black "Ubangi" masks with curly black wigs, gold earrings, and black leggings with a hammer and sickle painted on one rear pocket and a Star of David on the other. Their placards read, "I demands jobs, missionaries, white girls, and welfare too." One of the Nazis brandished a long plastic rattle; he would periodically leap into the air, shaking the rattle and screaming in imitation of a jungle witch doctor.[35] The Nazis were eventually acquitted by the Los Angeles County Appellate Court, reversing a lower court conviction for disturbing the peace and endangering public peace.

In early May 1965, Rockwell traveled to Flint, Michigan, to give a speech at Flint Junior College, but when he arrived the director of student affairs denied him permission to speak. Later in the week, there were several student protests of that action as a restriction on academic freedom. Dr. Lawrence Jarvie, the superintendent of community education, tried to convince the students that the cancellation had been not for censorship but security. Jarvie stated, "Wherever Mr. Rockwell has appeared, violence has resulted, to the point of riots."[36] The FJC administration was so angry and embarrassed by the Rockwell debacle that it expelled Robert Beam, president of student government, for engineering the visit.

While Rockwell was touring the country, Matt Koehl was leading demonstrations in the District of Columbia. On May 8, he led six Nazis on a picket in front of the White House for six hours with placards:

Gas Jew-Communist Traitors
Down with Six Million Lie

Two weeks later Koehl led eleven Nazis in a demonstration at the Chilean embassy to protest the conviction of Chilean Nazi Franz Pfeiffer for bombing a synagogue. The ANP placards read:

Free Franz Pfeiffer
Free Chilean Nazi Leader
End Dictatorship in Chile

On May 27, Rockwell appeared in Arlington Domestic Relations Court to answer a request from his ex-wife for increased support payments. Rockwell complained to the judge that his political beliefs impaired his earning power, the IRS was hounding him, and the party owed seven months' back rent on the headquarters. He mentioned the prospect of a new job in Richmond that would pay him $25,000 per year—the governorship. Ex-wife Judy, who had been receiving $150 per month since 1961, asked for a $50-per-month increase. Rockwell offered to split the difference with Judge Berton Kramer, at $175 per month. Judge Kramer agreed.[37]

Throughout the spring Rockwell had been writing a political "correspondence course" he called *Legal, Psychological & Political Warfare*. The course utilized his years of expertise in street agitation, propaganda, demonstrations, and legal maneuvering. On June 4, 1965, he sent out the following letter to supporters, offering the course for $95:

Dear Supporter:

I sincerely believe you simply MUST have the kind of hard-boiled, practical KNOW-HOW we are offering in our new, down-to-earth course in Legal, Psychological and Political Warfare. You need this information in the struggle you are already putting up, if you are to be as effective as possible, and still stay out of Jew and nigger jails.

In fact, I am SO sure that you will agree with me that you MUST have this practical know-how that I am sending this first lesson to you with no obligation whatsoever—absolutely FREE. Whether you enroll in the Course, or not, keep this first lesson and SEE if it does not help make you strong and powerful in our battle against Jew-communism and race-mixing!

There are twenty-five more lessons like this one in the complete course. . . . Read and think about what this FIRST lesson will mean to you and your fight with the enemies of our Race and Nation. Then decide if you can AFFORD to be without this priceless, practical, COMBAT information. . . .

Whatever you do, you must act NOW to get in on this year's course! Don't wind up sitting in some jail cell wishing you had known some simple fact which would have brought victory instead of time as a prisoner of Jews and niggers!

For Race and Nation!
Lincoln Rockwell[38]

Although sales of the course never reached Rockwell's expectations, the manual did provide excellent advice on "guerrilla theater," jails, court hearings, and various methods of protest.

Rockwell traveled to Dallas in late June to inform the unit that the time had come for it to "switch from an educational program to a program of agitation." Robert Surrey presented a white Chevrolet three-quarter-ton pickup to Rockwell for use in his campaign. The pickup had a walk-in camper attached to the box; the roof was outfitted with a removable speaking platform, a high-tech public-address system with a Grundig power amplifier, a wooden podium with a thick piece of plate steel inside to protect Rockwell from bullets, and a trapdoor for entrance and exit to the roof.

The Dallas unit went into action on July 4. Hundreds of Dallas citizens came downtown in ninety-six-degree heat to watch a "Spirit of 1776" theme parade that featured local dignitaries, pretty girls twirling batons, brass bands, marching servicemen, and a swastika float by the Dallas unit of the American Nazi Party. Adorning each side of a hay wagon were white placards: "America White—Africa Black."[39] The float was decorated with a four-foot-high swastika, the Stars and Stripes, and a Confederate flag. The use of the Confederate flag was an idea of the Klan followers who had switched to the ANP; Rockwell used the flag in his gubernatorial campaign to capitalize on the strong "states rights" sympathies of the South.

In late July 1965, Rockwell delivered more than a thousand signatures to the Virginia State Board of Elections, qualifying him for the November election. On July 23 the party rented a small storefront at 22 North Seventh Street in Richmond as a campaign headquarters for the White Majority Party. Above the "Rockwell for Governor" banner in the window flew Confederate, United States, and Virginia flags. In his campaign Rockwell pledged to "maintain the Constitution and the White Race"; his slogan—Vote Right; Vote White; Vote Rockwell.

ANP supporter Frank Smith volunteered the use of his Lincoln Continental to help with the campaign. Since Smith was unable to drive the car due to poor vision, Colonel Welch hitched a ride to Maine to drive Smith and the car down to Richmond. They stopped in Arlington on the way to pick up several thousand "Rockwell for Governor" pamphlets. Smith immediately took a liking to the attractive twenty-three-year-old party secretary, Claudia McCullers. On her desk sat a large "broomstick" Mauser pistol. Smith picked up the gun and said, "This looks like a good weapon, whose gun is this?"

"It belongs to Captain Lloyd," replied McCullers. Captain Lloyd had purchased the Mauser from the Greentop Gun Shop in Lanover County, Virginia, in 1962 for seventy dollars. He kept the pistol in a desk drawer in Richmond in case there was trouble.[40]

At national headquarters in Arlington, Alan Welch led ten Nazis in a picket in front of the District Building to protest home rule for the District of Columbia. The Nazis carried placards that read:

Home Rule Means Nigger Rule
Down With Home Rule
No Black Rule in D.C.
Remember White Victims of Black Crime

On August 4, ten ANP members picketed in front of Shaw Junior High School in Washington, D.C., "to protest in a peaceful and orderly manner Martin Luther King's presence in the national capital and to point out he has a communist background, and yet is honored by the United States government." The Nazis carried pickets reading:

America for Whites, Africa for Blacks

Down with M. L. Coon [a communist hammer through the C in "Coon"]

That evening, at a rally on Forty-eighth Street and Deane Avenue, thousands of blacks awaited King's arrival, along with two Nazis and a film crew from California working on a documentary on the ANP. When King arrived, Troopers Doug Niles and Harold Booker jumped the fence surrounding the event and charged him, yelling "Heil Hitler." Niles carried a canister of yellow and red paint to squirt on King but was intercepted by police before he or Booker neared King. The next day the ANP staged a ten-man anti-King picket at the White House; King was inside, visiting the president.

On August 9, a procession of five hundred leftists led by Robert Moses and David Dellinger marched from the Washington Monument to the Capitol. When the marchers attempted to enter the Capitol grounds they were stopped by police; the marchers responded by squatting on the spot. At that moment two Nazis in mufti ran at the two leaders, squirting both Moses and Dellinger with red paint, red for communist. The Nazis were immediately arrested for disorderly conduct.

On August 11, 1965, a week-long riot erupted in the Watts district of Los Angeles. Thousands of African-American rioters, protesting police brutality, terrified Los Angeles and the country with the most destructive civil disorder in the nation's peacetime history. Rioters attacked white motorists, overturned and burned automobiles, exchanged gunfire with police, and looted and burned stores to the battle cry of "Burn, baby, burn!" When order was finally restored, thirty-five people had been killed, more than a thousand wounded, four thousand arrested, and nearly a thousand buildings looted, damaged, or destroyed. Property damage was estimated at $200 million.

The Johnson administration responded by pushing an "anti-poverty" bill through Congress appropriating $790 million in 1964 and $1.5 billion in 1965. Johnson ordered $29 million in programs for the Los Angeles area.

Millions of whites across the country viewed the rioting as part of the civil rights movement. Reactionaries saw the events as communist-inspired revolution. For Rockwell, the timing was perfect. Anarchy in the streets put fear into the hearts and minds of white people—he could capitalize on it. Exploitation of racial fear was a faster road to power than anti-Semitism. As money began to pour into the party treasury, Rockwell stepped up his campaign, producing a one-hour publicity film.

The first part of the film was an introduction by Robert Surrey of the Dallas unit, who, explaining that "as a former leader of the John Birch Society" he was interested in right-wing organizations, questioned Rockwell about the aims and purpose of the White Majority Party. The second segment was more testimonial in nature, giving Rockwell the opportunity to express his anti-Jewish, anti-black sentiments. Because of the relatively high cost—$111 per copy—only a few films were manufactured. They were shipped to headquarters units around the country in hopes of generating contributions for the campaign.

Meanwhile in Texas the Dallas unit staged an anti–school integration demonstration at the South Cliff High School in a white neighborhood of well-kept homes. While most of the stormtroopers were picketing South Cliff High, Trooper Al Gray attempted to register a rented monkey as a student in the first grade at Ennin Elementary School in Dallas. Gray was arrested for disturbing the peace. Not to be outdone by the Dallas unit, Rockwell arranged for a live monkey to be put on display in a cage in the Richmond campaign headquarters window, with a sign reading "Martin Luther Coon."

On September 5 and again on September 20 the Dallas unit picketed the Dallas Zoo with placards proclaiming the NAAMAG—National Association for the Advancement of Monkeys, Apes, and Gorillas—a caricature of the NAACP. The Nazis carried placards:

Free the Monkeys
First Men in Space!
Monkeys Need Public Education Too[41]

The Dallas city attorney's office reacted by drafting an ordinance prohibiting the distribution of literature in the zoo.[42]

Rockwell delivered dozens of speeches throughout Virginia that summer and fall. One particular night in September he spoke in front of a crowd of one hundred people in Fredricksburg City Park. He attacked the previous two governors of the state, Lindsay Almond, Jr., and

Albertis Harrison, Jr., for "selling out" the white people, and attacked the Democratic nominee, Mills Godwin, Jr., who had recently criticized the Ku Klux Klan:

> He says he's going to try to get rid of the Ku Klux Klan but not those black terrorists and rioters. All he says he's going to do is get rid of the defense organizations of the white people. I think he's running for a federal judgeship.[43]

Rockwell ended his speech with vigor, raising a Winchester lever-action rifle and shouting, "All of you ought to own one of these."

On September 13, 1965, Rockwell appeared live on Channel 13 in Lynchburg, Virginia, for a speech and call-in question-and-answer session. In the week following his appearance nearly $300 in contributions came into the party coffers. The next week he purchased more television time, this time a one-hour slot on station WRVA-TV in Richmond for $658, which included seven twenty-second spot announcements to advertise his appearance.

Rockwell brandishes a rifle on the campaign trail and tells the audience to prepare for black rioters.

When the program commenced the announcer introduced Rockwell's campaign manager, Robert Lloyd. The camera panned over to the blond, clean-cut, all-American-looking Nazi. Lloyd described Rockwell as a man who had served America loyally for almost twenty years as a fighter pilot in the U.S. Navy, a man who had "gathered hundreds of thousands of white, Christian, young people like myself who are fed up with communism and race-mixing in our beloved America and our great state of Virginia."

Rockwell went on camera and spoke on the dangers of communism and race mixing. He predicted that if his opponents were elected it would only fuel race riots like Watts and a continued subservience to the federal government. He illustrated the danger with Cuban-printed pamphlets instructing blacks how to overthrow the U.S. government. He ended his speech after forty-five minutes to take questions by telephone, but most of the calls flooding into the station's switchboard were either obscene or denunciatory and could not be aired.

The FBI's Richmond field office proposed yet another COINTELPRO operation against the party. This time the target was the deputy commander, Alan Welch. Since Welch was extremely active in the day-to-day operations of the party, the Bureau believed that if Rockwell lost faith in Welch during the critical campaign for governor, a severe disruption in ANP activities would result.[44]

Unlike in the proposed COINTELPRO actions against Koehl, the Bureau authorized Richmond to send the following letter, complete with spelling errors, to the Dallas field office, where it was to be forwarded to Rockwell at the Arlington headquarters:

George Lincoln Rockwell
928 North Randolph Street
Arlington, VA

I have been a loyal follower of you for three years and am in complete sympathy with all you are trying to accomplish. yours is the only voice in our society today which courageously speaks the truth. And I want you to know that I am supporting you in your cindiacy for Governor of the State of Virginia.

Rockwell appearing on television during his 1965 campaign for the governorship of Virginia.

I know your berdens are heavy and that you must rely upon other persons to handle much of the day-to-day work of your organization. When you are at Headquarters, you can, and do, keep our operations running smoothly; however, while you are away there is a traitor carrying on the operations at home. This individual is not a traitor to the ideas of National Socialism in which we all believe but he is a physical traitor.

Alan Welch is a traitor to the Nazi Party. Not only is his mind warped but he is nothing but a damn queer. He interviews potential applicants to the Party and rejects those he believes are too manly. He attempted to engage an ANP member in an unnatural sex affair about three months ago. This is known to several of the Party members and we are sickened that a person of such low contemptible morals is in the Party, much less one of its high officers. . . . I hope you can find some way to replace this man who is doing so much to injure our great Party.

> A hopeful member from
> your best chapter.

By postmarking the letter from Dallas the Bureau hoped to perplex Rockwell and add to what was perceived to be his general paranoia.

In late September, Rockwell received the letter from Dallas and immediately contacted the FBI, because he felt it had violated federal law. He told the special agent that the "vicious" letter had disrupted his organization and was a source of great worry to him "as it cast a spell on one of his most trusted workers." The Bureau, of course, did nothing about the letter; it was quite pleased by Rockwell's reaction to the COINTELPRO scheme. The agents circulated a memo congratulating themselves on the success of the endeavor, describing how Rockwell was "wracking his brain" to identify the "spy" in the ANP-Dallas.[45]

On September 20, Rockwell and John Patler walked into the radio studio of WNBC in Rockefeller Plaza, New York City, to tape an interview with John Nabel, host of an all-night radio program. When Nabel asked Rockwell about his followers, Rockwell said, "We have very few. . . . I'm not comparing myself with this Man, but if you had asked Jesus Christ that question, in truth, He would have had to say that He had only twelve followers. And one of them turned out to be a rat! I'm in much the same position."[46] The interview never got on the air. The program's managers decided it was in poor taste and would serve no good purpose.

On September 24, 1965, twenty-year-old Nazi Robert Bruce disrupted a session of the U.S. House of Representatives by showering the floor with racist handbills and hurling a Nazi flag into the chamber. Bruce handcuffed his wrist to a metal handrail before flinging hundreds of one-way "boat tickets to Africa" onto the members of Congress. As security guards attempted to remove him from the gallery Bruce shouted "Long live Rockwell" and "Down with home rule."

At the end of September the ANP in the guise of the White Majority Party was ejected from the Virginia State Fair. Rockwell had set up a booth at the fair to promote his gubernatorial campaign. On display in his booth was a live monkey in a glass cage with a sign: "Residence of Dr. Martin Luther Coon." Beneath the cage was another sign that read "Ah Wants Full Equality. Ah's voting for Godwin." This outrageous display caused a stir among fair-goers and officials. On September 28 the Atlantic Rural Exposition, which operated the fair, obtained an injunction from the county circuit court prohibiting the White Majority Party from operating the booth.[47]

Once the ejection was official Rockwell was ordered to remove everything from the grounds. Having neither manpower nor transportation to do so at that moment he made arrangements to remove it the following day. Fearful that fair organizers would dump his display materials outdoors, Rockwell and Frank Smith decided to stay the night in the booth. They spent a long, miserable night in the fair building before the sun finally came up. Rockwell and Smith were anxious to pack the materials and get some much-needed breakfast. Captain Lloyd was scheduled to pick them up at daylight but failed to arrive. Rockwell angrily paced the floor, muttering, "Where is Lloyd? Where is Captain Lloyd? His is supposed to show up. How come he leaves me here?"

Lloyd finally drove up; he had been somewhere with Elaine, one of the two party secretaries. As the weeks went by Lloyd's attention continued to drift, being more focused on Elaine than election activities. On another occasion Lloyd arranged a rally, but no one could find the site. When the location was discovered it turned out to be a farmer's field. By the end of the year he was asked to withdraw from the party until he could devote his full attention to his duties.[48]

On October 6, a twenty-five-dollar-a-plate banquet for Republican gubernatorial candidate Linwood Holton took place in the Marriott Twin Bridges Hotel across the Potomac from Washington. Over 480 people attended the black-tie affair, including Richard Nixon. Holton addressed the audience and criticized his Democratic opponent, Mills

Godwin, Jr., for refusing to debate him. Suddenly, the attention of the audience and speaker was disrupted when ANP Deputy Commander Alan Welch stood up at a dinner table and shouted, "Are you willing to appear with George Lincoln Rockwell?"

Candidate Holton was stunned. The packed house was silent. "Are you willing to appear with George Lincoln Rockwell?" Welch yelled again. Holton's supporters regained their senses and ejected Welch from the hall.[49] Welch was disgusted at Holton's claim that he invited anyone and everyone to debate him on the issues. Rockwell—a registered candidate—had been refused participation in a statewide debate. A few days later at the same Marriott hotel, the Democratic gubernatorial candidate, Mills Godwin, was the featured dinner guest. Shortly after Godwin began his speech, ANP Officer Matt Koehl strode forward and shouted, "If you believe in equality, would you debate Mr. Rockwell?" The Democrats were prepared for the outburst; a group of men converged on the Nazi and escorted him from the building.[50]

On October 16, Rockwell gave a speech atop the ANP camper at a rally in Richmond. He told the dozens of listeners his political opponents were not telling the true nature of the "nigger threat to white, Christian America." He asserted that the civil rights movement was being directed by Cuban and Russian communists and that the race riots in Rochester, Danville, New York, and Los Angeles were all part of a "master plan" of terror: "The top officials of this state and those in the federal government are a bunch of cowards. Until you get a Wallace, you haven't got anything." He declared to the audience that the rioting in Watts had "cowed that city's entire police force and now they want to take your guns away. Remember, a free America is an armed America."[51]

Rockwell purchased two five-minute time slots on WRC-TV, the NBC affiliate in Washington, D.C., to deliver a political message. For $880 cash, Rockwell purchased a 7:25 P.M. time slot on October 28 and 29. The studio was extremely apprehensive about the public reaction to Rockwell's heavy-handed anti-black remarks, but NBC officials had no choice in the matter because election regulations required them to grant television access for campaign messages if the candidate had the money to purchase air time. The first broadcast generated more than a hundred calls, of mixed sympathies. The second message, on October 29, was practically ignored by the public.

In late October, Abe Rosenthal, the metropolitan editor of the *New*

York Times, received a tip that Dan Burros, former national secretary of the ANP and king kleagle (chief organizer) of the United Klans of America in the New York City area, was Jewish. Rosenthal assigned reporter McCandlish Phillips, a "born again," evangelical, fundamentalist Christian, to do a background check on Burros and see if the tip could be substantiated. Phillips discovered that Burros had been a star pupil at a Hebrew school in a Queens synagogue and had had a bar mitzvah at age thirteen. Phillips tried to contact Burros on several occasions, with no success. Finally, in the early morning of October 29, he spotted Burros leaving his Queens apartment and followed him to a barbershop. Phillips confronted the crew-cut Burros when he emerged, and they walked to a nearby luncheonette. After Phillips recited Burros's Klan and Nazi credentials, he asked, "There's one thing about you I can't figure out, it doesn't fit the picture. Your parents were married in a Jewish wedding ceremony."

"You're not going to print that!" Burros snapped. "I'll have to retaliate, do you understand? If you publish that, I'll come and get you and kill you. I don't care what happens. I'll be ruined. This is all I've got to live for." They left the restaurant and walked into the street. Phillips turned to Burros: "I'm through asking questions. I just want to talk to you for a few minutes as one human being to another human being." Burros made no reply. "I've been told that you feel trapped in this movement, that you think you can't get out. But there is an exit for you. I want to quote a verse from the Bible, a verse that has been meaningful for me: 'If any man be in Christ, he is a new creature; old things are passed away. Behold all things are become new.'"

"You're trying to con me," Burros sneered. "I'm not, I mean it," Phillips answered. Dan Burros walked away, back to his apartment in Queens.

Throughout that day Burros telephoned the *Times* with threats against Phillips. That evening he took a bus to the home of fellow Klansman and one time ANP sympathizer Roy Frankhouser in Reading, Pennsylvania. The next morning, October 31, Burros left Frankhouser's house to pick up the Sunday edition of the *Times* at a newsstand. The bold headline leapt from the page, sending a shock through his body:

STATE KLAN LEADER HIDES SECRET OF JEWISH ORIGIN

Burros stormed back to Frankhouser's home seething with rage, kicking furniture throughout the house in an unstoppable rampage. He found Frankhouser's nickel-plated .32-caliber revolver and yelled, "I'm ruined!" He put the barrel of the pistol to his chest and shouted, "Long live the white race! I've got nothing to live for!" He pulled the trigger, put the pistol to his head, and fired another round into his brain. The twenty-eight-year-old Nazi turned Klansman was dead.[52]

Rockwell's eulogy in the *Stormtrooper* told how Burros's life had been "steeped in racist revolutionary causes" like the ANP, the Minutemen, and finally the Klan. With his suicide Burros had "ended his miserably sad life of lies. . . . The Burros Episode is but one more indication of the madness of the people known as Jews. . . . They are a unique people with a distinct mass affliction of mental disorders . . . symptoms of paranoia, delusions of grandeur, and delusions of persecution. . . . Dan Burros was the product of this unfortunate Jewish psychosis. It cost him his life."[53]

Matt Koehl, Rockwell, and Alan Welch (left to right) in November 1965 at a press conference after Dan Burros's suicide. Burros, a former Nazi, shot himself after the *New York Times* exposed his Jewish heritage.

AP/Wide World Photos

Privately, Rockwell was stunned and saddened by the death. He admired Burros's talent at writing propaganda, his ability to condense an idea down to its most elemental meaning in such a way that it was impossible not to understand and remember it. He had been a "brilliant young man and hugely dedicated to the Cause . . . and he worked like a Trojan as a printer." Koehl remembers that Burros had not looked like a typical Jew and probably had a fair amount of "Aryan blood." Rockwell believed that whatever differences they might have had, Burros had been a sincere "righteous Jew" and that something could have been worked out whereby Burros could have continued to serve the National Socialist cause in some capacity and averted the tragedy.[54] Burros's exposure was not the result of FBI COINTELPRO action; Bureau files indicate that no action was ever directed against him. According to the *Washington Evening Star*, a more likely possibility was that his exposure was orchestrated by a Jewish organization.[55]

The November election took place. Rockwell garnered 5,730 votes for the White Majority Party, slightly under 1 percent of the total vote. Most conservatives rallied behind William Story, a Bircher and militant segregationist; he received 69,348 votes. The election was won by Democrat Godwin. Rockwell told the press, "I had figured realistically that I would get about three thousand votes." He called the results "amazing, considering the press blackout." Privately, Rockwell was very disappointed by the election results, attributing defeat to several factors: the local rallies had been poorly attended because the party had been unable to purchase sufficient advertising on radio and in newspapers; and his few television appearances were all but unadvertised, and poorly scheduled.

He told his followers there were two significant reasons for his failure. One was the Jewish community's silent treatment. Rockwell had expected the Jewish community to react strongly in the media to his candidacy; instead of "taking the bait" as he hoped, it had ignored him and denied him valuable publicity. The other primary reason for his failure was prosperity: the masses did not need him. How could he make revolutionaries out of people with full stomachs, two-car garages, and color televisions? Hitler had made almost no progress until the German economy collapsed and Bolshevik terror reigned in the streets. White Americans were simply too fat, too soft, too satiated with "bread and circus" to respond to him.

The vote total confirmed to Rockwell that he was now in the third phase of the ANP "struggle for power." The first phase—to make himself known to the masses—had been accomplished. The second phase—dissemination of the party program—was also accomplished. The third phase, under way, was organizing the people within the movement. The fourth phase—attainment of power through the votes of the newly won masses—would have to wait. Economic conditions were simply too good.

After the election it was business as usual for the ANP. On November 12, ten Nazis picketed the U.S. State Department to protest the refusal of the United States to recognize the racist government of Rhodesia. The Nazis carried placards:

Protect White People of Rhodesia
Arm White Rhodesia
White Man Fight
G. Washington 1776—Ian Smith 1965

On November 16, Rockwell and two bodyguards drove the camper to a trailer park just outside Duluth, Minnesota. Student organizer Martin Jordan picked him up and gave him a tour of the freshwater port of Duluth before taking him to a local radio station for an interview. Campus security officers were incensed at student organizers for breaking security precautions, but Rockwell sided with the students, declaring that the "most dangerous thing is a big police escort."

His speech commenced in Kirby Hall to an overflow crowd of a thousand spectators. He told the group that a power blackout that had occurred the week before on the East Coast was no coincidence; the same thing would happen all over the country: "It's a dress rehearsal for what they [the communists] have in mind." He asserted that the Jewish-led overthrow of the Russian monarchy in World War I had been financed by "a bunch of Wall Street Jews," who had paid Leon Trotsky to leave New York City and run the revolution. "Communism is a movement by atheistic Jews; Karl Marx was a Jew. . . . Trotsky was a Jew." The disintegration of the country was the next topic: "Civilization is disintegrating. It's the same thing that happened in Rome. Homosexuality is on the rise, just as it was in the last days of Rome. But America isn't dying of old age. It's being poisoned by the conspiracy." He told the audience he hated communism so much that if there were a legal means available, he would have no compunctions about killing Gus Hall.[56]

The *Mesabi Daily News* blasted the college students for inviting Rockwell and Hall to campus:

> It is a disgrace to a great institution of learning...a small core of young people who are basically out of tune with the traditions of America. These are the persons who in the guise of academic freedom, would injure the cause of education. They are simply rebels against constituted authority, the fine disciplines....A few well chosen expulsions could be in order.[57]

The International Longshoremen's Association of the AFL-CIO also condemned the speakers as un-American: "A communist and a Nazi have no free speech, particularly in a taxpayers' institution such as the University." The Minnesota Branch of the ACLU supported the students' right to academic freedom: "The University of Minnesota at Duluth has been and is operating under a policy on campus speakers which allows full access to all information on current topics."[58]

From Duluth the Nazis crossed the liberal bastion of Minnesota into Grand Forks, North Dakota, for an evening speech in the Prairie State Ballroom at the University of North Dakota. Rockwell told the audience that Hitler had not killed six million Jews in World War II, that analysis of the prewar and postwar population figures listed in the *World Almanac* showed it to be "numerically impossible." He ended his talk by saying he would like to be remembered "as the man who preserved the white people and stopped the fighting. I would like to be known as one who brought nobility and courage to the white man."[59] The audience was very polite. There was no booing or heckling.

On November 27, a large antiwar protest took place in the streets of Washington. More than twenty thousand protesters milled around the White House in what was dubbed the March on Washington for Peace in Vietnam. Some of the peace marchers carried Vietcong flags, sparking brief outbursts of violence between peace marchers and hecklers. One group, calling itself the U.S. Committee to Aid the National Liberation Front of South Vietnam, handed out literature in front of the White House calling for the defeat of the U.S. "aggressors" and the Vietnamese "traitors." Over six hundred policemen were on duty to control the crowd.

The ANP had been given a permit for a nearby counter-demonstration that day. Four ANP troopers distributed leaflets from the Ad Hoc Committee of Patriots to Stand Up for Our Boys in Vietnam. The leaflets advertised "free gasoline and matches" for any "peace creeps" willing to perform self-immolation (self-immolation by Vietnamese Buddhist monks was committed on several occasions in the 1960s as a means of protesting the war in Vietnam). While the uniformed Nazis handed out literature next to the ANP camper, Rockwell and several troopers, incognito in hippie clothing with hair combed in front of their eyes, infiltrated the peace marchers. Their objective: to seize North Vietnamese and Vietcong flags. Rockwell spotted a youth holding a red flag with a single gold star. He stalked the flag carrier until the right moment, then abruptly ripped the flag from his grasp and tore it to pieces. The marchers were outraged. Several attacked Rockwell and beat him, but police interceded and placed him in custody for disorderly conduct. "I was going to put the flag carrier under citizen's arrest but a cop got me first. I'm as guilty as hell, but I'd do it again. They've got no right to carry those flags," Rockwell told reporters. He forfeited ten dollars collateral.[60]

Author's collection

Rockwell seizes a North Vietnamese flag at a Washington peace rally.

Three other ANP troopers were arrested in similar flag incidents. Matt Koehl spotted a flag, but his attempt to rip it from the staff failed. The flag bearer retaliated, beating Koehl with the staff until two other Nazis jumped into the fray and brought him down on the hard asphalt. All were arrested for disorderly conduct.

The Western Division–ANP held a counter-protest on the same day against peace marchers in Los Angeles. The California Nazis drove a truck with a public-address system alongside the peace marchers and denigrated the peace marchers as they walked the streets. The Nazi truck had banners hung from the sides that read:

Kill Reds in Vietnam

Investigate Peace Creeps not KKK

Peace Creeps Are Traitors[61]

On November 30, 1965, the ANP vacated its campaign headquarters at 22 North Seventh Street in Richmond. A few days later Rockwell filed an expenditure report for his gubernatorial campaign totaling $20,631, including $6,857 for an automobile, $4,067 for advertising, $2,205 for printing and mailing of brochures, and $3,979 for opening and operating the headquarters. The next day seven Internal Revenue Service agents seized everything at ANP headquarters for nonpayment of $5,000 in back withholding and corporate income taxes for the years 1963, 1964, and 1965. The agents allowed party members to remove their personal belongings before they padlocked the door. The seizure was not totally unexpected; Rockwell had been negotiating with IRS officials for several months on the tax issue.[62] He estimated the value of the seized goods at between $20,000 and $30,000. The seizure did not affect the barracks, since it was a dwelling and not a place of business. The main problem confronting the party was not the seizure of equipment but the loss of the headquarters building. After five years of near-rent-free usage, Floyd Fleming decided to sell the property to a contractor for $30,000. The party had to vacate by January 15, 1966.

Rockwell filed a $100,000 suit against Treasury Secretary Henry Fowler and three agents of the Internal Revenue Service, claiming that the party officers had been "arbitrarily, unlawfully and wrongfully evicted from their premises." In addition, Rockwell asked Judge Oren Lewis for a temporary injunction to block the public auction of the seized party property, scheduled to be held the week of December 27 unless back taxes of $3,489 were paid.[63]

Senator Clifford Case (R-N.J.), criticized IRS Commissioner Sheldon Cohen, asserting that his scheduled auction of Nazi items put the federal government "in the position of purveying for profit the same stock-in-trade as the American Nazi Party."[64] The IRS, facing a court injunction and Republican Senator Case, postponed the auction until after the hearing before Judge Lewis.

On December 7, Rockwell spoke to a large crowd in Cahn Auditorium at Northwestern University in Evanston, Illinois. The school received complaints from the ADL, Hillel, and the Jewish War Veterans. The speech was restricted to students and faculty; no incidents occurred.[65]

Three weeks later, on December 20, the SDS sponsored a Rockwell speech in Altgeld Auditorium at Northern Illinois University. Rockwell gave two separate, hour-long speeches to capacity crowds of nine hundred people. Both speeches received considerable heckling and booing, and he had to dodge at least one egg. Heavy security kept the event from getting out of hand.[66]

On Christmas, December 25, in Dallas, Texas, five ANP members in stormtrooper attire marched in front of the Statler-Hilton Hotel in protest of an Israel bond banquet inside. With anti-Jewish placards in hand, the Nazis paraded as hundreds of guests arrived for the dinner, which featured the presentation of the Israel Freedom Medallion to the Zale Foundation for helping advance the economic development of Israel. As more and more guests arrived, the Nazis came under verbal attack by guests who took offense at the Nazi placards, which read "A Jew Is a Jew, Is a Jew, Is a Jew," with a depiction of a large beaked nose with a dollar sign in front of it. Catcalls turned into pushing and shoving, a fistfight broke out, and a free-for-all ensued. It took more than a dozen policemen to break up the fight. Two ANP members and a bystander were booked for disturbing the peace.[67]

The year 1965 ended with a last-ditch effort to get copies of the *Rockwell Report* printed. Since the party was now without a press because of the IRS seizure, Robert Surrey arranged for three thousand copies to be printed by an associate in Simmsport, Louisiana, and mailed to Dallas for collation and distribution. All party publications were suspended for the next four months.

Nineteen sixty-five was a year of mixed results. The party received publicity for Robert Lloyd's romp across the House floor and Rockwell's gubernatorial campaign. Nazi stunts in Washington, Dallas, and Glendale received local coverage, but little in the way of national exposure. The party opened a small unit in San Francisco and also received a powerful new printing press.

There were also setbacks. Rockwell's confrontation with King in Selma ended in failure. The FBI COINTELPRO attacks were weakening the party in Chicago and Arlington. His gubernatorial campaign was both costly and tiring, and the skimpy vote total revealed minute support even in Virginia. The loss of the Arlington headquarters was exacerbated by the IRS seizure of equipment.

Looking forward, Rockwell was excited about the country's apparent destabilization. The Watts riots invigorated him, reaffirming his belief that anarchy was being inspired and directed by communists. The urban riots, the peace marches, and the government's escalation of the war in Vietnam were issues Rockwell could exploit. His party was changing, too. Rockwell decided the time was right to meld National Socialism with Christian Identity. In August he tapped Western Division leader Ralph Forbes to become a Christian Identity minister.[68] His strident racial views, his flair for the dramatic and his loyalty to Rockwell made Forbes the perfect man for the job. California was an ideal location; there were numerous Identity ministries successfully operating there. Forbes would be the first Nazi officer to preside over a flock.

By fusing Christian Identity and National Socialism, Rockwell hoped to maximize the synergies of the groups and broaden the potential membership for each group. Nazis could find religious justification and legitimization in the church; Identity members could find political expression for their theology in the ANP. A "riot" could now be expressed as "religion" under the guise of the Identity Church. The push was on within the party to legitimize the cause, to deemphasize Nazism and push racial issues to the forefront. Racial issues could be easily exploited, because they played upon the nativist fears of the white population. To Rockwell's satisfaction, the country seemed to be sliding toward anarchy.

11
1966: WHITE POWER

You're working every day to pay taxes to breed little black
bastards. . . . You're subsidizing Negro mothers who
produce this little black scum for pay, and then when
they don't have any place to live, they want to come and
take your house and neighborhood.

> — Rockwell, Marquette Park,
> Chicago, 1966

Civil unrest in the United States and the battle casualties in Vietnam
continued to increase in 1966. By the year's end, five thousand servicemen had been killed, and war protests increased dramatically. Urban
ghetto riots increased fourfold over 1965. Another long, hot summer of
rioting, public discord, and black militance would unfold in Cleveland,
Chicago, New York, San Francisco, Atlanta, and Oakland.

Rockwell's greatest triumph occurred in 1966, during the Open
Housing rioting in Chicago. He stepped forward to lead the angry people
of Chicago and channel their hatred and hostility into a focused movement against Martin Luther King, Jr. Although his attachment to the
Open Housing violence was parasitic—he was not an instigator of the
white anger—Rockwell was too much of an opportunist and showman
to miss a chance to stir the pot. He also coined the phrase "White
Power" in Chicago to rally the white people around a single cause. John
Patler coined another phrase that summer, "The color of your skin is
your uniform." The de-Nazification of the party had begun. Ideology
would not stand in the way of the pursuit of power.

Rockwell's $100,000 suit against the Internal Revenue Service was
dismissed on January 3, 1966. Judge Lewis ruled that Rockwell had "no
standing" to collect damages, that IRS seizure of party property had
been in accordance with the law. Rockwell told reporters that the seizure
"got me out of action as far as putting out literature is concerned . . .

[but] as long as the Constitution exists at all, I'm in business. . . . What they got is our physical plant, but we are actually a spiritual movement."[1]

The party was unable to shift its party headquarters to the barracks on Wilson Boulevard because the property was not zoned commercial. The IRS eventually returned most of the seized items. Commissioner Cohen assessed numerous items—pictures of Hitler, swastika armbands, hate literature—as of no value; only the ANP office furniture and photographic and printing equipment would be sold at public auction.

The FBI COINTELPRO operatives seized the opportunity to attack the party. They produced a scheme to send a phony letter to the party's most ardent financial backers as well as rank-and-file members and sympathizers. The theme of the letter was "do not send money" to the ANP to help combat the IRS because their names would be exposed to the government. The letter read:

Dear Contributor:

As you know from the newspapers, the Jews in Washington have tried to finish their plot against us and have seized all the worthwhile property belonging to the Party and our beloved Commander, George Lincoln Rockwell. We are fighting them as best we know how and can assure you that National Socialism will win out over the treachery placed upon us.

We are confident that our fight to regain our property will prevail; therefore, we request that you do not send any money to National Headquarters or to our Dallas, Los Angeles, or Chicago chapters. We are afraid that the federal government will obtain your name if you send money and they will harass you as they are harassing us. We do not want you to be compromised and would rather you remain in the background until the air clears.

We would be desirous of obtaining your well wishes but please, I repeat, do not send money for fear of reprisal.

If you have received our previous letters requesting that you help us financially, please disregard, because we believe the threat of reprisal is imminent and do not wish to bring harm to you.

American Nazi Party National Headquarters[2]

The FBI skullduggery had little or no impact on the party. Matt Koehl later recalled that hard-core support remained intact.

On January 9, Rockwell arrived in Houston, Texas, for a speech at Rice University sponsored by the Weiss College speakers series. His speech was repeatedly interrupted by hecklers both inside and outside the auditorium. At one point a group of hecklers outside the building chanted "Speak louder, speak louder." Another group crawled onto the roof of the building and ran back and forth to make noise in the hall. Rockwell told the crowd, "I'm used to it. A lot of people prejudge me and want to raise hell and drown out facts, but they can't do it. No amount of hissing and booing can stop me from telling you the truth." [3] The appearance featured a debate with Ben Levy, chairman of the Houston Socialist Forum. Each man bemoaned the difficulty of presenting his ideas to the nation. Levy said the American Socialist Party "hasn't got the dough to buy even one minute of national television time." Rockwell told the students his views were barred from national television because the networks were owned by "Russian Jews."

On January 24, the ANP and the White Party of America worked together to disrupt the SNCC. The event was coordinated by two Canadians who had infiltrated SNCC and had devised a scheme to jam SNCC phone lines with nuisance calls. SNCC was spearheading a boycott of the Capital Transit Bus Lines in the District of Columbia, an effort which required coordination of car pools. The jammed SNCC telephone lines caused people to be stranded throughout the city, and the boycott was crippled.

On January 29, Rockwell arrived at Love Field in Dallas, where he was met by eight khaki-clad stormtroopers who snapped to attention and gave the Nazi stiff-arm salute. He told reporters he was in Dallas to stage a demonstration and provoke an arrest in order to prove a new city ordinance, aimed at the ANP, unconstitutional. The ordinance was designed to restrict the activities of extremist groups if they "interfere with public assembly or tend to incite riots by deprecating any group's ethnic origin." The ordinance read:

> Any person singularly or in concert with others, who, by the use of placards, signs, devices, uniforms or other paraphernalia which knowingly deprecates the ethnic origin of, or advocates the denial of Civil Rights to, any group, race or color of people, interferes with or attempts to interfere with a lawful public or private assembly, with intent to provoke an immediate breach of the peace, or with knowledge that he is likely to incite an immediate breach of peace, shall be deemed to have committed the offense of disorderly conduct. [4]

Rockwell called the ordinance (an outgrowth of the December 25, 1965, incident at the Statler-Hilton Hotel where two Nazis had been arrested for picketing the Israel bond banquet) "among the most unconstitutional I have ever run into. . . . I am coming to Dallas to break the ordinance as a test of the law."[5] (Fred Weldon, the Dallas ACLU president, stated, "We do not feel any wrong motives are involved, but there is a failure to take into account the constitutional law as it had developed in recent years.")[6] Later that day he carried a picket in front of the Praetorian Building, which housed the offices of the Anti-Defamation

Rockwell pickets alone in Dallas to protest a city ordinance meant to control hate groups.

League. Except for a handful of newsmen and a few plainclothes policemen, the picket received little attention until a bystander walked up to Rockwell and spit full in his face. A startled Rockwell turned to the bystanders and yelled, "Aren't there any cops around? Did you see him spit in my face?" After marching five minutes in nineteen-degree cold and wind, Rockwell put down his picket sign and held a brief press conference: "I think this proves the ordinance is invalid and the city knows it."

Rockwell remained in Dallas to help plan a demonstration about Walter Jenkins, President Johnson's personal advisor. Jenkins had been arrested for engaging in homosexual activity in a men's room at a YMCA. After his arrest for "disorderly conduct," reporters discovered that Jenkins had been arrested on the same charge in the same washroom five years earlier.[7] Rockwell wanted to exploit the close relationship between the president and Jenkins. Two weeks later the Dallas unit commenced a picket in front of Jenkins's home, then went after Dallas Mayor Erik Jonsson. They reproduced a photograph of Jonsson with Roy Wilkins of the NAACP on a leaflet with two swastikas and the caption "For his outstanding and unceasing service in behalf of the Jew-Nigger Bloc, the Dallas Unit of the American Nazi Party does hereby bestow upon Erik Jonsson the title of Honorary Nigger."[8] ANP headquarters sent stormtroopers to demonstrate in front of the White House for a full week, with placards reading "Is LBJ Queer?" and "How Many More Queers in the White House?"

Nazis picket the White House after Walter Jenkins— a close advisor of President Johnson— was arrested for homosexual activity in a YMCA men's room.

Author's collection

They also disrupted a gay-lesbian convention at the Sheraton Park Hotel in the District of Columbia. Robert Lloyd burst in on the meeting with a large box wrapped in pink paper labeled "EMERGENCY SHIP-MENT! Rush to: Queer Convention. 24 Qts Vaseline." Lloyd yelled for Rabbi Eugene Lippman (the featured speaker) so he could deliver the package. Lloyd was arrested for disorderly conduct and fined ten dollars.

In New York a student group at Columbia University called Humanitas invited Rockwell to speak. Rockwell sent John Patler to New York on February 8 to discuss arrangements with Dotson Rader, chairman of Humanitas. Patler asked for the two-hundred-dollar honorarium in advance, that there be no placards inside McMillin Theatre, and a student introduction. As he was about to leave Rader's apartment, the telephone rang. It was Rockwell. The New York Police Department had called to warn Rockwell that the outstanding warrant against him would be served if he tried to speak at Columbia. Rockwell instructed Patler to cancel the engagement: "The Jew Vets are out to get my ass. I can't chance coming."

Rader and Patler argued with Rockwell, trying to change his mind. Rockwell finally agreed to make the speech but demanded an attorney be put on retainer and that a secret entry to McMillin Theatre be arranged to avoid police intervention. Rader set to work arranging the new details. He informed Columbia's security staff of the arrival requirements and that Rockwell would seclude himself at his own apartment before the speech rather than stay at the Astor Hotel as planned. His attempts to secure legal counsel met with failure; Rader was turned down by more than twenty lawyers.

The next evening Rader and several Columbia associates picked up Patler and drove to Newark Airport to await Rockwell's arrival. Rockwell stepped onto the concourse wearing a raincoat and dark glasses, with his trademark corncob pipe. He introduced himself to the collegians, turned to Patler, and said, "How's it going, John?" Patler smiled. They crammed into a car and headed into New York. Rockwell asked for his money and handed the check to Patler. When he asked about the attorney, Rader told him no one would take the job. "Stop the fucking car!" Rockwell shouted. "No!" Patler cried, "I'll get Berger if anything happens."[9] Rockwell agreed, and they continued on. They parked a block from Rader's apartment and took the elevator up to the seventeenth floor—one floor above Rader's apartment—in case detectives or hoodlums were lurking on Rader's floor. Patler walked down the stairs to sixteen, found no one in the hallway, and waved the others forward.

Outside McMillin Theatre, a small army of policemen, including eighteen on horseback, worked the streets trying to keep order. More than 150 anti-Rockwell protesters marched outside the theater with signs:

Smash Fascism
Don't Listen to Nazi Rockwell
It Can't Happen Here

A line of people over two city blocks long waited for admittance. Inside the theater a janitor discovered a small black box behind a water cooler, making a ticking sound. A police bomb squad opened the box and found an alarm clock and a maze of wires made to look like a bomb. A thorough search of the building followed.

When it was time for Rockwell to leave Rader's apartment, police detectives were waiting in the hallway and promptly arrested him; Columbia security had given away Rockwell's whereabouts.[10] The warrant directed any police officer in New York State to convey Rockwell not to the nearest jail but to one particular jail, "The Tombs," on the Lower East Side. Rockwell feared that this notorious hellhole was run by "niggers," Jews, and hoodlums who would do anything for money and would see to it that he "fell out of a bunk." Ordinarily an arrest on such a minor charge as disorderly conduct was of no concern; bail was quite low, between ten and a hundred dollars. Rockwell was worried because every time ANP members were arrested on such charges in New York City or Philadelphia, bail was set in the thousands. If this happened while he was locked up in "The Tombs," he might never leave his cell alive.

When police finished booking him, two jailers took him to the stairway and led him down the rusty iron stairs. Step after step, he could feel the temperature drop as he descended into the prison. On the last flight of stairs he could hear hollering and shouting from the caged men. At the bottom of the stairway stood two beefy black guards with smiles on their faces. The jailers led him to a steel door, opened it, and pushed him inside. He looked around and realized he was in solitary confinement.

After a few hours he was brought before Criminal Court Judge James Watson, an African American. An attorney for the Jewish War Veterans, the complainant, demanded the highest possible bail for Rockwell. Watson told him, "Let me say that in this court everyone has equal justice under the law, whether he be the lowest or the highest." [11] Rockwell was released on one hundred dollars cash bond. During his arraignment a bystander rushed at Rockwell screaming, "The only good Nazi is a dead Nazi!" Police restrained the man, but he continued shouting that his mother, sisters, and brothers had been killed by Nazis. He was frisked by police and ushered out of the courtroom. Outside he told reporters that he had heard of Rockwell's arrest and impending court appearance on the radio and had resolved "to try and get my hands on him." When a reporter asked what he would have done had he reached Rockwell, the man removed a dime from his pocket, placed it between his teeth, and bent it double, then silently held it out in reply. [12]

Martin Berger, a twenty-seven-year-old Jewish lawyer, defended Rockwell for the American Civil Liberties Union. Berger received anonymous telephone threats and open criticism for his action. For his part, Rockwell told Berger, "If there were more Jews like you, I'd be out of business." [13] The next morning Rockwell made a brief appearance in criminal court to plead not guilty to the charge of disorderly conduct.

His trial was set for March, before a three-judge panel. He quietly slipped out of the courtroom and into a waiting car for a return trip to Arlington and the safety of the ANP barracks.

In early February, the ANP reopened a unit in San Francisco, under the direction of Alan Vincent, Clyde Irwin having dropped out. The unit referred to itself as the Bay Area Unit–American Nazi Party (BAUANP); it had an initial membership of five men. They regularly passed out leaflets near the Berkeley campus to respond to the frequent distribution of literature by "communists." On March 5, 1966, Vincent was kicked in the "seat of the pants" by a nineteen-year-old female student who objected to his "Hitler Was Right" placard. Lynda Koolish was arrested and charged with assault and battery. The BAUANP conducted regular pickets of the San Francisco W. E. B. DuBois Club and movie theaters showing *A Patch of Blue,* a story of interracial love.[14]

On February 18, the IRS auctioned the seized ANP items. Thirty prospective buyers, curiosity seekers, and newsmen and four ANP members gathered around the front porch of the old headquarters building at 928 North Randolph Street to watch the IRS sell office furniture, photo and printing equipment, American flags, file cabinets, an addressing machine, and various office supplies for a total of $734. Rockwell was not in attendance, but Alan Welch, John Patler, and Doug Niles stood nearby. Welch told a reporter, "We're just watching the vultures pick the carcass." Rockwell made arrangements for William Pierce to purchase essential items for the party, for which he was reimbursed. The net proceeds from the sale were far short of the IRS lien of $3,489. The IRS was anxious to lay claim to the party's $10,000 printing press, but Rockwell insisted it had been rented to the party. Rockwell was forced to reveal the owner of the press; two IRS agents appeared at George Ware's house demanding proof of the rental to Rockwell. Fully prepared for this eventuality, Ware took the men to his local bank and displayed the notarized copy of his agreement with Rockwell.[15] Rockwell's long-standing policy of having no substantial property in his own name had paid a big dividend. There was practically nothing of value for the IRS to seize—no automobiles, no weapons, no printing press, no real estate. Rockwell kept most of the party money in his hip pocket.

In mid-February, Rockwell sent a letter to Karl Allen's White Party in Alexandria offering amnesty to the ex-ANP members: all was forgiven, and he would take them back into the fold. Rockwell was desperate for manpower. With only eight men attached to national headquarters, the party was unable to conduct significant activity in the District of Columbia. He was impressed that the White Party had sustained itself for three years. The ex-ANP men declined to go back into the party: Rockwell had not changed the party's corporate structure.

On March 26, hundreds of peace marchers stood in front of the White House in an antiwar demonstration called the International Days of Protest, organized by the National Coordinating Committee to End the War in Vietnam. The ANP parked the camper on the grass on the north side of Lafayette Park and draped on its side a large swastika banner that read "Stand Up for Our Boys in Viet Nam." With a stormtrooper on each side, Rockwell blasted the "peace-creeps" for cowardice and treachery. Across Pennsylvania Avenue two party members burned a gasoline-drenched North Vietnamese flag on the sidewalk outside the White House. The two Nazis were led off by police, shouting "Sieg Heil! Down with communism! Long live Commander Rockwell!"[16]

The IRS seizure of headquarters had crippled the party's production of literature. Rockwell dispatched men to scout the area for an alternative site for a printing facility. They found a five-acre tract of land with a 15-by-110-foot chicken coop in Spotsylvania County, Virginia. Supporter George Ware purchased the building, and the block structure was quickly upgraded. The party went to considerable expense to clean and equip it with up-to-date wiring, a printing press, photo equipment, two bedrooms, and a kitchen. By April the party was back in the printing business.

Simultaneously, Rockwell mailed a "notice to all members and supporters" that the party was separating its business and order department from the "combat section." Robert and Mary Surrey, the ex-Birchers, of Dallas would now be in charge of all business operations—literature, subscriptions, sales, and fund-raising—and the money would continue to go to Arlington. Alan Welch recalls that the decision to delegate the business office to Dallas was a response to the IRS attack, to keep the mailing list far away from Washington. The party was on its back financially and the "Surreys were a godsend." Rockwell saw them as pure-hearted and honorable, and they enjoyed his full confidence in their professionalism and integrity.[17]

The Western Division–ANP was also occupying a new headquarters, the rent on Ralph Forbes's home having increased fourfold. Forbes found a suitable home in El Monte, California, at 4375 Peck Road. On

April 20, 1966, Rockwell arrived in California for a speech at Stanislaus College, in Turlock. Two days later the Western Division held the First Annual California State Convention of the ANP, a three-day conference at the new headquarters. Rockwell and Patler were present for an outdoor rally along with thirty Western Division supporters to celebrate what would have been the seventy-seventh birthday of Adolf Hitler. A crowd of fifty people gathered outside the home to heckle. Soon the unruly mob was throwing rocks, one of which hit Patler in the eye, knocking him off the porch. Police dispersed the crowd, and Patler was taken to the emergency room for treatment.

On May 2, a beautiful spring Sunday in Seattle, Rockwell and several ANP members prepared for an outdoor speech atop their camper near Westlake Mall, directly beneath a monorail. With a "STAND UP FOR OUR BOYS IN VIET NAM" banner hanging from the side of the vehicle, Rockwell stepped up to the stars-and-bars-painted rostrum to begin his speech to more than five hundred people. He thanked the police department and the city of Seattle for allowing him to speak. He promised there would be no violence during the rally, "unless someone brings a Viet Cong flag."

"And there's a Viet Cong flag," he shouted, pointing into the audience. "Just remember as you look at this flag, it is killing Americans."[18] A bystander grabbed the flag from the demonstrator, threw it to the ground, and stamped on it. "Thank God, you've got some patriots in Seattle," Rockwell yelled. Someone from the crowd tossed the flag up to Rockwell. He grabbed the flag at each end and ripped the five-pointed star symbol in two pieces. The crowd roared with approval.

Seeing their flag being dissected at the hands of a Nazi, several antiwar youths charged the Nazi camper and tore the swastika banner from its moorings. A scuffle erupted between ANP members and the youths; police interceded and quelled the fighting. The Nazis folded up their equipment, loaded it back on the truck and drove off within minutes. A reporter questioned the man who had carried the flag about his intentions. The flag bearer responded, "I represent the people of Viet Nam. This is the flag of the Vietnamese people. I fly this flag to show my love toward the Viet people."[19]

On May 5, the *Washington Daily News* ran a story about an attempt by Rockwell to purchase Hitler's yacht, the *Ostwind*. John Lyman had purchased the sleek racing yawl from the U.S. Navy in 1951 for

$25,000. His price to Rockwell, or anyone else, was $90,000. Hitler had used the boat, with a fine mahogany hull and teak decks inlaid with silver swastikas, for cruises in the Baltic. The U.S. Navy had captured it as a prize in 1945 and used it as a training ship at the Naval Academy. When the upkeep on the old wooden hull became too expensive, the Navy had sold it. Rockwell told the press he was hoping to raise the money from a rich Texan and use the boat as a floating propaganda center for the World Union of National Socialists. Of course, the idea of Rockwell at the helm of the *Ostwind*, with swastika raised high on the mast, was "unthinkable" to the Jewish War Veterans. National JWV Commander Milton Waldor declared,

> The Nazi party would do better to spend its resources for psychiatric treatment for its adherents. I cannot believe that the Coast Guard would permit the Nazis to sail from port to port along our coasts, or up the Mississippi, spewing venom and hate from loudspeakers and flaunting the swastika.[20]

The entire boat scheme was, of course, another publicity stunt. Rockwell had no money.

On May 23, 1966, Rockwell spoke to two thousand students in the Finch Fieldhouse at Central Michigan University in Mount Pleasant. Rockwell told the audience,

> My policy is too radical for the people of today.... My purpose is to train leaders, not ruffians or troublemakers. We are a counter-insurgency group, dedicated to fighting the communist revolution that is slowly taking its toll on the country.

He discussed the Watts riots, predicting even worse racial problems for the coming year:

> Most liberals are sincere in their efforts for civil rights, and most Negroes are people who want to improve themselves. But these people have been infiltrated by communist agitators who wish to throw this country into a state of upheaval and make it ready for revolution.[21]

The next day, Rockwell met a Canadian Nazi, John Beatty, on the middle of the Queenston-Lewiston Bridge spanning the Niagara River. Unable to cross the border, the two Nazis held a conference in the no-man's-land between the U.S.-Canadian immigration gates at either end of the bridge. The men discussed holding a world Nazi congress in Canada within six months. It never materialized.

ANP sympathizer Frank Smith came up with an idea for an ANP

Memorial Day dedication in Portland, Maine. Being a Navy man, Rockwell thought it only fitting to take advantage of an opportunity to honor fellow seamen in the traditional way in his home state. On May 30, Rockwell, Patler, Smith, and Mike Luteman departed in Smith's black Lincoln Continental, adorned with a red-and-black swastika flag on each side of the hood. Matt Koehl, Frank Niles, and secretary Claudia McCullers followed in the party camper. All participants wore civilian clothing; some wore swastika armbands. In Boston Smith arranged for thirteen motorcyclists to escort the procession, which Rockwell dubbed the "Iron Cross Brigade." When the entourage stopped for gasoline and a cup of coffee at a small roadside restaurant the owner of the establishment turned blue in the face as the black leather–clad bikers and Nazis entered. The other customers quickly departed. After a twenty-minute coffee break, the Nazis and the "Iron Cross Brigade" left the restaurant and continued north.[22]

When Rockwell's car reached Maine, the procession was joined by Maine state police, FBI agents, and newspaper reporters. This was the kind of high-publicity trip Rockwell enjoyed: a large contingent of troops to repel attackers, considerable effort by state and local authorities to ensure safe passage, and copious press coverage. When the Nazi entourage reached the Veterans Memorial Bridge outside Portland, it was met by City Manager Graham Watt, Police Chief Leon Webber, and a phalanx of Portland policemen wearing riot helmets and holding nightsticks. After a brief consultation the Nazis were escorted through the center of the city onto Commercial Street along the waterfront. The procession came to a halt when the motorcycle of one of the bikers fell on the railroad tracks. Three hundred local citizens watching from East End Beach reacted gleefully to the mishap.

The Nazis disembarked on the Eastern Promenade, where Rockwell and Patler carried a wreath to the end of a short quay. Rockwell paused while the television cameramen set up their equipment. Puffing slowly on his corncob pipe, he looked out on the spectacle he had created—hundreds of angry citizens, dozens of policemen, and reporters gathered around like vultures near a carcass. The cameramen gave the go-ahead.

"This is in honor of American fighting men and white Christian fighting men I have seen all over the world who gave their lives for this country." He threw the wreath into the harbor. "Let's have a few moments of silence for our fighting men in Viet Nam."

The moment the wreath hit the water, a middle-aged man in an eighteen-foot boat started his outboard motor and sped over the wreath in a futile attempt to sink it. Rockwell gave no reaction. Asked by reporters why he was making the dedication, Rockwell said, "It was about time someone demonstrated to offset the peace-creeps who are undermining our fighting men in Viet Nam."[23] Rockwell stayed in Maine for a few days. He visited his father for the last time.

In mid-1966, the party launched a quarterly journal called *National Socialist World. NSW* was the final step in a multilevel propaganda effort. Like other party literature, *NSW* was designed to win the hearts and minds of readers, but the focus this time was scholarly, intellectual types. *NSW* was the brainchild of William Pierce, a thirty-two-year-old assistant physics professor from Oregon who had recently moved east. Pierce had wanted to produce a journal of National Socialist ideas but lacked the necessary equipment. He struck a deal with Rockwell to split the cost of the journal evenly, Rockwell supplying the physical plant and labor while Pierce controlled content and handled editorial responsibilities. When the first issue was ready, Rockwell was unable to deliver his share of the financing, so Pierce paid for it. The journal broke even after the fourth issue, ultimately reaching a total circulation of one thousand.[24]

Alan Welch called it quits in June. Since 1964 he had pushed himself at a breakneck pace that had left him in a state of physical, spiritual, and emotional exhaustion. He had given everything, his job, his family, his social life. He gave too much; he wound up with debilitating migraine headaches that plagued him for the next thirty years. He never lost his awe of Rockwell, an "unending fount of creativity and courage." Welch believed that no matter what horrifying, monstrous thing confronted Rockwell, he kept his sense of humor, a humor that pulled the party through the worst scrapes.[25]

In New York, a three-judge criminal court panel dismissed all charges against Rockwell for the rotunda riot in 1960. The dismissal was based on the fact that Rockwell's appearance at the Supreme Court Building had been in connection with a court case and not to make a speech. His comments had been in reply to questions put to him by newsmen, not to incite the crowd of bystanders. Judge Simon Silver declared, "No valid purpose would be served by a trial here"; he commended the district attorney's office for its nineteen-page "scholarly brief" and praised the ACLU for defending Rockwell.[26] In response, Rockwell mailed an official complaint to the FBI on July 6, detailing violations of his constitutional rights and conspiracy against him by New York City officials. The Justice Department took no action regarding the complaint.[27]

In California, the Western Division staged pickets of the NAACP national convention. The first event took place on July 5, 1966, when four Nazis in uniform and Ralph Forbes dressed as a cleric circled the Statler-Hilton Hotel in Los Angeles with placards denouncing the Jewish leadership of the NAACP. The next evening, four uniformed Nazis picketed the front of the First Methodist Church in Los Angeles, where Vice President Hubert Humphrey was scheduled to address NAACP delegates. The Nazis carried placards reading:

Jew Kaplan Heads NAACP
White Man Fight
H.H.H. Had a Great Fall
Communism Is Jewish

The Western Division also sent three troopers to picket a movie theater showing the Western genre film *Duel at Diablo,* in which black actor Sidney Poitier portrayed a cowboy. The Nazis carried signs that read:

Negro Cowboys—That's Jewish
Only the Jews Would Mix the Races

In addition to the three Nazis in stormtrooper uniform, a fourth Nazi, wearing a hula skirt, cowboy boots, and a "Ubangi" mask over his face, kept yelling, "I'm a nigger cowboy!"[28] A crowd of two hundred bystanders watched the spectacle until the Nazis were attacked by teenagers and eventually arrested.

Martin Luther King now decided it was time to test nonviolence in the North. His previous excursion out of the Deep South had been a venture into Watts shortly after the riots. His reception by fellow blacks had been a slap in the face; comments like "Martin Luther Who?", "Get out of here Dr. King! We don't need you!" and "They're just sending another nigger down here to tell us what we need" had been common.[29]

King's target was Chicago. It had a teeming black population of more than a million, most of it jammed into two ghettos on the South and West Sides. Unemployment was rampant (one out of three people was on relief), the public schools had de facto segregation, and the housing areas were slums. Chicago was an ideal focus for a civil rights campaign. King declared, "If we can break the backbone of discrimination in Chicago, we can do it in all the cities of this country."[30]

While King was attempting nonviolence in Chicago, the "Black Power" movement was gathering momentum, creating a schism in the civil rights movement and driving fear into the hearts of whites. Stokely Carmichael, who had coined the phrase during a march in Mississippi, now headed the Student Nonviolent Coordinating Committee (SNCC).[31] Adherents of Black Power believed the old goal of integration was no longer viable or relevant. They also believed the black man ought to hit back when hit by a white man, repudiating the doctrine of nonviolence that had heretofore propelled the civil rights movement. Even Robert Lucas, the leader of CORE, described nonviolence as a "dying philosophy" that could no longer "be sold to the black people."[32] Adam Clayton Powell hailed Black Power as "a working philosophy for a new breed of cats—tough, proud young Negroes who categorically refuse to compromise or negotiate any longer for their rights...who reject old-line established, white financed, white controlled, white-washed leadership."[33] Carmichael had a slightly more militant view: "When you talk of Black Power, you talk of building a movement that will smash everything Western Civilization has created."[34]

Few agreed on what Black Power meant in terms of specifics. SNCC had never clearly defined it or the objectives or programs for achieving it, and the old-line civil rights leaders condemned it. Roy Wilkins called Black Power "separatism...wicked fanaticism...ranging race against race...in the end only black death." Bayard Rustin stated, "Black Power not only lacks any real value for the civil rights movement, but its propagation is positively harmful. It diverts the movement from any meaningful debate over strategy and tactics, it isolates the Negro community, and it encourages the growth of anti-Negro forces."[35] For the common man, Black Power did not mean seizing power through armed revolution; the idea that 11 percent of the population could take control of the most powerful nation on earth was ridiculous. A more palatable interpretation of Black Power was to make it synonymous with "black pride"—the concepts of self-respect and self-reliance, pride in black history and culture. Across the country in the big cities, de rigueur Black Power symbolism could be seen in the bristling Afro hairstyle, dashiki shirts, medallions, and the clenched-fist salute.

On July 28, Rockwell and Stokely Carmichael were guests on the CBS television show *At Random*. Rockwell reveled in the opportunity to embarrass Carmichael while also exposing Jewish backing of the civil rights movement. But he found Carmichael a bit more slippery and aloof than he had anticipated. Carmichael kept his voice low and calm, deflecting and countering Rockwell's barbs. However, he did admit that SNCC was in dire financial straits because Jewish money was drying up as a result of the group's increasingly militant stance.

In late July, the seventh month of his open-housing campaign in Chicago, King decided to amass his resources and make a strike on a strategic target to draw public attention to his cause. The catalyst for the operation would be open-housing marches through white suburban neighborhoods to pressure the city and local real estate agencies into ending discrimination against blacks. On Saturday, July 30, 1966, a large contingent of black demonstrators led by Al Raby and Jesse Jackson marched through Marquette Park and the nearby white neighborhoods. They were pelted with a barrage of rocks, bottles, and bricks by white onlookers, a few of whom were arrested. The next day an indignant Al Raby again led marchers through Marquette Park. Swarms of white men ran into the park and overturned every car driven by the marchers. Ice picks and single-edged razors punctured and slashed tires, and youths with lighter fluid set them on fire. Any car bearing the bumper sticker "Union to End Slums" was singled out and totally destroyed. The evening sky was illuminated by burning automobiles.

On August 5 King led a march through the same area and was stunned not only by the rock that hit him in the head but by the outright hatred of the inhabitants. This was unlike anything King had encountered in the South; it was not as simple a problem as exposing the vicious tactics of James Clark or Bull Connor. King said of the experience, "I have seen many demonstrations in the South, but I have never seen any so hostile and so hateful as I have seen here today." [36]

In the Arlington barracks, the Nazis tracked the situation on television. They cheered each time the cameras panned to the burning cars or a fallen marcher. Chicago presented Rockwell with his greatest opportunity. The violence was a result of mob rule; with no leadership, the whites were reacting purely on the basis of racial homogeneity. If he could stand before them as their leader he could not only organize the aimless, undirected mob into political action but also extract some desperately needed funds for the party. He discussed the situation in a "special report on Chicago" that was mailed to supporters.

> The White working people of Chicago FINALLY have been attacked in their very homes by the black scum, and have risen up in their righteous wrath to hand us THE opportunity of a lifetime.[37]

This was a call to action, a time to get out in the streets and agitate. The Chicagoans were not refined William Buckley–type conservatives but tough working men who would not stand for a "black invasion" of their neighborhoods. It would be Rockwell's finest hour.

In the weeks that followed, more violence flared with each open-housing demonstration. The ANP-Chicago unit, led by Chris Vidnjevich, took the point position in the fray, distributing ANP "White Power" literature and placards throughout the troubled neighborhoods, urging residents to join an armed "White Guard" to repel the "nigger criminals." The usually dormant unit was flooded with hundreds of residents stopping by 1314 Ohio Street for Nazi literature and White Power placards; blue-collar Americans were parading through the streets with swastika placards.

On August 14, John Patler flew into Chicago with several thousand White Power signs. He met with local ANP leaders Vidnjevich and his girlfriend, Barbara Warren (a.k.a. Erica Himmler), at Chicago headquarters to devise a strategy for a Gage Park rally that afternoon. The Nazis arrived at the park well in advance to hand out hundreds of White Power signs and swastika placards. When the open-housing marchers arrived they were met by thousands of swastikas and White Power signs. Soon bricks and bottles were flying into the middle of the procession. Dozens of whites were arrested. When the march was over, a crowd of two thousand whites gathered in Marquette Park, where the ANP set up a speaking area and passed out White Power signs. Patler stood on a bench and spoke: "If Negroes can march into white areas, we can march into Negro areas. Buy yourselves guns and teach your wives to use them too."

After Patler's speech a mob of three hundred men raged through the park, hurtling bottles and rocks at every passing car that contained blacks. When police tried to make arrests the mob turned on them until warning shots were fired. Two policemen were injured, and thirteen people were arrested. One policeman said it had been the closest thing to war he had ever seen.[38]

A Chicago reporter telephoned Arlington for Rockwell's comments. Rockwell told the reporter he was planning a march through a black area of Chicago on September 10 to determine if there was a double standard for law enforcement in Chicago:

> I want to see if the Negroes get the same rough treatment from the police that the white kids got when the Negroes invaded white neighborhoods. . . . We won't wear our Nazi uniforms, but we will probably carry placards. We'll have quite a few preachers with us, too. We'll stop every once in a while and we will pray that the Negroes will all go back to Africa, peacefully.
>
> I want to keep the march peaceful. If our side were to attack the Negroes, it would be a catastrophe for me. This would wreck the whole purpose of the march, which is to either force the police to fight the Negroes in our behalf, or if they don't, to prove there is a double standard of law enforcement.
>
> If the police don't fight the Negroes, it will cause an uprising among the white community. If some of my members or I are shot or beaten, it would prove the police protect the Negroes, but not the white people.[39]

In reaction to Rockwell's statement, Chicago Police Superintendent Orlando Wilson told the press that ANP demonstrators would be protected by police if they marched in black areas: "We don't discriminate in the use of officers in the enforcement of law. As long as they keep to the sidewalks, this is legal." Local whites were asked about the demonstrations taking place in their neighborhoods. One man replied:

> The people have invested all their hard-earned savings in their homes, their churches, and the hospitals. They can't afford a slum. It would be a tragedy. The neighborhood is one hundred percent united against niggers coming in. Their houses would be blown up!

Another man said:

> We've worked hard for what we have here and don't want to give it up. It would be just a matter of time before the neighborhood deteriorates after the Negroes move in.

Another declared:

> If the Nazis are building an organization as a buffer against the niggers, thousands will join it.[40]

Later that week Rockwell departed Arlington in the camper and drove sixteen hours to Chicago. On August 21, the Nazis brought the ANP camper to Marquette Park for a rally that afternoon. As the day wore on more than two thousand people congregated around it. Patler climbed through the hatch in the camper roof and began to speak. After several rounds of applause, Chris Vidnjevich stepped to the microphone and gave a brief talk. He too was showered with applause. Finally, Patler returned to the microphone to introduce Rockwell.

The crowd roared with an exuberance that Rockwell had never experienced before. Unlike college audiences applauding out of respect, these people needed him. He focused his initial attack upon the blacks:

We are paying, you are paying, you're working every day to pay taxes to breed little black bastards.... You're subsidizing Negro mothers who produce this little black scum for pay, and then when they don't have any place to live, they want to come and take your house and neighborhood.

These black people that now want equal opportunities, equal this and equal that, and want to live in this house and that house, move into your neighborhood, these same people for thousands of years lived on the richest continent on the face of this earth in Africa. They had more territory, more natural resources.... There were thousands of varieties of docile animals all over Africa—buffalo, horses, cattle—and they never dreamed of catching one and using them to work. Not once! You know what they worked? They worked their women! They harnessed up their women to their plow....

They never dreamed about a wheel.... They were pushing things around on sticks. The greatest coastline in the world... miles and miles of water in every direction: they never made a sail, all they ever did was sit on a log and drift up and down some place—probably drinking some kind of wine.

Do you know how the slaves got here? They were sold by their mothers and daddies for money to Arab slave traders. They were sold by their own people. These are our equals that sell their kids?

Then he shifted his attack on the Jews:

You begin to understand they're [blacks] too stupid to organize themselves. I'll tell you who's doing it... the Communists. I'm going to tell you the story of the NAACP. You know who organized it? Sixteen Jews and one almost-white nigger. You know where all the money for the race-mixing activity comes from—all these marches of Mr. Coon—you know who pays for it? The Jews.... Stokely Carmichael admitted it... openly admitted that they're [SNCC] two hundred thousand in debt. Coon isn't in debt. I know that Coon is doing great, because Jews are pouring the money into Mr. Coon.

A man in the crowd attempted to heckle Rockwell but was shouted down by the other bystanders.[41] Rockwell told the crowd he would personally lead a White Power march on September 10 through the "blackest and rottenest section of Chicago." He concluded his speech by asking the crowd to shout "White Power" loud enough for "Martin Luther Coon" to hear it across town. Over and over again, when Rockwell yelled "WHITE!" the crowd responded "POWER!"[42]

Rockwell climbed down from the camper to walk among the crowd and shake hands while Patler and Vidnjevich moved through the audience with baskets collecting donations. When they returned to the

Rockwell riles a crowd in Chicago's Marquette Park in August 1966.

camper their baskets were filled with more than $1,500. After eight long, heart-breaking years of hardship, desertion, and physical attacks, here at long last was a legion of white Americans accepting him as their leader. He was moved to tears.[43]

Although Rockwell did not have a permit to hold a rally in a public park, police did not arrest him. They swore out a warrant for his arrest and kept it for a more opportune moment. Two other white supremacists were not so lucky. Charles "Connie" Lynch of the National States Rights Party and Evan Lewis of the Ku Klux Klan were both arrested for giving a speech in Marquette Park without a permit.[44]

Rockwell returned to Arlington and issued an emotional fund-raising letter to every supporter, asking for donations to organize the people of Chicago into a unit. The "organizing" Rockwell had in mind involved five hundred uniforms, boots, police helmets, armbands, a radio command car, ten thousand "Back to Africa" placards, a hundred thousand instruction sheets, chartered buses, and travel expenses. The total amount of donations "needed" for the September White Power march totaled $41,000 (such an enormous amount of money could also be used to pay the IRS and purchase a building in Arlington for a new ANP headquarters). To entice even the stingiest supporter, Rockwell promised that if the police were overwhelmed by black attackers, the White Power marchers would "pile up the coons like cord wood."[45]

The mayor of Chicago, Richard Daley, told the press that hate groups should stay out of Chicago: "We don't want any people that come into our city for the purpose of agitation, regardless of who they are." He defended the city's injunction against King's "open occupancy" marches, an injunction that limited the marches to one a day, in daylight, in non-rush hours, with no more than five hundred participants, and after seven-day written notice to the police. King had called the injunction "immoral," but Daley replied, "On the contrary, I think it's a great moral issue." Daley went on to say that Chicagoans should be able to live wherever they wanted to, "but let's not kid ourselves. . . . How do you integrate if other people move out?"[46]

King's marches evoked considerable negative response from the public. The loudest grumbling came from Northern liberals who approved of civil rights campaigns in the South but were reluctant to support such action in the North.[47] King decided to intensify the situation: he announced a march through the nearby town of Cicero. Cicero had a population of nearly seventy thousand people, but not a single black lived there.[48] When the word came out of King's plan, SCLC officers were bombarded with negative feedback from religious and civic groups. No nationwide support was forthcoming, and few outsiders pledged their help. Why would liberals support voting rights in the Deep South but turn their backs on open housing in the North? Was the civil rights movement suddenly unfashionable, or was King tasting the bitter fruit of hypocrisy?

There were several factors working against King. Chicago was the first time King had challenged de facto segregation. Unlike de jure segregation of the South—where Jim Crow laws mandated the separation of blacks and whites at restaurants, lunch counters, hotels, schools, and theaters—the de facto segregation of the North was based on customs, legally sanctioned but not legally imposed. De facto segregation was a much more formidable system than de jure segregation, because there was no involved law to abolish or uphold. King had also gone public with his opposition to the war in Vietnam. Many blacks felt his stance on Vietnam was damaging to the civil rights movement. Democrats in Congress who were supporting the war in Vietnam saw King as ungrateful and unpatriotic.

The Cook County Sheriff, Richard Ogilvie, urged Dr. King to call off his open-housing march in Cicero. Ogilvie told reporters that if King insisted on marching in Cicero, the white reaction "will make Gage Park look like a tea party." He sent a telegram urging King to abandon his plan "in the interest of public safety." King refused to cancel the Cicero march:

> We fully intend to have the march. We have talked with Ogilvie about this and announced our plans last Saturday. We feel that we have honored in good faith his request for seven days' notice. In fact we gave eight days' notice. We feel that if Chicago is to be an open city, then metropolitan Chicago will have to resolve this problem. And Cicero is part of metropolitan Chicago.[49]

Race hatred was strong in the all-white middle-class suburb, creating an extremely sensitive and violent situation. Ogilvie also blamed the violence at previous marches on "young hoodlums." He therefore also threatened Rockwell with arrest if he appeared in any part of Cook County. Asked on what charge, he said, "I'll think of something."[50] Word of Ogilvie's comments provoked Rockwell to action. On August 29 he walked into the sheriff's office to see if charges would be placed against him. Ogilvie asked, "Are you George Lincoln Rockwell?" "Yes sir," Rockwell replied. "Did you call the press here?" the sheriff asked. Again Rockwell replied, "Yes sir." Sheriff Ogilvie said, "You are under arrest for disorderly conduct."

From the time he entered the sheriff's office until the arrest was less than five minutes. He was charged with "refusing to leave the office of the Cook County Sheriff"; he posted a bond of twenty-five dollars.[51] The arrest received nationwide exposure, including an editorial in the *Washington Evening Star* in support of Rockwell:

> Sheriff Ogilvie, we think, has let himself be played for a sucker. Under the circumstances, the arrest of Rockwell was not only stupid; it was plainly illegal. Certainly no court will sustain it. But it will give Rockwell something to talk about the next time he mounts the stump.[52]

Rockwell filed two suits in Federal District Court in Chicago, one for dismissal for disorderly conduct charges, the other to force the Chicago park district commissioner to grant him a permit to lead a rally in Gage Park. Judge Joseph Perry denied both requests. Marchers would have to use the sidewalk to avoid charges of parading without a permit. One party member told the press that "thousands of whites have promised to come and they'll scare these apes back into the trees."[53] An evening rally at the Chicago Coliseum was also planned. The Jewish War Veterans petitioned Judge Perry to issue an injunction to prevent the Nazis from holding White Power rallies or marches in Chicago, contending that the rallies would incite riots. Perry denied the injunction.

At noon on September 10, 1966, the Nazi march began, at Fifty-fifth and Western Avenue in the Englewood section of southwest Chicago. The turnout of 250 people was far short of the three thousand marchers Rockwell had predicted. Four hundred blue-helmeted policemen surrounded the White Power marchers as they walked two abreast from Gage Park south on Western Avenue. At 12:12 police halted the procession to place Rockwell under arrest for "holding a public meeting and soliciting funds in a city park without a permit." A Rockwell supporter wearing minister's clothing attempted to stop the arrest and was himself also arrested. He identified himself as "Reverend" Ralph Forbes, pastor of "the Second Covenant Church of Jesus Christ" in Los Angeles. He was also known as Captain Ralph Forbes of the Western Division of the American Nazi Party. John Patler and Christopher Vidnjevich took command of the marchers, many of whom wore swastika armbands and White Power T-shirts and carried placards that read:

Stop the Black Riots
Mayor Daley, Where Is "Your" Negro Neighbor?

Scattered violence occurred, but only three youths were arrested. Rockwell was held for eight hours while six stormtroopers marched in protest outside the police station. The Nazis told reporters the Jewish War Veterans had pressured police into keeping Rockwell locked up so he would miss the ANP rally at the Coliseum that evening. Rockwell was released at 8:00 P.M., but the rally was a flop; most supporters thought the rally had been canceled due to his arrest—only sixty-five people showed up. The poor turnout was financially crippling. The party had paid $1,000 to rent the arena and expected to recoup its costs. Rockwell pleaded guilty on the charges of holding a rally and soliciting funds without a permit and was fined four hundred dollars.

On September 12, Chicago leader Vidnjevich announced plans to march through the predominantly Jewish neighborhood of Hyde Park the following Sunday and demanded police protection: "The niggers were docile when we marched but the Jews might try to kill us." He also asserted that the Jews were behind the Negro activism: "The Jews are the real troublemakers. . . . They're the ones—we're going to march right through their neighborhoods and spit in their eyes."[54] The Jewish War Veterans succeeded in getting a federal order against Rockwell and the ANP, prohibiting the Nazis from demonstrating on Jewish high holy days. The temporary restraining order prohibited the party from "organizing or participating in any march or demonstration on public property or else-where" in Jewish neighborhoods during the Jewish holidays.[55] When the order expired on September 22, another was presented to the court. Federal Judge Joseph Perry issued a permanent injunction against the ANP. The judge based his ruling on the constitutional guarantees of freedom of religion.

As the judge read his ruling, Rockwell stood to voice his displeasure. "Will you remain seated until I am through?" asked the judge. "You're not commander here." When the judge finished reading, he immediately called out the next case. Rockwell stood to speak. "There is no comment necessary. There is the Court of Appeals!" the judge shouted.[56] Rockwell left the courtroom.

AP/Wide World Photos

Patler, Rockwell, and "Reverend" Ralph Forbes lead the White Power march through Chicago on September 10, 1966.

The FBI continued to mount COINTELPRO operations against the ANP. It devised a plan to cause a rift between the ANP and the United Klans of America. In late August the Western Division–ANP held a rally in San Francisco. Nazi leader Alan Vincent invited William Fowler, chairman of the California United Klans of America, to speak from the Nazi rostrum. Fowler spoke at length about the "Negro problem" and was followed by a Ralph Forbes harangue concerning the Vietnam war. FBI COINTELPRO operatives requisitioned photographs of the event from the San Francisco Police Department, then sent a fabricated letter to Klan followers, Rockwell, and ANP leaders throughout the country in hopes of causing distrust and dissension among their ranks. The Bureau wanted to create a wide split not only between the ANP and the Klan but also between Imperial Wizard Robert Shelton of United Klans for America and William Fowler, the local California leader of the United Klans of America:

> The pictures you see are of interest to all who swear allegiance to the Ku Klux Klan. Recently the American Nazi Party held a rally in Northern California. Now the Klan has no beef because the Nazi Party holds a rally, but what should concern the Klan is the fact that the man speaking at the microphone is William Fowler, Chairman of the California Ku Klux Klan, United Klans of America....

The Klan stands for Christianity and decency, the Klan stands for this great country of ours, the Klan stands for the rights of the White Man... but, never should we be accused of needing the Nazi storm troopers to get our message across to the American people.

And what of these uniformed storm troopers who stand alongside our "Klan representative" at this rally, wearing the swastika of the Nazi Party[?] Needless to say, fellow Klansmen, these are the followers of the crooked George Lincoln Rockwell, the psychopathic agnostic who laughs at the name of Christ. Rockwell is great when it comes to playing boyish tricks, but have you ever noticed that it really is not Rockwell himself who performs these publicity seeking stunts[?] Oh no, it is always some poor lame-brained nut who performs for the "Commander" and who sits in jail while the "Commander" quietly counts his money and dreams of new worlds to conquer....

Be assured that our Imperial Wizard, Robert Shelton will not tolerate the actions of Fowler in California. Fowler does not speak for the United Klans of America.[57]

Rockwell did not deliberately antagonize the Klan like he did Ed Fields or Billy James Hargis. The various Klan organizations were large in number, and they had a long history of repressing blacks—something Rockwell admired. However, he disagreed with their lynch-mob tactics, which could be crushed by the Justice Department, and anti-Catholicism prevented would-be cooperation from other right-wing individuals and groups. He believed that Klan leaders had failed the people because of their "cowardice and stupidity." Once they had failed completely, the people would have only one place to turn, and that would be the American Nazi Party.[58]

The Harvard Law–Graduate Democratic Club was to sponsor a Rockwell speech in Austen Hall on September 26, but the club's executive committee decided at an eleventh-hour meeting to renege on Rockwell's contract, which provided air fare and lodging expenses (ninety-two dollars) plus a twenty-five-dollar honorarium. Club vice-president James Conahan had invited Rockwell, Communist Party theoretician Herbert Aptheker, Socialist Party leader Norman Thomas, and Barry Goldwater for a panel discussion called "Spectrum," but shortly after the invitations became public the Jewish War Veterans had pressured the Democratic National College Committee to force the Harvard group to rescind Rockwell's invitation.

On the day before his appearance, the Democratic Club's executive committee voted 7–4 to break Rockwell's contract and pay him nothing, but it could not notify Rockwell of the decision. When Rockwell's plane landed in Boston, a student gave him the bad news. It did not faze him. His college appearances were not about money—they were about spreading the message.

From the moment Rockwell took the stage he set about embarrassing the Democratic Club, exposing every detail of the contract debacle. He threatened to sue for breach of contract, but he refrained, because this was a perfect example of how the United States was living under the "tyranny of the Jews." Embarrassed by the executive board's cowardice, the members of the Democratic Club voted 55–6 to honor the contract and pay the full amount of Rockwell's expenses.[59]

On October 3, Rockwell spoke before two thousand California Western University students and faculty in Golden Gymnasium, the first speaker in a series called "Freedom in America: Politics '66," sponsored by the Academic Board of Associated Students. Leery of another Ed Cherry–type assault, Rockwell positioned Bill Kirstein—party secretary of the Western Division—to his left. Kirstein continuously scanned the audience while another trooper monitored the front-row seats. There were no incidents.[60]

On October 7, twenty-six members of an organization known as the Action Coordinating Committee to End Segregation in the Suburbs (ACCESS) marched from Gum Springs, a predominantly black section of Fairfax County, to Alexandria, Virginia. Preceding the parade on horseback was American Nazi Officer Frank Drager. Drager, mocking the event with a Paul Revere reenactment, carried a placard reading "The Niggers Are Coming." Two days later Matt Koehl led a detachment of stormtroopers on a picket in front of Arlington's Buckingham Theater protesting ACCESS.

On October 22, 1966, the Western Division held a rally in San Francisco, between City Hall and Civic Center Plaza. The Nazis parked Rockwell's camper and draped the White Power banner over the side. Eighteen stormtroopers stood at attention in front of the camper holding White Power placards while a massive crowd of four thousand counter-demonstrators gathered around the Nazi display holding signs:

Abolish Hate
Defeat Fascism
Keep Racism Out of San Francisco
Go Home Nazis

ANP Officer Alan Vincent climbed atop the camper and addressed the boisterous crowd before being shouted down and pelted with eggs. Next, Rockwell climbed atop the camper and met the same results; this time a bottle shattered against the camper. He screamed at the swarming mass of counter-protesters, "I'm going to stay up here until you dirty finks let me speak," but a policeman climbed aboard the trailer and announced that the rally was over.

Rockwell and troopers descended into the camper and attempted to drive off, but the crowd made it virtually impossible to leave. A woman slammed a weighted purse into the camper window, sending shards of glass inside. A policeman attempted to put the woman under arrest, but she smacked him in the chest with the purse so hard the officer suffered a heart attack and had to be hospitalized. Skirmishes ensued between the crowd and police as the camper finally pulled out of the area. Police were forced to release all arrested individuals from their paddy wagon when the mob engulfed it, chanting "Let Them Go. . . . Let Them Go." During the melee a bystander suffered a heart attack and died at the scene.[61]

On October 25, the Dallas unit picketed a speech by Arthur Goldberg, the U.S. ambassador to the United Nations, at Southern Methodist University. While Goldberg was explaining his three-point plan for an "honorable" peace in Vietnam, Al Gray, a member of the ANP Dallas unit, led two other Nazis outside McFarlin Auditorium with placards:

U.N.—Red Front
Jews and Niggers Use the U.N.

A scuffle broke out with a bystander, and the Nazis were arrested.[62]

Rockwell's invitation to speak at Western Maryland College on November 28 came under extreme criticism from the Jewish War Veterans. The state commander, Norman Kolodner, stated, "We believe in freedom of speech but do not think that people should be given an opportunity such as this to try and warp the minds of our collegiate youth." Kolodner suggested the college show a film of American soldiers fighting Nazis in World War II and liberating Nazi prison camps. School administrators took a safe, defensive posture:

> The invitation was extended against the advice of the college administration, which believes, emphatically, that Rockwell's philosophy is diametrically opposite to everything for which the college stands as an institution of higher education.[63]

After condemning his invitation, schools typically patted themselves on the back for having "unqualified commitment to the principle of academic freedom." By placing responsibility on the student group tendering the invitation, administrators retained the option of saying "I told you so" if the event went sour or that it had been "a search for Truth" if the event was successful. Rockwell arrived on the Western Maryland College campus and spoke to a capacity crowd in Alumni Hall. Several members of the faculty marched with pickets outside the hall, but his appearance was without incident.[64]

On November 30, Rockwell spoke in front of a packed house at Brown University. The invitation did not come easily. The initial invitation had been granted by the Faunce House Board of Governors, a student body that administered student union activities, but in late October the board rescinded the invitation because of community pressure and criticism by the president of Brown, Ray Heffner. Faunce House issued the following statement:

> We invited him to speak about the white backlash because we feel that a direct confrontation with the most extreme view, no matter how repulsive, is justified by the intellectual maturity of the students and by the policies and traditions of this university, reaffirmed by President Keeney in 1963 when he said:
>
>> Communists, fascist, racists and bigots may be invited to speak on campus, so that our students may get a closer understanding of these people in their belief and partly so they themselves may be exposed to our beliefs and environment.[65]

Rockwell complained in the *Brown University Alumni Monthly:*

> While I speak at universities and colleges over America, my own University treats me like a colored step-child. . . . I make no secret of the fact that I believe the reason for this is the capture of a grand old New England college by Jewish and communistic radicals who are turning our kids into arrogant, ignorant, hell-raising peace-creeps, willing traitors to the greatest nation ever to appear on earth.[66]

In the wake of the cancellation an ad hoc free speech group formed a coalition called Open Mind. When its constitution was approved by the university, Open Mind reissued an invitation to Rockwell. Opposition to the speech was widespread. The Brown chapter of the Jewish students' organization Hillel ran a campaign to educate students about Nazism: a movie on the rise of Nazism was shown each week; the campus radio station, WBRU-AM, replayed taped interviews with Rockwell; and ANP literature was put on display.

On the day of his speech, over forty uniformed police, university security personnel, and FBI agents dispersed throughout Alumnae Hall. When the auditorium was filled to capacity, hundreds of students attempted to force their way in, breaking windows in the process. The audience responded to Rockwell's "facts" with applause, puzzlement, amazement, and laughter. Rockwell thought his speech "went over well" and congratulated the leaders of Open Mind for tendering the invitation. "The group wanted an anti-communist to speak after all the communists who have spoken at Brown," he was reported to have said.[67]

On December 3, twenty-one-year-old Michael Pullis was on duty at the party's secluded property in Spotsylvania, Virginia. He paced in boredom through the long building. Although the doors were all locked from the inside, Pullis wore a sidearm. The pistol and khaki uniform gave him a sense of power. Pullis enjoyed playing with his pistol—spinning it, twirling it on one finger, practicing a fast draw. On this occasion he was twirling the revolver in his right hand when it slipped from his grip and crashed to the floor. Had he watched a few more John Wayne movies he might have known the danger of keeping a live round of ammunition in the cylinder beneath the hammer. The hammer of the pistol hit the floor and discharged a .22-caliber bullet into Pullis's lower stomach and upward, deep into his chest. He staggered toward the telephone on the other end of the building but fell to the floor. He died of internal bleeding.

Frank Drager found Pullis dead on the floor; he called William Pierce, who came out to examine the scene. The medical examiner concluded that the death was accidental because of the nature of the wound and lack of a suicide note. Rockwell was numbed when he heard the news. He asked Koehl to break the news to the family but at the last minute took the unpleasant task on himself. On December 6, a brief graveside service was held at a nearby cemetery; Pullis's father and mother were the only people in attendance. When the five-minute service was over, the parents returned to New Jersey. They were shocked to learn their son had been a Nazi; he had told them he was working on a farm.[68]

On December 12, Rockwell drove the camper to Oneonta State University College for one of the rowdiest college events of his career.

His invitation had been tendered by the Student Council on Human Rights, which asked him to speak on "Human Rights and American Nazism." Forty-five minutes before his talk, all 750 seats in Alumni Hall were filled. Hundreds of students outside the hall rushed the firemen guarding the doors and pushed them out of the way. The heavy wooden doors broke off at the hinges, allowing hundreds of students to flood in. A thrill-seeking atmosphere permeated the event; never had an event—play, sporting event, or lecturer—drawn such a huge audience.[69]

The introduction, by the student chairman, Emile Gurstelle, was immediately disrupted by a bearded man named Stephen Jacoby. Jacoby walked up to the stage: "I'm not going to let that son-of-a-bitch speak unless the cops protect him." Gurstelle tried to continue his introduction, but Jacoby continued his tirade. "Has it been that long? Are you that young?" Jacoby asked the crowd if they wanted to hear Rockwell speak. "YES," roared the audience. Police came onstage and dragged Jacoby off to jail.

Rockwell gave his typical speech but was heckled throughout. When it was over he confided to reporters:

> That was one of the hairiest sessions . . . about as wild a session as I've ever seen. You get this in the streets but you don't get it on college campuses. I just think they let it go too far.[70]

In Rockwell's camper a reporter asked, "Do you believe all of this you preach?" Astonished by the man's query, Rockwell took his corncob pipe from his mouth and explained very slowly, in low voice, "This has cost me the most beautiful wife in the world. Seven kids. All my relatives. I was a commander in the Navy and a half-year away from a pension. Certainly, I believe all of this."[71]

By fall of 1966, the ANP had 190 members, but only ten attached to national headquarters; of the ten, half were stationed at Spotsylvania. Rockwell was in dire need of additional men, and he was completely perplexed as to why his success in Chicago had failed to recruit more followers.

In mid-December, Rockwell called Frank Smith to ask if Claudia would come to Arlington to help with some typing. They agreed to come down and spend Christmas through New Year's at ANP barracks. Rockwell needed Claudia to type up several hundred pages of the manuscript for his new book, *White Power*. Claudia slaved over the typewriter day in and day out, sometimes working late into the night. One evening Rockwell told Smith, "I'm losing John in the spring."

"What's the matter?" Smith asked. Rockwell said nothing more. Smith went downstairs to confront Patler. "John, the Commander tells me you are leaving the party. Is this true?"

"That's right," Patler replied. "I am going to leave it to take care of my family responsibility." Smith pressed him: "John, do you recall that Captain Lloyd did the very same thing? You were very bitter against Captain Lloyd for leaving the party. Now how come, here's a situation where you have a choice concerning your family, you are going to do the very same thing?" Now visibly irritated, Patler spoke with more volume and force: "It affects me personally, I am looking at things in a different light. . . . The best thing for me is to separate cleanly from the party and just take care of the family."

Smith continued to press the issue: "John, I don't think it's fair. If you were sincere in anything you ever told me about fighting for our race and our people here in this country, at least you will make some endeavor to continue your work." Being accused of hypocrisy was the last straw for Patler; he erupted into one of his volcanic fits of rage and stormed out of the barracks. The schism between Rockwell and Patler was growing wider.[72]

During the days that Claudia was typing his manuscript, Rockwell went to the Capitol to visit his childhood friend Stanley Tupper, now a Republican congressman for Maine. Dressed in a dark suit, Rockwell introduced himself to the receptionist as "Mr. Hunt" from Hebron Academy, in Maine. Tupper was a bit perplexed when his guest was announced; Mr. Hunt was dead. When the receptionist escorted "Mr. Hunt" into his office, Tupper understood why Rockwell used a pseudonym: he was attempting to spare Tupper public embarrassment. They shook hands and spoke of the "old days" for the better part of thirty minutes. Here was the "Linc" that Tupper remembered—charming, witty, candid. There was no trace of racism.

When their visit was over they shook hands for a final time. Rockwell looked Tupper in the eye and said, "We've done well, Stan; you in Congress, me the head of the American Nazi Party."

Tupper was astonished by the comparison: "Linc, why? Why don't you get away from it?" Rockwell hesitated for a moment and looked away as if he might be on the verge of a confession. He turned to Tupper and said, "I've got a tiger by the tail. . . . I will be killed." There was nothing more to say. After Rockwell departed, Tupper's receptionist asked, "Who was that good-looking gentleman?" "That," sighed Tupper, "was George Lincoln Rockwell."[73]

———

Another turbulent year came to a close. The IRS seizure had caused a small operational slowdown, but the loss of the headquarters building in Arlington was more damaging. The party eventually acquired the chicken coop in Spotsylvania to house its printing operations, but the distance between Arlington and Spotsylvania created isolation among men and operational problems for the party.

There were the new developments in party personnel. William Pierce helped the party by purchasing the crucial items at the IRS auction and creating the *National Socialist World* for the party's intellectual audience. Alan Welch quit, Alan Vincent became the new leader of the San Francisco unit, and Trooper Mike Pullis accidentally killed himself. Although the party was expanding the scope of its operations nationally, on the local level it was severely undermanned.

The FBI continued the COINTELPRO attacks, but neither of its efforts—the bogus funding letter to sympathizers or the Klan/ANP dissension letter—had much impact on the organization. For Rockwell, the success in Chicago, along with the *Playboy* interview, published that April, were the highlights of the year. He was also relieved to have the arrest warrant in New York dismissed. It had been a worry since 1960. The irony is that after all the legal rigmarole, he never spoke in Union Square.

Rockwell looked with optimism to 1967. He had several changes in mind for the American Nazi Party, the first of which was to change its name to the National Socialist White People's Party. He was encouraged by the militance of the Black Power movement and the scale of urban rioting. If the country's social fabric continued to deteriorate, he believed, there was a chance he could be elected to the presidency in 1972.

There was also the growing dissension between Rockwell and John Patler, which threatened to spill out into the open. Patler felt Rockwell was too controlling and condescending; Rockwell saw Patler as emotionally immature, making intra-Party cliques to further his own ends. They were headed for a showdown.

12

1967: "AN EVIL GENIUS"

Fifteen or twenty minutes after I'm president there won't
be any Red China. I'm going to be the guy that pushes
the button.
— Rockwell, Fort Hays State College, 1967

Nineteen sixty-seven was a year of tremendous civil unrest. The antiwar
movement was getting stronger. Begun primarily by students, clergy, aca-
demics, and civil rights leaders, it was now gaining broad support from
the middle class. Battle casualties in Vietnam surged to 9,353—greater
than all previous years combined. The previous urban rioting paled in
comparison to what was to come in 1967. Dozens of people were killed,
thousands were arrested, and property damage exceeded a half billion
dollars. Newark and Detroit suffered the worst rioting in U.S. history.
Sniper fire, lootings, and fire bombs wreaked havoc on the cities. Businesses closed, baseball games were postponed, and the airlines canceled
flights. The country seemed to be tearing apart at the seams.

Rockwell's party was undergoing changes, too. His quest for power
necessitated a minor reshaping of the party and a subtle shift in ideology.
On January 1, Rockwell sent out a national directive to all party members and supporters. It was time for the party's transformation to the
next phase of development. Certain tactical changes were necessary. First
and foremost the party would officially change its name to the National
Socialist White People's Party (NSWPP). "Sieg Heil," which sounded too
foreign, was to be supplanted by "White Power." Rockwell wrote,

We must strive, among our White family of people, to include all and
alienate no white non-Jews. Each white nationality must practice the rule

of finding a "happy medium" for the application of National Socialism in its own country in accordance with its own particular socio-political situation.

Although Patler was the main instigator for the name change, it was evident to Rockwell that if the blue-collar, white working people of Chicago were willing to use the White Power moniker, people in other cities would be too. The edict went out to all units of the ANP, but the transition to the new name was gradual; the organization would be known as the American Nazi Party for the rest of Rockwell's life.

Rockwell also issued the "Ten Points" of NSWPP. Unlike the earlier "tenets" of the ANP, which were directed exclusively at Jews, each point of the new program focused on a different issue.

TEN POINTS of American National Socialism:

1. America must be all white. Blacks must be deported.

2. Jewish domination of our culture, financial and national affairs must be smashed.

3. Communism, Zionism, and all other forms of treason must be exterminated.

4. The rights of a man's home, his family, and private property must be held sacred.

5. The right of law-abiding white people to keep and bear arms at all times and all places shall not be infringed.

6. Crime and riots in the streets will be smashed by the just and immediate use of power.

7. We will fight wars only for America, and then we will fight to total and immediate victory, using all available weapons.

8. Productive free enterprise, large and small business, and neighborhood stores must be encouraged and protected.

9. Every productive, working American must have a decent job, lifetime economic security and wholesome living conditions for himself and his family.

10. Youth, our future leaders, must have unlimited educational opportunities and help in setting up family-life.[1]

On January 10, Rockwell and Frank Drager arrived in Clinton, New York, for a speech at Hamilton College, sponsored by the Root-Jessup Public Affairs Council. Rockwell walked into the chapel dressed in a dark suit, a reel-to-reel tape recorder slung over his shoulder, while bodyguard Drager kept a watchful eye on the surroundings. In a brief press conference before the speech he told reporters "he couldn't win the presidency until someone like [Ronald] Reagan got in."[2]

Before Rockwell took the stage, students had been given tracts urging them to walk out at the conclusion of his speech in protest of his ideology. The event was closed to the public because of limited seating. Rockwell told the overflow audience of seven hundred that the key to the "communist revolution" under way in America was suppressed news: "Three Russian Jews control everything you see on the boob tube. . . . You'll never see a black criminal on television. They're always pictured as doctors, lawyers or some such professional man."[3] He pointed out that FBI statistics listed 85 percent of all crime as committed by blacks: "A white woman can't walk across Washington without being raped by a Negro. Not even the ugly ones!"[4] The audience roared with laughter. The speech concluded after fifty minutes, and the floor was opened for questions, but the students obeyed the tract and filed out in quiet protest.

Two weeks later, Rockwell flew into Spokane, Washington, and proceeded by car to Pullman for a speech at Washington State University. He gave a forty-five-minute interview to members of the student newspaper, *Daily Evergreen*, before stepping to the podium before a thousand students: "I want to talk about Jews."

He offered $1,000 to anyone who could disprove his "unimpeachable" facts that the Russian revolution had been orchestrated by Jews; that wealthy New York Jews financed Leon Trotsky's departure from New York to promote revolution in Russia; that Trotsky as head of the Red Army after the Bolshevik revolution had been responsible for killing twenty million Christians: "Communism is a Jewish operation. They've got you helping them. . . . In this country you can't criticize Jews. If you do you will be called a fascist, a bigot."

He complained that Americans had been fooled by communists time and time again with the help of public figures like Eleanor Roosevelt and Dean Acheson: "Take for example Castro's visit to the U.S. after he took control of Cuba. Ed Sullivan had him on his TV show and with his arm around Castro said, 'Here is the George Washington of Cuba.' When Castro got back to Cuba, he screamed 'I'm a Marxist.'" Rockwell collected his two-hundred-dollar honorarium and drove off to Central Washington State College.[5]

Washington State University received letters and telegrams criticizing his appearance. One writer demanded a public apology from the university to all non-Christians and the resignation of student advisor Dr. George Condon. Another letter, from a group calling itself the Deport Rockwell Committee, asked that Rockwell "be exported to Siberia or some such, and that state senators do not allocate any money to Pullman, or other colleges wanting [a] NAZI regime and Rockwell in this country."[6]

Rockwell appeared at Oregon State University for back-to-back speeches in the eight-hundred-seat home economics auditorium. Dozens of students waited in pouring rain outside the auditorium, hoping to gain admittance to either speech; most did not get in. The excluded students went to the Memorial Union ballroom to cluster around loudspeakers on which the speech could be heard broadcast over campus radio. After his introduction, complete silence filled the auditorium; it was as if the devil himself had taken the podium. "My mission is to put the searchlight on the termites and expose their undermining technique. . . . I'm determined to tell what is in my heart, in spite of terrorism, yellow armbands, and Stars of David. It is important to expose the truth," he said[7]

After the speech he collected his honorarium of $150 and departed for the University of Oregon in Eugene for a speech that evening. At a press conference in Eugene he told reporters, "Negroes don't fit in our society. They can't compete. They don't think ahead. . . . Negroes are biologically and functionally not suited to compete in our modern civilization. They are better suited to sit under a coconut tree and wait for the nuts to fall."[8]

That evening he spoke to a packed house of 7,300 people in McArthur Court, while a dozen members of Students for a Democratic Society marched in protest outside the arena. He covered the usual topics and was heartily applauded when he attacked Johnson's incremental method of fighting the Vietnam conflict:[9] "I think the war in Vietnam is designed to keep LBJ's economy going. We ought to go over there and win it! All we gotta do is go over there and blast them with everything we've got!"[10]

He lost his composure to hecklers halfway through the speech, when he tried to explain his theory that white voters cancel each other out by voting variously Democrat or Republican, while blacks vote only for black candidates and Jews vote pro-Jewish. "Senator Eastland and Adam Clayton Powell are both Democrats. You tell me what Adam Clayton Powell and Eastland have in common." As he paused for dramatic effect, a heckler yelled out, "They're both Jews!" The audience roared. It was laughing at Rockwell. Visibly stunned, Rockwell shouted,

"I'll tell you, peace-creeps and Jew-lovers, you wait until these people get tired of your creepism and communism. They'll get you so bad, you'll wish Hitler would come over here and rescue you!"[11]

When the speech was over he collected his $211 honorarium and drove on to Portland to catch a plane. In just one day he had spoken to nearly ten thousand students, but his gross receipts for the entire day were only $361. His marketing skills were successful, but his lack of business acumen was costing him thousands of dollars. He could have easily charged half the gate receipts for every appearance.

On January 26, a blizzard hit the Chicago area, dumping a record snowfall. Rockwell was in San Diego trying to get a flight back to Chicago for his court appearance, but there were no flights into the snow-clogged city. When the airports reopened, Rockwell filed a petition for a change of venue. His petition maintained that he had been falsely arrested by Sheriff Ogilvie, that all the witnesses to the arrest had been Jewish, and that the primary witness, Reginald Holzer, also Jewish, had since become a judge of the very court that would try him. The petition also detailed failings of his attorney and the probable bias of a jury composed of Jewish citizens. The petition was denied.

Patler, on temporary assignment with the Chicago unit, asked Rockwell to be excused from party business to help tend to his father-in-law in Arlington, who had suffered a heart attack. Rockwell promised to fly Patler back to Arlington if he would stay on a few more days, and he agreed. When it came time to leave for a speech in Wisconsin, Rockwell attempted to renege; the two men argued vehemently. Patler insisted he would not take a bus and finally coaxed the plane fare from Rockwell.

Rockwell and two stormtroopers left Chicago in the party's now-beat-up Chevrolet camper for a speech at Lawrence College in Appleton, Wisconsin, on February 8. His speech at Lawrence was almost canceled because of pressure from veterans groups, Jewish leaders, local citizens, and faculty members. A majority of student senators voted to cancel his appearance, but a minority faction made an end run and called for a school-wide referendum, which supported his appearance. Ironically, while American soldiers were dying at the hands of the Vietnamese communists, American Communist Party spokesman

Herbert Aptheker had appeared at Lawrence University the month before Rockwell with no commotion or protest.

When the ANP camper arrived in Appleton, at the Conway Motor Hotel, Rockwell gave a press conference for six TV stations, eight radio stations, and twelve newspapers. He told the journalists he was disappointed his upcoming speech was closed to the public, because many local conservatives wanted to hear him speak; but the closed-door session would also exclude the Jewish War Veterans, who often resorted to "force and violence."[12]

Lawrence administrators treated Rockwell like a leper. He was forbidden to have lunch on campus and was ordered to leave immediately after his speech was completed. All requests to conduct a live interview with Rockwell on the campus radio station were denied. The 1,200 seats in Memorial Chapel filled quickly. Outside the auditorium seventy-five anti-Rockwell protesters braved freezing weather to demonstrate. Five Nazi supporters formed their own picket line and marched next to the anti-Rockwell group. At 8:00 P.M. Rockwell stepped to the podium and began his address to a capacity crowd. He was in top form, making the audience laugh, then stunning it into silence. There were no boos, no walkouts. He told the audience he considered it "one of the highest honors of my life to speak in the home community of the late Joseph McCarthy. I consider him one of the greatest Americans who ever lived."

Through the evening Rockwell gave examples of "prominent Jews who are communists." He slammed Herbert Aptheker, Picasso, Jacob Epstein, and Allen Ginsberg. He told the audience it had cost him his family and career to stand up and refute Judaism: "You can discover who is a dictator in any country by finding out who you can't criticize. You can criticize any nationality in the country... Irish, Pollocks, Negroes, Catholics, but you can't criticize the Jews."

Switching his attack from Jews to blacks, he shouted, "I don't have to say that Negroes are inferior.... I just have to tell you to wait until five thousand of them come to Appleton and you get a dose of them.... Then you'll find out for yourself." He claimed that "85 percent" of all the crime committed in the United States was "committed by the black people." He also made reference to the recent blizzard in Chicago: "During the storm all the white people were out helping each

WE MUST END OUR PRESENT IMMIGRATION SYSTEM WHICH DISCRIMINATES AGAINST NON-WHITES...

LBJ

FBI

The American Nazi worldview: communist Jews, allied with violent blacks, manipulating the U.S. government. Drawn by John Patler.

other, but the black people were out looting. . . . All of this is nothing but facts; when I say it, it's labeled as hate." Rockwell was ushered from the auditorium and into a waiting automobile, which whisked him back to the ANP camper.[13]

In reaction to Rockwell's appearance at Lawrence, two Wisconsin state senators, Norman Sussman (Democrat from Milwaukee) and Gordon Roseleip (Republican from Darlington), cosponsored a resolution calling for Wisconsin higher educational institutions to bar "hatemongers" of "non-philosophies" from state-supported schools. The resolution would permit only speakers with "some point to make or information to give or some belief to represent that can be said to be educational."[14]

From Appleton the camper went west to Minneapolis, where Rockwell gave a speech before an overflow crowd of 1,400 people jammed into Coffman Ballroom at the University of Minnesota; eight hundred students listened to the speech on closed-circuit audio. While Rockwell only pocketed a couple of hundred dollars in honorarium, the Committee for Free Speech raked in over $1,400 in ticket sales.[15]

From Minneapolis the ANP camper went south to Des Moines, Iowa, for a speech at Drake University on February 13, 1967. Where one school might be embroiled in a battle with community members, veterans groups, and faculty over his appearance, the next might be as calm and serene as if Ralph Nader were coming to its campus. Such was the contrast between the seething Appleton and the complacent Des Moines.

Rockwell was the first of four controversial speakers invited to Drake University to participate in a program called "Dissent '67." There were no protests, no commotion; Rockwell was afforded the same respect as any other speaker. A full house of 1,500 people listened to Rockwell complain about the "kosher racket." With great fervor, Rockwell explained that the U and K symbols on food labels indicated "blessed" products or kosher food. He insisted that all consumers were paying higher prices for groceries because Jewish rabbis forced manufacturers to pay for the blessing on their food products. The "racket" was so secret that no manufacturer would divulge the amount of payment or know if his competitor was paying the same fee for a similar product. "Do you think the Jews would allow a stormtrooper to stand in a factory and put swastikas on the little cans?" Rockwell asked.[16]

Rockwell returned to Wisconsin for a restricted speech at the State University at Eau Claire on February 16, sponsored by the Young Democrats and Young Republican Clubs. Community opposition was widespread, yet restrained; opponents did not want to give Rockwell additional press coverage. A student group sponsored a film of German Nazi atrocities, while a citizens group purchased full-page advertisements in local newspapers depicting World War II Nazis taking away civilians at gunpoint.

On the evening of the speech, the weather in northwest Wisconsin was bitterly cold. While a dozen anti-Rockwell protesters braved below-freezing temperatures outside the field house, the temperature inside was rising, as 3,500 people anxiously awaited Rockwell's appearance. A hush fell over the crowd as Dr. Karl Andresen, the faculty advisor to the Young Democrats, approached the podium to start his introduction:

I am sure Mr. Rockwell appreciates that I am standing here with somewhat mixed feelings. The last time I was this close to a Nazi was in my hometown in Nazi-occupied Norway in 1944, when I was being marched down the street with a machine pistol in my back, surrounded by three Nazis. . . .

Mr. Rockwell, tonight you will be speaking to a group of young American men and women who are growing up in a confused and confusing world . . . to some who have prejudices against Negroes, Jews, and other minorities. I am grateful that your presence here tonight will be a timely reminder that such prejudice is a part of the Fascist ideology and not of the democratic, regardless of race, creed, and color. . . .

Finally, let me comment in answer to those who opposed the right of students to hear the speaker for tonight. . . . The true test of freedom is to be willing not to silence the idea we abhor. This view is based on the faith that error, when absurd, when vicious, will refute itself. . . . May the day never come when pressures from groups outside our college communities will dictate which speakers American college students may or may not hear.[17]

Rockwell followed with his usual crusade against Jews, blacks, communists, and nationally managed news. He pocketed $288 for his appearance; the school collected more than $3,000.

The following afternoon, February 17, Rockwell gave a speech in the Student Center of Western Michigan University. Admission was free, and the event was open to the public. He told a capacity crowd that "our country is in the midst of a communist revolution and my followers and I are a counter-revolutionary movement."[18]

From Michigan Rockwell made his way to Mankato State College in Minnesota, where on February 28 he spoke before a capacity crowd of two thousand. With students packed in doorways and sitting in the aisles and on window ledges, Rockwell slammed the government for conducting a half hearted war in Vietnam:

> This is the worst war in history and though we could win, the liberals won't let us. We shouldn't be in the war, but we are, so we should win. If the leaders allowed the military to fight, victory could be realized. . . . We could win in three days if they let our boys go in and use everything they have. I hope to get in power, and if I do, I can finish this war off with the Boy Scouts.

Rockwell ended his talk with an appeal for "white power."

> There is Jewish supremacy in Israel and black supremacy in the Congo. Why can't we have white supremacy here? Quit dividing yourselves. . . . The Negroes don't play this game, they vote black. The Jews aren't stupid enough to play Republicans and Democrats either. They vote for whoever is most pro-Jewish. The only way to save the country is to start voting white. The only answer is white power.[19]

His next appearance was at Wake Forest College in North Carolina on March 3, to take part in a "Challenge" speakers program sponsored by the student government. Rockwell told the 2,500 students in Wait Chapel that misinformation was ruining the United States and that the source of the misinformation was the "communist conspiracy," run by Jews. Near the end of his speech he was interrupted by Robert Grant, a black defensive tackle on the football team, who walked in front of the audience and said, "Negroes have given as much time and sweat to the development of America as white people." The audience stood and gave Grant a standing ovation. Rockwell tried to continue but was disrupted more than twenty times by hecklers; he later called the audience the most "pro-Negro group" he had ever seen.[20]

On March 12, Rockwell began a sweep through the Midwest with a speech at Stout State University in Menomonie, Wisconsin, before 1,500 people. The meeting was sponsored by the Society on Intellectual Freedom and was open to the public. The next day he spoke at the University of Wisconsin at Waukesha, sponsored by the Young Democrats as part of a lecture series on the "American Political Spectrum."

His next stop was Wisconsin State University at River Falls, where he spoke to more than 2,500 people in Karges Gym. The highlight of the evening was a debate between Rockwell and history professor Edward Peterson. Peterson told the audience he was not anxious to appear in a debate with Rockwell but did so in remembrance of a Jewish boy he served with in the Second World War who had given his life for the United States.

During the course of the evening Rockwell received the most severe intellectual attacks from professors he had ever experienced. Political science professor Raymond Anderson, who was originally scheduled to debate but had withdrawn when a topic could not be chosen, slammed Rockwell in his introduction:

> These students did not come here to listen to any nonsense about an international Jewish communist conspiracy.... They will laugh at any attempt on your part to tell them that the letter K stamped on cans of food constitutes a part of an international Jewish-Communist conspiracy. They are not interested in your views on Vietnam ... [or] in tales about civil rights movement being dominated by the International Jewish communist conspiracy....
>
> These students came to listen to you defend the philosophy of the Nazi Party. Tell them about the myth of the superiority of the Aryan race.... Explain the reasons for the deliberate murder of six million Jews by the Nazi Party during the time that Hitler was in power in Germany.

Rockwell took the stage and began his counter-attack:

> Well, thank you, Dr. Anderson, and let me thank you especially for writing my speech in advance.... He [Anderson] says I use a different technique in the streets than I do here. Of course! Of course! In the streets is when I'm agitating and people are running up and down shouting and having sit-ins and lie-ins and crawl-ins and riot-ins and TV-stealings and

looting and so forth. I use a different technique when I'm at a college. . . . Let me ask you fellows this, the gentlemen in the audience. Do you approach girls the same way you talk about them in the fraternity house? You do not! You give them the whole bit, the whole line and it works very well, you use whatever presentation is necessary under the circumstances. So do I, I'm not stupid. . . .

I fought in World War II and I fought to win. In Korea we fought to draw and now in Viet Nam we're fighting to lose. And here's what they'll do to you. . . . They are going to give you a flashlight and a pistol and send you into tunnels after the Vietcong rats down there in those tunnels and do you know why they send you down there with a pistol and a flashlight? Because you can't use tear gas to flush them out; tear gas is reserved for the girls at the University of Mississippi. You can't use it on communists.[21]

Tear gas was actually used by the U.S. Army in Vietnam.

When the speech concluded, the Rockwell-Peterson debate commenced. Although an underdog, Peterson used Rockwell's own logic for his attack.

Peterson: Wouldn't you have to concede that the Jewish minority of Western civilization/United States has performed far beyond what its number would have indicated?

Rockwell: I agree, sir, I have never said the Jews are inferior. . . . I find the Jews intellectually superior. I think they're the greatest businessmen in the world and they've taken control of this country. I think they're pretty damn clever!

Peterson: If they're that superior—by your own logic—shouldn't we do what the Jews tell us to do and stop fooling around as an inferior people?

The topic of Holocaust denial was raised.

Rockwell: I most certainly do deny that the Germans exterminated or purposefully murdered and killed innocent people in the concentration camps. . . . Hitler took all of these sabotaging, bloody communists and put them in concentration camps and put them to work. And they were not exterminated, he printed money for them. I have the money with the Star of David on it—Moses and his tablets. He put tattoos on them to get their numbers. Now does this sound like they were going to exterminate them? The Germans were the most efficient people in the world—they had ten years—and if you don't think they could have exterminated those Jews in ten years then you're wrong. The Jews in the concentration camps died of disease, they died of hunger.... They were not exterminated.

Peterson: There are unimpeachable documents...read the Nuremberg trial documents.... In 1941, unimpeachable evidence, is the Wannsee Conference.... It was determined to send all the Jews away, which I think is like your plan for taking care of the Negro problem—send them away. By 1943–44 there is absolutely no question in anybody's mind who's looked at the documents that millions were killed. Now some people will say it wasn't six million, it was only three million. Now this is a numbers game; as far as I am concerned, a single person who is killed for so foolish a reason as his race, is a crime.

On March 15, the ANP camper rolled into Fargo, North Dakota, where Rockwell and Ralph Abernathy of SCLC gave speeches as part of Civil Rights Day at North Dakota State University. Rockwell's speech commenced in Festival Hall before a packed house of 1,500 people. After the speech a panel of NDSU students and faculty offered rebuttals. A panel member, Professor Arif Hayat from India, told Rockwell, "Perhaps when you get old and sit back and reflect on what you have contributed to your cause, you might find that your life has been worthless in terms of contributions to this world."[22]

His next stop was Fort Hays State College in Hays, Kansas. The school was embattled with the local community over his appearance. Local VFW and American Legion posts openly criticized the invitation and demanded a rebuttal speaker to reiterate American ideals to the students, but the student council stood fast on its decision to invite Rockwell and dismissed the rebuttal idea.

Rockwell took the stage before a capacity crowd of 1,800 people in the Sheridan Coliseum; the general public was allowed to attend. After being greeted with light applause, he blasted Jews, communists, and blacks, and he ripped the Johnson administration for lying to the American people: "The utmost tragedy of our time is sending our boys to Vietnam and not letting them win." He told the students that after he was elected president he would eliminate Chinese communists: "Fifteen or twenty minutes after I'm president there won't be any Red

China. I'm going to be the guy that pushes the button." The crowd gasped in disbelief.

He concluded his forty-five minute speech by thanking the students for inviting him to their campus. Silence filled the auditorium. Not a single person in the audience clapped in applause. Rockwell was stunned: "Do you hate me that much? This is the first time I've failed to be applauded at a college. . . . I wonder whether this is spontaneous or preplanned."[23]

Rockwell departed for Kansas State University in Manhattan. His appearance in Weber Hall had been funded by a student program called News and Views. Security was tight. The previous night an effigy of Rockwell had been hung from a tree on campus; a student had telephoned the school newspaper, the *Collegian*, to claim responsibility. The caller told the newspaper staff that his grandparents had been killed in a German concentration camp during World War II and that for this reason he would kill Rockwell. Over thirty state and local police were dispersed throughout the auditorium, and several FBI agents covered the exits.

An audience of some three thousand crammed into the arena, many wearing black ribbons around their arms as a symbol of dissent and in memory of those who died under Nazism. Nonetheless, Rockwell captivated the audience throughout his hour-long speech. He covered his usual topics, diverging somewhat to state: "Malcolm X was one of the greatest men that ever lived, but Martin Luther King is a fink."[24] He drew applause for his stands on Vietnam, inflation, and Cuba.

Meanwhile, in the spring of 1967, John Patler produced his final copy of the *Stormtrooper*, titled "The Untold Story of Benito Mussolini." This edition contained not only Mussolini's life story but Patler's too. In the "Know Your Party Officers" column Patler retraced his upbringing and political activities. He reminisced about the ANP's greatest battles, the weekly rallies on the Mall in Washington, the riot in Boston where they were almost killed, the "Hate Bus" through the South. He boasted that practically all cartooning, layout, and design of party literature and successful public events had been coordinated and planned by him. Patler was leaving the party, and this was his farewell issue. For eight years he had been a faithful disciple of Commander Rockwell. Now he was disillusioned, not only with the party but with Rockwell. The dissension between the two men had outgrown their need for each other. On one occasion Rockwell had remonstrated with Patler for calling the other troopers "blue-eyed devils." Patler denied the accusation, claiming that Elijah Muhammad had made the comment in a Muslim publication that "only pigs and blue-eyed devils ate green peas." Patler had found the quote so hilarious that he mentioned it in the barracks mess hall. Somehow his meaning was misconstrued by other members to mean that he hated "blue-eyed devils" because his Greek lineage made him feel inferior—less Nordic, less Aryan.

On another occasion Patler had taken Rockwell to task for squandering party funds on three personal vacations in 1966. This was a bone of contention among many of the troopers, not just Patler. Unlike Elijah Muhammad, who became rich off the Nation of Islam, Rockwell never had more than a few thousand dollars to his name. Double standards existed wherever Rockwell was involved. He frequently had special meals prepared for him by his secretary, Barbara von Goetz, while the other troopers ate the slop in the mess hall.

The breaking point between Rockwell and Patler occurred in late March, when Patler "abandoned his post" in Spotsylvania. Patler hated the isolation from his wife and two young boys; he left and returned to Arlington. When Rockwell learned of the matter, he personally went to Spotsylvania to cut the lock on Patler's room and move his personal effects to Arlington.[25] Rockwell dictated a discharge letter, citing numerous charges against Patler: abandoning his post, gross insubordination and insulting conduct to superiors, neglect of duties (specifically, failure to produce more than two *Stormtroopers* in one year), promotion of dissension among the ranks, promotion of distrust by non-Nordic members of the party, and usurpation of authority. The letter directed his immediate dismissal. He was allowed to appeal, if he wished, at party court the weekend of the convention of June 9–11. Matt Koehl supervised while Patler removed his possessions from the barracks. As Patler packed away his gear he muttered a refrain over and over, "He's making a big mistake, he'll be sorry."[26]

On March 31, Rockwell appeared before 2,700 students in Memorial Hall on the campus of Bowling Green University in Ohio. The students laughed at his jokes and applauded at the conclusion, ignoring the student council resolution calling for silence after his speech.[27] From Ohio he went to the University of Washington and then on to Sonoma State College in Rohnert Park, California. There were no incidents.

On April 12, hundreds of protesters opposing capital punishment picketed outside San Quentin prison in California, against the execution of Aaron Mitchell, an African-American lifelong criminal sentenced to die for killing a Sacramento policeman during a restaurant robbery. Rockwell staged a counter-demonstration with a large placard that read "GAS—The Only Cure for Black Crime and Red Treason." With only one ANP supporter to accompany him, Rockwell marched right into the midst of the hundreds of protesters. A protester attacked him from behind and knocked the placard from his hands; Rockwell's assistant charged the attacker and laid him out with a combination punch. Rockwell picked up the placard and continued picketing.

Rockwell spoke at the University of California–Santa Barbara on April 14. The school newspaper, *El Gaucho*, asked attendees not to applaud or boo, but it grossly underestimated Rockwell's ability as an entertainer. Time and time again he brought laughter from the nine hundred students packed into Campbell Hall. The sellout crowd heard Rockwell give his usual speech, but he also went out of his way to praise Ronald Reagan. Rockwell found it "encouraging" that Reagan had been elected governor of California, but he was somewhat suspicious, calling Reagan an "ex-pinko." In a campus interview, Rockwell said, "For a state that could elect Reagan, it'll be ripe for me in a few years."[28] He went on to say that "America is full of people who have no discipline, no order, no sense of responsibility, and get their kicks out of plain raising hell." When asked about racial superiority, he stated, "I do believe in evolution. People generally believe that if you give Bantus [a tribe in Central Africa] a good environment, they'll all turn into Beethovens, Bachs, and Shakespeares...and I think this is insanity. It's a matter of breed.... This is like saying that if you give enough oats to a plug draft horse, you'll make him win races."[29]

On April 20, Rockwell spoke before four thousand students in the auditorium of Michigan State University in East Lansing. The speech was carried on loudspeakers outside the auditorium, where an additional three thousand students gathered. Four days later, on April 24, Rockwell spoke before two thousand students in Carney Hall at Kansas State

College in Pittsburg, Kansas. While Rockwell was giving his speech, thirty-five students marched in protest outside the auditorium. Rockwell spoke against international atheistic Jews, race riots, and the mass media, and he called President Johnson a "crook surrounded by queers."

The next day, April 25, Rockwell appeared before 600 students in a packed Krehbiel Auditorium at Bethel College in North Newton, Kansas. He told the students they were "hypocrites and cowards who like the Negroes until they move in next door to you."[30] That evening he appeared before 870 students in Wilner Auditorium at Wichita State University in Kansas, while a procession of forty local NAACP members picketed outside the building with placards with the Star of David and "6,000,000" beneath the phrase "It Could Happen Here Baby—the All-American City."

Rockwell then drove to Chicago to stand trial for disorderly conduct, obstructing a peace officer, and criminal trespass. On May 15, after a six-day trial, Rockwell was convicted by a Cook County jury. Rockwell told reporters, "I am utterly shocked that such a thing can happen in this country. I'm too disturbed at various aspects of this trial to make further comment now."[31] Judge Maurice Lee of Chicago sentenced Rockwell to three months in jail and fined him $500. Rockwell appealed the decision and returned to Arlington after posting a $5,000 bond.

On May 16 Rockwell appeared before a thousand students in Royce Hall on the campus of UCLA. After a showing of Leni Riefenstahl's Nazi propaganda film *Triumph of the Will*, Rockwell gave his speech. He was continually disrupted by a group of students trying to rally the crowd to assault Rockwell. When the students moved to block the exits to the auditorium, campus police quickly removed Rockwell by way of an underground exit.

The party's three-day national convention commenced at the barracks on June 9. All party officers and supporters were requested to attend the leadership conference, which would institute internal changes. Leaders from around the country converged on Arlington for the meeting. The first issue was discussion and clarification of the name change to the National Socialist White People's Party. Rockwell emphasized it was time to de-Nazify the party and explained that the transition to NSWPP was complete. Rockwell announced that a printing company of Dallas had just completed the tenth chapter of his second book,

White Power. One thousand copies had been printed to be sold at ten dollars each.

The topic of amalgamating Karl Allen's White Party into the NSWPP was raised, and an invitation was tendered to WPA headquarters for a meeting at the party barracks. The officers of the White Party discussed Rockwell's amalgamation proposal and decided to hear his offer. On June 10, the members of the White Party arrived at the barracks, but they received a cold reception from Nazi personnel. The Nazis directed the WPA men to sit in the center of the room and wait for the commander. There was no friendliness or camaraderie between the groups; the pistol-packing Nazis formed a perimeter around the White Party men.

Rockwell made his grand appearance with no hint of congeniality. He opened a copy of *Mein Kampf* and read aloud a section about the communists coming to a Nazi meeting to beat up the opposition. The White Party men were shocked and insulted by the reading. Without a word, they stood and walked out of the meeting en masse. Ralph Forbes, temporarily back from California, ran after Karl Allen to explain that the commander had meant no harm, but Allen would have none of it. Rockwell had made a deliberate or thoughtless slight, and now there was no chance of reconciling with the men from the WPA.[32]

Behind the scenes, in closed-door meetings, Rockwell attempted secret negotiations to bring John Patler back into the organization. Rockwell asked Chris Vidnjevich, the gung-ho six-year ANP veteran and leader of the Chicago unit, to talk with Patler and see if he could be persuaded to rejoin the party. Vidnjevich met with Patler on three occasions. Patler was very bitter about his dismissal, erupting into fits of rage: "Rockwell is an evil genius and he must be stopped." After hearing this a few times, Vidnjevich said, "Well, it sounds like you are back in your old gang in New York." "That's right, and we're going to stop him," Patler responded.[33]

On the afternoon of June 28, 1967, Rockwell and a college student returned to the barracks after a brief interview. As Rockwell turned the car into the heavily wooded barracks driveway he slammed on the brakes: a large branch blocked the road. Figuring that juveniles had placed the small roadblock, Rockwell asked the student to remove it. As the student stepped out of the car a gunshot rang out from the bushes less than fifteen yards away. The bullet ricocheted off the roof of the car, inches from Rockwell's head. Rockwell mistook the gunshot for a cherry bomb. He jumped from the car and ran into the woods to chase what he imagined were teenage pranksters. The thick kudzu-covered undergrowth of the woods was too difficult to penetrate, so he ran to Wilson Boulevard in hope of capturing them on the side street adjacent to the woods—the likely escape route.

According to an account of the incident that he told to Matt Koehl, as he turned the corner onto the side street he caught a glimpse from behind of two assailants. One matched John Patler's physique in every way, according to Koehl, and the accomplice was tall. When Rockwell returned to the vehicle he noticed a scratch from a bullet in the roof of the car and fully realized what had just happened. He notified the police and filed a petition for permission to carry a handgun (but was denied).[34]

Rockwell immediately beefed up security around the barracks. He posted a guard, installed floodlights, and kept three watchdogs in the yard. The next week he typed up his will, giving Matt Koehl control over his remains in the event of his death. He specified that his body be interred with military honors in Arlington National Cemetery, as was his right as a veteran of the armed forces. He arranged a dinner with some of his family. Five family members visited Arlington, and they went out to dinner together. He also saw two of his daughters from his first marriage.

Rockwell was very disturbed by the assassination attempt. When Barbara von Goetz asked if he had chased Patler, he refused to talk about the incident. He believed that to ambush him the way he did, the shooter must have had inside information on his whereabouts, information to which only a few party members were privy. Suspecting treachery, he telephoned Frank Smith in Maine to arrange a secret meeting in Arlington. Smith obliged and met Rockwell at a nearby restaurant to discuss the assassination attempt. According to Smith, Rockwell told him that the physical builds of the assassins he chased were completely unfamiliar to him, contradicting what he'd told Koehl, and that if he was killed, he wanted Smith to look into the matter thoroughly.[35]

In early July the final issue of the *Rockwell Report* came off the press bearing the ominous title "Assassin Misses Commander." After seven years of publication, Rockwell had decided to amalgamate the *Rockwell Report* with the new party paper, which had the same name as Rockwell's latest book, *White Power*. The final issue gave the full details of the botched assassination attempt and also included twenty-three photos from the party archives, a sentimental tribute to men who had contributed to the party, and a retrospective of the various missions: a picket of the White House led by Robert Lloyd, troopers posing in front of the second "Hate Bus," Karl Allen and David Petersen in ape suits leading a civil rights march, a battered Rockwell after an expert beating at the German Orphans home, campaign pictures from the Virginia gubernatorial campaign, the Nazi march through Chicago, a rally in Marquette Park, Western Division demonstrations and fisticuffs, collating *This Time the World* in the basement at the barracks, the Alex Haley interview for *Playboy*, and speeches from different cities and colleges. Rockwell seemed to have had a premonition of his death. He had created a visual eulogy.

On August 25, Rockwell rolled out of bed at 6:30 A.M. and had breakfast with the other men. He stripped off his bedding, bundled his dirty clothes with the sheets, and threw the bundle into the back of a car. He spent the remainder of the morning tinkering on a typewriter-improving invention that he hoped to perfect and patent.

The party planned a trip into the District of Columbia that afternoon to distribute the debut issue of *White Power*. At 11:30 A.M., Rockwell went to wash his clothes, telling his men, "I'll be back in a minute." The Speedy Laundromat was across Wilson Boulevard from the barracks, in the Dominion Hills Shopping Center. He parked the car and took his clothes inside. As he struggled to stuff his clothes into one machine, a Mrs. Ruby Pierce emptied an adjacent machine so he could wash all his clothes at the same time.

He loaded both machines, dumped in soap and worked the coin levers. He turned to Mrs. Pierce and said, "Oh, I forgot something." He walked out to the car, parked in front of the Laundromat, backed out of the space, and put the car in drive. Twenty feet away, on the flat roof of the Laundromat, a man steadied the sights of the long-barreled "broomstick" Mauser pistol on Rockwell. He squeezed the trigger twice. Two gunshots blasted through the windshield on the driver's side. One bullet hit Rockwell square in the chest. The other missed and passed through the front seat. Rockwell rolled to the passenger seat; the driverless car coasted slowly forward and bumped into a parked car. He opened the passenger door and tumbled out onto the parking lot.

Staggering to his feet, he pointed to the roof of the shopping center, wobbled for an instant; then his knees buckled, and he fell to the pavement. Rockwell was dead, at age forty-nine.

In Tom's Barber Shop, barbers Jim Cummings and Tom Blackney heard the shots from the roof. They charged out the door and ran to get around back before the assassin escaped. As they neared the end of the stores they spotted a man running along the side of the building. With the barbers cutting off his escape route, the man turned around and ran for the rear of the shopping center. He vaulted a wall into a residential neighborhood and ran into a wooded park. Cummings told police the man wore a dark trench coat, dark pants, and possibly a yellow shirt.

Forty-five minutes after the shooting, Arlington Police Inspector Raymond Cole spotted a man standing at a bus stop about a half mile from the shopping center. Cole recognized the man as one of Rockwell's followers and called for backup. When the reinforcements arrived, the officers converged on the suspect, who bolted into a residential area, where he was arrested. The suspect, dressed in soaking wet dark pants and a perspiration-soaked yellow shirt, was John Patler.[36]

The final curtain.

13

WHERE'S THE BLEACH?

> Being prepared to die is one of the greatest secrets of
> living. . . . I know this is irrational, but I believe that I was
> placed here for a purpose and I think God has something
> to do with it.
>
> — Rockwell, to Alex Haley,
> *Playboy* magazine

Dozens of bystanders congregated around Rockwell's body in the parking
lot. A reporter took witness Mrs. Ruby Pierce aside and asked if she knew
it was Rockwell she had been talking with in the Laundromat and asked
her feelings about his life and death. Mrs. Pierce gave a roundabout
response:

> I know that Mr. Rockwell is a man that has an opinion. And I know that
> we have the greatest country on Earth, and I know that it's only great
> because we have the freedom of speech. Whether we be Jews, or
> Catholics, or Protestants, or Negro, all of them have their own little pet
> grievances, all of them have their little pet groups. And for that reason I
> never opposed Rockwell in any way. . . .
>
> I will remember Mr. Rockwell as a tall, handsome, neatly dressed man
> that came into the Laundromat very graciously. And I was impressed with
> the charm of this individual and I was most happy that I could give him
> this second washing machine, and I will remember him just that way, as
> a very charming man.[1]

John Hancock, the manager of the Laundromat, told reporters that
Rockwell "remembered he had forgotten his bleach" and was going to
get some. That evening he spoke with reporters on Patler's arrest:

> I saw a picture of the man they picked up on TV tonight, and I'm sure he's
> the one Rockwell and some other boy were chasing that day in June. I
> almost ran over him. I was in my car on Wilson Boulevard when

Rockwell turned into his driveway, and I saw him and the boy with him dive out the door on the passenger's side and then run along Wilson Boulevard.... I turned into the street leading to my house, a man ran out of the bushes on one side, across the road, and into the bushes on the other side.... I had to step real hard on the brakes to avoid hitting him.[2]

Patler was charged with first-degree murder, and bond was set at $50,000. Former Arlington County School Board member Helen Lane agreed to represent him as his attorney. Matt Koehl, now the senior officer and heir apparent of the ANP, told reporters:

Whoever did it, it is of benefit only to the blacks and Jews of this country. It is a defeat for every white man. He was my commander. I think he'll go down in history as one of the greatest living Americans and one of the greatest white men of all time.... I believe that despite what happened here, his death will inspire a victory for the white men of the country.... He wanted his work to go on.[3]

Karl Allen, leader of the White Party, was getting off his shift as manager of the Prince Karl Hotel in the District of Columbia when he heard the news. Although estranged from Rockwell for several years, he realized "the movement" had lost its leader. That evening Karl Allen, Seth Ryan, Bernie Davids, and Chris Bailey, all ex-ANP members, gathered at the White Party headquarters, on King Street in Alexandria, to discuss Rockwell's death. Seth Ryan, who hated Patler, reminded his fellow White Party members of the Black Muslims' embarrassment following Malcolm X's assassination. He suggested they defend Patler—guilty or not—to deflect media attention from the movement to Rockwell's natural enemies. The men agreed with his logic and decided to create the Free Patler Committee.

In England, Colin Jordan was sitting out an eighteen-month jail sentence when he learned of Rockwell's death. His thoughts were consumed by a "crushing sorrow that such a great leader of men in the Cause, capable of great things in the future, should be lost in the moment of an assassin's bullet."[4]

Ed Fields was driving in his car when news of the killing came over the radio. He was stunned to learn that Patler was the accused killer, but he never doubted his guilt.[5]

The Jewish community's reaction was mixed. Samuel Samuels, the national commander of the Jewish War Veterans, stated, "The killer... has done a great disservice to the nation in the elimination of Rockwell by making a martyr of a despicable enemy of America." Samuels said his organization would continue to cooperate with other organizations to "eliminate permanently the teaching of brutality, hatred, inhumanity, and fanaticism, wherever they are found in our American community."[6]

Rabbi Arthur Lelyveld, president of the American Jewish Congress, declared, "George Lincoln Rockwell, after years of operation, never enrolled more than a handful of followers, attracted no support from any business, political, civic or religious leader and made no impact on American life."[7]

Alan Welch was driving his new Volkswagen in Houston when the news came over the radio. He pulled the car over to the shoulder and sat in shock. Rockwell had been the finest leader he had ever encountered. He had led by example, he had been fair, just, honorable, courageous, and incredibly intelligent. He had never talked down to people; he had made them feel like they were worth something. And he had made things work when others gave up. Welch had recalled a phone call from Rockwell a few months earlier; Rockwell had said someone was trying to kill him and that he wanted Welch to come back to Arlington. Welch had thought it was a ploy to get him to return. He was shocked to learn that Patler was the killer. The incident left him devastated and thoroughly depressed.[8]

Barbara von Goetz was working in the District of Columbia when Floyd Fleming telephoned her with the news. She was stunned. Rockwell had always told people he would be shot—now it had happened. She told Fleming she was relieved it had been a quick death and that he would not suffer the rest of his life as a paraplegic.

Arlington police searched the entire escape route for the murder weapon but concentrated their efforts on a stream in Bon Air Park called Four-Mile Run. Patrolman Francis Beakes discovered a pistol wedged beneath a rock in six inches of water, Robert Lloyd's 7.63 mm Mauser. It was halfway between the assassination site and the bus stop where Patler had been arrested.

While authorities were putting together their case, the strange odyssey of Rockwell's burial began. An autopsy by Arlington medical examiner Dr. John Judson revealed that the Mauser bullet had entered to the right

Police study the assassination site where Patler conducted his sneak attack.

of Rockwell's heart, causing massive damage to the major blood vessels; death had come in one or two minutes from massive hemorrhaging. When Judson released the body for burial, conflicting claims arose from Rockwell's family, which wanted a burial on Southport Island, Maine, and Matt Koehl, who laid claim to the body as specified in Rockwell's will. Rockwell's family capitulated on August 27, informing authorities it would no longer contest the ANP's claim to the body.

Meanwhile, the FBI director, J. Edgar Hoover, kept a close eye on the proceedings. In an internal FBI memo he scrawled his displeasure at the tardiness of his information: "I read all of this in this morning's paper. I got this memo at 1:42 P.M., Aug. 28—ancient news!"[9]

The Defense Department approved Rockwell's burial in Culpeper National Cemetery but insisted that no Nazi regalia be displayed. The official statement read:

> Unseemly demonstrations, such as the wearing of the uniform, insignia and emblems or the display of flags or banners of the American Nazi Party or its members will not be permitted in ceremonies at a national cemetery.
>
> A national cemetery is a permanent shrine in honor of the dead of the armed forces of this country. Burial ceremonies must be conducted with

dignity and with proper concern for the sensibilities of those whose loved ones lie there.[10]

It turned down the ANP request for an "all-Caucasian" military honor guard but had no objection to Rockwell's interment in Nazi uniform. The only official requirement was for a casket covered with an American flag.

On Tuesday morning, August 29, the ANP funeral procession left Arlington on the sixty-five-mile journey to the cemetery. A white Cadillac convertible carrying six uniformed Nazis led the cortege, followed by the hearse, adorned with a giant swastika wreath. When the cortege arrived in Culpeper, at 11:00 A.M., Matt Koehl, dressed in a dark suit and with Rockwell's personal copy of *Mein Kampf* clutched in his hands, led a contingent of fifteen stormtroopers in full Nazi attire. Blocking the entrance gate of the cemetery were state and local police as well as sixty-six military policemen flown in by helicopter from Fort Belvoir just minutes before the procession arrived. Surrounding the Nazis outside the gate were dozens of reporters and over three hundred Culpeper citizens.

The superintendent of the cemetery, Edward Maxwell, met with Koehl to explain the Defense Department ruling that no Nazi insignia would be allowed in the cemetery. Appealing to Koehl on the basis of good taste and cooperation, Maxwell urged that his men remove the swastika armbands and lapel pins from their clothing so they could proceed to the graveside. Koehl told Maxwell they had come in good faith and intended to bury Rockwell with the honors of the party. For the next six hours each group waited for the other to back down.

With the funeral cortege blocked from the cemetery, the two trailing cars in the procession were forced to stop on tracks of the Southern Railroad that intersected the short road to the cemetery. Suddenly the warning signals flashed on and a clanging bell signaled the approach of a train. The lead car was able to inch forward off the tracks, but the second car, carrying Arlington police detective Walter Kaddle, was directly in the way of the freight train. Kaddle slammed the car in reverse and backed off the tracks just seconds before a freight train thundered over the crossing.

As the day wore on tempers grew short. At 3:30 P.M., U.S. Army Provost Marshal Major General Carl Turner grabbed a bullhorn and told Matt Koehl he had fifteen minutes to comply with Army regulations. The first arrest came when a uniformed Army private first class, James DeWitt, broke ranks and joined the Nazi entourage; he was

Nazi Chris Vidnjevich attempts to rally the crowd at the Culpeper National Cemetery after MPs blocked Rockwell's burial procession.

AP/Wide World Photos

immediately arrested by MPs. ANP supporter Doug Niles then jumped on the roof of the hearse and yelled, "You ain't gonna stop me, you two-star, communist swine. Let's go." The driver of the hearse edged the vehicle forward a few inches until the grill touched the five-foot, six-inch general. Niles lunged at the MPs and was arrested. Chris

Vidnjevich from Chicago jumped on the roof of the hearse to rally the Nazis.

"Now you see what the Jews are doing, they are keeping us out of here. It's Jewish power. What we need is white power." Vidnjevich led the group in a "Heil Hitler" before leaping into a double column of MPs and being arrested. Fellow Nazi Mike Steward also attempted to crash the MPs and was likewise arrested.[11] Fifteen minutes later nothing had changed. General Turner picked up the bullhorn and spoke again.

"Mr. Koehl, in view of your refusal to comply with the regulations of the Department of the Army, the Department of the Army has withdrawn its approval for the burial of George Lincoln Rockwell in this cemetery." Koehl yelled back, "I cannot allow the body to be buried against the express wishes of Commander Rockwell! I will remain in custody of the body!"

"That is your problem," answered General Turner.

The Nazis started booing and shouting, "Heil Hitler! Traitor! Dirty Jewish swine!" Koehl got in the last word: "Twenty years he served in the Navy and you won't let him be buried. The commander fought in two wars and he can't even be buried in a military cemetery. Commander Rockwell's being treated like a dog."[12] Koehl and the undertaker returned to the hearse and led the funeral procession back to Arlington.

The body was stored at the funeral home for the night while the ANP contemplated its next move. Unwilling to inter the body in a national cemetery under the government's conditions, Koehl was forced to make a decision. On August 30, 1967, Rockwell's body was cremated. The ashes were kept under armed guard at party barracks.

Meanwhile, Patler had his first court appearance in Arlington County. As he walked into court under heavy guard, a spectator in the second row lunged at him screaming, "Patler, you filthy swine! You assassin!"[13] Six policemen subdued Australian Eric Wenberg, resident of ANP headquarters. He was handcuffed and removed from court, still screaming, "You filthy assassin! Long live the American Nazi Party! Long live Matt Koehl!"[14] Later in the day Wenberg was brought back into the courtroom and found guilty of contempt of court. Judge L. Jackson Embrey gave him the maximum sentence of ten days in jail and a fifty-dollar fine. Wenberg was deported the next month.

Arlington County police uncovered several damning pieces of evidence against John Patler. Three cartridge cases and four bullets were recovered at the Highland County farm of Sam Ervin, Patler's father-in-law, where a neighbor had seen Patler target-shooting against a white oak tree in July. The evidence was sent to an FBI laboratory for examination; it was confirmed that all four bullets and three cartridge cases had been fired by Lloyd's gun. The correlation of bullet to murder weapon was the first evidence linking Patler with the murder weapon.

Patler maintained his innocence throughout the proceedings. His team of attorneys, Thomas Harrigan, Thomas Morris, and Helen Lane, presented other possible motives for the slaying. Robert Lloyd, the original owner of the pistol, had been discharged from the ANP in 1966 (but reinstated as deputy commander by Koehl immediately after Rockwell's death). The defense team wanted to shift suspicion to Koehl, since he had the most to gain by the killing. Koehl was perhaps too reclusive to be the triggerman, but Robert Lloyd was not. Some people (party members included) believed the killing was actually a coup. It elevated Rockwell to martyr status and turned the reins of the organization to Koehl, a strident Hitlerite.

It was no secret that Lloyd and Patler did not like each other. Lloyd told police that in 1964, before their falling-out, he had loaned the pistol to Patler. When he asked for its return Patler said it had been stolen. But Frank Smith testified for the defense that he had seen the gun in Lloyd's possession in Richmond during the gubernatorial campaign. Defense attorney Harrigan also argued that Rockwell had decided spontaneously to visit a Laundromat and there had been no way for Patler to have known of Rockwell's sudden decision. Only Koehl knew that Rockwell was going to do his laundry that day.

In December, Patler took the stand to explain why he had been at the bus stop shortly after the shooting. He said that after a dispute with his wife about his methods of disciplining their son, he had stormed out of the house fifteen minutes before noon and walked at a rapid pace because he was so angry. He realized that the argument had been foolish and decided to return home by bus.

The question remains: How did Patler know Rockwell was going to be at the Laundromat? Conspiracy theorists want to believe Matt Koehl was involved. He had used the same car earlier in the day and surely had noticed Rockwell's dirty laundry on the rear seat. He could have telephoned Patler to tell him Rockwell was planning to do his wash. But Koehl did not seem to have a motive. He was already the number-two man in an ever-shrinking organization and had shown no signs of dissatisfaction with Rockwell's leadership, just lack of funds.

Someone other than Koehl could have telephoned Patler from the barracks. Besides Koehl, Robert Bruce, Donald Parsons, and George Parker had been there. However, testimony revealed that Patler and his wife, Alice, had been running errands that morning, and there was no evidence that Patler had placed any calls then himself. Police captain Raymond Cole felt Rockwell was a creature of habit who kept to certain routines and that Patler would have known this, having lived with him for so many years.

In any event, no concrete evidence of a conspiracy was ever proven. The scenario presented by the prosecution was that Patler had acted alone, fueled by rage after being discarded from the party by the man who had been his father figure for ten years. He had had motive, means, and opportunity. It was also asserted that Patler had been the most likely participant in the barracks driveway shooting in June. (Although Rockwell wrote of chasing two men after the ambush, he privately told William Pierce there had only been one. Rockwell's reasons for the discrepancy are unclear, but he may have wanted to exaggerate the danger he was in.) Patler had analyzed the area, he knew Rockwell's habits, and he had stalked and waited for his opportunity to stop the "evil genius."

Ninety-one witnesses were called to the stand. One testified that she had seen Patler standing at a bank across from the barracks two days before the shooting. The Commonwealth attorney, William Hassan, presented a witness who had found a cap and a reversible raincoat in a neighbor's yard on the escape route within an hour after the shooting. Two ANP men testified that Patler had worn the same type of coat.

The defense introduced evidence regarding Patler's shoes. An FBI agent testified that it was impossible to state with certainty that the tar on them was the same as that on the roof of the Laundromat. They also did not show evidence of roofing gravel. Moreover, imprint samples taken from the roof were of a size 11½ shoe—much bigger than Patler's size.

Captain Raymond Cole, who had apprehended Patler after the shooting, testified that when Patler was arrested, his dark colored pants had been pulled up to his knees and that his shirt had been soaking wet. Hassan told the jury that Patler's pants had been wet because he knelt in a stream to lodge the murder weapon between two rocks. Hassan, who had been at odds with Rockwell for so many years, was making the finest, most compelling argument of his career to convict Rockwell's killer.

"I ask you, if you determine John Patler guilty of a crime of lying in wait, an assassination, a killing from ambush, give him the chair."[15] Patler's slim brunette wife burst into shrieks, yelling, "No! No! No!" then fainted to the floor. She was carried from the courtroom and taken by ambulance to Arlington Hospital. The all-white jury of ten men and two women returned to the courtroom after thirty hours of deliberation. A guilty verdict was handed down and a twenty-year sentence, the minimum for the crime, meted out.

In February 1968, Patler's attorneys asked Circuit Court Judge Charles Russell for an appeal of his conviction. Defense attorney Harrigan cited twenty-two errors in the three-week trial, including the use of "identification" witnesses by Hassan who had testified they saw a man resembling Patler running from the scene only after seeing him in a police station, in court, or in a newspaper photograph. Harrigan also pointed out that testimony by FBI analysts regarding a footprint found on the roof of the shopping center failed to match the tread in Patler's tennis shoes. Judge Russell denied the appeal and imposed the twenty-year prison term but delayed execution of the sentence because the defense lawyers appealed to the Virginia Supreme Court. Patler, who remained free on $40,000 bond until the disposition of the appeal, said, "I think the court, the jury, and Commonwealth have made a terrible mistake, and because of that mistake, an innocent man is going to be deprived of twenty years of his life and a great injustice has been done. Ever since my arrest, events have been a stampede to judgment."[16]

The Virginia Supreme Court affirmed Patler's conviction in November 1970. On December 4 his $40,000 bond was revoked by Judge Russell, and Patler went to prison. In 1972, the U.S. Supreme Court also refused to review his case. Patler was paroled from the Pulaski Correctional Unit in August 1975 but violated his parole and returned to prison for an additional six years.

In 1968, the American Civil Liberties Union filed suit against the Pentagon to allow Nazi regalia during burial at Culpeper National

Cemetery. In November 1969 the U.S. 4th Circuit Court of Appeals upheld the ruling of the circuit court prohibiting such a burial.[17] Thus ended Koehl's battle to inter Rockwell's ashes with Nazi-uniformed pallbearers. The New Order, the successor organization of the NSWPP, maintains custody of Rockwell's ashes at a secret location.

EPILOGUE

The battle of our times—if there is to be any battle—
is for the survival of the White race.
— Rockwell, *In Hoc Signo Vinces*

At the time of Rockwell's death there was no formal provision for party succession. Koehl, as the ranking officer, technically could have assumed leadership, but he felt that under the circumstances, a broader mandate was necessary. In early September he convened a special council of sixteen leading party members and officers. He opened the session with the question of succession, telling those present to consider every possibility, including themselves. He left the room to allow uninhibited deliberation. When he returned, they announced that he was the only conceivable candidate to become party leader.

"Are you sure?" Koehl asked. "Bear in mind that we are a National Socialist organization operating on the Leadership Principle . . . I alone will retain the responsibility for making the final decisions."[1] Again, in a rare display of unanimity, all confirmed that Koehl should become the new national leader of the party, even William Pierce, Robert Lloyd, and the Surreys, all of whom would later defect over differences in policy.

According to Koehl, the party had no more than one hundred members and approximately two hundred registered supporters when Rockwell died. Under his leadership, the party consolidated, shutting down the California and Chicago units and transferring Ralph Forbes and Chris Vidnjevich to Arlington. The party was evicted from the barracks on Wilson Boulevard in 1968 and abandoned the Spotsylvania property.

Arlington County eventually purchased "Hatemonger Hill" from the Kerns and tore down the mansion. Ironically, it transformed the property into a park, complete with a swimming pool, for the enjoyment of Arlington's ethnically diverse citizens.

Koehl, Pierce, and Lloyd led the remaining members of the NSWPP into the 1970s. They purchased a headquarters building at 2507 North Franklin Road in Arlington in June 1968. They continued to pursue the second phase in movement development that Rockwell had initiated with a name change to National Socialist White People's Party. The American Nazi Party had been a suitable name for the rough-and-tumble, anything-goes first phase of party operations, a gimmick to attract public attention. The second phase required an image make-over to emphasize the actual ideals and goals of National Socialism.

To some extent, inroads were made in this direction. The new National Socialist White People's Party entered candidates in a number of small local elections, usually attracting about 5 percent of the vote with its all-out National Socialist platform. In a Milwaukee school board race, it managed to garner one in every five voters. The ambition was to parlay this support into more formidable electoral undertakings. But the reality of achieving higher office never materialized. A number of serious internal problems gradually became more and more apparent. The party lacked qualified candidates, staff, and infrastructure, and it faced perpetual personnel turnover.

Koehl believed that a clearer understanding and appreciation of fundamental Hitlerian ideals and values were needed by party adherents. Toward that end, a moratorium on negative literature was put into effect in 1978 to shift emphasis to the positive goals of National Socialism. The immediate effect on the party was the sudden jettisoning of the mindless haters.

Koehl realized the social conditions around the country had also changed. America was at peace, and its economy had not collapsed. Gone were the urban riots, the Vietnam War, student activism, and revolutionary ferment. In their place were mass consumerism and the often successful pursuit of the American Dream by an emerging demographic that was decidedly less white. These events prompted Koehl to reexamine the entire movement and its mission. He believed he was witnessing the collapse of an entire civilization—an old order—resting upon a false spiritual foundation. It became obvious to him that what had to replace this decadent civilization was a "New Order," one based on a new spiritual outlook.

Accordingly, the NSWPP was officially renamed the New Order on January 1, 1983, and restructured as a religious organization. As such, the New Order did not require government approval or seek IRS tax-exempt status; it sought the same rights and treatment granted to other religious bodies in accordance with the U.S. Constitution. Anyone attempting to deprive its adherents of their civil rights would be in violation of the law and—theoretically—subject to all applicable penalties and restrictions.

Koehl believes this "living faith of Adolf Hitler" is still very much in its infancy and will grow over an extended period of time. He explains:

> Today we have only the rudiments. We are laying a foundation. The elaboration of our doctrines and the development of those formal usages and structures, such as one normally associates with the older religions, will involve the work of generations and centuries. But what is time when one is talking seriously about religion? How long did the Christians have to wait for Constantine to deliver a decadent Roman Empire into their hands? How often over the millennia did Diaspora Jewry repeat the ancient formula, "Next year in Jerusalem?" If it be the will of heaven, we too can tarry a bit.[2]

Although there were those who disagreed with the changes and quit the movement, new recruits took up the cause fervently and the overall quality of support improved significantly.

The New Order moved from Arlington to Milwaukee, Wisconsin, in 1985. Arlington was not a central location, and the high cost of living in the area made it difficult to continue. There was also the stigma of a continued existence in what the right wing considered an increasingly corrupt and alien "Beltway" environment. The current focus of the New Order became the development of necessary infrastructure to facilitate informational outreach and educational training, rather than formal membership-gathering.

Koehl is convinced today that Rockwell would have eventually came to the same conclusion regarding the evolution of National Socialism in the United States, that it should be a religious movement rather than a political party: "Had he started out in today's world, there is little question but that he would have brought the full force of his dynamic personality directly into a Hitlerian religious ministry."[3]

Although all traces of the Nazis have vanished from Arlington, the legacy of Rockwell and the American Nazi Party lives on. Rockwell's dubious place in history is firmly established as the seminal force of post–World War II National Socialism in America and as the originator of the Holocaust denial movement. Rockwell's Holocaust-denial platform—that the Jews invented the story of the Holocaust to legitimize Israel and extract reparations from Germany, and that they perpetuate the myth by their control of the media and Hollywood—is still used by "Holocaust revisionists" of today. This denial, once the exclusive domain of the fringe, is now being cunningly introduced to the public in both academic and media outlets. It may become even more prevalent as the Holocaust survivors succumb to old age, leaving no witnesses to refute the charges. Rockwell's disciples continue his work.

Besides leading the New Order, Matt Koehl also presides over the World Union of National Socialists. However, the rigid, monolithic structure originally envisioned by Rockwell and Jordan never materialized. The realities of national agendas, geographic distances, separate operations, and lack of staff proved insurmountable. Most National Socialist activity around the world has been conducted by national entities with minimal coordination by the World Union. In recognition of these obstacles, WUNS was formally restructured in 1992 as the authoritative policy-making body of the National Socialist movement rather than as the membership organization it had been.

William Pierce split with NSWPP in July 1970 to form Youth for Wallace, in support of George Wallace's run for the presidency. It served as a recruiting tool for a follow-up group he formed with Willis Carto, called the National Youth Alliance. When Carto and Pierce split up, Pierce renamed his group the National Alliance and established headquarters in Hillsboro, West Virginia. The National Alliance prints and distributes the *National Vanguard* and maintains an Internet web site, and Pierce conducts a weekly program called *American Dissident Voices,* broadcast over the Internet and shortwave radio. Pierce also wrote two widely read right-wing underground novellas, *The Turner Diaries* (1978) and *Hunter* (1979). *The Turner Diaries* presents a futuristic world in which antigovernment "patriots" blow up federal buildings and wreak havoc upon "race-traitors." *Hunter* is the story of a man who single-handedly "exterminates" mixed couples, Mossad agents, liberals, blacks, and Jews.

The Turner Diaries inspired a Nazi terrorist group in the 1980s called The Order, or Silent Brotherhood. The text became the modus operandi for this group, which used it as a blueprint for bank robberies, armored car heists, and counterfeiting operations, which brought it more than six million dollars. It also assassinated Jewish talk show host Alan Berg in Denver, Colorado, in 1984. All the members of the group were eventually imprisoned or killed. In 1995, the Oklahoma City federal building was destroyed by right-wing fanatic Timothy McVeigh using a rented truck loaded with a fertilizer bomb; in *The Turner Diaries*, a similar method is used to destroy FBI headquarters in Washington.

Ralph Forbes, leader of the ANP's Western Division, served as David Duke's 1988 presidential campaign manager. In 1990, Forbes ran for lieutenant governor of Arkansas as a Republican and won 46 percent of the primary vote but lost to a conservative African American in a runoff election. James Warner is the leader of the Christian Defense League and sells right-wing books from a mail-order outlet in Louisiana. The National States Rights Party folded in the mid-1980s; today Ed Fields publishes *The Truth at Last* in Marietta, Georgia.

Rockwell's other former officers and stormtroopers are scattered around the country. Most are politically inactive and lead quiet lives. There are no American Nazi Party reunions. John Patler was given unsupervised release from prison in July 1983. He changed his name back to Patsalos and lives in seclusion on the East Coast. His brother George murdered his live-in girlfriend and was sentenced to life in prison in 1997.

With the fall of the Berlin Wall and the crumbling of the Soviet "evil empire," communism is no longer the focus of the American right. A belief has evolved that the U.S. government has lost its way. Right-wingers see it as being on the verge of bankruptcy and run by leftist New World Order fanatics with the help of the ever-present "international Jewish financiers." They see federal law enforcement officers using deadly force to reconcile what they consider to be state concerns at Waco and Ruby Ridge. They see their tax dollars being soaked up by a regulatory jungle or given away to foreign nations or illegal aliens.

There are vast differences between the right-wing extremism of Rockwell's era and the modern right-wing extremist. Unlike the old right, which appealed to patriotism and love of country, and strove to change America by way of the Constitution, the new right believes the entire political system is a farce, that it must be destroyed and rebuilt in a new political image. The new right believes the government is Zionist-controlled; they call it the Zionist Occupied Government, or ZOG. Rockwell believed there were individual "crypto-communists" within the government, but he held some high federal officials, such as J. Edgar Hoover, in the highest regard. The new right considers law enforcement, especially federal agencies such as the Bureau of Alcohol, Tobacco, and Firearms and the FBI, as enemies to be destroyed, servants of a corrupt order. Rockwell believed law enforcement officers were ultimately on his side and secretly sympathetic to his movement but bound by oath to perform their duties.

Several similarities between the old right and the new right have remained. Most common is the belief in a vast and sinister conspiracy—a paranoid style of politics where the root of all evil can be traced back or attributed to someone or some thing. Both groups believe in the superiority of the white race. Both groups relish the display of symbols such as swastikas and lightning bolts. But the new right has become "high-tech" in its communications, using AM-FM, shortwave, phone dialers, computer bulletin boards, the Internet, and rock music to disseminate ideas.

The arrival of neo-Nazi skinheads in the 1980s was a new development in the right-wing extremist movement. Although they were of British origin, their youth subculture of punk rock music, nihilism, and self-disfigurement was easily transplanted to the United States. By the early 1990s there were several thousand skinheads in the country, many of whom were simply hard-drinking rowdies devoted to punk music and their exclusive counterculture clique. Others were hardened urban racists meaning to break heads and stomp their boots on those they despised.

Skinhead methods are repulsive to most Rockwell-era adherents. Koehl describes them as

> homeless orphans, the pitiful product of alienation and anomie in a society which they correctly perceive as offering them nothing but hostility and hopelessness . . . the crude rage of the disenfranchised. Their reaction is to strike out—here and now—to get it out of their systems, regardless of any possible consequences. But using their bald heads as battering rams, rather than instruments of higher thought, is hardly a recipe for success. Such immature behavior tends toward puerile yahooism,

moronic spectacle and worse, and is therefore counterproductive to the efforts of any constructive cause.[4]

There is certainly no reason to believe the end of anti-Semitism is in sight, but there is no reason to be overly excited about or fearful of its existence. Barry Rubin, a professor at Hebrew University, Jerusalem, writes:

> Never before...has anti-Semitism been less significant than at present. One can count the number of skinheads, anti-Jewish groups in post-Soviet Eastern Europe, synagogue desecrations, or articles denying the Holocaust, but however distressing the continued existence of this scourge may be, its quantity is still minor and the significance on Western society and the lives of Jews even less.[5]

Indeed, the numerous anti-Semitic journals and organizations have the equivalent public impact of a doomsday lunatic preaching on a busy street corner—the masses pay no attention. However, if a mass movement of anti-Semitism were to evolve, it would certainly include many of the fringe groups, but it would not spring forth from them, nor would it be led by them.

Racists are utilizing two very important tools today: the Internet and rock music. Both media provide an avenue to reach the minds of youths at their most critical years of development. The Internet provides access to chat rooms and web pages where people can trade news and views, video and audio presentations, encrypted messages, merchandise distribution, and rally announcements. There are also "how to" manuals on constructing explosives and modifying weapons. To those with access to a computer and an Internet service provider, these items are available instantaneously and free of charge.

Music is the other medium that could help perpetuate a white power movement for future generations. The financial success of the numerous independent record labels created in the 1980s proved that the major labels had not cornered the market. In fact, thousands of youths rejected the staid middle-of-the-road music of the major labels and FM radio station playlists for alternative college radio stations pumping out original music on their low-power transmitters.

Resistance Records is an independent label formed in Detroit in the 1990s. The label has signed more than a dozen of the best racist bands and formed a distribution network in the United States, Europe, South Africa, and South America. Sales for 1996 were more than $300,000. Resistance also publishes a full-color music magazine and has a presence on the World Wide Web.

An official with Oregon's Communities Against Hate attests to the power of music at drawing young people: "It's probably the most successful organizing tool white supremacist skinheads have. Kids get into the scene because of the music, and then they're introduced to the politics."[6]

The scenario for radical anti-Semitism might continue by way of underground guerrilla warfare bands, using leaderless resistance. But a crisis—perhaps a perceived governmental restriction of constitutionally guaranteed civil liberties, a nuclear explosion, an economic catastrophe—could be the catalyst for a societal breakdown that could ultimately lead to the creation of pogroms against various groups, not just Jews. With the proper leader and an intelligently crafted ideology, the extremist right may find its way into the political mainstream. Rockwell's prediction of economic catastrophe and race war may never materialize. But if the economy collapsed, would desperate Americans look for another Roosevelt to redistribute the wealth? Or would some turn to another George Lincoln Rockwell to provide the solution?

The White Power movement is perhaps Rockwell's most enduring legacy. Gone was the criterion of being Nordic or Aryan; gone was the Nativist, anti-Catholic prejudice of the Ku Klux Klan. Now anyone white and non-Jewish could belong to a worldwide racist movement that had no internal racial or ethnic hierarchy.

Rockwell also popularized, even commercialized, anti-black and anti-Jewish propaganda, rife with dark humor. Through vehicles such as a "Boat Ticket to Africa," "The Diary of Ann Fink," or a Hatenanny recording of "We's Non-Violent Niggers," Rockwell tried to insert his influence into mainstream American culture. These comic book–level works actually appealed to vast numbers of prejudiced Americans. He established the precedent of American Nazis joining the Christian Identity Church, a place where racist beliefs and anti-Semitism coexisted under one church roof. This, too, has been carried forward to the next generation.

Rockwell was never close to grabbing the brass ring of political power, and the American Nazi Party's maximum membership at any one time never exceeded two hundred. Some writers and pundits are quick to dismiss his impact as minimal and his life's work a failure. However, he is recognized by today's organized racists as the progenitor of contemporary racism. It is very likely that three separate movements created by him—Holocaust denial, White Power, and the melding of Nazism with Christian Identity—will extend well into the twenty-first century.

Hatred like George Lincoln Rockwell's is eternal. It is something that each generation must contend with, something that every person must reconcile within themselves. We must each look within ourselves to see whether the light that is in us is not really darkness.

NOTES

Key to Abbreviations

AHP = Alex Haley Papers, Schomburg Center for Research in Black Culture, New York Public Library

GLR/USN = George Lincoln Rockwell, serial no. 106684, Department of Navy Personnel Records

PST = *Portland (Maine) Sunday Telegram*

WES = *Washington Evening Star*

NSB = *National Socialist Bulletin,* American Nazi Party

NYT = *New York Times*

TTTW = *This Time the World,* George Lincoln Rockwell (Reedy, W. Va.: Liberty Bell Publications, 1979)

UPI = United Press International

WP = *Washington Post*

WDN = *Washington Daily News*

Introduction

1. Roger Foss, interviewed by author, 14 June 1994.
2. *NYT,* 22 June 1960.
3. *Blood in the Face,* videocassette by James Ridgeway (Right Thinking Productions: 1991).

Chapter 1: Political Sleep

1. *Portland (Maine) Evening Press,* 3 March 1978; *PST,* 5 July 1931, 17 February 1935; *Portland (Maine) Press Herald,* 4 March 1978; George "Doc"

Rockwell papers, Boothbay Region Historical Society and Museum, Boothbay Harbor, Maine.

2. George Lincoln Rockwell, *TTTW,* 18.

3. Frederick Simonelli, "American Fuehrer: George Lincoln Rockwell and the American Nazi Party" (Ph.D. diss., University of Nevada–Reno, 1995), 13, 18.

4. Tupper was elected to three terms as a Maine Republican to the House of Representatives and served as ambassador to Canada in 1967.

5. The record, along with all of "Doc" Rockwell's show business memorabilia, was destroyed in 1971 when Slipshod Manor burned to the ground.

6. Stanley Tupper, interviewed by author, Boothbay Harbor, Maine, 25 April 1994.

7. Lewis became a superior court judge in Alaska.

8. *TTTW,* 5; Eben Lewis, telephone interview, May 1996.

9. Tupper interview.

10. Simonelli, "American Fuehrer," 14.

11. Ibid., 15.

12. *TTTW,* 4.

13. Ibid., 21.

14. GLR/USN.

15. *TTTW,* 26.

16. Ibid., 28–29.

17. Tupper interview.

18. Ibid.

19. *TTTW,* 32.

20. *TTTW,* 41.

21. GLR/USN.

22. The few surviving charts are prized possessions among the locals of Boothbay Harbor; reproductions are available from the Boothbay Region Historical Society and Museum.

23. *TTTW,* 69.

24. Ibid., 70.

25. *TTTW,* 71; *Portland (Maine) Sunday Telegram & Press Herald,* 28 May 1950.

26. *Portland (Maine) Sunday Telegram & Press Herald,* 28 May 1950.

Chapter 2: Awakening

1. *TTTW,* 83–84.

2. GLR/USN.

3. Roberta Feuerlicht, *Joe McCarthy and McCarthyism: The Hate That Haunts America* (New York: McGraw-Hill, 1972), 68.

4. *Common Sense* depicted communism as "Judaism." It primarily attacked Jews and to a lesser extent blacks, but was sympathetic to the former Nazi regime in Germany.

5. *TTTW*, 78.

6. C.N.C., of Glendale, Calif., was extremely anti-Jewish. It believed the nation and white race were being threatened by anti-Christian, racially "mongrelizing" forces such as communism and internationalism.

7. *TTTW*, 83.

8. Ibid., 89.

9. Simonelli, "American Fuehrer," 36.

10. *TTTW*, 92.

11. Ibid., 94.

12. GLR/USN.

13. The Zwicker hearings led to the downfall of Joe McCarthy.

14. Feuerlicht, *Joe McCarthy and McCarthyism*, 119.

15. GLR/USN.

16. *TTTW*, 109.

17. Ibid., 110.

18. Adolf Hitler, *Mein Kampf* (New York: Reynal & Hitchcock, 1941), 197.

19. *TTTW*, 114.

20. FBI Files 105-70374 Monograph *American Nazi Party; TTTW*, 121.

21. DeWest Hooker, interviewed by author, Washington, D.C., 12 September 1993.

22. *TTTW*, 134.

23. The Columbian Workers Movement formed in Atlanta in 1946. Membership was made up of returning World War II veterans. Burke designed the famous Thunderbolt symbol for the group and published two editions of a newspaper by the same name before he was incarcerated for sixteen months for "usurpation of police powers."

24. Emory Burke, interviewed by author, Montgomery, Alabama, 22 August 1995.

25. William L. Pierce, "George Lincoln Rockwell: A National Socialist Life," *National Socialist World* (Winter 1967), 13–36; Wallace Allen, interviewed by author via telephone, 11 April 1994.

26. *The Virginian* was a white-supremacy, anti-Jewish magazine.

27. FBI File: "George Lincoln Rockwell/Am. Nazi Party," 105-70374 (hereafter FBI BuFile: 105-70374).

Chapter 3: 1958: Battle Call

1. *TTTW*, 164; Pierce, "George Lincoln Rockwell," 13–36.

2. Etta Bick, "Ethnic Linkage and Foreign Policy: A Study of the Linkage Role of American Jews in Relations Between the United States and Israel, 1956–1968" (Ph.D. diss., City University New York, 1983), 140.

3. FBI BuFile: 105-70374.

4. Rockwell's Atlanta associates were so repulsed by the "kike" signs that they printed their own for the demonstration. See M. F. Green, *The Temple Bombing* (Reading, Penn.: Addison-Wesley, 1996).

5. *TTTW*, 167.

6. FBI BuFile: 105-70374.

7. Ibid.

8. *WES*, 17 October 1958.

9. *WES*, 18 October 1958.

10. Ibid.; FBI BuFile: 105-70374.

11. *WES*, 17 October 1958.

12. *WES*, 23 October 1958.

13. *WES*, 30 October 1958.

14. FBI BuFile: 97-3835-2.

15. Ibid.

16. FBI BuFile: 105-70374.

17. *TTTW*, 174.

18. Simonelli, "American Fuehrer," 49–51.

19. John Patler, "Know Your Party Officers," *Stormtrooper*, vol. 6, no. 1 (1967), 23–32.

20. Ibid.

21. Dr. Pierre Rube, "Report of John Patler," Morrisania City Hospital, Mental Hygiene Clinic, New York City, 26 October 1956. (From *Commonwealth of Virginia vs. John Patler*, exhibit #1a).

22. Ibid.

23. Patler, "Know Your Party Officers," 23–32.

24. *TTTW*, 176.

Chapter 4: 1959: The Armor of Fearlessness

1. FBI BuFile: 105-70374.

2. Ibid.

3. Ibid.

4. FBI BuFile: 97-3835.

5. Ibid.

6. FBI BuFile: 105-70374.

7. Ibid.

8. Ibid.

9. Ibid.

10. *WES*, 5 June 1959.

11. *The Rockwell Report*, vol. 2, no. 5 (15 December 1962), 4.

12. Ibid., 3.

13. Hans Staudinger, *The Inner Nazi: A Critical Analysis of Mein Kampf* (Baton Rouge: Louisiana State University Press, 1981), 82–83.

14. *Mein Kampf*, 174.

15. Anti-Defamation League of B'nai B'rith, *FACTS* (September 1960), 163.

16. FBI BuFile: 105-70374.

17. *WES*, 13 May 1959.

18. *WES*, 17 May 1959.

19. FBI BuFile: 105-70374.

20. Earl Shaffer, interviewed by author, Arlington, Virginia, 21 October 1994.

21. Hitler's birthday, April 20, is celebrated annually by National Socialists.

22. *WES*, 22 April 1959; *TTTW*, 181–82.

23. *WES*, 22 April 1959.

24. Charles Russell, "Memorandum of Amicus Curiae," filed 5 June 1959, Arlington County Courthouse.

25. *WES*, 5 May 1959.

26. FBI BuFile: 105-70374.

27. *WES*, 22 June 1959.

28. FBI BuFile: 105-70374.

29. Ibid.

30. *TTTW*, 188–90.

31. Ibid., 191.

32. *Mein Kampf*, vol. 1, ch. 12, 488.

33. William Pierce, interviewed by author, Hillsboro, West Virginia, 27 April 1996.

34. *Mein Kampf*, vol. 2, ch. 7, 723.

Chapter 5: 1960: The Ultimate Weapon

1. *WES*, 11 January 1960.

2. FBI BuFile: 105-70374; *Northern Virginia Sun*, 12 January 1960.

3. Joseph Kirman, "Major Programs of the B'nai B'rith Anti-Defamation League: 1945–1965" (Ph.D. diss., New York University, 1967), 170.

4. Oscar Cohen, "The Swastika 'Epidemic' and Anti-Semitism in America, (New York: Anti-Defamation League of B'nai B'rith), 1960, 3–5.

5. Isaac Franck, "Statement on George Lincoln Rockwell by the Washington Jewish Community Council," January 1960, American Jewish Archives.

6. GLR/USN.

7. George Lincoln Rockwell, *In Hoc Signo Vinces*, January 1960.

8. ADL, *FACTS* 13, 164.

9. FBI BuFile: 105-70374; *WP*, 16 February 1960.

10. FBI BuFile: 105-70374; *WP*, 24 February 1960.

11. *WES*, 11 February 1960.

12. "Memorandum on ACLU Representation of Nazi Handbill Distributions in Washington, D.C.," 1 March 1960, American Jewish Archives.

13. *WES*, 26 February 1960.

14. Foss interview; Foss diaries.

15. FBI BuFile: 139-1049.

16. "Rockwell's Hate Literature Distributions," Jewish Community Council of Greater Washington, 18 March 1960, American Jewish Archives.

17. FBI BuFile: 105-70374.

18. Ibid.

19. Foss interview.

20. Ibid.

21. Ibid.

22. Gerald L. K. Smith Collection, box 53, Bentley Historical Library, University of Michigan.

23. FBI BuFile: 105-70374; *WES,* 11 June 1960.

24. *WES,* 12 June 1960.

25. FBI BuFile: 105-70374; *NYT,* 18 June 1960.

26. FBI BuFile: 105-70374.

27. FBI BuFile: 105-70374; *The Worker,* 19 June 1960.

28. Ibid.

29. FBI BuFile: 105-70374.

30. *NYT,* 22 June 1960.

31. Ibid.

32. FBI BuFile: 105-70374; UPI, 24 June 1960.

33. Foss interview.

34. A. M. Rosenthal and Arthur Gelb, *One More Victim* (New York: New American Library, 1967), 102.

35. Foss interview.

36. Ibid.

37. Rosenthal and Gelb, *One More Victim,* 101.

38. "The Burros Business," *The Rockwell Report* October–November 1965, 7.

39. Rosenthal and Gelb, *One More Victim,* 106.

40. Foss interview.

41. Ibid.

42. Ibid.

43. FBI BuFile: 105-70374; *WDN,* 15 August 1960.

44. Foss interview.

45. Ibid.

46. *WDN,* 16 August 1960; Foss interview; ADL, *FACTS* 13, 165.

47. *TTTW,* 217.

48. FBI BuFile: 105-70374.

49. *WES,* 6 July 1960.

50. Foss interview.

51. Rosenthal and Gelb, *One More Victim,* 121; *WES,* 31 July 1960, 21 September 1960.

52. *WES,* 28 July 1960.

53. Ibid.

54. *TTTW,* 219–224.

55. Foss interview.

56. *TTTW,* 227.

57. ADL, *FACTS* 13, 166; *NYT,* 5 August 1960.

58. FBI BuFile: 105-70374; *WDN,* 12 August 1960; FBI Registration Section, "Foss statement," 19 August 1960.

59. FBI BuFile: 105-70374; *WP,* 14 August 1960.

60. Foss interview.

61. *NYT,* 31 August 1960.

62. FBI BuFile: 105-70374; *WES,* 30 August 1960.

63. FBI BuFile: 105-70374.

64. FBI BuFile: 105-70374; *WDN,* 13 October 1960.

65. FBI BuFile: 105-70374; *Los Angeles Mirror,* 2 November 1960.

66. Matt Koehl, interviewed by author, Arlington, Virginia, 29 April 1996.

Chapter 6: 1961: This Time the World

1. Trumbo was blacklisted and imprisoned for his refusal to answer the questions of the House Un-American Activities Committee.

2. Foss interview.

3. *Daily Record, (Boston, Mass.)* 16 January 1961.

4. *WES,* 16 January 1961; *National Socialist Bulletin* (January 1961), 5; *ADL Bulletin* (April 1961), 6; *Portland (Maine) Press-Herald,* 16 January 1961.

5. *Daily Record,* 16 January 1961.

6. *WES,* 16 January 1961; *Portland (Maine) Press-Herald,* 16 January 1961.

7. Stan Tupper, interviewed by author, Boothbay Harbor, Maine, April 1994.

8. *WES,* 30 January 1961; *NYT,* 31 January 1961.

9. *WES,* 1 February 1961.

10. *WES,* 15 February 1961.

11. *WES,* 14 February 1961.

12. *New York Journal American,* 15 February 1961.

13. *WES,* 9 June 1961.

14. Isaac Franck, Jewish Community Council memo of 28 February 1961, Arlington County Library, Virginia Room Collection.

15. Kirman, "Major Programs," 183–84.

16. Ben Bagdikian, "The Gentle Suppression," *Columbia Journalism Review* (Spring 1965), 16–19.

17. James K. Warner, "Swastika Smearbund," Arlington County Library, Virginia Room Collection.

18. *NSB,* 20 April 1961; Foss interview; Karl Allen, interviewed by author, 16 June 1994; Bernard Davids interview, May 1995, October 1997.

19. Foss interview; FBI BuFile: 105-70374; *NSB,* 20 April 1961.

20. FBI BuFile: 105-70374.

21. Ibid.

22. This passage suggests that Hitler used anti-Semitism merely for political purposes, when in fact he was an uncontrollable Jew-hater. When the Eastern Front was collapsing he used his precious rail transportation to move Jews to death camps rather than to resupply troops. Such a strategically incomprehensible choice can be explained only by a priority system in which the destruction of Jews was as important as military victory. Rauschning, *Hitler Speaks,* 234.

23. *Boston Traveler,* 28 March 1961.

24. *The Rockwell Report*, 15 September 1962, 4.

25. Kirman, "Major Programs," 326.

26. *WES*, 22 May 1961.

27. *State Times (Baton Rouge, Louisiana)*, 23 May 1961.

28. *The Shreveport (Louisiana) Times*, 26 May 1961.

29. *The Rockwell Report*, 1 January 1962, 4.

30. Claude A. Clegg, *An Original Man* (New York: St. Martin's Press 1997), 152–53.

31. *WDN*, 25 June 1961.

32. Allen and Koehl interviews.

33. *WES*, 8 July 1961.

34. *WDN*, 20 July 1961.

35. "Citizens Concerned" minutes (1961), Arlington County Library, Virginia Room Collection.

36. *WES*, 30 July 1961.

37. *WES*, 4 August 1961.

38. *WES*, 9 August 1961.

39. Allen interview.

40. Ibid.

41. *WP*, 20 September 1961.

42. *WES*, 29 September 1961.

43. Allen interview.

44. FBI BuFile: 105-70374.

Chapter 7: 1962: A World Union of National Socialists

1. *Sunbury Daily Item*, 22 January 1962.

2. Benjamin Davis was a leader in the Communist Party of America.

3. FBI BuFile: 105-70374.

4. Ibid.

5. *The Stormtrooper*, March–August 1964 and February 1962, 6–11; *Chicago Sun-Times*, 26 February 1962.

6. ADL, *FACTS*, vol. 15, no. 2 (October 1963), 278–79.

7. *Muhammad Speaks*, April 1962; *The Stormtrooper*, February 1962.

8. *The Stormtrooper*, February 1962.

9. "Report of Manny Lansky-Pacific Coast Area Director—JWV," 19 March 1962, American Jewish Archives.

10. *Daily Aztec*, 8 March 1962, San Diego State College.

11. *Daily Aztec*, 9 March 1962, San Diego State College.

12. Ibid.

13. Ibid.

14. Ibid.

15. Ibid.

16. *New York World Telegram and Sun*, 16 March 1962.

17. *Daily Aztec*, 9 March 1962, San Diego State College.

18. *Texas Observer*, 11 March 1962.

19. FBI BuFile: 105-70374; *Los Angeles Times*, 25 March 1962.

20. FBI BuFile: 105-70374.

21. WES, 4 April 1962; Allen interview.

22. Chris Bailey, interviewed by author, Alexandria, Virginia, October 1994.

23. Office of Naval Intelligence, "Memorandum to FBI," Department of the Navy, FOIA 100-44-1238.

24. Foss interview.

25. FBI BuFile: 105-70374.

26. FBI BuFile: 105-70374; *Los Angeles Times*, 8 May 1962.

27. FBI BuFile: 105-70374.

28. Hargis operated the Christian Crusade from Tulsa, Oklahoma. His organization's literature reached millions of readers and his radio broadcasts were carried by hundreds of stations.

29. Matt Koehl interview.

30. ADL, *FACTS*, vol. 15, no. 2 (October 1963), 274.

31. *WP*, 12 March 1962.

32. Article of Incorporation, Arlington County Courthouse, book 32, pp. 522–24.

33. *WP*, 18 July 1962.

34. *The Rockwell Report*, no. 19 (15 July 1962), 2–3.

35. Colin Jordan, interview by letter, 1994.

36. *The Stormtrooper*, no. 3 (November 1962), 6–10, 20–31.

37. WES, 6 August 1962, 9 August 1962; *The Stormtrooper*, no. 3 (November 1962); Colin Jordan correspondence.

38. Davids interview.

39. Colin Jordan, John Tyndall, and Matt Koehl all insist the Cotswold Agreement was genuine.

40. FBI BuFile: 105-70374.

41. Simonelli, "American Fuehrer," 177.

42. *The Rockwell Report*, 15 September 1962.

43. "Resolutions Regarding George Lincoln Rockwell and the American Nazi Party 1963–1966," National Museum of American Jewish Military History, Washington, D.C.

44. AHP.

45. E. R. Fields, interviewed by author, Atlanta, Georgia, August 1995.

46. FBI Monograph, *American Nazi Party*.

47. *Birmingham (Alabama) Post-Herald*, 30 September 1964.

48. FBI BuFile: 105-70374; Fields interview.

49. FBI BuFile: 105-70374.

50. *WES*, 27–28 September 1962.

51. "Letter to Roy James," Eugene "Bull" Connor Papers [10F6], Birmingham Public Library.

52. Taylor Branch, *Parting the Waters: America in the King Years 1954–63* (New York: Simon & Schuster, 1988), 654–55.

53. James declined to be interviewed.

54. FBI BuFile: 105-70374; *Birmingham (Alabama) News*, 28 September 1962.

55. "Letter to Roy James," Eugene "Bull" Connor Papers [10F6], Birmingham Public Library.

56. *The Rockwell Report*, vol. 2, no 2 (1 November 1962), 5–6.

57. *Carletonian*, 26 September 1962, Carleton College, Minnesota.

58. Rockwell speech, audiocassette from Carleton College Archives, Carleton College, Minnesota.

59. Ibid.

60. Davids interview.

61. FBI BuFile: 105-70374.

62. *The Rockwell Report*, vol. 2, no. 3 (15 November 1962), 5–6.

63. Ibid., 2–3.

64. Alan Welch, interview by letter, 1997.

65. *WES*, 19 January 1963.

66. "George Lincoln Rockwell: A Myth or a Real Threat to America's Peace?" *Private Affairs*, June 1982.

Chapter 8: 1963: March on Washington

1. Susan Canedy, *American Nazis: A Democratic Dilemma* (Menlo Park, Calif.: Markgraf Publication, 1990), 163–65.

2. *Facts on File*, vol. 23 (1963).

3. David J. Garrow, *Bearing the Cross* (New York: William Morrow, 1986), 232.

4. Ibid.

5. *Richmond (Virginia) Times-Dispatch*, 15 February 1963.

6. Mary Blake French, interviewed by author, Arlington, Virginia, 21 October 1994; *Virginia Gazette*, 23 August 1963; *The Flat Hat*, 20 January 1964.

7. The American Jewish Committee and B'nai B'rith were hostile to Zionism before World War I, reflecting the view that Jews had found their "Zion" in the United States and that a Jewish state was unnecessary. Following the war both organizations came under sharp criticism by the American Jewish Congress for their position. The American Jewish Committee feared in particular, however, that the creation of a Jewish nation might raise doubts among Christians about the "dual loyalty" of American Jews. See Berman.

8. University of Virginia Library Archives, Alderman Library—Special Collections, box 8851.

9. Rockwell was born in Bloomington, Illinois.

10. *Miami Herald*, 26 February 1963.

11. FBI BuFile: 105-70374.

12. *Miami Herald*, 4 March 1963.

13. Allen interview; Davids interview.

14. Allen interview.

15. Allen interview; Foss interview; *The Stormtrooper,* March–April 1963.

16. Allen interview.

17. Foss interview.

18. *Intra-Party Confidential Newsletter,* vol. 1, no. 4 (16 April 1963).

19. FBI BuFile: 105-70374; *New York Herald-Tribune,* 28 April 1963; *Los Angeles Examiner,* 5 May 1963.

20. FBI BuFile: 105-70374; *Los Angeles Examiner,* 7 May 1963; ADL, *FACTS,* vol. 15, no. 2 (October 1963), 279.

21. *The Rockwell Report,* vol. 2, no. 10 (1 March 1963), 2.

22. *The Rockwell Report,* vol. 2, no. 16 (1 June 1963), 4–5.

23. Kirman, "Major Programs," 184.

24. Davids interview.

25. Allen interview.

26. Ibid.

27. Ibid.

28. Ibid.

29. Ibid.

30. *Intra-Party Confidential Newsletter,* vol. 1, no. 12 (15 June 1963); *The Stormtrooper,* vol. 2, no. 3, May–June 1963.

31. GLK Smith Collection, "G. L. Rockwell," box 53, Michigan Historical Collections, Bentley Historical Library, University of Michigan.

32. *John Birch Society Bulletin,* January 1963.

33. FBI BuFile: 105-70374.

34. *Intra-Party Confidential Newsletter,* vol. 1, no. 18 (8 August 1963).

35. Allen interview.

36. Ibid.

37. FBI BuFile: 44-359.

38. FBI BuFile: 105-70374.

39. *WES,* 31 July 1963.

40. Taylor Branch, *Pillar of Fire: America in the King Years 1963–65* (New York: Simon & Schuster, 1998), 114.

41. Garrow, *Bearing the Cross,* 276; Branch, *Pillar of Fire,* 133.

42. *Intra-Party Confidential Newsletter,* vol. 1, no. 18 (8 August 1963); *The Stormtrooper,* vol. 2, no. 4 (July–August 1963).

43. *Intra-Party Confidential Newsletter* (1 September 1963); *The Stormtrooper,* vol. 2, no. 4 (July–August 1963); Allen interview.

44. *WP,* 29 August 1963.

45. *WES,* 28 August 1963.

46. Allen interview.

47. Jim Haskins, *The March on Washington* (New York: HarperCollins, 1993), 71–73.

48. James Forman, *The Making of Black Revolutionaries* (New York: Macmillan, 1972), 336.

49. Benjamin Muse, *The American Negro Revolution* (Bloomington: Indiana University Press, 1968), 26.

50. *Intra-Party Confidential Newsletter,* vol. 1, no. 22 (1 September 1963).

51. Extremely rare, available to collectors at three to five hundred dollars. Letter to author from Andrew S. Thomas of Richard Avedon Studio, 1994.

52. *WP,* 15 October 1963; *Intra-Party Confidential Newsletter,* vol. 1, no. 27 (15 October 1963); *The Stormtrooper,* vol. 2, no. 5 (September–October 1963); *Eagle,* 11 October 1963, American University.

53. *WES,* 15 October 1963.

54. *Los Angeles Times,* 24 October 1963.

55. FBI BuFile: 105-70374.

56. Ibid.; Allen interview.

57. *Danville (Virginia) Register,* 16 November 1963.

58. "Petition for the Redress of Grievances," author's files.

Chapter 9: 1964: America for Whites

1. *Hofstra Chronicle,* 3 February 1964, Hofstra University.

2. Ibid.

3. Rockwell speech, audiocassette from Hofstra University Archives (tape FT9).

4. Ibid.

5. *Collegian,* 19 February 1964, Colorado State University.

6. Ibid.

7. FBI BuFile: 105-70374; *Denver (Colorado) Post,* 20 February 1964; *Collegian,* 20 February 1964, Colorado State University.

8. Lew Cor [GLR], "When the Nazis Tried Human Vivisection," *Sir!* (March 1958).

9. Rockwell speech, audiocassette from University of Kansas Archives, Student Union Activities Minority Opinion Forum (tape T71, T586).

10. Ibid.

11. *Daily Kansas,* 24 February 1964.

12. *Intra-Party Confidential Newsletter,* 1964.

13. Ibid.

14. *WES,* 27 February 1964.

15. *Minnesota Daily,* 11 March 1964, University of Minnesota.

16. *Minnesota Daily,* 4 March 1964, University of Minnesota.

17. *Minnesota Daily,* 10 March 1964, University of Minnesota.

18. Barbara von Goetz correspondence, 3 December 1997.

19. FBI BuFile: 105-70374.

20. Ibid.

21. *National Review,* 19 September 1967; *WES,* 1 September 1967; FBI BuFile: 105-70374.

22. Ibid.

23. Confidential correspondence with priest, August 1997.

24. *National Review,* 19 September 1967.

25. Matt Koehl correspondence, 26 July 1997.

26. AHP.

27. Simonelli, "American Fuehrer," 224.

28. Muse, *The American Negro Revolution,* 91.

29. *Detroit News,* 15 May 1964.

30. *Mirror,* 22 May 1964, Colorado State College–Greeley.

31. FBI BuFile: 105-70374.

32. *University of Washington Daily,* 29 May 1964, Seattle, Washington.

33. *University of Washington Daily,* 2 June 1964, Seattle, Washington.

34. AHP.

35. WES, 9 June 1964.

36. *The Stormtrooper,* vol. 3, no. 2 (March–August 1964).

37. Muse, *The American Negro Revolution,* 92.

38. WES, 5 July 1964.

39. Matt Koehl correspondence, 21 November 1997; *The Rockwell Report,* October–November 1965, 9–11.

40. Everett Dirksen, Republican leader of the Senate 1959–1969; gave crucial support to Johnson's civil rights legislation.

41. *The Stormtrooper,* September–October 1964.

42. Renny Connell, "Television and Politics in the 1960s" (master's thesis, Florida Atlantic, 1972).

43. *Long Beach Independent,* 4 September 1964; *The Stormtrooper,* September–October 1964.

44. *Glendale News-Press,* 9 October 1964; *The Stormtrooper,* September–October 1964.

45. *Michigan Daily,* 17 September 1964, University of Michigan–Ann Arbor.

46. Ibid.

47. *Michigan Daily,* 14 October 1964, University of Michigan–Ann Arbor.

48. Editorial by Jeremy Raven, *Michigan Daily,* 15 October 1964, University of Michigan–Ann Arbor.

49. *Honolulu Advertiser,* 20 October 1964; *Honolulu Star-Bulletin,* 20 October 1964; *Ka Leo O,* 23 October 1964.

50. *NYT,* 1 November 1964; WES, 26 October 1964.

51. The contemporaneous term "denial" was not used in Rockwell's era. Today it connotes a "movement."

52. Many of Hitler's early Nazis—Ernst Rohm in particular—were pederasts.

53. Hitler's Nazis killed between fifteen and twenty-five thousand homosexuals during WWII. See Richard Plant, *The Pink Triangle,* 235.

54. Canadian Broadcasting Corporation, *This Hour Has Seven Days,* 25 October 1964.

55. *Golden Gator,* 29 October 1964, San Francisco State College.

56. *Stanford Daily,* 6 November 1964, Stanford University.

57. *Stanford Daily*, 11 November 1964, Stanford University.

58. *Stanford Daily*, 12 November 1964, Stanford University.

59. *Stanford Daily*, 13 November 1964, Stanford University.

60. *Stanford Daily*, 17 November 1964, Stanford University.

61. *Stanford Daily*, 9 November 1964, Stanford University.

62. FBI BuFile: 105-70374; *Dallas Morning News*, 23 November 1964; Jerald Walraven, interviewed by author via telephone, 1995.

63. *San Jose Mercury*, 28 November 1964.

64. FBI BuFile: 157-9-00 (COINTELPRO).

65. Real name was Bierbaum (birth certificate from Wisconsin).

66. FBI BuFile: 159-9-41 (COINTELPRO).

67. FBI BuFile: 105-70374; University of Kansas Collection, Ephemeral 1341.1.

68. *Burbank (California) Leader*, 8 December 1964.

69. FBI BuFile: 105-70374.

Chapter 10: 1965: Rockwell for Governor

1. *The Rockwell Report*, March 1965.

2. FBI BuFile: 105-70374; UPI, 12 January 1965.

3. Matt Koehl correspondence, 21 November 1997.

4. FBI BuFile: 105-70374; *Meridian (Mississippi) Star*, 17 January 1965; *The Rockwell Report*, January 1965, 2–12.

5. The local press incorrectly identified Robinson as a member of the ANP rather than NSRP, a mistake repeated by Garrow and others.

6. George Breitman, ed., *Malcolm X Speaks* (New York: Pathfinder, 1965); *The Rockwell Report*, January 1965, 11.

7. AHP. See Clegg.

8. *Glendale News-Press*, 29 December 1964.

9. *Burbank (California) Leader*, 12 February 1965.

10. *San Francisco Chronicle*, 26 January 1965.

11. *San Francisco Chronicle*, 27 January 1965.

12. *The Rockwell Report*, February 1965, 11; George Ware, interviewed by author via telephone, 1993.

13. Alex Haley, "George Lincoln Rockwell," *Playboy*, April 1966, 71–72, 74, 76–82, 154, 156.

14. *Geneseo Lamron*, 5 February 1965, State University of New York–Geneseo.

15. *Stylus*, 5 February 1965, State University of New York–Brockport.

16. *The Rockwell Report*, February 1965, 15.

17. AHP.

18. FBI BuFile: 157-9-9-5 (COINTELPRO).

19. Ibid.

20. Ibid.

21. *The Rockwell Report*, March 1965, 7–11.

22. *The Rockwell Report*, March 1965, 13.

23. FBI BuFile: 174-1-53-9.

24. FBI BuFile: 105-70374.

25. *Colorado Daily*, 8 April 1965.

26. *Ohio University Post*, vol. 54, no. 91 (19 April 1965).

27. Ibid.; *The Stormtrooper*, Summer 1965.

28. *WES*, 20 April 1965.

29. *WES*, 25 April 1965.

30. *Intra-Party Confidential Newsletter*, March 1964.

31. FBI BuFile: 105-70374.

32. Ibid.

33. Rockwell speech, audiocassette of the Michael Jackson Program, University of Kansas, Wilcox Collection, RH, WL tape 462.

34. *Glendale News-Press*, 30 April 1965.

35. FBI BuFile: 105-70374.

36. *The (Flint, Michigan) Journal*, 25 February 1965, 5 May 1965, 6 May 1965.

37. *WES*, 27 May 1965.

38. FBI BuFile: 105-70374.

39. *Dallas Morning News*, 4 July 1965.

40. *Commonwealth of Virginia vs. John Patler*, Arlington County, Virginia (C-5575).

41. Walraven interview, 1995.

42. *Dallas Times Herald*, 30 September 1965.

43. *WES*, 13 September 1965.

44. FBI BuFile: 157-9-41 (COINTELPRO).

45. Ibid.

46. FBI BuFile: 105-70374; *WDN*, 13 December 1967.

47. *WES*, 29 September 1965.

48. *Commonwealth of Virginia vs. John Patler*, Arlington County, Virginia (C-5575).

49. *WES*, 6 October 1965.

50. *WES*, 9 October 1965.

51. FBI BuFile: 105-70374; *Richmond (Virginia) Times-Dispatch*, 16 October 1965.

52. Rosenthal and Gelb, *One More Victim*, 205–227; FBI BuFile: 105-70374.

53. *The Stormtrooper*, Spring 1966, 28.

54. Matt Koehl correspondence, 21 November 1997; Alan Welch correspondence, 13 November 1997; *The Rockwell Report*, October–November 1965, 7–9.

55. FBI BuFile: 105-70374; *NYT*, 31 October 1965; *New York Herald-Tribune*, 7 November 1965, 8 November 1965; *Newsweek*, 15 November 1965; *WES*, 16 August 1975; FBI BuFile: 157-3323.

56. *Duluth (Minnesota) News-Tribune*, 17 November 1965.

57. *Mesabi Daily News*, 15 November 1965.

58. Ibid.

59. *Dakota Student,* 12 November 1965, University of North Dakota–Grand Forks.

60. *WES,* 27 November 1965.

61. FBI BuFile: 105-70374.

62. *WES,* 3 December 1965.

63. *WES,* 14 December 1965.

64. Ibid.

65. *Daily Northwestern,* 3 December 1965, Northwestern University–Evanston, Illinois.

66. *Northern Star,* 22 December 1965, Northern Illinois University.

67. FBI BuFile: 105-70374; *NYT,* 28 December 1965.

68. Simonelli, "American Fuehrer," 227.

Chapter 11: 1966: White Power

1. *WES,* 3 February 1966.

2. FBI BuFile: 157-9-41 (COINTELPRO).

3. FBI BuFile: 105-70374; *The Rice Thresher,* 6 January 1966.

4. *Dallas Morning News,* 18 January 1966.

5. *Dallas Times Herald,* 19 January 1966.

6. *Dallas Morning News,* 20 January 1966.

7. Doris Kearns, *Lyndon Johnson and the American Dream* (New York: Harper & Row, 1976), 207.

8. Jerald Walraven interview, text in author's files.

9. Martin Berger was a Jewish attorney who occasionally worked for the ACLU.

10. Dotson Rader, "The Deadly Friendship," *The New Republic,* 23 September 1967; FBI BuFile: 105-70374; UPI, 9 February 1966; *WP,* 10 February 1966; *WES,* 10 February 1966.

11. FBI BuFile: 105-70374; UPI, 9 February 1966; *The Rockwell Report,* March 1966, 7–10.

12. FBI BuFile: 105-70374; UPI, 9 February 1966.

13. *WES,* 11 February 1966.

14. The W. E. B. DuBois Club of America (DCA) was a national Marxist youth organization chartered by the Communist Party.

15. George Ware, interviewed by author via telephone, 1993.

16. WES, 26 March 1966.

17. Matt Koehl correspondence, 21 November 1997; Alan Welch correspondence, 13 November 1997.

18. Total U.S. battle casualties topped five thousand by the end of 1966.

19. *Seattle Post-Intelligencer,* 2 May 1966.

20. FBI BuFile: 105-70374; *WDN,* 5 May 1966.

21. *Daily Times News* (Portland, Michigan), 24 May 1966; *CM-Life,* 27 May 1966.

22. Frank Smith, interviewed by author via telephone, April 1994.

23. *Portland (Maine) Press-Herald,* 31 May 1966.

24. Pierce interview.

25. Alan Welch correspondence, 13 November 1997.

26. *WES*, 28 June 1966.

27. FBI BuFile: 44-33591.

28. *Glendale News-Press*, 27 July 1966.

29. "Tough Years Ahead," *Newsweek*, 30 August 1965, 19.

30. *NYT*, 11 October 1965, 44.

31. "Black Power: Politics of Frustration," *Newsweek*, 11 July 1966, 26.

32. "Negro Leaders Dividing—The Effect," *US News & World Report*, 18 July 1966, 32.

33. Muse, *The American Negro Revolution*, 242.

34. Ibid., 244.

35. Ibid.

36. *NYT*, 6 August 1966; *Chicago Daily News*, 6 August 1966.

37. Rockwell, "Commander's Special Report on Chicago," University of Kansas, Wilcox Collection RH, WL Eph 1341.2.

38. FBI BuFile: 105-70374; *Chicago Daily News*, 16 August 1966.

39. Ibid.

40. *NYT*, 21 August 1966.

41. *Chicago Tribune*, 22 August 1966.

42. FBI BuFile: 105-70374.

43. Rockwell, "Commander's Special Report on Chicago."

44. *Chicago Tribune*, 22 August 1966; FBI BuFile: 105-70374.

45. Rockwell, "Commander's Special Report on Chicago."

46. *Chicago Sun Times*, 23 August 1966.

47. "Victory in the North," *Newsweek*, 5 September 1966, 20.

48. "Urban Powder Kegs," *Senior Scholastic*, 23 September 1966, 19.

49. Ibid.

50. *NYT*, 22 August 1966; FBI BuFile: 105-70374.

51. FBI BuFile: 44-0-7039.

52. *WES*, 2 September 1966.

53. *NYT*, 11 September 1966.

54. *NYT*, 12 September 1966.

55. Ibid.

56. Ibid.

57. FBI BuFile: 157-9-26-6 (COINTELPRO).

58. *The Rockwell Report*, 1 January 1962, 2–4.

59. *Harvard Law Record*, 29 September 1966, 6 October 1966, 14 October 1966; *Harvard Crimson*, 27–29 September 1966, 30 September 1966, 1 October 1966.

60. FBI BuFile: 105-70374; *San Diego Evening Tribune*, 4 October 1966.

61. FBI BuFile: 105-70374.

62. *Longview Morning Journal*, 27 October 1966; *Dallas Times Herald*, 26 October 1966.

63. *WES,* 20 November 1966.

64. *The Gold Bug,* 2 December 1966, Western Maryland College.

65. *Providence Journal,* 22 October 1966.

66. *Rhode Island Herald,* 9 December 1966.

67. *Pembroke Record,* 2 December 1966.

68. William Pierce interview; *Free Lance-Star (Fredricksburg, Virginia),* 5 December 1966, 7 December 1966; Matt Koehl interview.

69. *State Times,* 16 December 1966, State University College–Oneonta, New York.

70. *Oneonta (New York) Daily Star,* 13 December 1966.

71. Ibid.

72. *Commonwealth of Virginia vs. John Patler,* Arlington County, Virginia (C-5575).

73. Stanley Tupper interview, 1994.

Chapter 12: 1967: "An Evil Genius"

1. *White Power,* vol. 7, no. 1 (September 1967), 4.

2. *Utica (New York) Observer-Dispatch,* 11 January 1967.

3. *Oneonta (New York) Dispatch,* 11 January 1967; *Rome (New York) Sentinel,* 11 January 1967.

4. *The Hamilton Spectator,* 13 January 1967, Hamilton College, Clinton, New York.

5. *Daily Evergreen,* 27 January 1967, Washington State University, Pullman, Washington.

6. "Complaints," Washington State University Archives, 205 Office of the President file 19:01.

7. *Oregon Stater,* 1967, vol. 27, no. 4 (February–March 1967) Oregon State University Alumni Association; *Daily Barometer,* 20 January 1967, 26–27 January 1967, Oregon State University.

8. *Oregon Daily Emerald,* 27 January 1967, University of Oregon, Eugene, Oregon; *Eugene (Oregon) Register Guard,* 27 January 1967.

9. U.S. battle casualties for the year 1967 surged to 9,377, nearly twice the figure for 1966.

10. *Eugene (Oregon) Register Guard,* 27 January 1967.

11. *Corvallis (Oregon) Gazette-Times,* 26–28 January 1967; *Oregon Daily Emerald,* 27 January 1967; *(Portland) Oregonian,* 27 January 1967.

12. *Lawrentian,* 9 February 1967, Lawrence College, Appleton, Wisconsin.

13. *Post-Crescent (Appleton, Wisconsin),* 4 February 1967, 9 February 1967, 26 August 1967; *Lawrentian,* 9 February 1967; *Oshkosh (Wisconsin) Northwestern,* 9 February 1967; *Neenah-Menasha (Wisconsin) News,* 9 February 1967; *The Milwaukee Journal,* 9 February 1967; *Milwaukee State News,* 9 February 1967.

14. *Post-Crescent,* 15 February 1967.

15. *Minnesota Daily,* 10 February 1967, University of Minnesota.

16. *Times-Delphic,* 15 February 1967, Drake University.

17. Hilda Carter and John Jenswold, *The University of Wisconsin–Eau Claire: A History 1916–1976* (Eau Claire: University Wisconsin–Eau Claire Foundation, 1976).

18. *Western Herald*, 21 February 1967, Western Michigan University–Kalamazoo.

19. *Mankato Free Press*, 1 March 1967; *College Reporter*, 2 March 1967, Mankato State College.

20. *The Old Gold and Black*, 6 March 1967, Wake Forest University; *Winston–Salem Journal*, 4 March 1967.

21. In reaction to this statement, a professor wrote the secretary of defense for the official U.S. policy on tear gas use in Vietnam. The secretary of defense responded: "Local commanders have the authority to use tear gas...when it is considered to be the most effective weapon in any given situation, and the Viet Cong by now are aware that such is the case." *Student Voice*, 17 April 1967.

22. *Fargo (North Dakota) Forum*, 16 March 1967.

23. *Hays (Kansas) Daily News*, 17 March 1967.

24. *Kansas State Collegian*, 17 March 1967, Manhattan, Kansas.

25. *Commonwealth of Virginia vs. John Patler*, Arlington County, Virginia (C-5575).

26. Matt Koehl interview.

27. *The B-G News*, 4 April 1967, Bowling Green State University.

28. *El Gaucho*, vol. 47, no. 95 (17 April 1967), University of California–Santa Barbara.

29. Ibid.

30. *Bethel Collegian*, vol. 55, no. 13 (5 May 1967), North Newton, Kansas.

31. *WES*, 16 May 1967.

32. Karl Allen interview.

33. *Commonwealth of Virginia vs. John Patler*, Arlington County, Virginia (C-5575), 1881.

34. *The Rockwell Report*, July 1967; *WES*, 29 June 1967.

35. *Commonwealth of Virginia vs. John Patler*, Arlington County, Virginia (C-5575); Barbara von Goetz interview; Matt Koehl interview.

36. *WDN*, 26 August 1967; *NYT*, 25 August 1967.

Chapter 13: Where's the Bleach?

1. Mrs. Ruby Pierce interview, *Blood in the Face*, videocassette by James Ridgeway (Right Thinking Productions, 1991).

2. "Two Shots Fired from Store Roof," clip file, Virginia Room, Arlington County Library, Arlington, Virginia.

3. *NYT*, 25 August 1967.

4. Colin Jordan correspondence, 1994.

5. Edward R. Fields interview.

6. "Jewish War Veteran Commander Speaks Out on Rockwell Death" 25 August 1967, American Jewish Archives.

7. Press Release, American Jewish Congress, 25 August 1967, American Jewish Archives.

8. Alan Welch correspondence, 13 November 1997.

9. FBI BuFile: 105-70374.

10. *WDN*, 29 August 1967.

11. *WDN*, 30 August 1967.

12. *NYT*, 30 August 1967; *Newsweek*, 4 September 1967; *WES*, 29 August 1967; *New York Daily News*, 30 August 1967; *WDN*, 30 August 1967; FBI BuFile: 105-70374.

13. *WDN*, 29 August 1967.

14. Ibid.

15. *WES*, 16 December 1967.

16. FBI BuFile: 105-70374.

17. *WES*, 14 March 1969.

Epilogue

1. The Leadership Principle is based on the premise that when a person is placed in charge of an organization (be it military, church, or business) or operation, that person is given full authority to accomplish his or her task, subject to full accountability. Thus, responsibility is achieved by holding an identifiable person accountable, rather than some anonymous, majority-rule or committee-type decision-making body where no one takes the blame or credit.

2. Matt Koehl correspondence, 30 January 1998.

3. Matt Koehl correspondence, 25 November 1997.

4. Matt Koehl correspondence, 30 January 1998.

5. Jerome Chanes, *Antisemitism in America Today: Outspoken Experts Explode the Myth* (New York: Simon & Schuster, 1998), 120.

6. *Intelligence Report*, Southern Poverty Law Center, Winter 1998.

BIBLIOGRAPHY

Books

Archer, Jules. *The Incredible Sixties*. New York: Harcourt-Brace-Jovanovich, 1986.

Berman, Aaron. *Nazism, the Jews, and American Zionism 1933–1948*. Detroit: Wayne State University Press, 1990.

Bledsoe, Thomas. *Or We'll All Hang Separately: The Highlander Idea*. Boston: Beacon Press, 1969.

Branch, Taylor. *Parting the Waters: America in the King Years 1954–63*. New York: Simon & Schuster, 1988.

———. *Pillar of Fire: America in the King Years 1963–65*. New York: Simon & Schuster, 1998.

Breitman, George, ed. *Malcolm X Speaks*. New York: Pathfinder, 1965.

Candey, Susan. *American Nazis: A Democratic Dilemma*. Menlo Park, Calif.: Markgraf Publication, 1990.

Carson, Clayborne. *In Struggle: SNCC and the Black Awakening of the 1960's*. Cambridge, Mass.: Harvard University Press, 1981.

———. *Malcolm X: The FBI File*. New York: Carroll & Graf, 1991.

Carter, Hilda, and John Jenswold. *The University of Wisconsin–Eau Claire: A History 1916–1976*. Eau Claire: UW–Eau Claire Foundation, 1976.

Chanes, Jerome, ed. *Antisemitism in America Today: Outspoken Experts Explode the Myths*. New York: Birch Lane Press, 1995.

Clegg, Claude Andrew, III. *An Original Man: The Life and Times of Elijah Muhammad*. New York: St. Martin's Press, 1997.

Dinnerstein, Leonard. *Anti-Semitism in America*. New York: Oxford University Press, 1994.

Dornberg, John. *Munich 1923: The Story of Hitler's First Grab for Power*. New York: Harper & Row, 1982.

Evanzz, Karl. *The Judas Factor: The Plot to Kill Malcolm X.* New York: Thunder's Mouth Press, 1992.

Farmer, James. *Lay Bare the Heart.* New York: Arbor House, 1985.

Feuerlicht, Roberta. *Joe McCarthy and McCarthyism: The Hate That Haunts America.* New York: McGraw-Hill, 1972.

Finch, Phillip. *God, Guts, and Guns.* New York: Putnam, 1983.

Ford, Henry, Sr. *The International Jew.* W. Va: Liberty Bell Publications, 1993.

Foreman, James. *The Making of Black Revolutionaries.* New York: Macmillan, 1972.

Forster, Arnold, and Benjamin Epstein. *The New Anti-Semitism.* New York: McGraw-Hill, 1974.

Garrow, David. *Bearing the Cross: Martin Luther King, Jr., and the Southern Christian Leadership Conference.* New York: William Morrow, 1986.

———. *Protest at Selma: Martin Luther King and the Voting Rights Act of 1965.* New Haven, Conn.: Yale University Press, 1978.

Gentile, Thomas. *March on Washington: August 28, 1963.* New York: Doubleday, 1983.

Glock, Charles, and Rodney Stark. *Christian Beliefs and Anti-Semitism.* New York: Harper & Row, 1966.

Greene, Melissa Fay. *The Temple Bombing.* Reading, Penn.: Addision-Wesley, 1996.

Haley, Alex. *Malcolm X.* New York: Grove Press, 1965.

Haskins, James. *The March on Washington.* New York: HarperCollins, 1993.

Hernton, Calvin. *White Papers for White Americans.* New York: Doubleday, 1982.

Hitler, Adolf. *Mein Kampf.* New York: Reynal & Hitchcock, 1941.

Hoffer, Eric. *The True Believer.* New York: Harper, 1951.

Horton, Aimee. *The Highlander Folk School: A History of Its Major Programs 1932–1961.* New York: Carlson Publishing, 1989.

Howe, Irving. *The American Communist Party: A Critical History.* New York: Praeger, 1962.

Kearns, Doris. *Lyndon Johnson and the American Dream.* New York: Harper & Row, 1976.

Lipstadt, Deborah. *Denying the Holocaust.* New York: Free Press, 1992.

Muse, Benjamin. *The American Negro Revolution: From Nonviolence to Black Power 1963–1967.* Bloomington: Indiana University Press, 1968.

Pierce, William L. *Hunter.* Hillsboro, W.Va.: National Vanguard Books, 1983.

———. *The Turner Diaries.* Hillsboro, W.Va.: National Vanguard Books, 1978.

Rauschning, Herman. *Hitler Speaks.* New York: Putnam, 1940.

Ridgeway, James. *Blood in the Face: The Ku Klux Klan, Aryan Nations, Nazi Skinheads & the Rise of a New White Culture.* New York: Thunder's Mouth Press, 1991.

Rockwell, George Lincoln. *This Time the World.* Reedy, W.Va.: Liberty Bell Publications, 1979.

———. *White Power.* Reedy, W.Va.: Liberty Bell Publications, 1977.

Rosenthal, A. M., and Arthur Gelb. *One More Victim*. New York: New American Library, 1967.

Scales, Junius, and Richard Nickson. *Cause at Heart: A Former Communist Remembers*. Athens: University of Georgia, 1987.

Staudinger, Hans. *The Inner Nazi: A Critical Analysis of* Mein Kampf. Baton Rouge: Louisiana State University, 1981.

Volkman, Ernest. *A Legacy of Hate: Anti-Semitism in America*. New York: Franklin Watts, 1982.

Wade, Wyn Craig. *The Fiery Cross: The Ku Klux Klan in America 1954–63*. New York: Simon & Schuster, 1987.

Weisbord, Robert, and Arthur Stein. *Bittersweet Encounter: The Afro-American and the American Jew*. Westport, Conn.: Negro University Press, 1970.

Periodicals

Anti-Defamation League Bulletin (April 1961).

Bagdikian, Ben H. "Two Bigots: A Study in Contrasts." *ADL Bulletin* (December 1958).

Buckley, William F., Jr. "The Conscience of George Lincoln Rockwell." *National Review* (September 1967).

Cor, Lew [GLR]. "When the Nazis Tried Human Viviscetion." *Sir!* (March 1958).

FACTS 13, no. 10 (September 1960); 15, no. 2 (October 1963).

Fields, Edward R. "Rockwell Suit Settled." *Thunderbolt*, no. 71 (October 1965).

Hollander, Zander. "Fiasco for a Fuehrer." *ADL Bulletin* (April 1959).

Ianniello, Lynne. "Rockwell on the Campus." *ADL Bulletin* (April 1963).

Intra-Party Confidential Newsletter (March 1963–March 1964).

McGovern, Michael. "The Problems of a Fuehrer." *ADL Bulletin* (November 1966).

Muhammad Speaks (April 1962).

National Socialist Bulletin, no. 1–6 (1960–1961).

National Socialist World (Spring 1966–Winter 1967).

Newsweek, "Tough Years Ahead" (30 August 1965); "Black Power: Politics of Frustration" (11 July 1966); "Victory in the North" (5 September 1966).

Playboy, interview by Alex Haley (April 1966).

Podhoretz, Norman. "A Few Words Concerning This Picture." *Esquire* (March 1963).

Rader, Dotson. "The Deadly Friendship." *The New Republic* (23 September 1967).

Shapiro, Fred C. "The Last Word (We Hope) on George Lincoln Rockwell." *Esquire* (February 1967).

Senior Scholastic, "Urban Powderkegs" (23 September 1966).

The Rockwell Report (October 1961–July 1967).

The Stormtrooper (February 1962–September 1967).

U.S. Lady (December 1955).
U.S. News & World Report, "Negro Leaders Dividing—The Effect" (18 July 1966).
White Power (1 September 1967).
White Power Newsletter 1967.

Newspapers

Baton Rouge (Louisiana) State Times, 23 May 1961.
Birmingham News, 28 September 1962.
Birmingham Post-Herald, 30 September 1964.
Boston Traveler, 28 March 1961.
Burbank (California) Leader, 8 December 1964, 12 February 1965.
Capital Times (Madison), 9 February 1967.
Chicago-American, 26 February 1963.
Chicago Daily News, 16 August 1966.
Chicago Sun Times, 26 February 1962, 23 August 1966.
Chicago Tribune, 22 August 1966.
Colorado Daily, 8 April 1965.
Corvallis Gazette-Times, 26–28 January 1967.
Daily Kansan, 24 February 1964.
Daily Record (Boston), 16 January 1961.
Daily Sentinel-Tribune (Bowling Green), 1 April 1967.
Daily Times News (Mt. Pleasant, Michigan), 24 May 1966.
Dallas Morning News, 23 November 1964, 4 July 1965, 18 January 1966, 20 January 1966.
Dallas Times Herald, 30 September 1965, 19 January 1966, 26 October 1966.
Detroit News, 15 May 1964.
Denver Post, 20 February 1964.
Duluth News-Tribune, 17 November 1965.
Eau Claire (Wisconsin) Daily Telegram, 16 February 1967.
Eau Claire (Wisconsin) Leader-Telegram, 6 February 1967, 10 February 1967.
Eugene Register Guard, 26–27 January 1967.
Fargo (North Dakota) Forum, 16 March 1967.
Fredericksburg (Virginia) Free Lance-Star, 5 December 1966, 7 December 1966.
Flint (Michigan) Journal, 25 February 1965, 5–6 May 1965.
Glendale News-Press, 9 October 1964, 29 December 1964, 30 April 1965, 27 July 1966.
Hays (Kansas) Daily News, 15–17 March 1967.
Honolulu Advertiser, 20 October 1964.
Honolulu Star-Bulletin, 20 October 1964.
Long Beach(California) Independent, 4 September 1964.
Longview Morning Journal, 27 October 1966.

Los Angeles Evening Herald, 26 October 1960.

Los Angeles Examiner, 5–7 May 1963.

Los Angeles Mirror, 2 November 1960.

Los Angeles Times, 25 March 1962, 8 May 1962, 24 October 1963, 4 February 1994.

Mankato Free Press, 1 March 1967.

Meridian (Mississippi) Star, 17 January 1965.

Mesabi Daily News, 15 November 1965.

Miami Herald, 26 February 1963, 4 March 1963.

Milwaukee Journal, 9 February 1967.

Milwaukee State News, 9 February 1967.

Neenah-Menasha News, 9 February 1967.

New York Daily News, 24 June 1960, 30 August 1967.

New York Herald Tribune, 28 April 1963, 7 November 1965, 8 November 1965.

New York Journal American, 15 February 1961.

New York Post, 24 June 1960.

New York Times, 18 June 1960, 22 June 1960, 5 August 1960, 31 August 1960, 31 August 1961, 2 April 1964, 1 November 1964, 11 October 1965, 31 October 1965, 28 December 1965, 21–22 August 1966, 11–12 September 1966, 1 October 1966, 25 August 1967, 30 August 1967, 4 March 1978.

Northern Virginia Sun, 1 December 1960.

Oneonta (New York) Daily Star, 13 December 1966.

Oneonta (New York) Dispatch, 11 January 1967.

Oregonian, 27 January 1967.

Oshkosh-Northwestern, 9 February 1967.

Portland (Maine) Evening Press, 3 March 1978.

Portland (Maine) Sunday Telegram, 5 July 1931, 17 February 1935, 28 May 1950.

Post-Crescent, 4 February 1967, 9 February 1967, 15 February 1967, 26 August 1967.

Providence Journal, 22 October 1966.

Rhode Island Herald, 9 December 1967.

Richmond (Virginia) Times-Dispatch, 12 February 1963, 16 October 1965.

Rome (New York) Mercury, 11 January 1967.

San Diego Evening Tribune, 4 October 1966.

San Francisco Chronicle, 26–27 January 1965, 13 April 1967.

San Jose Mercury, 28 November 1964.

Seattle Post-Intelligencer, 2 May 1966.

Shreveport Times, 26 May 1961.

Sunbury Daily Item, 22 January 1962.

Texas Observer, 11 March 1962.

Times-Picayune, 3 June 1962.

Utica (New York) Observer-Dispatch, 11 January 1967.

Virginia Gazette, 23 August 1963.

Washington Daily News, 12–13 August 1960, 15–16 August 1960, 20 July 1961, 25 June 1961, 5 May 1966, 26 August 1967, 29 August 1967, 30 August 1967, 13 December 1967.

Washington Evening Star, 17–18 October 1958, 23 October 1958, 30 October 1958, 22 April 1959, 5 May 1959, 13 May 1959, 17 May 1959, 5 June 1959, 22 June 1959, 11 January 1960, 11 February 1960, 26 February 1960, 11–12 June 1960, 6 July 1960, 15 July 1960, 28 July 1960, 31 July 1960, 30 August 1960, 21 September 1960, 16 January 1961, 30 January 1961, 1 February 1961, 14–15 February 1961, 22 May 1961, 9 June 1961, 6 July 1961, 30 July 1961, 4 August 1961, 9 August 1961, 29 September 1961, 17 March 1962, 4 April 1962, 6 August 1962, 9 August 1962, 27–28 September 1962, 3 January 1963, 19 January 1963, 25 February 1963, 28 April 1963, 31 July 1963, 28 August 1963, 15 October 1963, 27 February 1964, 9 June 1964, 5 July 1964, 18 September 1964, 26 October 1964, 20 April 1965, 25 April 1965, 27 May 1965, 13 September 1965, 29 September 1965, 6 October 1965, 9 October 1965, 27 November 1965, 3 December 1965, 14 December 1965, 3 February 1966, 10–11 February 1966, 26 March 1966, 28 June 1966, 2 September 1966, 20 November 1966, 16 May 1967, 29 June 1967, 29 August 1967, 1 September 1967, 16 December 1967, 14 March 1969, 16 August 1975.

Washington Post, 16 February 1960, 24 February 1960, 14 August 1960, 20 September 1961, 12 March 1962, 18 July 1962, 29 August 1963, 15 October 1963, 10 February 1966.

Wichita (Kansas) Beacon, 24 April 1967, 25 April 1967.

Wichita (Kansas) Eagle, 24 April 1967, 25 April 1967.

Winston-Salem (North Carolina) Journal, 4 March 1967.

Worker, 19 June 1960.

Collegiate Newspapers

Bethel Collegian (Newton, Kansas), 5 May 1967.

Bowling Green News, 4 April 1967, 8 March 1967, 30–31 March 1967.

Brown Daily Herald, 20 October 1966.

Carletonian (Carleton College), 26 September 1962.

CM-Life (Central Michigan), 13 May 1967, 27 May 1967.

College Reporter (Mankato), 2 March 1967.

Collegian (Western Washington State College), 16 October 1964.

Collegian (Colorado State University), 19–20 February 1964.

Dakota Student (University of North Dakota–Grand Forks), 12 November 1965.

Daily Aztec (San Diego State), 9 March 1962.

Daily Barometer (University of Oregon), 20 January 1967, 26–27 January 1967.

Daily Evergreen (Washington State–Pullman), 27 January 1967.

Daily Northwestern (Northwestern), 3 December 1965.

Drake Times-Delphic, 15 February 1967.

Eagle (American University), 11 October 1963, 15 October 1963, 18 October 1963.

El Gaucho (University of California–Santa Barbara), 17 April 1967.

Flat Hat (Virginia), 10 January 1964.

Geneseo Lamron (SUNY–Geneseo), 5 February 1965.

Gold Bug (Western Maryland College), 2 December 1966.

Golden Gator (San Francisco State College), 29 October 1964.

Hamilton Spectator (Clinton, New York), 13 January 1967.

Harvard Crimson, 27–30 September 1966, 1 October 1966.

Harvard Law Record, 29 September 1966, 6 October 1966, 14 October 1966.

Hofstra Chronicle, 3 February 1964.

Ka Leo O, 23 October 1964.

Kansas State Collegian (Manhattan), 17 March 1967.

Lawrentian (Lawrence College), 19 February 1967.

Michigan Daily (Ann Arbor), 14–17 September 1964.

Minnesota Daily, 4 March 1964, 10–11 March 1964, 10 February 1967.

Mirror (Colorado State), 22 May 1964.

Northern Star (Northern Illinois University), 22 December 1965.

Ohio University Post (Athens), 19 April 1965.

Old Gold and Black (Wake Forest), 6 March 1967.

Oregon Daily Emerald, 26–27 January 1967.

Oregon Stater (Oregon State), February–March 1967.

Pembroke Record (Rhode Island), 2 December 1966.

Rice Thresher, 6 January 1966.

Stanford Daily, 6 November 1964, 9 November 1964, 11–13 November 1964, 17 November 1964.

State College Leader (Fort Hays State), 16 February 1967, 23 February 1967, 16 March 1967, 27 March 1967.

State Times (SUNY–Oneonta), 16 December 1966.

Student Voice (University of Wisconsin–River Falls), 17 April 1967.

Stylus (SUNY–Brockport), 5 February 1967.

Sunflower (Wichita State University), 7 April 1967, 25 April 1967, 2 May 1967.

Washington Daily (University of Washington), 29 May 1964, 2 June 1964.

Western Herald (Western Michigan University–Kalamazoo), 21 February 1967.

Theses and Dissertations

Barnett, Bernice M. "A Structural Analysis of the Civil Rights Movement and the Leadership Roles of Martin Luther King Jr." Ph.D. diss., University of Georgia, 1989.

Beaver, Gene M. "The Beliefs of the Citizens' Councils: A Study in Segregationist Thought." Master's thesis, California State–Fullerton, 1968.

Bick, Etta Zablocki. "Ethnic Linkage and Foreign Policy: A Study of the Linkage Role of American Jews in Relations Between the United States and Israel, 1956–1968." Ph.D. diss., City University–New York, 1983.

Coleman, Susie H. "Martin Luther King's Chicago Campaign: An Experiment in Paradox." Master's thesis, Austin Peay State University, 1969.

Connell, Renny. "Television and Politics in the 1960's." Master's thesis, Florida Atlantic University, 1972.

Davison, Donald L. "The Political Consequences of the Voting Rights Act of 1965." Ph.D. diss., Washington University, 1985.

Geels, James H. "The German-American Bund: Fifth Column or Deutschtum?" Master's thesis, North Texas State, 1975.

Goldberg, David. "The Philosophical Foundations of Racism." Ph.D. diss., City University–New York, 1984.

Greenbaum, Keith R. "Anti-Semitism and Racism in Politics: The Populist Connection." Ph.D. Diss., Brown University, 1993.

Keith, Elvin W. "A Comparison of Selected Old and New Right Wing Groups: Involvement with Law Enforcement." Master's thesis, Western Michigan University, 1989.

Kirman, Joseph. "Major Programs of the B'nai B'rith Anti–Defamation League: 1945–1965." Ph.D. diss., New York University, 1967.

Kohl, Paul R. "Who Stole the Soul? Rock and Roll, Race, and Rebellion." Ph.D. diss., University of Utah, 1994.

Lewis, Rand C. "Right-Wing Extremism in West Germany, 1945–1989: A Nazi Legacy." Ph.D. diss., University of Idaho, 1989.

Norman, Barbara. "The Black Muslims: A Historical Analysis." Ph.D. diss., University of Oklahoma, 1985.

Peled, Yoav. "Class, Nation, and Culture: The Debate over Jewish Nationality in the Russian Revolutionary Movement, 1893–1906." Ph.D. diss., University of California–Los Angeles, 1982.

Richberg, Velma Deloris. "The Highlander Folk School Involvement in the Civil Rights Movement from 1957 to 1961." Master's thesis, Fisk University, 1973.

Romaine, Anne Cooke. "The Mississippi Freedom Democratic Party Through August 1964." Master's thesis, University of Virginia, 1970.

Simonelli, Frederick J. "American Fuehrer: George Lincoln Rockwell and the American Nazi Party." Ph.D. diss., University of Nevada–Reno, 1995.

Sobisch, Andreas. "Right-Wing Extremism in Western Democracies: Testing Forty Years of Theory." Ph.D. diss., Emory University, 1993.

Young, John Wesley. "Totalitarian Language: Orwell's Newspeak and Its Nazi and Communist Predecessors." Ph.D. diss., University of Virginia, 1987.

Federal Government FOIA Releases

Federal Bureau of Investigation, U.S. Department of Justice

44-0-000	Civil Rights Violations (New Orleans)
44-0-7039	Civil Rights Violations (Cook County, Ill.)
44-33591	Civil Rights Violations (New York City)
44-359	Civil Rights Violations (Emporia)

97-3835-2	Registrations Act
100-44-1238	"Memorandum to FBI." Office of Naval Intelligence, Department of the Navy
105-70374-1	Monograph on ANP
105-70374	Main File: George Lincoln Rockwell/ANP
139-1049	Unauthorized Publication or Use of Communications.
157-00	Racial Matters
157-3323	Dan Burros
157-9-1	COINTELPRO
174-1-59	Bombing Matters–Threats
175-43-1	Threat Against the President

Department of the Navy Personnel Records
Christopher Bailey
Schuyler Ferris
George Lincoln Rockwell

Interviews

Allen, Karl R. Interviewed by author, 14 June 1994.
Allen, Wallace. Interviewed by author, Atlanta, Ga., 12 April 1994.
Bailey, Christopher. Interviewed by author, Alexandria, Va., 24 October 1994.
Brown, Mike. Interviewed by author via telephone, 18 August 1995.
Burke, Emory. Interviewed by author, Montgomery, Ala., 22 August 1995.
Davids, Bernard. Interviewed by author, 10 May 1995, 4 October 1997.
Eddy, T. R. Interviewed by author via telephone, 23 July 1994.
Ferris, Schuyler. Interviewed by author, Falls Church, Va., 30 September 1993.
Fields, Edward R. Interviewed by author, Atlanta, Ga., 21 August 1995.
Foss, Roger. Interviewed by author, 14 June 1994.
French, Mary Blake. Interviewed by author, Arlington, Va., 21 October 1994.
Hooker, DeWest. Interviewed by author, Washington, D.C., 30 September 1993.
Jordan, Colin. Correspondence with author, 1994.
Koehl, Matthias. Interviewed by author, Arlington, Va., 26 April 1996.
Lagoulis, Speros. Interviewed by author via telephone, Boston, Mass., 22 October 1997.
Pierce, William L. Interviewed by author, Hillsboro, W.Va., 25 April 1996.
Shaffer, Earl. Interviewed by author, Arlington, Va., 21 October 1994.
Smith, Francis J. Interviewed by author via telephone, 8 April 1994.
Tupper, Stanley. Interviewed by author, Boothbay Harbor, Maine, 25 April 1994.
Tyndall, John. Correspondence with author, 23 March 1995.
von Goetz, Barbara. Correspondence with author, 5 December 1997.
Walraven, Jerald. Interviewed by author via telephone, 21 May 1995.
Ware, George. Interviewed by author via telephone, 16 May 1993.
Welch, Alan J. Correspondence with author, 13 November 1997.

ANP Literature, Pamphlets, and Propaganda

"A Halfpenny Hitler." Reprint, *London Jewish Chronicle,* 24 February 1961 (University of Iowa).

"A Negro World." (University of Iowa).

"American Nazi Victory! Jews Again Provoked into Stupid, Illegal Attack!" 1959 (University of Iowa).

"Anatomy of a Smear." Early WUFENS tract circa 1958–1959 (Author's files).

"And They Call Me a 'Jew Spy'!" G. L. Rockwell, 1960 (University of Iowa).

"Avenge Ole Miss!" 1963 (Wilcox Collection).

"Brotherhood Nigger-Talk Dictionary" (Wilcox Collection).

"Commander's Special Report on Chicago" (Wilcox Collection).

"Eichmann Speaks!" 1962 (Wilcox Collection).

"Facts, Doctrines, and the Ideas of the American Nazi Party" (Author's files).

"From Ivory Tower to Privy Wall: On the Art of Propaganda" *National Socialist World,* Spring 1966.

"Here Comes Whiteman." Comic by John Patler (Wilcox Collection).

"How the CIA Swindled IKE, DICK, and YOU with the Great U-2 Hoax." (Author's files).

"How to Get Out or Stay Out of the Insane Asylum." G. L. Rockwell, 1960 (Author's Files).

"How You Can Beat the Federal Race-Mixers." 1965 election material (California State–Fullerton).

"If It Can Happen to Rockwell It Can Happen to You!" (University of Iowa).

"In Hoc Signo Vinces." G. L. Rockwell, 1960 (Author's files).

"Jew-Dominated Philadelphia Resorts to Terror..." (Author's files).

"Jews Driven to Terrorism to Stop Us!" 1960 (Author's files).

"Keep the White Vigil Going" (Wilcox Collection).

"Kidnapping and Torture of Eichmann by Israeli Criminals." Early ANP tract. (Author's files).

"Last Minute News and Special Offer!" Pre-orders for *This Time the World.* (Author's files).

"Legal, Psychological, & Political Warfare." G. L. Rockwell, 1965 (Liberty Bell Publications, W.Va.).

"Must Men Starve to Get Justice in Philadelphia?" (Author's files).

"Niggers! You Too Can Be a Jew!" (University of Iowa).

"Official Stormtroopers Manual." Dan Burros, 1961 (Author's files).

"Petition for Redress of Grievances." 1963 post-mutiny tract (Author's files).

"Program of the World Union of National Socialists" (University of Iowa).

"Prospects for Victory." ANP–Western Division (Author's files).

"Rank, Uniform and Insignia of the Stormtroopers." John Patler, 1961 (University of Iowa).

"Should We Lynch Rockwell?" (University of Iowa).

"Special Message from the Commander." G. L. Rockwell, 1963 (University of Iowa).

"The Arithmetic of Patriotism" 1961 (University of Iowa).
"The Barry Goldwater Record" (Wilcox Collection).
"The Big Lie: Who Told It?" (University of Wisconsin–River Falls Archives).
"The Diary of Ann Fink" (Wilcox Collection).
"The Difference Between National Socialism and Communism" (University of Iowa).
"The Eichmann Farce." G. L. Rockwell, 1961 (University of Iowa).
"The Jews Admit Collapse of Their Press Conspiracy" (University of Iowa).
"To All Who Would Like to See Commander Rockwell the Next Governor of Virginia" (Wilcox Collection).
"U.S. Nazis Ruled Legal!" (University of Iowa).
"United White Vote for Rockwell" (University of Iowa).
"Virginia Stands Fast in Face of Jewish Pressure" (University of Iowa).
"Was Lincoln a Bigot?" (Wilcox Collection).
"We Challenge the Jews" (University of Iowa).
"We Drive to Top of International Anti-Jew Movement in One Year" (University of Iowa).
"We Speak! Beginning of End for the Jews!" (Author's files).
"What's behind 'Mr. Hate.'" (Author's files).
"White Men Are Starving for You." Post "Hate Bus" tract (Author's files).
"White Men Organize White Guard: A Call to Arms from George Lincoln Rockwell" (University of Iowa).
"Why Is a Nazi? The Story of Lincoln Rockwell & the American Nazi Party" (Author's files).
"Why the Swastika?" G. L. Rockwell (Wilcox Collection).

Records (single)

"Ship Those Niggers Back" and "We's Non-Violent Niggers," by Odis Cochran and the Three Bigots (Labadie Collection).
"Who Needs Niggers? and "We Don't Want No Niggers for Neighbors," by G. L. Rockwell and the Coon Hunters (Labadie Collection).
"Nazi Rockwell! A Portrait in Sound." Helios Records Inc., 1973 (Labadie Collection).

Television and Video

Blood in the Face. Videocassette by James Ridgeway, Right Thinking Productions, 1991.
Roots: The Next Generations. Episode VII. Directed by John Erman. Warner Bros., 1977.
This Hour Has Seven Days. Canadian Broadcasting Corporation, 25 October 1964.

This Time the World. 16mm B&W movie produced by Marlin Johnson. Sun Film Corporation, 1967.

Miscellaneous Documents

"Bigot Seeking Buildup: The 'News' Techniques of George Lincoln Rockwell." American Jewish Committee. May 1962. Wilcox Collection.

"Citizens Concerned" minutes, 1961. Arlington County Library—Virginia Room.

"Community Relations." Rockwell's Appearance at Harvard, by Robert Segal. Jewish Community Council, 4 October 1966, (Boston) American Jewish Archives.

"Complaints." Washington State University Archives. Office of the President. File 19:01.

"Exposé of Rockwell Outfit *(Swastika Smearbund)*." Joel D. Wolfsohn. Jewish Community Council of Greater Washington. Arlington County Library—Virginia Room.

"Jewish War Veteran Commander Speaks Out on Rockwell's Death." 25 August 1967. American Jewish Archives.

"Letter to Roy James." Eugene "Bull" Connor Papers (10F6). Birmingham Public Library.

"Letter from Arnold Forster (ADL) to Charles Posner (JCRC) regarding Rockwell prosecution." 24 May 1963. American Jewish Archives.

"Letter from Edwin Lukas (American Jewish Committee) to Charles Posner (Jewish Community Relations Committee) regarding libel charges against Rockwell." 27 May 1963. American Jewish Archives.

"Memorandum on ACLU Representation of Nazi Handbill Distributions in Washington, D.C., March, 1960." American Jewish Archives.

"Memorandum on (ANP) picketing of *Exodus.*" Isaiah Terman. 13 February 1961. American Jewish Archives.

"Press Release (on Rockwell's assassination) American Jewish Congress." Rabbi Arthur Lelyveld, 25 August 1967. American Jewish Archives.

"Report of Manny Lansky—Pacific Coast Area Director–JWV." 19 March 1962. American Jewish Archives.

"Rockwell's Hate Literature Distributions." Jewish Community Council of Greater Washington, 18 March 1960. American Jewish Archives.

"Rockwell's Picketing *(Exodus)* on February 20." Jewish Community Council of Greater Washington, 28 February 1961. Arlington County Library—Virginia Room.

"Statement of George Lincoln Rockwell" by the Washington Jewish Community Council. Isaac Franck, January 1960. American Jewish Archives.

"The Swastika 'Epidemic' and Anti-Semitism in America." Oscar Cohen, published by ADL, 1960.

"Votes Cast for Governor, Lt. Governor, Attorney General—General Election, November 2, 1965." Levin Nock Davis, State Board of Elections, Virginia.

Arlington County Records

"Articles of Incorporation." Book 29, pp. 44–46; Book 32, pp. 522–24.
Commonwealth of Virginia vs. John Patler (C-5575).
"Report of John Patler." Dr. Pierre Rube, Morrisania City Hospital Hygiene Clinic, New York City, 26 October 1956.
"Memorandum of Amicus Curiae..." Charles Russell, 5 July 1959.

Papers and Archival Collections

American Jewish Archives, Cincinnati, Ohio
Arlington County Library, Virginia Room, Arlington, Va.
Bentley Historical Library, University of Michigan, Ann Arbor, Mich.
Brown University Archives, Brown University, R.I.
Boothbay Region Historical Society & Museum, Boothbay Harbor, Maine
Hofstra University Archives, Axinn Library, Hempstead, N.Y.
Jerald Walraven Papers, Private.
Karl Allen Papers, Private.
Labadie Collection, University of Michigan, Ann Arbor, Mich.
National Museum of American Jewish Military History, Washington, D.C.
Roger Foss Papers, Private.
Schomburg Center for Research in Black Culture, New York Public Library, N.Y.
T. R. Eddy Papers, Private.
University of Virginia, Alderman Library, Special Collections, Charlottesville, Va.
Wilcox Collection, University of Kansas, Lawrence, Kans.

INDEX

ABOUT THE AUTHOR

William Schmaltz is a native of St. Paul and a graduate of the University of Wisconsin–River Falls. He lives in Stillwater, Minnesota, with his wife and three children.